Charles Beard

The English Reformation of the Sixteenth Century

In it's Relation to Modern Thought and Knowledge. Second Edition

Charles Beard

The English Reformation of the Sixteenth Century
In it's Relation to Modern Thought and Knowledge. Second Edition

ISBN/EAN: 9783744704519

Printed in Europe, USA, Canada, Australia, Japan

Cover: Foto ©Lupo / pixelio.de

More available books at **www.hansebooks.com**

THE HIBBERT LECTURES, 1883.

THE REFORMATION

Of the Sixteenth Century

IN ITS RELATION TO

MODERN THOUGHT AND KNOWLEDGE.

LECTURES

DELIVERED AT OXFORD AND IN LONDON,

IN APRIL, MAY AND JUNE, 1883.

BY

CHARLES BEARD, B.A.

SECOND EDITION.

WILLIAMS AND NORGATE,
14, HENRIETTA STREET, COVENT GARDEN, LONDON;
AND 20, SOUTH FREDERICK STREET, EDINBURGH.

1885.

Luther du!—grosser, verkannter Mann! Du hast uns von dem Joche der Tradition erlöset: wer erlöset uns von dem unerträglichern Joche des Buchstabens! Wer bringt uns endlich ein Christenthum, wie du es itzt lehren würdest, wie es Christus selbst lehren würde!

LESSING.

TO

LEYSON LEWIS,

IN

GRATEFUL ACKNOWLEDGMENT OF THIRTY-FIVE YEARS'

UNBROKEN FRIENDSHIP.

PREFACE.

THE only word of preface which this book needs is a request to the reader that he will look at it in the light of its expressed purpose. I have not tried to write, even within the smallest compass, a history of the Reformation, but only to show the relation in which its results stand to modern knowledge and modern thought. There are many chapters omitted which I would gladly have written; and critics who have read themselves deeply into certain parts of the story, may look for much in these pages which they will not find. Should I have proved to the satisfaction of only a few that if theology in this age is to keep abreast of advancing science, and to continue to answer to the inexhaustible religious wants of men, a new Reformation is needed, it will be enough.

It was in 1483 that Luther was born. I thank the Hibbert Trustees for the opportunity which they have afforded me of adding my humble wreath to the various tributes of honour, affection and gratitude, which in his native country will greet the Four-hundredth anniversary of his birth.

CHARLES BEARD.

June, 1883.

CONTENTS.

LECTURE I.
REFORM BEFORE THE REFORMATION 1

LECTURE II.
THE REVIVAL OF LETTERS IN ITALY AND GERMANY . . 35

LECTURE III.
THE REFORMATION IN ITS EXTERNAL ASPECTS . . . 76

LECTURE IV.
THE PRINCIPLES OF THE REFORMATION . . . 112

LECTURE V.
THE REFORMATION IN RELATION TO REASON AND LIBERTY . 147

LECTURE VI.
THE SECTS OF THE REFORMATION 184

LECTURE VII.
THE REFORMATION IN SWITZERLAND 225

LECTURE VIII.
THE RISE OF PROTESTANT SCHOLASTICISM . . . 262

LECTURE IX.

The Reformation in England 300

LECTURE X.

The Growth of the Critical Spirit. . . . 336

LECTURE XI.

The Development of Philosophical Method and Scientific Investigation 370

LECTURE XII.

Conclusion 401

LECTURE I.

REFORM BEFORE THE REFORMATION.

To look upon the Reformation of the sixteenth century as only the substitution of one set of theological doctrines for another, or the cleansing of the Church from notorious abuses and corruptions, or even a return of Christianity to something like primitive purity and simplicity, is to take an inadequate view of its nature and importance. Granting that it was any or all of these things, the further questions arise, What were the forces which produced it, and why did they operate exactly at that time and in that way? From the beginning of the thirteenth century to the end of the fifteenth, a lively sense of the need of reformation was never absent from the Church, and repeated efforts were made to effect it. Why did they all fail? Why was it left for the reaction of schism, and the existence of Protestant communions in face of the old Church, to produce that reform of discipline and morals which the Council of Constanz found impossible? Whence originated the transfer of religion from the objective to the subjective side of things, which marks the transition from Catholicism to Protestantism? Were the forces which produced these results exhausted in calling the Reformation into being, or are they still active and bearing fruit? In other words, was the Reformation a finished process, or do its principles still ask to be carried to a further logical development?

These questions will receive such complete answer as I am able to give them in the course of Lectures to which this is the introduction. At the same time, that the future direction of our inquiry may be indicated, it is necessary to answer them briefly and provisionally now. The Reformation, in the view which I shall take of it, was not, primarily, a theological, a religious, an ecclesiastical movement at all. It was part of a general awakening of the human intellect, which had already begun in the fourteenth century, and which the revival of classical learning and the invention of the art of printing urged on with accelerating rapidity in the fifteenth. It was the life of the Renaissance infused into religion, under the influence of men of the grave and earnest Teutonic race. It was a partial reaction from the ecclesiastical and ascetic mood of the middle ages to Hellenic ways of thinking: a return to nature which was not a rebellion against God, an appeal to reason which left room for loyal allegiance to the Bible and to Christ. But this intellectual movement was wider than the Reformation, and when from various causes the Reformation was arrested in its development, was only just beginning to manifest itself in its full scope and force. From it have proceeded the physical, the historical, the critical researches which during the last three centuries have so immensely widened the area of human knowledge. The forces which, in the fifteenth and sixteenth centuries, first began to operate on a large scale, are the forces that have enabled us to look, not only at the physical universe in itself and in its relations to mankind, but at the whole past history of our race, with new eyes. And the question towards which the inquiries, in which I hope to have your kind encouragement and co-operation, will all converge, is this: Inasmuch as our outlook upon the physical world is quite other than that of the Reformers —as our knowledge of antiquity, both sacred and secular, has, since their day, been greatly widened and made more accurate—as these changes directly and largely affect our conceptions of God, of the Divine government, of the nature and authority of Scripture, of the importance to be attached to the opinions of Christian antiquity—what ought to be our intellectual attitude towards the creeds and confessions bequeathed to us by the Reformation?

During the whole of the three centuries which preceded the Reformation, two facts impressed themselves deeply— yet from time to time with varying intensity—upon the minds of thoughtful and pious Churchmen in Western Europe: first, that the Church was one, authoritative, divine; and next, that it stood in urgent need of practical amendment. The Latin was to such the only Church; the Greek and the lesser Eastern communions were too far off and too little known to strike their imagination; with all kindred races they owned one spiritual allegiance. One Pope, one Emperor, the sun and moon in the intellectual sky, who have inferiors but no equals, together make up a logically perfect system, embracing things spiritual and things temporal. Nor did this feeling of the unity of the Church greatly depend upon the audacity with which Papal claims were made, or the extent to which they were acknowledged: it was perhaps equally strong when Innocent III. had raised the political influence of Rome to its highest pitch, and when a succession of disregarded Pontiffs held their court in the Babylonian captivity of Avignon. It chiefly depended upon the fact that the tradition of Latin Christianity had come down from antiquity in one clear, unruffled stream. The very recollection of an Arian Church had long passed away; while, whatever heresies of later date had arisen, had either been completely rooted out, or existed in the heart of the Church only in a condition of suspended vitality. Men's ignorance of the true story of the past had been bolstered up by carefully devised fictions: the Donation of Constantine was held to be as indisputable a fact as the Council of Nicæa: the forged decretals of Isidore lay at the basis of all Papal law. The majestic oneness of the Church in creed, in ritual, in discipline—the conduct of worship in a sacred tongue, which at once overpassed all national distinctions, and by strong and tender ties connected the present with the past—the graduated hierarchy, which united every meanest servant of the Church with the Pope in sole supremacy at its head—all combined to make the idea of open separation from the mystic body of Christ one that the boldest spirits did not dare to entertain.

At the same time, dissatisfaction with the Church's practical working was deep and widespread. There can be no greater mistake than to suppose it to have been confined to the age immediately preceding the Reformation, or to have been exaggerated by schismatics in order to justify their schism. All through the centuries of which I am speaking, the thirteenth, the fourteenth, the fifteenth, these complaints perpetually recur: now finding a voice in scorn and invective meant to reach the popular ear; now lending an undertone of seriousness to poetical *persiflage;* sometimes furnishing matter for the airy scorn of the learned—oftenest perhaps of all, the sad burthen of writers filled with a prophetic aspiration after truth and goodness. They touch the same points: the decline of monastic fervour and purity, the heaping up of wealth by both secular and regular clergy, the scandals created by the enforcement of clerical celibacy, the corruptions and exactions of the Papal see. Luther has been blamed for strong speech on these things, but he does not speak one whit more strongly than Petrarch: if Erasmus' Colloquies and Adages are full of contemptuous scorn of monks and nuns, so is Boccaccio's Decameron. The very abuse which started both Luther and Zwingli on their reforming career—that of the indulgences—was of old standing: Tetzel himself could hardly have been more shameless than Chaucer's Pardoner; John XXIII. flooded Europe with these commodities; John Wessel, in the generation immediately before Luther, attacked the whole theory on which they rested even more roundly than he. Indeed, the student of the latter half of the fifteenth century is surprised to find how little that is new it contributes to the approaching convulsion. There may indeed have been a feeling that, as so many methods of reform had been tried in vain, some bolder surgery than had yet been applied to the running sores of the Church was imperatively needed. But men were still crying out against the old abuses, without knowing from what quarter of the heavens the reviving and reforming wind would blow.

The efforts which the Church made through these three centuries to amend herself, may be divided (though not chronologically) into three classes, which I will call, for convenience' sake, the Catholic, the Mystic, the Biblical. But before I proceed to speak of each of these, I must premise that this, like every other classification of the same kind, must not be taken as rigidly true to fact; that the several tendencies which it implies mutually act and re-act; and that a difference of opinion may often justifiably arise as to the category in which a particular movement of reform ought to be placed. First, then, of the Catholic.

It appears from what I have already said that nothing could be less fair to the mediæval Church than to suppose it sunk in torpid self-satisfaction, profoundly unconscious of its weaknesses and its sins. It had its own ideal of the religious life, which, if not ours, was yet a high one: if it produced many worldly Bishops, many profligate Popes, it never was without saintly recluses and learned theologians. But this ideal is one which, above all others, carries within itself the necessity of fallings away and risings again in those who try to realize it. It involves the exclusive training of one part of human nature at the expense of another: not merely the mastery of the spirit over the flesh, but the abject slavery of the flesh to the spirit intent upon unearthly things. The virgin is purer than the wife; the monk is nobler than the man. The crown of piety is sought in detachment from the world: it is safest to shun temptation even at the cost of avoiding duty: better close the eyes at once to all beauty, better wholly turn away the heart from earthly delight, than run the risk of being caught in the net of self-pleasing. The salvation of a man's own soul is the one, all-absorbing object of life: compared with it, what other end is worth toil and patience? by the side of the Beatific Vision, what splendour of worldly success would not show poor and common? Reflections of this kind first drove Benedict to his cave in the inaccessible cliff above the Anio; and when in after years Benedictine abbeys had grown rich, and Benedictine monks idle and luxurious, reflections of this kind led to the foundation of new orders and the enactment of more stringent rules. So Robert first, and then Stephen Harding established Citeaux; so, when Citeaux was growing too prosperous, St. Bernard led away his little colony to Clairvaux. This is the story of all monastic orders both before and since the Reformation: a period of fervent zeal, of unbounded self-sacrifice, of miracles of self-conquest; and then a time of slow relaxation, ending often in shameful license, yet followed after a while by another spasm of reform. Such efforts of religious revival carry within them the earnest of their own failure; they are the attempt "to wind ourselves too high, for sinful man beneath the sky;" they involve an outrage upon essential principles of human nature, which in the long run always avenge repression by rebellion.

The close of the twelfth and the beginning of the thirteenth century were marked by a great outbreak of anti-sacerdotalism over a large part of Europe. At the very moment when Innocent III. had vindicated the Papal power to the utmost against Emperors and Kings, it was assailed by a widespread domestic conspiracy. This conspiracy assumed different forms: among the Waldenses, of whom I shall speak more particularly in another connection, it was Biblical; the Albigenses were declared to be tainted with Manichæan heresy; there were other less famous sects which seemed to anticipate the intellectual and moral extravagances of the Anabaptists of the sixteenth century. But one hatred and contempt of the priesthood characterized the whole movement. Their ignorance, their worldliness, their avarice, their profligacy, had alienated men from the Church. It seemed as if whole provinces were about to be permanently lost to Rome. I need not dwell upon the various forms of forcible repression with which this religious upheaval was met; the principal result of the rebellion was to call into existence the two great mendicant orders, the Dominican and the Franciscan. Did the heretical teachers lead the people astray by the magic of their eloquence?—let the Dominicans outpreach them. Was the wealth of the clergy a perpetual stumbling-block to piety?—let the Franciscans show the world an example of poverty as naked as Christ's. The two new orders spread through Europe with startling rapidity: unconfined in monastic houses, their members pervaded every parish: by means of their lay brotherhoods, they permeated all classes of society: they were a Papal militia, independent of the Bishops, and owning allegiance only to their own generals and the Pope. Soon they laid hold on the Universities, and helped to give its form to scholastic theology: Thomas Aquinas is the boast of the Dominican order; Bonaventura, Duns Scotus, William of Ockham, were Franciscans. But the universal fate of monastic orders overtook them. Notwithstanding their rigid vows of poverty, they grew rich like the Benedictines before them, and with riches came idleness and moral laxity. A not unnatural shame drove some of the Franciscans, who recollected the marriage of their founder with his mystic bride Poverty, into almost open revolt: the Spiritual Franciscans, as they were called, made an earnest attempt to return to the old simplicity. But the inevitable tendencies of the system were too strong for them; and by the time of the Reformation the mendicant orders were the shame, not the stay, of the Papacy.

The self-reforming effort of the Church took another shape at the close of the fourteenth century. The captivity at Avignon had ended, but it had ended in schism. The world was scandalized by the spectacle of rival Popes disputing for the honour of the triple crown. Wearied by thirty years of this disgraceful strife, the Church, by an almost desperate effort of independence, took matters into its own hands, and a Council was convened at Pisa, in 1409, neither by Pope nor by Emperor, but by the College of Cardinals. It was an august assembly: the presence of representatives of national Churches, of the Sacred College, of monastic orders, of famous Universities, enabled it to speak with almost the unanimous voice of Western Christendom; while it acquired a still greater weight from the fact that it was a living protest in favour of the doctrine that the Church was above the Pope, not the Pope above the Church. Its first and indeed its most important act was to depose both the rival Popes, Benedict XIII. and Gregory XII., and to elect Alexander V., once a Franciscan friar, in their room. It was not a happy choice. When, after a reign of ten months, the new Pope died, all he had done for the Church was to have dissolved the Council, and to have issued a bull giving quite unprecedented privileges to the mendicant orders. His successor was Balthazar Cossa, who, under the name of John XXIII., gave the Church a foretaste of the personal and administrative scandals which have made the Popes of the Reformation a by-word. And now indeed, if ever, the hour of the Church's self-amendment seemed to have struck. The reigning Pope shocked the universal conscience. The deposed Popes still lived, and still maintained their claims. A strong party, of which Gerson, the famous Chancellor of the University of Paris, was the head, was in favour of radical reform. Germany, in the person of Sigismund, the last Emperor of the house of Luxemburg, intervened with decisive force: nothing lay so near to Sigismund's heart, who, though infirm of will, was a man of fine impulses, as the cleansing of the Church from scandals which were fast becoming intolerable. The Council of Pisa afforded an apt precedent: if a Council could depose two Popes, why not three? At last the stress of politics in Italy threw John into the hands of the Emperor, and with the assent of the former, though hardly with his goodwill, another general Council assembled at Constanz in 1414. The three Popes were summoned to appear before a tribunal which assumed to have the right of adjudicating upon their claims. At last, reformation was made a distinct and avowed end of ecclesiastical policy. The Council set before itself three objects to be attained: to unite the Church under one acknowledged Pope; to reform it in its head and in its members; to extirpate all heretical and erroneous doctrines.

Unhappily for the good name of the Council of Constanz, the third of these objects was allowed precedence over the other two. The trial and condemnation of John Huss, who had come to Constanz under an imperial safe-conduct—the penal fire which was lighted in the meadow by the lakeside, first for him, and then for his friend and follower Jerome of Prague—the "blush of Sigismund," not the only mute protest of a royal conscience, drugged by ecclesiastical casuistry, which history records—the principle, deliberately laid down by the Council, that faith need not and ought not to be kept with heretics—are things which must not detain us here. John XXIII. was persuaded or forced, not only to abdicate, but to acknowledge a long and black bead-roll of sins; and then the issue was joined. The Church was without an autocratic head: should she not use the opportunity to purge herself of scandals? The Emperor, with his Germans, took the side of reform: Gerson, powerfully aided by Hallam, Bishop of Salisbury, gave to it the whole weight of his intellectual and personal ascendency. Nor could there be any doubt as to what at least the Chancellor wanted. Doctrinal reform was not in his thoughts: the shame of Huss's death rests on him, not less than on his colleagues. But his treatise, "On the Way to unite and reform the Church in a General Council," written in 1410, after the disappointment at Pisa, which still survives, breathes as regards all practical matters the spirit which prevailed at Wittenberg a century afterwards. He draws a sharp distinction between "the one, holy and Catholic Church," of which Christ is the sole head, and the Apostolic Church over which the Pope presides. He asserts that the Council is above the Pope, "above him in authority, above him in dignity, above him in office;" that Popes are but men, liable to error and to sin; that a Pope is "in all things subject, like any other Christian, to the precept and commandment of Christ." He laughs at the idea that while long-descended secular princes may be deposed for the good of their subjects, a Pope cannot, who owed his dignity to the votes of Cardinals, and "whose father and grandfather probably could not get beans enough to eat." "Should the son of a Venetian fisherman be allowed to hold the Papacy to the detriment of the whole Church commonwealth?"[1] Still, with the concurrence of all these favouring circumstances, the opportunity was missed. It was decided (the death of Hallam at this moment had something to do with it) first to give the Church a new head, and then to proceed to its reformation. The choice fell upon Cardinal Colonna,

---

[1] "Si propter salvationem unius regni, unius provinciæ, deponitur unus Rex, unus Princeps sæcularis, qui per successionem perpetuam descendit: multo magis unus Papa, unus Prælatus est deponendus, qui per electionem Cardinalium fuit institutus, cujus pater et avus forsan ventres implere non sufficiebant fabis. Durum enim est dicere quod filius unius Veneti piscatoris papatum debeat tenere cum detrimento totius reipublicæ ecclesiasticæ.".... "Papa, ut Papa, est homo, et ut homo, sic est Papa, et ut Papa potest peccare, et ut homo, potest errare.—Subjicitur ergo, ut alter Christianus in omnibus præcepto et mandato Christi.".... "Sed numquid tale Concilium, ubi Papa non præsidet, est supra Papam? Certe sic. Superius in auctoritate, superius in dignitate, superius in officio. Tali enim Concilio ipse Papa in omnibus tenetur obedire, tale Concilium potest potestatem Papæ limitare quia tali Concilio, cum repræsentet Ecclesiam universalem, claves ligandi et solvendi sunt concessæ. Tale Concilium jura papalia potest tollere, a tali Concilio nullus potest appellare, tale Concilium potest Papam eligere, privare et deponere, tale Concilium potest jura nova condere, et facta ac antiqua destruere, talis etiam Concilii constitutiones, statuta et regulæ sunt immutabiles et indispensabiles per quamcumquam personam inferiorem Concilio." Gerson, "De modis uniendi ac reformandi Ecclesiam in Concilio universali," quoted by Gieseler, Kirchengeschichte, Vol. II. Part iv. pp. 15, 16.

who took the name of Martin V., and straightway proceeded to act in accordance with true Papal precedent. His first measure was to confirm all the regulations which had obtained in the Papal Chancery, and with them, therefore, the whole series of practical abuses of which the Church so bitterly complained. His next step was to break the force of the general league for reform, by concluding separate concordats with the Transalpine nations—treaties which seemed to promise much, while they really conceded little. The Pope's personal character did the rest: his office recovered the respect of which the schism and the profligacy of John XXIII. had deprived it: and the Council, which had preceded its election of the Pope by a declaration that it would not dissolve until reforms were achieved, separated without any other result than the kindling of the Hussite war.

This was the age of reforming Councils. I cannot pause to tell in detail the story of the Council of Basel, which assembled twelve years after the dissolution of the Council of Constanz, and for substantially the same purposes. The same forces, too, met in conflict: on one side, the Emperor Sigismund, still eager for reform; on the other, Pope Eugenius IV., intent upon preserving the Papal prerogative intact, and trying to draw off the attention of Christendom from reform at Basel to a treaty of union with the Greek Church at Ferrara and Florence. Nor is it necessary to narrate the way in which the adroit management of Æneas Sylvius Piccolomini—afterwards Pope Pius II.—who at the right moment transferred his services from the Imperial to the Papal side, broke up the Council of Basel, and once more handed over the Church to the autocracy of Rome.

The attempt to secure disciplinary reform by means of general Councils had hopelessly failed, shattered against long prescription and the baser ambitions of men. Thomas of Sarzana—Nicholas V.—ruled in Rome, a wise and liberal patron of that classical revival which was to prove the true dissolvent of Papal supremacy. Under the long administration of Frederick III., in whom the House of Hapsburg again succeeded to the Imperial throne, the empire was torn by internal dissensions. The misfortunes of Henry VI.'s reign, and the subsequent Wars of the Roses, occupied all England's attention. Charles VII. of France was busy winning back his kingdom from the English, and Louis XI. in consolidating it, by crafty treachery. If the Church were to be reformed, it was clear that it must be by the application of more powerful forces than had yet been tried. But Europe was too busy with wars and schemes of dynastic ambition to think of reforming it.

I pass now to a series of manifestations also within the Church, which I have called Mystic, and which cannot justly be neglected in any enumeration of internal efforts of reform. The mystic is one who claims to be able to see God and divine things with the inner vision of the soul—a direct apprehension, as the bodily eye apprehends colour, as the bodily ear apprehends sound. His method, so far as he has one, is simply contemplative: he does not argue, or generalize, or infer: he reflects, broods, waits for light. He prepares for Divine communion by a process of self-purification: he detaches his spirit from earthly cares and passions: he studies to be quiet, that his still soul may reflect the face of God. He usually sits loose to active duty: for him, the felt presence of

God dwarfs the world and makes it common: he is so dazzled by the glory of the one great Object of contemplation, that he sees and cares for little else. But the morals of mysticism are almost always sweet and good, even if there be a faint odour of cloister incense about them; though at the same time there are more ways than one from mysticism to immorality, all leading through the Pantheism into which mystics are ever apt to fall. For shall not one who is mystically incorporate with God live in a region above law? And if God be the ground and substance of all things, what justification is there for distinction between good and evil? But these are comparatively rare aberrations, and the essential weakness of mysticism lies in another direction. It much rather consists in the fact that mysticism cannot formulate itself in such a way as to appeal to universal apprehension. It affirms, it does not reason: all the mystic can say to another is, I see, I feel, I know; and if he speaks to no corresponding faculty, his words fall to the ground. Indeed, the mystic is always more or less indistinct in utterance: he sees, or thinks he sees, more than he can tell: the realities which he contemplates are too vast, too splendid, too many-sided, to be confined within limits of human words: he looks at them, now in this aspect, now in that, and his reports, while each true to the vision of the moment, have a sound of inconsistency with each other. So mysticism usually fails to propagate and perpetuate itself: the mystic faculty is a gift of God, not an aptitude that can be communicated by man to man: its appearance in the Church is as that breath of the Spirit which bloweth where it listeth.

The monastic life, one might think, would be so favourable to the development of this phase of religiousness, as to make it wonderful, not that the Catholic Church has produced so many mystics, but that she is not the mother of more. But it is a characteristic of mysticism that it is singularly independent of creeds and churches. It is less a matter of belief, or of ecclesiastical environment, than of individual mood and capacity. As a Raphael must have painted, though he had not been born just when Italian art was putting forth its brightest blossoms, so Tauler, I venture to think, would have been a mystic, even had he received his education in the Oxford of to-day. Give a mystic the thought of God, and his mind wants and can contain no more: from a soul so filled, all peculiarities of ecclesiastical time and place drop away as useless shell or indifferent garment. This is the reason why the works of great mystics have always been the world's favourite books of devotion: they move in a region above diversities of creed: they reach that which is common to every age and sex. The "Imitation of Christ" is a more Catholic book than Protestant translators are always willing to have it appear, but the Catholic trappings of the thought do not vex the Evangelical reader; while it would be difficult to find out from internal evidence whether the *Theologia Germanica* was written before or after the Reformation. And so I think it is hardly fair to represent the Catholic mystics of the middle ages as precursors of Luther. He was of kin to them, as indeed all the world's great religious teachers form but one family; but I do not see that they specifically smoothed his way. In so far, indeed, as mysticism is an intensely personal and individual thing, bringing the single soul face to face with God, without the intervention of priest or sacrament, it accords with the subjective principle of Protestantism. But on the whole it is truer to look upon Catholic mysticism as the effort of pious souls within the church to get rid of superficial corruptions and defacements by going down to the ultimate ground of religious reality.

Mysticism, on the one side, stands so nearly related to all spiritual religion, while, on the other, it is capable of running into such excesses of extravagance and fanaticism, as often to make it very difficult to decide who are to be included in the category of mystics. The centuries of which I am speaking were so far from being marked by a dead level of orthodox obedience, as, on the contrary, to be crowded with sects which ran their brief course of enthusiastic activity, and then either died of spiritual inanition or perished under persecution. Some mystics stand out in their separate individuality; others are founders of schools or hierophants of sects. Mysticism develops itself in many different directions: now it is simply poetical, spending a wealth of metaphor to express that which is inexpressible; now losing itself in Pantheistic speculation; again springing up in strong moral aspiration; or, once more, animating millenarian, almost revolutionary hopes. Such, for instance, was the mysticism of the Fratricelli, the heretical Franciscans, who, not content with trying to bring back the order to the standard of simplicity and purity set up by its founder, meditated mystic revolution. Their book was the "Introduction to the Everlasting Gospel,"[1] a work of doubtful author-

---

[1] In 1254, the Bishop of Paris sent to Innocent IV. a book entitled, "Introductorius in Evangelium æternum, seu in libros Abbatis Joachim," which the next Pope, Alexander IV., condemned in a bull dated 1255.

ship, which brought together the characteristic ideas scattered through the books of Abbot Joachim of Flora, in the kingdom of Naples, an apocalyptic seer, who lived in the latter part of the twelfth century, and who, though the unconscious inspirer of much heresy and rebellion, is yet a canonized saint of the Catholic Church. In his view the world was growing old: the kingdom of the Father, which had lasted from Adam to Christ, was at an end: the kingdom of the Son, which was to close with the coming of Antichrist, was almost over;[1] and after a struggle with powers of evil, the kingdom of the Holy Ghost was about to begin. The actual carnal church was to pass away, as the synagogue had already done: the new spiritual church was to spring from that part of the order of St. Francis which had been faithful to its founder's spirit. It was to be a reign of poverty, humility, love, in which, therefore, Popes and Bishops had no part: all men were to be converted to Christ, and to love one another so fervently as to have all things in common: all wrongs were to be redressed, and all miseries to disappear. Not unconnected with this belief in the Everlasting Gospel, though possibly not directly inspired by it, were the revolts against Church authority of Gerard Sagarelli and Fra Dolcino of Novara, in Northern Italy, at the end of the thirteenth century,— revolts which, aiming at ecclesiastical reform by revolutionary means, were finally put down, with copious shed-

---

Its authorship is variously attributed to one of two Franciscans belonging to the severer party in the order, Gerhard and John of Parma. Hahn: Geschichte der Ketzer im Mittelalter, III. 160—162.

[1] The dates of the beginnings and endings of the three kingdoms are variously given by different authorities. Conf. Hahn, III. 106.

ding of blood. Then there were the Pantheistic mystics, the so-called Brethren of the Free Spirit, who from the thirteenth to the fifteenth century appear all along the course of the Rhine,[1] thence spreading into other parts of Germany, as well as into Switzerland and France, and more than once drawing down on themselves the censures of the Church. It is in this connection, perhaps, that Master Eckhart finds his fit place, a profound Pantheistic thinker, who from the philosophical side is now recognized as having anticipated some of the results of later metaphysical speculation in Germany. As a theologian, he was condemned by Pope John XXII.; as a mystic, he was the precursor of Tauler, some of whose published sermons are more correctly ascribed to him. Eckhart, if heretical in teaching, was pure in life; but over the Brethren of the Free Spirit some cloud of uncertainty and suspicion hangs, as if common morality did not well accord with the doctrine of the absorption of the Many in the One. Not so, however, with the Friends of God, a secret fellowship also belonging to the Rhineland, upon which recent research has thrown a much-needed light. You remember the mysterious layman who listened to the Dominican John Tauler, as he expounded, eloquently and successfully as he thought, the deep things of the kingdom, and then, after convincing him of his own unfitness to instruct others, condemned him to a silence

---

[1] The sect which appeared in Brussels about the beginning of the fifteenth century, under the name of *homines intelligentiæ*, seems to have been an offshoot of the Brethren of the Free Spirit. The tenets ascribed to them are a mixture of mystical Pantheism, with highly antinomian views of the relation between the sexes. They, too, held the fundamental doctrine of the "Everlasting Gospel" as to the three successive kingdoms. Hahn, II. 526.

which lasted for two years, and was finally broken only with much hesitation and many tears. That nameless one was Nicholas of Basel, the founder and head of the "Friends of God," who comes and goes in the church history of the time in this mysterious fashion, and at last falls into the hands of the Inquisition, with the usual result. What his peculiar mysticism was, may be seen in Tauler's Sermons, and in the *Theologia Germanica*, which, though later in date, belongs to the same school. Only in its outward form is his mysticism Catholic, and hardly Catholic even there: its essence is the suicide of self, the moral absorption of the spirit in that which is alone good.

The Tertiaries of the Franciscan order, men and women who were bound by its principles and animated by its spirit, without incurring the obligation of abandoning their place in the world, form a point of transition to some Christian communities, among whom was developed another form of Teutonic mysticism.[1] These were the Beghards and Beguines. The Beguines, societies of women who lived together, supporting themselves by the labour of their hands, and giving their spare time and strength to works of charity, first appear as early as the

---

[1] Hahn gives a place to all three sects among Biblical heretics. At the same time he says—and the remark is worth careful notice—"It should not be overlooked that the different parties embraced in this section pass into one another at many points. Thus the heretical Franciscan Tertiaries bore the names Fratricelli and Beghards: thus Gregory XI. places Beghards and Turlupins in one and the same category: thus the terms Lollhards, Beghards and Fratricelli, were synonymous: thus the Beghards and Fratricelli were confounded with the *Pauperes de Lugduno*, and the Beghards with the Rhenish Friends of God." Hahn, II. 420, 421.

eleventh century: a male community of the same kind, known as Beghards, was founded at Louvain in 1220: and both Beguines and Beghards multiplied rapidly in the Low Countries. They differed little from the older orders, except in the looseness of their association; their houses appear to have been independent of each other, and were not organized under a common head. The time of their decline came in the fourteenth century. It was the old story: the first love had waxed cold; they had learned to beg instead of working, and their houses had become no longer the refuge of the devout, but the resort of the lazy. But there were also fanatical Beghards, who in their profession of a mystical Pantheism are hardly to be distinguished from the Fratricelli and the Brethren of the Free Spirit, and whose ethical theories are subject to the same reproach. The greatest mystic of the Low Countries, unless we are to account Thomas à Kempis as such, was Johann Ruysbroeck, who from 1293 to 1381 lived a life remote from the public eye, and died Prior of a monastery of Augustinian Canons, at Grönendal, not far from Brussels. He was younger than Eckhart, whose influence he had felt, standing in the line of mystical ancestry, between that master and Tauler on the one hand, Gerhard Groot on the other. But in Groot, the founder of the Brethren of the Common Life, the mystical and the practical were subtly blended. He was born in the year 1340 at Deventer, and it was in that neighbourhood that his society chiefly flourished. It was the monastic life, in a kind of loose formation. The brethren took no irrevocable vows, lived simply, earned their bread by teaching children and copying books, and kept up a friendly intercourse with the world which they had left. A fine air of practical Christianity blows through these brotherhoods: their aim is to realize, under ascetic conditions, yet without fanaticism and exaggeration, the highest ideal of social life, and they succeed in no small degree. Presently we shall see that they rendered important services to education and classical literature in Holland; but their name would deserve to live if only that in training Thomas à Kempis they produced the "Imitation of Christ."[1] Out of the brotherhood had grown two houses of regular canons, in one of which, that of St. Agnes, near Zwoll, à Kempis passed almost the whole of his long and innocent life.

Of a book which has gone through many thousand editions, which has been translated into every European language, and which in actual religious influence probably stands next to the Bible, it is not necessary to speak at length. It is more Catholic in form than the *Theologia Germanica:* it is Catholic, too, in essence, inasmuch as its piety is the piety of the cloister, not of the world. With all its sweetness and its strength, there are large areas of human life which it does not touch: it deals so exclusively with the soul's personal relation to Christ, as to be justly obnoxious to the charge of being little more than a manual of sacred selfishness. But, such as it is, it is only fair that the Latin Church should have the whole credit of it. When we note the condition of that

---

[1] I adhere, until conclusive evidence to the contrary is produced, to the traditional belief which connects Thomas Hemerken with the "Imitation." Even if he were not the author, he did much to propagate the book and give it its vogue. An account of the latest literature on the subject, which is yet far from being fully investigated, will be found in the "Modern Review" for October, 1882, art. "Musica Ecclesiastica," by Alexander Gordon, M.A.

Church in the fifteenth century, with its life-blood poisoned by corruptions which only the spasm of revolution could cast out, and its destinies guided by Popes whose very vices were an ironical proof of Divine protection, it is pleasant to be able to turn to Thomas in his cell at Zwoll, meditating on those deep and piercing words which have expressed the love to Christ and the aspiration after goodness of every subsequent generation. But, I repeat, I do not claim him as a precursor of the Reformation, except in so far as all manifestations of true religion are parts of one silver thread, running through the coarse fabric of the ages. Of the *Theologia Germanica*, Luther said:[1] "And I will say, though it be boasting of myself, and 'I speak as a fool,' that, next to the Bible and St. Augustine, no book hath ever come into my hands whence I have learned, or would wish to learn, more of what God and Christ and man and all things are." Yet I cannot find any distinctive Lutheranism in it,—either the doctrine of the sole sufficiency of Scripture, or that of justification by faith alone. But all true mystics are a church apart, who cannot be prevented by distance of time, or sharp distinctions of sect and creed, from holding out to one another hands of genuine brotherhood.

We pass now to a third class of Reformers before the Reformation—the Biblical: men who, both in their religious method and the conclusions to which it led them, so closely resemble Luther and Zwingli as to excite wonder that they did not anticipate their success. Oldest and in some respects most interesting of these are the

---

[1] Preface to the Second Edition of 1518.

Waldenses, a still surviving church, the history of which goes back to the beginning of the twelfth century. The more accurate research of recent years traces the origin of the Waldenses to a double fountain, the streams from which soon mingled, and were thenceforth hard to be distinguished. On the one hand, there were the Vaudois, the "men of the valleys," who still hold their ancient seats in the mountains of Dauphiné and Piedmont; on the other, the so-called "Poor Men of Lyons," the followers of Peter Waldo, a rich merchant of that city, who gave himself up to apostolic work and adopted an apostolic simplicity of living. But the Waldenses, whatever their origin, were from the first Biblical Christians. They translated the Scriptures into their own tongue, and expounded them in their natural sense only. They maintained the universal priesthood of the believer. They struck a second blow at sacerdotal doctrine by denying the validity of sacraments administered by a wicked priest. Their only sacraments were Baptism and the Eucharist: they rejected purgatory, indulgences, prayers for the dead, invocation of saints. Their morals were unimpeached even by their enemies; while in "The Noble Lesson,"[1] a poem in the Provençal dialect, they have left an epitome of the Bible history which rises to a high ethical level, but which does not exhibit a trace of distinctively Augustinian theology. There was a moment in the history of the Waldenses which forcibly calls to mind the relations between Wesley and the Church of England. Forbidden to preach, excommunicated, banished, they

---

[1] "The Noble Lesson" may be found in Hahn, Vol. II. Appendix, pp. 628 et seq. For two distinct statements of Waldensian belief, see the same vol., pp. 138—140.

I. REFORM BEFORE THE REFORMATION. 25

went to Rome, where in 1179[1] the third Lateran Council was being held, and appealed to Pope Alexander III. for liberty to expound the Scriptures. It was denied them, not without some contempt; and their breach with the Church was made irreparable by a decree of Lucius III. (1183), in which, in company with other heretics, they were formally condemned. The development of Waldensian opinions and practice seems to have been two-fold: they spread over a large part of Europe with great rapidity, so that before they had been very long in existence it was said[2] that a Waldensian, who was travelling from Antwerp to Rome, could sleep every night at the house of a fellow-believer. They thus mingled with the half-secret sects[3] of which I have already spoken: if

---

[1] Hahn (II. 256), Neander, Kirchengeschichte (V. ii. p. 1192), both give the date 1170. But the third Lateran Council, the eleventh of the Œcumenical Councils, was held in 1179, which is the date for the interview between the Pope and the Waldenses given by Gieseler, K. G. II. ii. p. 556. We possess a curious account of this interview from the pen of an eye-witness, the English Franciscan, Walter de Mapes, in his book, *De Nugis Curialium*, preserved in MS. in the Bodleian Library, who, according to his own account, was ordered to confer with the Waldensian Deputies, and easily succeeded in exposing their ignorance. He calls them "Valdesios homines, idiotas, illiteratos (a primate ipsorum Valdo dictos qui fuerat civis Lugduni super Rhodanum): qui librum domino Papæ præsentaverunt lingua conscriptum Gallica, in quo textus et glossa Psalterii plurimorumque legis utriusque librorum continebatur." Hahn, II. 257, note.

[2] Abbot Trithemius, quoted by Erbkam, Geschichte der Protestantischen Sekten im Zeitalter der Reformation, p. 141.

[3] Early in the thirteenth century, certain heretics in Strasburg, whose tenets resembled those of the Waldenses, were condemned to the stake, though not with the result of extirpating heresy. For about the end of the fourteenth century appears at Strasburg, with affiliated communities in many cities of the Rhineland and Swabia, a sect called the *Winkeler*. This was probably a nickname given to them in allusion

hardly to be counted among mystics, they yet helped to give German mysticism a soberer and more scriptural tone. On the other hand, the Vaudois remained in their own valleys, as they still remain, faithful, under much persecution, to their ancestral principles; and when, about 1526, they opened communications with the Reformed Churches of Switzerland and Germany, they found that, if they had something to learn, they had nothing to unlearn. Here, it would seem, we have the Reformation, not merely in germ, but in blossom and in fruit; and yet, for the general purposes of European life, the tree was barren. The time of ingathering was not yet: the Waldenses were men born, as it were, out of due season.

The same is true of John Wiclif, who may be described as having re-discovered the Waldensian principles, though equally unable to carry them to a successful issue of reformation. The external contrast is striking. The Waldenses were poor and obscure men, illiterate except in their knowledge of Scripture, unsmiled upon by the powerful in Church and State, and hopelessly beaten in their first conflict with constituted authorities. Wiclif, on the con-

---

to the secret element in their association. Both in doctrine and in practice they were akin to the Waldenses. They denied the spiritual powers of the priesthood, and confessed to lay fathers, who, like the apostles, were twelve in number, travelling from place to place, and exercising a general supervision over the whole sect. They attended mass only to avoid suspicion; in their own meetings they heard sermons out of "great books," presumably the Bible. The *Ortlieber*, also a sect widely spread in Strasburg and its vicinity about the beginning of the thirteenth century, were the followers of one Ortlieb, who had studied in Paris under Amaury de Bène, and, unless much maligned, was an antinomian Pantheist. At a later period, the *Ortlieber* are not to be distinguished from the Brethren of the Free Spirit. Hahn, II. 362. C. Schmidt, in Herzog: Real-Encyclopädie, s. v. Winkeler, Ortlieber.

trary, was learned with all the learning of his time, a favourite teacher at Oxford, enjoying the patronage of a great political party, protected by Princes of the blood in his contest with the Bishops, and, whatever the traditional ill usage of his bones, dying in his bed and in peaceful possession of his benefice. But both Wiclif and the Waldenses attacked the Church on the same lines. He too was a Biblical reformer, appealing to the authority of Scripture, and placing it, in the vulgar tongue, in the hands of the people. He was an anti-sacerdotalist, not merely out of ethical disgust at the pretensions and vices of the clergy, but deliberately, as a matter of Christian theory. Given these two facts, and it is of comparatively little interest to know to what precise point of doctrinal negation he advanced; in them, the whole consequences of the Reformation, as it afterwards came to the birth, are shut up. Why was not Wiclif the Reformer at least of England? His teachings, as a matter of fact, never wholly died out of the people's heart, but lay there, silently preparing them for the new breath of inspiration when it came: his English Bible circulated secretly in manuscript, till it was lost in the first of that long series of translations which has but just reached its final term. But adverse forces, arising on every side, combined to crush the new religious movement. The House of Lancaster, which had given Wiclif his first great patron, when once it had ascended the throne with a doubtful title, found its account in an ecclesiastical alliance. The insurrection of the Commons, popularly associated with the name of Wat Tyler, brought suspicion on Lollardism, as the Peasants' War afterwards did on Luther. The Wars of the Roses engaged in dynastic struggle the whole heart and strength of the nation. Caxton had not yet set up his press in the Westminster Almonry. With the exception of Lord Cobham, who soon perished by fire, Wiclif does not seem to have left any one behind him with the capacities of a leader, and the statute *de hæretico comburendo* did the rest. The Reformation in England was left to illustrate the general law of European revival.

But while the influence of Wiclif in his own country thus passed away, or at least sank beneath the surface of society, it was strangely revived in a distant and almost alien land. The wife of Richard II., Anne, daughter of Charles IV., King of Bohemia, not only felt a deep personal interest in Wiclif's doctrines, but made herself the channel of communication between Oxford and Prague. Jerome Faulfisch—better known as Jerome of Prague— who after a brief interval of weakness sealed his faith by martyrdom at Constanz, had studied at Oxford, and had carried Wiclif's books with him to his own country. There had already been a movement of reformation in Bohemia, born of the universal and secular disapprobation of the morals of the clergy; and when the writings of Wiclif were brought to John Huss, they fell upon a prepared mind. I need not enter more particularly into the character of the Hussite reformation; it is sufficiently indicated by what I have already said. But it was national to a far greater degree than that of Wiclif: King and Queen, many great nobles and churchmen, a majority of the common people, were on the side of Huss; while the fierce and long war kindled by his shameful betrayal amply testifies to the hold which the new doctrines had acquired. In this war, which became a struggle of races between Sclav and Teuton, and in the internal dissensions which are a too sure accompaniment of religious revolution, the Bohemian reformation, as a united national movement, came to an end, though it was not finally stamped out till the House of Hapsburg and the Jesuits applied their united energies to the task. But I cannot find that it had done much for the rest of Europe. Huss was a precursor of Luther, inasmuch as he preceded him in time, but I scarcely think that he prepared his way. Differences of race and language set up a barrier, more impassable than any mountain chain, between Bohemia and Germany. The incidents of the Hussite war, the bloody exploits of Ziska, the signal victories of Procopius, could hardly be helpful in the propagation of religious ideas. What few traces there are of the influence of Huss[1] in German thought in the fifteenth century, are found rather in the region of religious socialism than in that of theology: he was a heretic of an alien race, the object only of hatred and of fear. When in his disputation with Eck at Leipzig, in 1519, Luther was pressed by his adversary to say whether he acknowledged the authority of the Council of Constanz and the justice of

---

[1] Huss was everywhere well received on his last memorable journey from Prague to Constanz. There is a story that some time in the course of the fifteenth century the Council of Bamberg imposed upon all citizens an oath of renunciation of the Hussite heresy. Hans Böheim, or Behem, whose name seems to point to a Bohemian origin, was a piper of Niklashausen, in Franconia, who in 1476 drew together a great concourse of people by his preaching of reform, and who finally, after some uproar and loss of life, was burned to death. But facts like these, of which there are more than one, seem to exhibit Huss as the precursor in Germany quite as much of the Peasants' War as of the Reformation. Compare, on this subject, Janssen: Geschichte des Deutschen Volkes seit dem Ausgang des Mittelalters, II. 393 et seq.

Huss's sentence,[1] he had the boldness to declare, though Duke George broke out into angry protest, that not all the doctrines condemned by the Council were heretical. But it is very significant that he hardly knew to what he was pledging himself. Before a year passed he had read Huss's books; he had received congratulatory letters from Bohemia, and he writes to Spalatin in February, 1520:[2] "I have hitherto unknowingly held and taught all John Huss's doctrines; in a like unknowingness has John Staupitz taught them; briefly, we are all unconscious Hussites. Paul and Augustine are Hussites to the letter." But in 1520, Luther was already Luther, and had plainly not become so by help of Huss.

It is the same with that succession of scholars of whom Ullmann has treated with so much fulness of learning in his book, "The Reformers before the Reformation." John of Goch, the founder and director of a Priory of Canonesses of St. Augustine, near Mechlin, whose life extends from 1400 to 1475,[3] held the sole authority of Scripture, by which he believed that the teachings of fathers and doctors were to be judged, condemned the Pelagian heresy as to grace and the Catholic doctrine of good works, declared the fallibility of the Church, announced a spiritual theory of the sacraments. John of Wesel preceded Luther at the University of Erfurt, where he taught about the middle of the century, was

---

[1] Luther's Werke, ed. Walch. XV. 1430.

[2] Luther's Briefe, ed. De Wette, I. No. 208, p. 425: "Ego imprudens hucusque omnia Johannis Huss et docui et tenui. docuit eadem imprudentia et Johannes Staupitz: breviter, sumus omnes Hussitæ ignorantes: denique Paulus et Augustinus ad verbum sunt Hussitæ."

[3] Ullmann: Reformers before the Reformation, Eng. Trans. I. 135.

afterwards a popular preacher in Mainz and in Worms, was tried for heresy, recanted, and died in prison in 1481. He, too, relies on the authority of Scripture, applying it to prove the unlawfulness of indulgences, which he condemns in seven propositions, hardly if at all less trenchant than Luther's well-known ninety-five. Then there was John Wessel, born at Gröningen about the year 1420, educated in the school at Zwoll conducted by the Brethren of the Common Life, and possibly therefore a pupil of Thomas à Kempis: wandering as scholar and teacher through many Universities, Cologne, Paris, Heidelberg: so great a doctor as to be adorned with the pompous title of *Lux Mundi:* the friend of Cardinal Bessarion and Francesco della Rovere, afterwards infamous as Sixtus IV.: connected with the classical revival in Germany as the teacher of Reuchlin and Rudolf Agricola: and dying at last at Gröningen, uncondemned, in 1489, when Luther was already six years old. Wessel held Protestant views on the authority of Scripture, and put forward a doctrine of justification by faith, though always the faith that worketh by love. But although the thought of these theologians was so distinctly on the lines of the Reformation, we cannot largely credit them with being its active precursors. John of Goch was essentially a recluse, whose writings were first published in the sixteenth century, with the express intention of showing how Lutheran men had been before Luther. John of Wesel's books were involved in their author's condemnation: of the only two which survive, one was first published in the sixteenth, the other not till the eighteenth century. So, too, with John Wessel's works: his *Farrago rerum theologicarum,* the first to be printed, appeared at Wittenberg in 1522.[1] A third edition of the same book, published at Basel in the same year, is preceded by a remarkable preface from the pen of Luther,[2] in which he declares the almost verbal identity of his own doctrine with that of Wessel, and expresses his wonder that the latter had not been more widely famous. But while so saying, he denies the existence of any actual link between himself and his predecessor: *sic pugnavi ut me solum esse putarem;* "I fought as thinking myself alone."

One very remarkable fact in connection with all these efforts of reform remains to be noticed. Not only did they accomplish no permanent amendment, but in spite of them the evil grew. The century which elapsed between the great reforming Councils and the outbreak of the Reformation was one more fruitful in scandals than any other. Not even in the days when Theodora and her daughter Marozia made and unmade Popes were there Pontiffs more utterly disregardful, not only of morality, but of decency, than Sixtus IV., Innocent VIII., Julius II., Clement VII. Alexander VI. is a proverb of human infamy. A scarcely veiled Paganism sat in the fisherman's chair in the person of Leo X. The fiscal oppressions of the Papacy were in no way lightened: the rapacity of Cardinals was unchecked: the sale of indulgences was shamelessly pressed. Not only was a large part of Germany governed by spiritual princes, but the Emperor Maximilian averred that the revenue which the

---

[1] Ullmann, Eng. Trans. II. 605, 606. The edition which Ullmann takes to be the earliest is without date or place. He supposes it to have been printed at Heidelberg.

[2] For Luther's preface to Wessel's book, see Seckendorf: Historia Lutheranismi, Book I. sec. 54, § cxxxiii. p. 226.

Roman Curia[1] drew from that country was a hundred times greater than his own. In Italy, the comparatively new abuse of nepotism had been introduced: each successive Pope busied himself, during his short tenure of power, in carving out principalities for the relatives who were, or were called, his nephews. But at the same time, the doctrinal system, on which these abuses of practice were supposed to rest, had been undergoing a steady development. While monastic orders were passing through alternate periods of reform and decay—while mystics were seeking truth and purity in withdrawal from the outer courts of creed and ritual into inner chambers of contemplation—the schoolmen were painfully building up, stone upon stone, an edifice of reasoned belief, the several parts of which, whatever we may think of the security of its foundations, were held together by good logical cement. The doctrines of the seven sacraments, of transubstantiation, of the power of the priest, of the heavenly treasure of merit and the prerogative of the Church to dispense it, of purgatory, of the invocation of saints, of the honour due to Mary, of her assumption and immaculate conception—were all reduced to a system, were bound one to another by argument and analogy were followed out to their logical consequences. This system reigned without a rival, supported alike by present authority and past prescription. Except in the mind of a daring thinker here and there, all remembrance of a period during which it was in process of formation had passed away, much more the recollection of a primitive and apostolic Church. The Papacy, with all that it in-

---

[1] Ranke: Deutsche Geschichte im Zeitalter der Reformation, I. 56.

volved, never seemed to be more firmly established than when Germany and Switzerland were ready to break out into open revolt against it.

Why did that revolt succeed, when so many other attempts at reform had failed? Why did Luther and Zwingli do what Wiclif and Huss had not done? Something no doubt is due to the great personal qualities of the men, something more to favouring political circumstance. But the main thing was, that the fulness of time had come, in the intellectual revival which was everywhere breathing life into the dry bones of European thought: in the renewed knowledge, first of classical, next of Christian antiquity, which, kindled at the old lamp of Hellas, had brightly shone in Italy, and from Italy had spread across the Alps: in the invention of the art of printing, and its rapid application to be the handmaid of the new learning. There was fresh oxygen now in the intellectual air, and the fire of reformation, once lighted, no longer burned fitfully and feebly, but with steady and consuming flame. The seed-bed of the human mind had been ploughed and harrowed and nourished, so that whatever living germ was committed to it could not but grow and flourish. The Reformation was part of a mightier movement than itself—the manifestation upon religious ground of the intellectual forces which inspire the speculation and have given us the science of to-day.

LECTURE II.

THE REVIVAL OF LETTERS IN ITALY AND GERMANY.

THE history of European thought is continuous: age grows out of age: in each generation lives and moves the quintessence of all that have preceded it. In dealing, therefore, with any great intellectual movement, it is impossible to select a starting-point which shall not be arbitrary: wherever you begin, you can always trace further back the positive process of development, the negative process of reaction. At the same time, there are epochs at which the human mind has more signally broken with the past, has more decisively entered upon a new path of progress, than at others; epochs, the significance of which, only partially apprehended at first, has been fully interpreted by the experience of ages. Such an epoch was that of the Revival of Letters in the fourteenth and fifteenth centuries. We do not give it too pompous a name when we call it the Renaissance, the Re-birth of the human intellect. Its characteristic and, to a large extent, its moving force, was a renewed interest in the masterpieces of classical antiquity, and an earnest attempt to imitate them. For many centuries men had suffered an unconscious intellectual imprisonment within limits prescribed by orthodox Christian belief and the scholastic philosophy, and now gradually awoke to the knowledge that there was a freer and a fairer world outside. In philosophy, the first step was to turn from meagre abridgments and jejune comments to the works of Plato and Aristotle themselves; the next, to learn from the Greeks the method of independent observation and reflection upon the universe; with this result, that when the lesson was thoroughly learned, modern science came slowly and hardly to the birth. The naturalness of the old Pagan life—not wholly unaccompanied by its license—re-asserted its charm, and powerfully combated the monastic ideal which mediæval Christianity had set up. But while the Renaissance was thus a rebellion, quite careless of results, against scholastic philosophy and ascetic theories of morals, it was, in its second stage, hardly less powerful within the limits of Christian belief and practice than beyond them. The curiosity which explored the records of classical, did not leave untouched those of Christian antiquity. An appeal was soon made from the canons and traditions of the Church, first to the Fathers and then to the New Testament itself. The Greek Testament, the Septuagint, the Hebrew Bible, took the place of the Vulgate in the hands of the learned. The Scriptures, in the vernacular languages of Europe, brought home to the minds of the people how widely different was the Church of the New Testament from the ecclesiastical system over which presided a Julius II. or a Leo X. Now at last the abortive efforts of reformation, which in the thirteenth, the fourteenth, the fifteenth centuries had flickered and died away, rose into a great and consuming flame of revolt, the end of which was the severance from the Papacy of a large part of Northern and Western Europe. But the Reformation itself was only an incomplete movement. The stores of knowledge which alone could make it complete were not accumulated till long after its progress had been arrested. Its rising tide broke itself in vain against the dull and obstinate superstition of the House of Hapsburg and the faithless ambition of the Valois' and the Bourbon. Its leaders were unable or afraid to follow its principles to their legitimate issue. A rebellion against Catholic scholasticism, it built up a new scholasticism of its own, upon assumptions hardly less arbitrary. It was met and checked by a counter-reformation, which not only prevented fresh conquests, but won back part of the ground that the Church had lost. But while the development of religious thought was thus practically stayed, the general movement of the human mind held on its triumphant way: Philosophy fearlessly sought for the word that should solve the enigma of the universe: Science gradually plumed her wings for the magnificent flights of discovery which she now makes with so superb a confidence: History reinterpreted the antiquity of the human race, and in disinterring the secrets of speech penetrated to a period beyond written record. We are in the full tide still of that flood of intellectual life which Petrarch witnessed in its first feeble rise. What wonder that theological landmarks which Luther and Calvin established in the sixteenth century have long been submerged!

It would lead us too far astray to discuss the primary causes of this great re-awakening of intellectual activity.

Probably the darkness of the dark ages has somewhat exaggerated by theological prejudice: within the limits imposed by the Church there may have been more movement of mind than some Protestant critics have been willing to admit. But whether the revival of classical learning were cause or effect of the first stirring among the dry bones of European thought, it soon came to be the characteristic feature of the Renaissance. Europe gradually awoke to the knowledge of what men had speculated and discovered and sung, before it had been lulled to sleep in the arms of the Church. It was no longer an offence against ecclesiastical propriety or good morals for a cleric to occupy himself with profane learning. Men went back for examples to a time beyond Jerome, who thought it impossible to be Christian and Ciceronian at once, and Augustine, who bewailed the hours he had lost in the company of Homer and Virgil. Presently teachers were brought from Constantinople, where Greek was still a living language: manuscripts of Greek poets and historians were collected and copied: the convent libraries of East and West were searched for remains of antiquity: the charm of Hellas began to work. Popes vied with merchant princes, and despots with both, in the encouragement of learning: Nicholas V., the founder of the Vatican Library, made Rome, during his pontificate, the centre of the classical reaction: the learned labours of Poggio, the honeyed verse of Politian, the Platonic academy of Ficino, suggest the name of Lorenzo de Medici: the Visconti and the Sforzas alike protected, flattered, pensioned Filelfo: Lorenzo Valla, Pontano, Sannazaro, grouped themselves round the Arragonese dynasty of Naples. When in the fifteenth century the humanists were in full force, the possibilities of the Italian tongue were left unimproved, though Dante and Petrarch in verse, and Boccaccio in prose, had already shown of what great things it was capable: what the men who thought themselves the literary kings of Italy cared for was to be able to write prose, for every phrase of which a precedent could be quoted from Cicero, and verses which, if not precisely Ovidian or Virgilian, might be mistaken for the work of Statius or Silius Italicus. The matter of prose or verse was of small importance: correctness of diction, elegance of form, were everything. The humanists attacked one another, flattered their patrons, rang the changes on classical imitation, in the full conviction that in their labours the golden age of literature had returned. They were the furthest possible from the knowledge that all that they were doing was to gain a mastery over classical methods of thought and speech, which another generation and a graver race might turn to good account.

The revival of letters in Italy neither led to any activity of theological thought nor produced any religious reformation. Lorenzo Valla[1] is the only humanist whose

---

[1] Valla's works were taken up by the Germans, and made to do duty a second time in the controversy against Rome. Ulrich von Hutten republished the pamphlet on the Donation of Constantine in 1517; Erasmus, the Notes on the New Testament in 1505. Valla may be credited with the honour of being the first critic in modern times who attempted to correct the text of the New Testament by comparison of MSS. "Si Laurentius, collatis aliquot vetustis atque emendatis Græcorum exemplaribus, quædam annotavit in N. T." Erasmus, Ep. ciii., ad Christopherum Fischerum. Opp. III. 98 C. It is a curious sample of the inconsistencies of this strange age that Pope Nicholas V. invited Valla, after he had been brought to trial by the Inquisition (whose clutches he escaped by a cynical profession of conformity to the

name can be mentioned in this connection. He exposed the fiction of the Donation of Constantine: he criticised the Latin of the Vulgate: he expressed doubts as to the authenticity of the Apostles' Creed: his Notes on the New Testament are the earliest work of modern Biblical criticism. But, with this single exception, the fashion of classical reaction carried all before it. There was no open rebellion against the Church; that was reserved for the time of Ochino and the Sozzini: the humanists, as a rule, were faithful to the common practice of Italy: they conformed and they disbelieved. The existing organization of Christianity they accepted as a fact, while to its dogmatic system they were profoundly indifferent, and, in common with Popes and Cardinals, laughed at its moral restraints. Those were days of open vice, of brazen-fronted license, when crime went straight to results of which it was not ashamed, and foul corruption poisoned the life-blood of society. And the humanists were neither better nor worse than their contemporaries. The frank naturalness of classical literature contained little that could brace them against the universal dissolution of morals; nor when Zion ran riot was it to be expected that austere modesty should have taken refuge upon Olympus. To some it may seem only an instance of perverted taste, to others it may indicate almost a degraded turn of mind, that when the exigencies of their verse required the mention of God, He figured as "*Jupiter Optimus, Maximus,*" or even as "*Superum Pater nim-*

Church), to Rome, to occupy the post of Apostolic writer, with a large salary. The purity of Valla's Latin style outweighed all other considerations with the humanist Pope.

bipotens" and "*regnator Olympi.*"[1] The greatest truths, the most awful realities of faith, were made to bend to artificial necessities of style. In a word, the classical revival filled the humanists' whole souls. Christian antiquity they despised, and they did not see that the morals of the Church needed to be reformed.

Two reasons may be given why the Italian Revival should have blossomed into Reformation only upon soil which was not Italian. The first is the Italian character, coupled with the peculiar relation of the nation to the Papacy. Italian religion has rarely been of the ethical kind. It is capable, perhaps beyond all others, of erotic rapture: it will kindle into the fiercest fanaticism; but it is very apt to cool into an easy cynicism, smiling at moral distinctions, the obligation of which it does not care to deny. Lorenzo de Medici, who writes with the same pen pious dramas and lascivious songs—who presides over a Platonic academy and intrigues to make his son a Cardinal, and strangles his country's liberties—is not more characteristic of the Italy of the Revival than Savonarola thundering in the Duomo, or kindling on the Piazza della Signoria the bonfire of Florentine gauds and vanities. The one represents Italy in her ordinary mood; the other, Italy in her moments of pious

---

[1] There are worse things even than these. In describing the death of Christ, Vida, in his Christiad, "introduces a gang of Gorgons, Harpies, Centaurs, Hydras, and the like. The bread of the Last Supper appears under the disguise of 'sinceram Cererem.' The wine mingled with gall offered to our Lord upon the cross is 'corrupti pocula Bacchi.'" Cardinal Bembo "described the Venetian Council bidding a Pope 'uti fidat diis immortalibus, quorum vices in terra gerit.'" Symonds: Renaissance in Italy: The Revival of Learning, pp. 399, 400.

excitement. We may compare her to the acolyte who has been all his life too close to the mysteries of the altar to have any reverence for them left. She knew what Popes and Cardinals and Bishops were. To her the perpetual rush of Christendom to Rome to join in the struggle for power and pelf was a familiar thing. No one was so well acquainted as she with the dissoluteness, the corruption, the cruelty of the sacred city. The very oppressions which goaded Germany and England to revolt, brought gold into her coffers: rents and tithes, exacted in every corner of Europe, were spent in Italy. Except Adrian VI., in the brevity of whose pontificate Rome openly rejoiced, every Pope of these ages was Italian. Of all nations, the Italian was that least likely to feel the moral reproach of a system which thus redounded to its own advantage. If reform was to come at all, it must spring from the heart of a race endowed with a deeper moral consciousness.

But, again, the humanists of the first century of the Revival were too much occupied in learning the lessons of classical antiquity to think of applying them or to find out that they had any application. In them the mind of Europe was undergoing a training which could not till later develop into creative effort. The classic languages of antiquity were being appropriated as literary instruments: the results of Greek and Roman thought were slowly sinking into men's minds, and so preparing them for fresh and independent activity. In the work of the Italian humanists there was no element of originality; nothing that they did is valued now for its own sake; or, if there be anything, it is the vernacular prose and verse of which they thought little. The century which is peculiarly their own is almost a blank in the history of Italian literature: we pass at a bound from Petrarch, Dante, Boccaccio, to Pulci, Boiardo, Ariosto. It was the second age of the Revival which became creative, and that was German, French, English. Italy handed on the torch of learning to the Transalpine nations: while she herself, always more careful of the form than of the matter of speech, continued the task of polishing her language, the graver Northern nations were shaking the foundations of thought. And to their aid came, at precisely the right moment, the invention of printing. It was about 1455 that Gutenberg sent out from his press at Mainz the first printed book, the Mazarin Bible. In the same year Reuchlin was born, and in 1467, Erasmus.

Germany, as we might naturally expect, was far behind Italy in the race of classical revival. In the latter, Latin, up to at least the fifteenth century, could hardly be said to be a dead language: it had never ceased to be the dialect of literature and the Church, and the Italians, in renewing their acquaintance with Roman orators and poets, seemed to themselves to be only reclaiming a neglected national inheritance. It was Italy, too, that had been in direct communication with the East, and by Italian teachers that the knowledge of Greek was communicated to the rest of Europe. The great Councils of Constanz and of Basel did something to bring the German and the Italian mind together. Poggio Bracciolini attended the first, then and afterwards, either in his own person or by deputy, searching the convent libraries of Germany and Switzerland for manuscripts of the classics. One result of the second was the appointment of Æneas

Sylvius Piccolomini, the celebrated Siennese diplomatist, as secretary to the Emperor Frederick, and his consequent residence for some years, between 1440 and 1450, at Vienna. He is a good representative of the Renaissance on its practical side: a man of letters, who, if not learned, was fully equipped with the culture of his times: a Churchman, who availed himself of the advantages of his calling, without submitting to its restraints: a politician, who, after spending years in the service of the Emperor, adroitly changed sides and made himself Pope. Germany, at the beginning of the fifteenth century, had already five Universities, those of Prague, Vienna, Erfurt, Heidelberg and Cologne, to which in 1409 Leipzig was added, and in 1419, Rostock.[1] But if we may judge from the report which Æneas Sylvius makes of the University of Vienna, the instruction given in these institutions was not worth much.[2] Too much

---

[1] The University of Prague was founded in 1348, Vienna in 1365, Erfurt in 1378, Heidelberg in 1385, Cologne in 1388. Erfurt will be recognized as the fountain of Lutheranism. Heidelberg was established with an express view to breadth and comprehensiveness of training. Cologne, on the contrary, was almost exclusively theological, and soon became the head-quarters of reaction. It was the chief seat of the Inquisition in Germany. Conf. Ullmann: Reformers before the Reformation, Eng. Trans. II. 278 et seq., 328 et seq.

[2] Maximum autem hujus gimnasii vitium est, quod nimis diutinam operam in dialectica, nimiumque temporis in re non magni fructus terunt. Qui magisterii artium titulo decorantur, hac una in arte maxime examinantur. Cæterum neque Musicæ neque Rethoricæ neque Arithmeticæ curam gerunt: quamvis metra quædam et epistolas ab aliis editas imperite exhibentem magistrandum compellant. Oratoria et Poetica apud eos penitus incognita, quibus omne studium in elenchis est variisque cavillationibus, solidi haudquaquam multum. Qui libros Aristotelis et aliorum philosophorum habeant raros invenies, commentariis plerumque utuntur." Æn. Sylvii Piccol. Opera Omnia, Basel, 1551, p. 719.

attention, he complains, was bestowed upon dialectics, and too much time spent on matters of little importance. Men who were decorated with the title of Master of Arts, were for the most part examined in dialectics alone. No attention was paid to music, or rhetoric, or arithmetic. Oratory and poetry were almost unknown. The books of Aristotle and other philosophers were rarely to be found: most men were content with commentaries. Piccolomini represents himself as the defender of poetry, or, as we should now say, of polite literature, among a coarsely practical generation, whose allegation was that poetry neither clothed nor fed them:[1] "only Justinian and Hippocrates filled the purse." "When I came to Austria as Imperial Secretary," he says, "I offended all who were counted men of mark among the Viennese, and who detested poetry as a pernicious and abominable thing."[2] He himself was proud of the title of poet, though without much pretension to it in the modern sense of the word: he had been solemnly crowned at Frankfort by the Emperor Frederick, and, till he became a Cardinal, signed all his letters, " Æneas Sylvius Poeta." But in espousing the cause of the poets and the historians against the schoolmen, he evidently had a hard battle to fight.

Some half-century later, Conrad Celtes could write to Momerlochus of Cologne : "In your city have I become acquainted with the empty and deceitful inferences of dialectics. No one here teaches the Latin grammar : no one studies the orators : Mathematics, Astronomy, Natural History, are unknown : Poetry is ridiculed : men draw back in horror from the books of Ovid and Cicero, as the Jew from swine flesh." Quoted by Hagen, Deutschlands Literarische und Religiöse Verhältnisse im Reformationszeitalter, I. 374.

[1] Opp. p. 619 : Ep. cxi. to Wilhelm von Stein.
[2] Opp. p. 937 : Ep. ccccii. to Sbigneus, Cardinal Archbishop of Krakau.

It was a little later than this that Rudolf Agricola, who deserves to be called the restorer of Greek learning in Germany, crossed the Alps in search of knowledge which he could find nowhere else. He was a pupil of Thomas à Kempis in one of the schools of the Brethren of the Common Life. To the merits of that fraternity in the matter of education I have already alluded: so far as was possible with the means at their command, they seem to have applied to teaching the principles of common sense, and to have directed the attention of their scholars from mere words to thoughts and things. But it was with something of a prophetic insight that à Kempis advised six of his best pupils to repair to Italy for a more thorough course of instruction than he could give them. These were Rudolf Lange, Count Moritz von Spiegelberg, Rudolf Agricola, Alexander Hegius, Ludwig Dringenberg, Antonius Liber. Only the three first followed—perhaps were able to follow—their teacher's advice: Lange and Spiegelberg, before they went to Italy, visiting the University of Erfurt, where at least one Italian humanist was teaching about 1460. Agricola followed them to Italy not long afterwards. There he formed a close friendship with Johann von Dalberg, afterwards Bishop of Worms and Curator of the University of Heidelberg, the result of which was an invitation in 1482 to introduce the new learning into that institution. The originally broad lines of the foundation accorded with the enlightened plans of the Curator and the new Professor; and Heidelberg, soon to be illustrated by the name of Melancthon, became the centre-point of the modern tendency, in opposition to the obscurantism of Cologne. Agricola was a fine example of the grave and religious German humanist: from à Kempis and the Brethren of the Common Life he had imbibed a real interest in theology, and, like Erasmus after him, was ready to dedicate all his erudition to the service of her whom he regarded as the Queen of sciences. His death in 1485, at the early age of forty-two, prevented him from playing the important part which he otherwise must have done in the literary and religious revival of Germany. But the movement was already too national in its aims and extent to suffer even a momentary hindrance from the loss of one man.

Of the other pupils of Thomas à Kempis, Dringenberg is known as the teacher of a school at Schlettstadt,[1] which, founded in 1450, soon numbered 900 pupils, and was the centre from which the new learning spread itself along the upper Rhine. Rudolf Lange was head of a similar school at Münster; Antonius Liber taught successively in Amsterdam, Kempen and Alkmar. But the most important of these schools was that founded in 1481 at Deventer by Alexander Hegius. Hegius, who had not crossed the Alps, possibly owed what knowledge of Greek he had to his old friend and schoolfellow Agricola.[2] No work that can be called original is attributed to him. But the glory of a schoolmaster is in his scholars; and the chief claim of Hegius to remembrance is, that he taught Erasmus the rudiments of learning.

---

[1] Now Schelestadt, on the western side of the Rhine, above Strasburg.

[2] Another distinguished scholar of Hegius, Hermann von dem Busche, says of him in a Latin epigram:

    Hoc duce, Westphales intravit Græcia muros,
      Et Monastriacas Pegasus auxit aquas.

The years during which Erasmus was laying the foundations of that unrivalled erudition which made him the first scholar of Europe—from 1480 to the end of the century—were years of rapid intellectual progress in Germany. Everywhere, but especially along the course of the Rhine, schools were being founded, libraries collected, classical authors translated and imitated, grammars and other school books compiled. After an interval of between thirty and forty years, during which no University had been founded, a new group came into existence. The zeal of a wise Burgomaster gave Greifswalde its University in 1456: a little later, Duke Albrecht of Austria founded Freiburg. Basel followed in 1460, Ingolstadt and Trier in 1472. In 1477, Duke Eberhard with the Beard established Tübingen, and in the same year Archbishop Diether, Mainz. Elector Frederick the Wise called Wittenberg into existence into 1502; while Joachim I., Elector of Brandenburg, incited by his minister, Eitelwolf vom Stein, who had been Dringenberg's pupil at Schlettstadt, gave Northern Germany a University at Frankfort-on-the-Oder in 1506. At the end of the century, almost every German city of importance possessed some educational institute, or, if not, at least a resident scholar, who kept up a close intercourse with the learned world, and raised the intellectual level of the place. Of Heidelberg and its University, now flourishing in renewed activity, I have already spoken. At Speier was Jacob Wimpheling, another pupil of Dringenberg's—the typical scholar of the Rhineland, bound by close friendship to all the votaries of the new learning—an author of very various activity, especially interested in education and the training of young men in the best scholarship. Over the Benedictine monastery of Spanheim presided Abbot Trithemius, the well-known annalist, who died, as he had lived, a Catholic—a pupil of Agricola's, who had collected a library of 2000 volumes, Hebrew, Greek and Latin. At Basel, already becoming a centre for printers and publishers, lived Sebastian Brandt, a teacher both of law and polite literature, the author of that pungent satire, the "Ship of Fools," which, with "Reinecke Fuchs," also belonging to this period, directed against the corruptions of the Church the batteries of a humour level to the apprehension of the common people. Freiburg was the home of Ulrich Zasius, the Rector of the Latin school, a learned jurist and a correspondent of Erasmus: Tübingen, that of Heinrich Bebel, an energetic and successful teacher, whose *Facetiæ* and "Triumph of Venus" show in the unrestrained freedom of their satire the less worthy side of the German revival: Augsburg, of Conrad Peutinger, a patrician of that free city, and its Secretary, who, having studied in Italy, where he enjoyed the friendship of Politian, had returned home to form a collection of antiquities, and to pursue the study of classical and German archæology.[1] Nürnberg, where the artists, who, with Albrecht Dürer at their head, made it almost a German Florence, were already at work, was the abode of Willibald Pirkheimer, one of the most characteristic

---

[1] The name of Conrad Peutinger is preserved among scholars by the famous *Tabula Peutingeriana*, an ancient map, based on an *Itinerarium* of the time of the Emperor Theodosius, which gave the military roads through the greater part of the Western Empire. Peutinger got it from Conrad Celtes, who had found it in a Benedictine monastery on the Tegernsee. It was, however, not published in a complete form till 1753.

figures of this period; like Peutinger, a patrician and servant of his native city, who had lingered long in Italy and brought home many Italian friendships; a votary as well as a patron of arts and letters, at once a translator of the Fathers and a writer of pasquinades; a stately burgher, not untouched by the self-indulgence which belonged to the Italian humanist; who welcomed Luther, yet had two sisters Abbesses, and who died at last satisfied with neither the old church nor the new. At Ingolstadt, a few years later, lived and taught Johann Eck, a humanist, who had not yet made the mistake of seeking notoriety in disputation with Luther, and who, though a Professor of Theology, eagerly associated himself with the classical revival. Turning our eyes northwards, we find, in the Saxon towns of Gotha and Erfurt, a company of friends devoted to one another and the new learning, of whom the chief was Mutianus Rufus, a Canon of Gotha, called by his admirers the German Cicero, and Eoban Hess, a Latin poet of great contemporary fame, who might in like fashion claim the name of Ovid or Virgil: the one, a grave scholar, who never committed his thoughts to writing, except in familiar letters, and who hid behind a decent conformity opinions with which neither Luther nor Eck would have sympathized;[1] the other, a joyous son of the Muses, who had an ode for every occasion and a feast for every friend. And besides

---

[1] Non incepit Christi religio cum illius incarnatione, sed fuit ante omnia sæcula, ut prima Christi nativitas. Quid enim aliud est verus Christus, verus Dei filius, quam, ut Paulus inquit, sapientia Dei, quæ non solum affuit Judæis in angusta Syriæ regione, sed Græcis et Italis et Germanis, quanquam vario ritu religiones observarentur. Mutianus Rufus, Ep. 36, quoted by Strauss, U. v. Hutten, I. 46.

these—to abridge a catalogue already too long—there were the travelling scholars, of whom Conrad Celtes, Hermann von dem Busche, and above all Ulrich von Hutten, may be taken as the type. These were the knights errant of the Revival, whom we find teaching in every University in turn, always eager to sow their knowledge broadcast, always ready for hot dispute with monks and schoolmen, and for the most part living a life of frank enjoyment. Germany was all astir with intellectual life: the fabric of old beliefs was tottering to its base: some new thing was coming, though as yet men hardly knew what.[1]

At the same time we must be careful to notice that the new movement is not as yet specifically directed against the Church. It rather produced an atmosphere in which the Church's tapers would not burn, and flickered out of themselves. Every variety of theological opinion obtained among the humanists. Some, as for instance Trithemius and Wimpheling, were always devout Catholics: Eck became the champion of the Church. Others, though not many, imitated the Italian scholars in their secret or open disregard of all religion. Erasmus, who had no sympathy with dogmatic Lutheranism, yet felt profoundly the errors and corruptions of the Church, and would have reformed them in his own way, is the type of another class. Others yet again, like Mutianus Rufus, yielded themselves to the stream of tendency at first, but when they found whither it was hurrying them,

---

[1] For many of the foregoing facts I am indebted to Hagen, "Deutschland's Literarische und Religiöse Verhältnisse im Reformationszeitalter," Vol. I.

drew back into orthodox conformity. But while the new scholars were thus, in part at least, unconscious of their goal, the monkish theologians, the disciples of the schoolmen, made no mistake. An unerring instinct told them that they had a mortal battle to fight with this arrogant generation of students, who would have nothing to say to Duns Scotus, and preferred Cicero to Thomas Aquinas. It was a hopeless struggle: not only the conflict of darkness with light, but between combatants on the one side stupidly and ludicrously ignorant, on the other equipped with the best learning of the age. And it marks the essentially literary character of the new movement, that the monks unanimously called their opponents "the poets," a word of contempt in clerical circles —"a brand mark," as Strauss remarks with somewhat rueful humour, "like Pantheist nowadays."[1]

The war was waged all over Germany. Argument was hardly possible: the poets despised the verbal subtleties of the scholastic theologians, while, on the other hand, the schoolmen blinked, like owls in sunshine, in the light of the new learning. But it was possible enough to silence intrusive teachers, to call hard names, to affix the stamp of heresy, to condemn, to excommunicate, to burn, if not men, at least books. At last, however, in a way almost without precedent, the two armies joined issue in one decisive battle, that of Reuchlin with the theologians of Cologne.[2] Johann Reuchlin, born at Pforzheim in 1455, is, with one exception, the greatest figure

---

[1] Strauss, U. v. Hutten, I. 49.

[2] I may refer here generally to Mayerhoff, Reuchlin und seine Zeit; L. Geiger, Johann Reuchlin; and D. F. Strauss, Ulrich v. Hutten, particularly Vol. I. chaps. vii. viii.

of the German revival. Men called him and Erasmus "the two eyes of Germany."[1] Entering at an early age into the service of the Counts of Würtemberg, his native princes, he had studied letters at Paris, law at Orleans: whatever Italy and the Greek scholars there resident could teach him, he had learned in repeated journeys to Rome and Florence: Hermolaus Barbarus had Græcized his name into Capnio: Argyropulos, when he heard him read and expound Thucydides, declared that in his person exiled Greece had fled across the Alps. But he was more of a theologian than a stylist: other men of his day wrote more elegant Latin prose than he, though none had done so much to promote the study of the classical languages by the compilation of dictionaries and grammars. But his especial merit was in connection with the Hebrew language, which he had taken up in deliberate opposition to the Pagan tendencies of the Italian humanists. Wherever he could find an instructed Hebrew, he took lessons of him, sparing no cost. Mutian heard a story in Bologna that he had given a Jew ten gold pieces for the explanation of a single obscure phrase. His Hebrew Grammar, though not absolutely the earliest to bear that name, is the first that deserves it.[2] Half a century later, Melancthon speaks of him as indisputably the introducer of

---

[1] U. v. Hutten says: "Duos Germaniæ oculos (Erasmum et Capnionem) omni studio amplexari debemus: per eos enim barbara esse desinit hæc natio." Mutian uses stronger language still: "Erasmus surgit super hominis vices. Divinus est, et venerandus religiose, pie, tanquam numen," quoted by Strauss, U. v. Hutten, I. 189.

[2] Reuchlin's "Rudimenta Hebraica" was published in 1506. Conrad Pellicanus, who had learned from Reuchlin nearly all the Hebrew he knew, issued in 1503 his "De modo legendi et intelligendi Hebræa." Mayerhoff, pp. 44, 45, 262.

Hebrew learning into Germany.[1] But Reuchlin, although he had spent a large part of his life in teaching and other purely literary occupations, was by profession a lawyer and a statesman, not a man of letters. He was a favourite servant of Eberhard with the Beard, the first Count of Würtemberg who assumed the title of Duke, and was sent by him on many embassies to the Papal and Imperial Courts. The Emperor had ennobled him: he was one of the Judges, elected by the Suabian League, to decide international disputes. No man was held in higher honour than he: the great humanists of Italy, as well as all the rising scholars of Germany, were his friends: Universities competed for his services: already on the verge of old age, he had retired into the country, and exchanged diplomacy for study and the breeding of white peacocks, when the great storm of his life burst upon him.

Hebrew was a dangerous thing to touch in those days. When Reuchlin in his earlier life lectured upon it in Heidelberg, he had to do it privately, for fear of the monks. The Jews, evermore an accursed people, had crucified the Lord: what could be plainer than that any one who tampered with their tongue was a heretic and an outcast? If the plea was urged that the Old Testa-

---

[1] Declamatio "De Capnione Phorcensi," Ph. Melanthonis Opp. Corpus Reformatorum, XI. 1006. Reuchlin's own language on this point is clear. In his "Consilium pro libris Judæorum nen abolendis," he says, in answer to the taunt of Pfefferkorn that he had not written his own Hebrew Grammar, "So ist doch vor mir nie kainer kummen, der sich understanden hab, die gantzen hebraische sprach inn ain buch zu reguliern, das sie moecht von den latinischen gefasst und empfangen werden, und solt den neid sein hertz zerbrechen, dannocht bin ich der erst." H. v. d. Hardt: Historia Literaria Reformationis, ii. 49.

ment was written in Hebrew, the ready answer was, that the Vulgate was the Bible of the Church, and quite good enough for any sound churchman. And Reuchlin had more than a philological interest in his Hebrew studies. Early in life he had come under the influence of John Wessel, of Gröningen, who exhorted him to study the Bible, and, if Melancthon is to be believed, taught him the rudiments of Hebrew. Like Erasmus, and unlike the Italian scholars, he applied himself to the ancient languages with a theological purpose. He had not scrupled to point out errors in the Vulgate, appealing from it to the Hebrew original; and when reproved for so doing, had replied in the true spirit of the Christian scholar: "I revere St. Jerome as an angel; I respect De Lyra as a master; but I adore Truth as a God."[1] But more than this, he was caught in the fantastic net of the Cabbalists, to whom Pico della Mirandola had first introduced him. He believed in mystic meanings of the words and letters of the Hebrew Scriptures. He taught a Canon of Bamberg how to find in one verse of Exodus the seventy-two unspeakable names of God.[2] This delusive shadow of erudition was the pre-occupation of his life; he expounded it in a treatise, *De verbo mirifico*, published in 1495, and again twenty years later in another, *De arte cabbalisticâ*, dedicated to Leo X. He was thus a man about whom hung an undefined suspicion of unsoundness: if, as the monkish saying went, every good grammarian was a heretic, how much more a man who dealt in such unlawful learning?

---

[1] Strauss, U. v. Hutten, I. 192. The influence of De Lyra's Commentary on Luther is well known. It was said, "Si Lyra non lyrasset, Lutherus non saltasset."

[2] Ibid. I. 191.

To Reuchlin, then, about the beginning of the year 1510, came a converted Jew, by name Johann Pfefferkorn, on a strange errand.[1] The visitor, who, if accounts may be trusted, was as unwholesome in appearance as in character, brought with him an order from the Emperor Maximilian, then busy with his campaign against Venice, requiring all Jews within the limits of the empire to bring their books to the town-halls of their respective abodes, to be submitted to the inspection of Pfefferkorn and such assistants as he might choose, and if they contained any insults to the Christian religion, to be straightway burned. This, then, was the purpose for the execution of which the aid of the greatest Hebrew scholar of the day was asked. For the time, Reuchlin got rid of his visitor upon allegation of some informality in the mandate, which his legal knowledge enabled him to point out. But Pfefferkorn was persistent, and, besides, had powerful friends behind him. Before long, Reuchlin was required by the Archbishop of Mainz, in pursuance of an imperial order, to give his opinion on the question, whether all Hebrew books, except the Old Testament, ought not to be forcibly taken from the Jews and burned. To this the scholar could give only one reply. He prepared a memoir, in which he divided Hebrew literature into seven categories, of which only one, and that doubtfully, was declared worthy of the fire: while the general conclusion was, "that the Jews' books should not be burned, but that with reasonable debate they should, by God's help, be gently and kindly brought over to our

---

[1] The most important documents in the controversy between Reuchlin and the Dominicans of Cologne will be found reprinted in Hermann v. d. Hardt: Historia Literaria Reformationis, Part ii.

faith"—an attempt which Reuchlin proposed to further by founding Chairs of Hebrew in the German Universities. This, however, was not what Pfefferkorn wanted; and the first result was a bitter personal controversy between him and Reuchlin, in which—so at least thought the friends of learning—the latter lost dignity, first by engaging such an adversary at all, and next by too much descending to his level. But now, as it was too plain that Pfefferkorn was no match for Reuchlin, who was supported by the whole of learned Germany, new batteries were unmasked. Behind Pfefferkorn were the Dominicans of Cologne; behind the Dominicans, the Inquisition. The Jew retires from the fray, but his place is taken by Jacob Hoogstraten, the chief Inquisitor. It is not a question now of collecting and burning Hebrew books, but of compelling Reuchlin to pay the penalties of heresy.

The story of the struggle, which lasted for six years, cannot now be told in detail. An attempt to condemn Reuchlin at a court of the Inquisition held at Mainz, broke down. A second inquiry, held by the Bishop of Speier, resulted in his acquittal, and the condemnation of his opponents in costs. Then the case went by appeal to Rome, where Hoogstraten appeared in person, confident in a full purse and the influence of the mendicant orders. But here, too, after long delays, a theological commission, over which the Archbishop of Nazareth presided, gave judgment in Reuchlin's favour. It proves, however, how much Leo both feared and hated the Dominicans and Franciscans, that he could not bring himself to strike a decisive blow against them, and that, instead of confirming the judgment of the court, he issued a *mandatum de supersedendo*, imposing silence on both parties.[1] But it is important to notice that it was by no means a struggle between the Church, as such, and the humanists. The Emperor seems soon to have become ashamed of the part which he had been made to play, and actually wrote to the Pope on behalf of Reuchlin. The Chapter of Mainz took the same side. The Pope himself was reported to have said privately that he would see that Reuchlin came to no harm. The persecuted scholar found many friends among the various clerical judges before whom the case was heard. His enemies were the mendicant orders and the Universities over which they had control; Paris, Mainz, Erfurt, Louvain, all pronounced against him, as Cologne had already done. The rage of the Dominicans when Hoogstraten was compelled to leave Rome without obtaining the desired con-

---

[1] The subsequent fortune of Reuchlin's case is worth recording. His enemies at Cologne had carried on the war for some time in books and pamphlets when Franz v. Sickingen, in his character of a general reformer of abuses, took up his cause, probably at Hutten's instigation. He addressed a letter to Hoogstraten, requiring the Dominicans to write to Rome to announce their retirement from the case, to cease from all persecution of Reuchlin, and to pay the costs in which they had been condemned at Speier. Should they fail to comply with these conditions, he signified his intention of ravaging the diocese of Cologne with fire and sword. It was impossible to argue with a master of legions: the conditions were accepted, the costs paid, and Hoogstraten laid down his office of Inquisitor. But *nullum tempus occurrit ecclesiæ*. Within a few months a favourable opportunity presented itself: the letter to Rome was declared to have been written under compulsion: Leo X., who by this time had been enlightened by events at Wittenberg, issued a brief, questioning the judgment given at Speier and condemning Reuchlin, and Hoogstraten was restored to his functions and dignities. Mayerhoff: Reuchlin, p. 241. Strauss: U. v. Hutten, II. 19 et seq. Geiger: Joh. Reuchlin, pp. 436 et seq.

demnation, knew no bounds: they denounced the Pope; they talked of appealing to a general Council; they even threatened schism. On the other hand, the scholars, the poets, rallied round Reuchlin, knowing that his cause was their own. All the men whom I have mentioned as the leaders in the literary movement, and many more, were his enthusiastic friends. They called themselves Reuchlinists: *Salve Reuchlinista*, was a common form of address in speech and writing. They defended his cause in prose and verse, serious argument and biting satire: they encouraged him in letters: even Erasmus so far forgot his habitual caution as to write to Pope and Cardinal on his behalf.[1] The printers and booksellers were on the same side: the complaint was made, both then and later, that the conservative party did not receive fair play from the new art of printing.[2] It was a struggle to the death, the young men against the old, the classics against the schoolmen, scholarship against ignorance, light against darkness.

One literary device, adopted by Reuchlin's friends to show the kind and extent of the support which was given him, was the publication in 1514 of a collection of letters addressed to him by the scholars of Germany. *Clarorum virorum Epistolæ ad Johannem Reuchlin.*[3] By this

---

[1] Erasmi Opp. III. Epp. clxviii. p. 146, clxxiv. p. 154.

[2] See a curious and angry confession, from the pen of a bitter enemy, of the favour in which the Lutherans stood with the printers and publishers. Cochlæus, Acta et scripta M. Lutheri, under the year 1522, p. 82.

[3] On the title-page of the "Illustrium virorum Epistolæ," a collection of letters which followed the Epp. Obsc. Vir. in 1519, and must not, therefore, be confounded with the "Clarorum virorum Epistolæ," published in 1514, was the notice, "Reuchlinistarum exercitum pagina

was suggested the idea of perhaps the most celebrated pasquinade recorded in the history of literature. If the illustrious men thus saluted and supported their champion, why should not the obscure men do the same? It was felt, however, that it would hardly do to select Hoogstraten as the recipient of these letters; inquisitors, however stupid and ignorant, are dangerous men to laugh at; and the figure-head put forward, therefore, was Ortuinus Gratius, Professor of polite literature at Cologne, and a scholar of Alexander Hegius at Deventer. To him, then, were addressed the *Epistolæ Obscurorum Virorum*, which burst upon amused and applauding Germany in the last months of 1515.[1] The book in its original form consisted of forty-one letters, written in the choicest bad Latin—not much worse Latin, it may be inferred, than the monks commonly used—and supposed to be addressed to Ortuinus Gratius by men of the party of reaction. The writers, who bear feigned and absurd names, propose to their leader the most ridiculous questions, complain of the treatment which they receive from the poets, are made to display as if unconsciously the most astounding ignorance, as well as a revolting coarseness of life and conversation, which has yet its

---

invenies mox sequenti." The letter of Joh. Cocleariligneus, in the Epp. Obsc. Vir. (Part ii. No. 59), contains a burlesque list of the same kind, as does also the "Carmen rithmicale Magistri Philippi Schlauraff" (Part ii. No. 9). Their opponents, in modern German literature, are the "Dunkelmänner," the "Finsterlinge," each of which terms is rather a play upon the word "obscuri" than a translation of it.

[1] The first edition of the Epp. Obsc. Vir. bore on its title-page the impress of Aldus of Venice: the second purported to have been printed at Rome. They were really printed, so far as it can now be ascertained, at Mainz or Hagenau.

comic side. Unlike other books of the same kind, the *Epistolæ Obscurorum Virorum* has not lost its power of amusement with lapse of time: the vileness of its Latinity is as quaint as ever: and it is a curious evidence—allowing for the caricature—of ways of living and thinking which literature might otherwise have been too dignified to record. A second part, adding seventy letters conceived in the same spirit to the first collection, followed in 1517. The effect was prodigious. The trial at Rome was in a state of suspended animation: but now *solvuntur risu tabulæ*. There were monks in Brabant, says Erasmus, who took the book seriously, as a genuine tribute of respect to Ortuinus; and Sir Thomas More sent him a similar report of English stupidity.[1] He himself was hugely delighted with the one or two of the letters which were sent him in proof before the publication of the whole: an old tradition affirms that his laughter over them cured him of a quinsy. But when all Germany was ringing with the blow that had been struck, and especially when the second part appeared, in which his own name was freely used, his characteristic timidity drove him to the other side; and in a letter to Cæsarius,[2] which Pfefferkorn and his friends did not fail to publish, he complained that the satire of the epistles was too personal. Luther[3] never cared for them: he is on the point of nailing his Theses on the Indulgences to the church door of Wittenberg, and is in much too serious a

---

[1] Erasmi Opp. III. Epp. dcccclxxix. p. 1110 C, Appendix lxxxvii. p. 1575 A.

[2] Erasmi Opp. III. Appendix, Ep. clx. p. 1622.

[3] Briefe, ed. De Wette, Epp. 20, 21, I. pp. 37, 38.

mood for such light-hearted trifling.[1] But the humanists, upon whom no shadow of the coming storm rested, were in an ecstacy of delight.

The dates alone are sufficient to show that the "Letters of the Obscure Men" were no such powerful factor in the production of the Reformation as has been sometimes alleged. Even if pasquinades played a more important part in popular revolutions than they do, the Reformation in 1516 was already too far prepared for the Letters greatly to help or hinder it. Who was their author? They have been commonly associated with the name of Ulrich von Hutten, a man of noble birth, whom love of literature made into a wandering scholar; through almost the whole of his brief life the sport of poverty and the prey of disease; the Lucian of Germany, whose prose and whose verse were equally pungent; who was the friend of Sickingen and of Luther, and who would have been the friend of Erasmus too if Erasmus would have permitted it; always a stout and not too scrupulous warrior for German freedom, and good letters, and—when it dawned—for new religious light. But we have the letter which Hutten, then at Bologna, wrote on receiving the first part of the book; and, unless it were deliberately intended to mislead, it is impossible to reconcile with it the supposition that he had any share in the authorship.

---

[1] Hoogstraten, in the dedication to Leo X. of a work published in 1519, was astute enough to point out to the Pope the close connection between Reuchlin's case and Luther's movement at Wittenberg. Reuchlin himself is reported to have said of Luther: "Gottlob, nun haben sie einen Mann gefunden, der ihnen so blutsaure Arbeit machen wird, dass sie mich alten Mann wohl in Frieden werden hinfahren lassen." Mayerhoff: Reuchlin, p. 234.

That he made large contributions to the second part is amply attested by internal evidence; among others, a most amusing letter in doggrel verse,[1] describing the adventures of an unhappy monk among the humanists of Germany, is plainly his. The critics are now settling down to the belief that while more Reuchlinists than one had a hand in the original volume, its conception and execution are chiefly due to Johann Jäger, better known as Crotus Rubianus, a scholar who was Hutten's earliest and closest friend. Its humour answers to what we know of his character. Had it been Hutten's, it would have had a sharper edge, a more definite moral purpose. The creator of the "obscure men" loves his puppets, while he laughs at their antic ways: no seriousness, as from a dissolving world, broods over him: the struggle between light and darkness is only matter for a capital joke. Hutten died, only thirty-five years old, penniless, friendless, solitary, worn out with conflict; Crotus lived to an obscure old age, returning at last, not without suspicion of sordid inducement, to the fold of Rome.[2]

The one name, however, in which the classical revival of Germany is summed up, is that of Erasmus. He is

---

[1] Epp. Obsc. Vir. Part ii. No. 9.

[2] Kampschulte, who, in his interesting book on the University of Erfurt, has given a minute account of the band of "poets" there assembled round Mutian and Eoban Hess, adheres to the idea that Hutten was associated with Crotus in the composition of the *first* part of the Epp. Obsc. Vir., and that the letter from Bologna was only part of a deliberate plan of concealment. He also names Eoban Hess himself and Petrejus (Peter Eberbach) as fellow-workers. He is, however, a little inclined, in the interest of his subject, to rush to conclusions not fully warranted by evidence. Kampschulte: Die Universität Erfurt in ihrem Verhältnisse zu dem Humanismus und der Reformation, Part i. pp. 192 et seq.

the typical northern scholar. No contemporary Italian humanist had so great a reputation: he was recognized on both sides of the Alps as the literary chief of Europe. Like Agricola and Reuchlin, he travelled for purposes of study: Paris and Rome, Bologna and Florence, were familiar to him: he corrected the press for Aldus at Venice: he learned Greek at Oxford and taught it at Cambridge: all the rising scholars of England looked up to him as their head. No one else wrote Latin with such ease and elegance: the letters which he exchanged with Popes, Cardinals, Kings, scholars, were eagerly read: his books had an enormous circulation. The "Praise of Folly," in its first imperfect form, went through seven editions in a few months,[1] and, when acknowledged and published by its author, was repeatedly reprinted. The "Adages," though a much longer and more learned work, were hardly, if at all, less popular. One bookseller, hearing that the University of Paris was about to condemn the "Colloquies,"[2] printed, as a measure of precaution, 24,000 copies. What income Erasmus derived from his works it would be difficult to say, but he was pensioned by more than one crowned head, and was in

---

[1] R. B. Drummond: Life of Erasmus, I. 201.

[2] The Colloquies were in fact condemned by the Sorbonne, afterwards solemnly burned in Spain, and finally placed by Rome (though only after Erasmus' death) in the *Index.* Müller: Erasmus, p. 242. "De Colloquiis damnatis, scholasticus erat ludus. Colineus quidam excuderat, ut aiunt, ad viginti quatuor millia Colloquiorum in modum Enchiridii, sed eleganter. Id fecerat non studio mei, sed amore questus. Quid multis ? Nihil erat in manibus præter Colloquia. Præcesserat nescio quis rumor, forte a typographo studiose sparsus, fore ut hoc opus interdiceretur. Ea res acuit emtorum aviditatem." Erasmi Opp. III. Ep. dxxxi. 1168 D.

the constant receipt of valuable presents.¹ There has been no such literary reputation since; for with the disuse of Latin as the universal language of educated men, passed away the possibility of a single Republic of Letters. England never acknowledged the supremacy of Voltaire; France never found out the greatness of Goethe. But before the sickly scholar of Basel—throwing on every controversy of the age the light of his genius and his learning, though too cautious to take a decisive part in any, the derider of monks, who yet clave to the Church, the Reformer who shrank from reform, the humanist who would not desert the Papacy—all Europe bowed.

To over-estimate the worth of what Erasmus did for scientific theology is simply impossible. Like most of the other great German humanists, he was a sincere Christian believer, who desired to apply the new knowledge furnished by the classical revival to the service of religious truth and the Church. As early as 1505 he republished the Notes on the New Testament by Lorenzo Valla, the single theological product of the Italian Revival. This was followed in 1516 by his edition of the New Testament in Greek,² with a Latin version and

---

¹ See a remarkable letter (No. 1103, Opp. Vol. III. p. 1284) to a Spanish correspondent, in which he recounts a long list of letters and gifts received from men of note.

² Erasmus' Greek Testament counts as the *editio princeps*. The Greek Text of the Complutensian Polyglot, so called from its having been printed at Alcala (Complutum), was out of the printer's hands as early as January, 1514; but Leo X.'s license to publish was not granted till March, 1520. This, too, was a critical edition, though it is now uncertain what MSS. were employed in its preparation. Erasmus' second edition was published in 1518, the third in 1522, the fourth

notes, printed by Froben at Basel—an edition which, it should not be forgotten, was the first attempt to form a correct text by collation of manuscripts. Subsequent editions, of which four were printed in the lifetime of Erasmus, were accompanied by paraphrases, which, however wordy and unnecessary they may seem to modern critics, were highly esteemed and of great use in popularizing a knowledge of the New Testament. To us, at least, it is interesting and important to know that the influence of Erasmus' version can be distinctly traced in those labours of Tyndale and Coverdale[1] which lie at the basis of our English Bible, and that in 1547 Edward VI. ordered a copy of his Paraphrases of the Gospels, in English, to be set up in every parish church.[2] But, besides this, the labour which other humanists applied to editing the classics, Erasmus largely reserved for the Fathers. He superintended the publication, with more or less addition of preface and comment, of the works of Cyprian, Jerome, Augustine, Irenæus, Basil, Chrysostom. His was a scholar's conception of reform :- he rightly apprehended the necessity of placing before men's eyes, in as unadulterated a form as possible, the records of Christian antiquity. Both his New Testament text and his editions of the Fathers have long been superseded; but it should be recollected that without the first neither Luther nor Tyndale could have made their translations from the Greek original, and that the second were the arsenal from

---

in 1527, the fifth in 1535. In 1536, Erasmus died. Conf. Scrivener: Introduction to the Criticism of the New Testament, chap. v.

[1] Westcott: General View of the History of the English Bible, pp. 179, 257.

[2] Westcott, p. 116. Milman: Latin Christianity, VI. 439.

which the Reformers drew all their weapons of Patristic controversy.

Erasmus had a keen eye for ecclesiastical abuses, and especially hated the monastic system. It had fastened the stain of illegitimacy upon his birth; it had robbed him of both his patrimony and his personal liberty. No one knew more than he of the ignorance, the self-indulgence, the bigotry of monks, or satirized them with a sharper pen. That the "Praise of Folly" and the "Colloquies" were in the hands of every educated man, meant that all the world was laughing at the follies and superstitions of popular religion. Erasmus might find fault with the satire of the *Epistolæ Obscurorum Virorum* as having a personal mark; but their humour, if more broadly comic, is certainly not more incisive than his own. On every side of his literary activity, therefore, Erasmus belonged to the religious humanists, who hoped that the revival of good letters might end in the reformation of the Church. And yet he stands apart from all the rest. In the burlesque enumeration of the friends of Reuchlin given by one of the obscure men, he finds only a doubtful place: "*Erasmus est homo pro se.*"[1] He does not march in line with the army of the Reuchlinists. While all the rest of the world is sure that new learning must lead to reformed faith, he professes not to see the connection. "What have I to do," he asks

---

[1] "Tunc quæsivi ab aliis an etiam Erasmus Roterodamus esset cum eis. Respondit mihi quidam kaufmannus dicens, 'Erasmus est homo pro se. Sed certum est quod nunquam erit amicus illorum theologorum et fratrum, et quod ipse manifeste in dictis et scriptis suis defendit et excusat Johannem Reuchlin, etiam scribens ad Papam.'" Epp. Obsc. Vir. Part ii. Ep. 59.

again and again, in various phrase, "with the cause of Reuchlin and of Luther?"[1] He hardly knows Reuchlin, he says; he has only seen him once or twice: the Cabbala and the Talmud are things that he does not care about. So with Luther: in the one letter which he writes to him before the correspondence which preceded their final rupture, he accepts his offer of friendship only coldly, and advises him to moderate his tone. To other correspondents he declares that he has not read the books of which all the world is talking: he even takes credit for an attempt to prevent Froben of Basel from printing Luther's works.[2] All this is in his letters to such men as Leo X., Cardinal Wolsey, the Elector Archbishop of Mainz: but there were times at which he knew himself and his true allies better. When in 1522 he published the third edition of his "Colloquies," it was found to contain a dialogue called the "Apotheosis of Reuchlin."[3]

---

[1] "Primum illud præfandum est, mihi neque cum Reuchlini negotio, neque cum Lutheri causa quicquam unquam fuisse. Cabala et Thalmud, quicquid hoc est, meo animo nunquam arrisit. . . . . Primum enim, quid rei bonis studiis cum fidei negotio? deinde, quid mihi cum causa Capnionis ac Lutheri?" Ep. 477, to the Elector Archbishop of Mainz, Opp. III. pp. 514 A, 516 F. Conf. Ep. to Wolsey, 317, III. p. 322 B, F.

[2] "Testatus sum te mihi ignotissimum esse, libros tuos nondum esse lectos: proinde nec improbare quicquam, nec probare." Ep. to Luther, 427, Opp. III. p. 444 F. "Lutherum non novi, nec libros illius unquam legi, nisi forte decem aut duodecim pagellas, easque carptim. . . . . Proinde minis etiam egi cum Johanne Frobenio typographo, ne quid operum illius excuderet." Ep. to Leo X., 529, III. p. 578 C.

[3] It is entitled, "De incomparabili heroe Joh. Reuchlino in divorum numerum relato." A Franciscan monk sees in a vision Reuchlin conducted into heaven by a choir of angels, under the especial escort of St. Jerome. The interlocutors in the dialogue express their intention of counting him among the Saints, and the whole winds up with a

The great Hebrew scholar was dead, and this was the eloquent and touching tribute which Erasmus laid upon his grave. Again, in 1520, Elector Frederick the Wise journeyed to Aachen, accompanied by his secretary, George Spalatin, to be present at the coronation of Charles V. "Thereby, at Cologne," says Spalatin, "the highly learned man, Erasmus Roterodamus, was with this Elector of Saxony, and talked with him of all manner of things; and was asked whether it was his opinion that Dr. Martin Luther had erred in his writing and preaching. Whereupon he answered, in Latin, 'Yea, indeed, in two things: that he has attacked, first, the Pope's crown, and next, the monks' bellies.' Thereupon this Elector smiled, and bethought him of this answer, hardly a year before his death."[1]

---

collect in his honour. "Amator humani generis Deus, qui donum linguarum, quo quondam Apostolos tuos ad Evangelii prædicationem per Spiritum tuum Sanctum cœlitus instruxeras, per electum famulum tuum Johannem Reuchlinum mundo renovasti," &c. &c. Erasmi Opp. I. p. 692 D.

[1] G. Spalatin: Leben und Zeitgeschichte Friedrichs des Weisen, 164. Erasmus' way of speaking of Luther and his work differed greatly according to his mood at the time and the person whom he was addressing. He not unfrequently recognized himself as the precursor of the Reformation. In a letter to Zwingli (Huld. Zuinglii Opera, edd. Schuler et Schulthess, VII. 310) he said, "videor mihi fere omnia docuisse, quæ docet Lutherus, nisi quod non tam atrociter, quodque abstinui a quibusdam ænigmatibus et paradoxis." The story of the egg that Erasmus laid, Luther hatched, seems to have been current at the time: Erasmus himself alludes to it (Ep. to Cæsarius, 719, III. p. 840 D): "Ego peperi ovum, Lutherus exclusit. Mirum vero dictum Minoritarum istorum, magna que et bona pulte dignum. Ego posui ovum gallinaceum, Lutherus exclusit pullum longe dissimillimum." Perhaps an extract from the letter before quoted to the Archbishop of Mainz best defines the position which he would like to have occupied had he not been driven from it by the remorseless logic of events: "De articulis, quos objiciunt Lu-

At first sight, this looks like mere time-serving; and no doubt there was in Erasmus a distinct element of both personal and intellectual timidity. He wished to stand well with all the world, and especially with his royal and ecclesiastical patrons: he was reluctant to do anything that might imperil his intellectual supremacy. It was one thing to scatter abroad general sarcasms, and another to face personal opposition: there was a cry for reformation of abuses with which it was easy to mingle his voice, yet at the same time to protest against ill-regulated zeal and ungoverned impetuosity. But to stop here is to take only a superficial view of the character and action of Erasmus. He believed in the dissolvent power upon old abuse of intellectual culture. The reform which he desired, and which he did so much to prepare, would, he thought, come slowly, gradually, surely, as the horizon of human knowledge widened, and men laid upon truth

there, in præsentia non disputo, tantum de modo et occasione disputo. Ausus est Lutherus de indulgentiis dubitare, sed de quibus alii prius nimis impudenter asseveraverant. Ausus est immoderatius loqui de potestate Rom. Pontificis, sed de qua isti nimis immoderate prius scripserant, quorum præcipui sunt tres prædicatores, Alvarus, Sylvester et Cardinalis Sancti Sixti. Ausus est Thomæ decreta contemnere, sed quæ Dominicani pene præferunt Evangeliis. Ausus est in materia Confessionis scrupulos aliquos discutere, sed in qua monachi sine fine illaqueant hominum conscientias. Ausus est ex parte negligere scholastica decreta, sed quibus ipsi nimium tribuant, et in quibus ipsi nihilo minus inter se dissentiunt; postremo, quæ subinde mutant, pro veteribus rescissis inducentes nova. Discruciabat hoc pias mentes, cum audirent in scholis fere nullam sermonem de doctrina Evangelica, sacros illos ab ecclesia jam olim probatos auctores haberi pro antiquatis: imo in sacris concionibus minimum audiri de Christo; de potestate Pontificis, de opinionibus recentium fere omnia. Totam orationem jam palam quæstum, adulationem, ambitionem, ac fucum præ se ferre. His imputandum opinor, etiamsi qua intemperantius scripsit Lutherus." Ep. 477, Opp. III. pp. 515, 516.

a firmer grasp. Such a reformation would involve no violent break with the past: there was no need of a rebellion against the Pope, or of an upturning of Europe, or of the founding of a new church upon the ruins of the old. Luther's masterful ways disturbed this literary dream: his theses against indulgences, his resistance to Papal argument and menace, his abjuration of his monastic vows, his marriage, his communion in both kinds, were so many successive blows against the only theory of reformation which Erasmus could entertain. Nor must it be forgotten that he was absolutely without sympathy for Luther's characteristic theology. Justification by faith was a thing abhorrent to him. Erasmus thought the progress of Lutheranism an injury to good morals as well as to good letters. His own theology—readers may find it in his *Enchiridion militis Christiani*[1]—was a strongly ethical faith, out of which the characteristic superstitions of Catholicism had disappeared, but which Luther would certainly have declared to be nought.[2] He is the Jerome of the Reformation, as

---

[1] The "Enchiridion" was written about 1501, and probably published not long after. But Erasmus reprinted it, with a letter in its defence, in 1518. We may take it therefore as representing his matured opinions.

[2] For a number of characteristically violent criticisms on Erasmus, see Luther's Tischreden, ed. Förstemann, sec. xxxvii. Nos. 106—135. The following are worth quoting. "Anno 36. 1 Augusti, Martinus Lutherus solus in speculationibus sedens creta in mensem scripsit. 'Res et verba Philippus. Verba sine re Erasmus. Res sine verbis M. Lutherus. Nec rem nec verba Carolostadius.'" Tisch. II. 409. Again: "Erasmus ist ein Feind aller Religion und ein sonderlicher Feind und Widersacher Christi, ein vollkommen Conterfeit und Ebenbild des Epicuri und Luciani. Dies hab ich, M. Luther, mit meiner eigenen Hand geschrieben Dir, mein lieber Sohn Johannes, und durch

Luther is its Augustine. But it is not wonderful that as time went on, as Luther's aims became more definite and his success more assured, Erasmus found it ever more difficult to preserve even the appearance of neutrality, and at last was forced by the solicitations and remonstrances of his friends to enter upon a controversy in which neither he nor Luther reaped many laurels. His book, *De Libero Arbitrio*, was published in 1524, and from that time to his death, in 1536, he watched the progress of the Reformation with jealous and jaundiced eyes.[1]

It is easy at this distance of time to see that, without the vigorous personality of Luther, little would have been accomplished for the reformation of the church; and that such a doctrine as that of justification by faith, in virtue of its capacity for popular impression and its innate motive power, was a main element in his success. But nothing can well be more unjust than to find fault with Erasmus for not being Luther, or even for unwillingness to place himself at Luther's side. Neither his strength nor his weakness was Luther's: he was a scholar,

---

Dich allen meinen Kindern und der heiligen Christlichen Kirchen." Tisch. II. 419. A more deliberate though hardly more favourable estimate may be found in Luther's letter to Amsdorf, Feb. 1534: Briefe, ed. De Wette, IV. 507.

[1] In 1534, Erasmus published a project of reform in his little work, "De amabili Ecclesiæ Concordia," an exposition of the seventy-third Psalm, undertaken at the request of Julius Pflug, Bishop of Naumburg. But he was then sixty-seven years of age, and within two years of his death: the Confession of Augsburg is already four years old, and there is no longer any room for reforming initiative, even had Erasmus been able to take it. We need not wonder, therefore, that there is little in the book beyond deprecation of abuse and excess, and a recommendation to all parties to live and let live in matters of religion.

not a religious reformer: a sickly man of letters, not a hero of faith. I should as little think of dwelling upon his timid caution in shifting his sails to suit the wind, as upon Luther's ungoverned violence of speech: like all men who play a great part, each had the defects of his qualities. But events have amply justified both. The Reformation that has been, is Luther's monument: perhaps the Reformation that is to be, will trace itself back to Erasmus. He was mistaken in thinking that the reforming efficacy of culture was of quick operation, or that no more sudden and sharp cautery than his own method supplied was needed to cure the abuses of the time. But he is the father of the theological scholarship of the Reformed Churches. His New Testament lies at the base of all subsequent textual criticism. His editions of the Fathers first made possible the study of Christian antiquity. He compassed what was then almost the whole of human knowledge, and brought it to bear upon religious truth. This is, after all, the scientific method, the only method which produces results safe from ultimate disturbance. Luther's personal inspiration still lives and works among men, who learn from him the secret of faith, who catch from him the contagion of heroism; but the spirit of Erasmus is the life of scientific criticism, the breath of modern scholarship.

There is a story[1] which, though of respectable anti-

---

[1] I cannot trace this story, in the form in which it is given in the text, further back than to a tract by J. L. Fabricius, "De Ludis Scenicis Dialexis Casuistica quinquepartita," first published at Heidelberg in 1663, and afterwards reprinted in Gronovius' "Thesaurus Græcarum Antiquitatum," Vol. VIII. 1699. But there is a curious record of a similar play performed before Francis I. in Paris in 1524, which was from the pen of Johann Lange, Prior of the Augustinian convent, and

quity, is perhaps more apt than authentic, that when Charles V. was holding the Diet of Augsburg in 1530, a party of actors asked leave to present before him a play in dumb show. Permission being granted, there entered the hall a masked figure, in a doctor's gown, upon whose back was a label, "Johann Reuchlin." He threw down upon the floor a bundle of sticks, some straight, some crooked, and so departed. Next followed another, in like attire, whose name was Erasmus of Rotterdam: for a long time he tried to make the crooked sticks square with the straight ones, and then, finding his labour in vain, retired in manifest disturbance of mind. The third masked figure was that of a monk, labelled Martin Luther, who, bringing in fire and fuel, set a light to the crooked sticks, and when the flame had caught them retired in his turn. Then came in one clad like an Emperor, who with drawn sword tried to keep the fire and the sticks apart, but, when the flame gathered strength all the more, went away in great anger. Last of all a Pope, bearing the name of Leo X., came in, wringing his hands, till, looking about him for help, he saw two jars, one full of oil, the other of water, and, rushing to them like a madman, seized the oil and poured it upon the fire, which, spreading itself all abroad,

---

afterwards Lutheran pastor, at Erfurt. This appears to have been printed in two different forms, though whether either or both are now extant I am unable to say. They are mentioned in Burckhard's "Commentatio de vita et fatis Ul. Hutteni," whence the "argumentum tragœdiæ" has been transferred by Dan. Gerdes to the second volume of his well-known "Historia Reformationis," where it will be found at p. 48 of the "Monumenta" in the Appendix. But the Paris play was not in dumb show, and both Hutten and a mendicant friar, "fraterculus, obeso et protentiore ventriculo, capite pingui," play a part in it.

compelled him to flee. Who these actors were no one knew; for without waiting for reward they disappeared. But the moral of their play was such as even Charles V. might draw.

LECTURE III.

THE REFORMATION IN ITS EXTERNAL ASPECTS.

THE specifically religious revolution in Germany which we call the Reformation, was part of a more general movement of thought from which it finally, though only gradually, disengaged itself. Germany, as we have already seen, had caught from Italy that impulse of renewed mental activity which was then diffusing itself over civilized Europe, and which even yet shows no sign of exhaustion. It shared in the universal revolt against ecclesiastical oppression, the long-standing disgust with clerical laxity and vice which at the beginning of the sixteenth century was made more intense by the shameless administration of successive Popes. And in this respect it had special reasons for discontent. It was the milch cow of the Papacy, which at once despised and drained it dry. An examination of the map reveals a state of things to which no other European country can show anything parallel.[1] At least a fourth of the whole

---

[1] See especially Spruner-Menke : Hand Atlas für die Geschichte des Mittelalters und der neueren Zeit. Map 43: Deutschland im Zeitraum der Reformation.

area of Germany was under ecclesiastical rule. On the extreme north-east were the wide domains of the Teutonic knights, not yet converted into an hereditary appanage of the House of Hohenzollern. On the north-west stretched in continuous line the dioceses of Bremen, Utrecht, Münster and Paderborn. The Bishopric of Liège occupied a not inconsiderable part of the Netherlands, while those of Metz and Strasburg covered the French frontier. The great Electoral Archbishoprics of Cologne, Trier and Mainz, ran along the course of the Rhine. In Central Germany, Hildesheim, Halberstadt, Magdeburg, Würzburg and Bamberg, were all ecclesiastical states, while Salzburg and Trent carried the line of clerical fortresses down to the confines of Italy. Whenever the Diet met, three out of the seven Electors who made up the first line of the political hierarchy were ecclesiastics, while the great Bishops successfully held their own with the crowd of minor potentates. It is quite true that the wealth and power of these Bishoprics made them objects of ambition to members of royal and noble families, and so usually prevented them from falling a prey to Italian rapacity; but they were not the less outworks of the Papacy, and instruments of Papal corruption and oppression. And it is not wonderful, therefore, that with other feelings of discontent mingled a desire for national independence of Italy. The cry for reform constantly took the shape of a demand for a *German* Council. The nation would willingly, if it could, settle its own ecclesiastical affairs. The Holy Roman Empire was yet much more than a pale shadow of the past, and if any Emperor had been found willing to put himself at the head of his Estates, in direct opposition to the Pope, he might have had a united people at his back.

It would be a great mistake to suppose that the necessity of reform in the Church was felt only by those whom we call Reformers. All through the struggle, which we may take as lasting from 1517, when Luther nailed his indulgence theses to the church door at Wittenberg, to 1552, when the Peace of Passau was signed, two voices are to be heard—that of the Protestants, who demand a reform of doctrine as well as of discipline; that of the Catholics, who are ashamed of abuses which they cannot deny, and angry at their own inability to correct them. Throughout all negociations between the opposed parties runs a thread of reference to a general Council or a national Assembly, which is to make the crooked straight. Though the precedents of Constanz and of Basel were not wholly encouraging, they were too recent to be forgotten. Even before the Papal bull had made its way to Wittenberg, Luther sought to turn aside its blow by an appeal to a general Council.[1] A little later, when the Diet of Worms was waiting for the Reformer's appearance, the Emperor asked from the

---

[1] The idea of appeal to a general Council was neither a new one nor confined to Germany. On the 19th of March, 1518, the Parliament of Paris, engaged in a controversy as to what were afterwards known as the Gallican liberties, appealed "au Pape mieux conseillé, et au premier concile general, legitiment assemblé," while, a few days after, the University, evidently not forgetful of the traditions of Gerson and Jean d'Ailly, followed with another appeal, "ad futurum concilium legitime ac in loco tuto (congregatum) et quod libere, et cum securitate adire poterimus." Gieseler, K. G. II. iv. p. 204, note. Köstlin, Martin Luther, I. 233, says that Luther in his appeal was careful to follow these precedents.

Estates a written statement of ecclesiastical oppression and abuses, a document to which Duke George of Saxony, the very representative of Catholic orthodoxy among the German princes, contributed a list of grievances which struck dismay into the heart of Aleander, the legate of Leo X.[1] When another legate, Chieregati, asked the Diet at Nürnberg, in 1522-3, why the Edict of Worms against Luther and his followers had not been enforced, he was answered by the production of 100 *gravamina*—a long and heavy bill of indictment brought by united Germany against the Church, which it was demanded should be tried by a national Council, to be held within a year in a German city, under the presidency of the Emperor.[2] Afterwards, when the opposition between parties had become more decisive and more bitter, Catholics were naturally reluctant to identify themselves with Protestant demands. But it is instructive to note how, during the latter part of the period of which I have spoken, the opposition to a Council comes chiefly from the side of the Pope. The Emperor desires it. The Protestants only ask for guarantees that it shall be equitable and independent. It is the Pope who refuses it, who puts it off, who seeks to retain it within the sphere of his own influence. At last it met at Trent in 1546, and after many adjournments accomplished its work. But long before this time, it had been seen that doctrinal accommodation was out of the question: all that the Council could now do was to re-settle Catholic faith on an authoritative basis. From it nevertheless dates that movement of counter-reformation which, while it poured

---

[1] Köstlin: Martin Luther, I. 435.

[2] Marheineke: Geschichte der Teutschen Reformation, I. 430.

fresh blood into the veins of the Church by renewing its religious life, at once removed its worst scandals, and enabled it to make a successful stand against aggressive Protestantism. In one aspect the Council of Trent sufficiently justifies the action of the Reformers. It was the tardy confession of the Papacy that at least disciplinary reform was imperatively necessary.

It need hardly be said, however, that the chief motive power of the Reformation was distinctively religious, and that it sprang in large part from the intense personal conviction and contagious faith of one man, Martin Luther. The humanism of the time at best provided an air in which the new thoughts could breathe and burn: no Reuchlin, no Erasmus, no Pirkheimer, would have dashed themselves, as did Luther at Worms, upon the serried spears of the Papal army. The condition of Germany, divided among so many princes and princelets, jealous of each other and kept apart by conflicting interests, was unfavourable to political action against Italy: three centuries were to elapse before it could be made one, and then only by the stern logic of force. The only manifestation of popular political life was in the free cities; nor, except through its religious consciousness, was there any means of banding the nation together and making it feel its power. But this is precisely what Luther did. Himself, as he gloried in saying, "a peasant and the son of a peasant," he never—but for one moment, when the Peasants' War seemed to threaten the work of his life with destruction—lost his deep and vivid sympathy with the people. His doctrine of the natural priesthood of the Christian believer was, within the limits of the Church, profoundly democratic. So, too, was that still more central article of his creed, justification by faith alone; for it made religion a matter entirely between Christ and the believing soul, needing the intervention of neither priest, nor visible church, nor sacrificial rite. Luther's rugged, yet always nervous and moving eloquence—his mastery over the German language, then just beginning to be a literary tongue—his deliberate use of popular phrases and proverbs—his translation of the Scriptures, which made the Bible everywhere a household book—the prayers, the catechisms, the hymns, in the composition of which he always had the common people in view—combined to make him a national leader, in a way which would have been impossible on any other than religious ground. When, all over Germany, from Lübeck and Bremen, where the Reformation triumphed, to Austria and Bavaria, where persecution at last succeeded in effacing it, men repeated Luther's prayers at night and morning, and taught their children the hymns in which he had embodied the essentials of the faith, and saw in the New Testament which he had given them how different was the primitive from the Papal Church, it was no wonder that their hearts went out to Wittenberg and the man who had thus made himself the representative of the best national aspirations. There was a moment at which it seemed possible that the religious enthusiasm which Luther inspired and led might take a political form. Under the influence of Ulrich von Hutten, he was more than half inclined to throw in his lot with the schemes of revolution cherished by Franz von Sickingen. But that movement ended in speedy and ignominious failure, and for the rest of his life Luther confined himself to a purely religious activity. He was a loyal subject of the Electors of Saxony. He never wavered in his allegiance to the Emperor, notwithstanding a thousand proofs that the Imperial and the Papal policies were, so far as he was concerned, substantially the same. He discouraged all leagues and alliances in defence of Protestantism which seemed to have an outlook towards war. He would have the Gospel triumph only in the strength of truth and patient endurance. This may have been a Utopian view, but it at once concentrated his religious influence and gave it something of a national tone and spirit.

Luther's was a singularly strong and intense nature. Only Catholic libellers have ever affected to doubt his absolute sincerity. One spirit ran through all his days, animating them by the same passionate piety. We do not know what were the inward conflicts which drove him into the Augustinian convent at Erfurt, in defiance of the wishes of a father whom he loved and honoured: the story of the thunder-storm in which a friend perished at his side, if more than a legend, only gives picturesque form to the crisis of a struggle which must have been spiritual, and was probably long and doubtful. But once a monk, he applied himself with eager earnestness to the ascetic life, fasting, praying, reading with unwearied assiduity, shrinking from no labour however painful, from no penance however disgusting. He exhausted the possibilities of this method of perfection before, with equal zeal, he applied himself to another and a better: "If ever a monk," he said, "had got to heaven by monkery, I should have been he."[1] From

---

[1] Wahr ist's, ein frommer Mönch bin ich gewesen, und so gestrenge meinen Orden gehalten, dass ichs sagen darf: ist je ein Mönch gen

the first, men augured great things of him. His father thought that a distinguished worldly career had been marred by his sudden entrance into the cloister. The Provincial of his Order, Staupitz, made him his special care, watched over him in his spiritual struggles, and designated him for work in the newly-founded University of Wittenberg. There is even a faint halo of prophecy about his head, as of one in whom the long-desired reform of the Church might find consummation. For good or evil, he draws men's eyes to himself: Frederick the Wise protected, though he never saw and only partially sympathized with him: Cardinal Cajetan, after his conference with him at Augsburg in 1518, is reported to have said:[1] "I will talk no more with this animal; for he has deep eyes, and wonderful speculations in his head." Luther's personal ascendancy throughout life was immense. He had not to wait for fame; it came to him unasked. Already, in 1519, Froben, the printer of Basel, writes to him, not only that the edition of his works which he had published is exhausted, but that the copies are dispersed through Italy, Spain, England, France and Brabant.[2] At the Frankfort fair of 1520, one bookseller alone sold 1400 copies of his books.[3] Within two or three years after the burning of the Pope's bull, he was a power

---

Himmel kommen durch Möncherey, so wollte ich auch hinein kommen sein: das werden mir zeugen alle meine Klostergesellen die mich gekannt haben. Denn ich hätte mich, wo es länger gewäret hätte, zu Tode gemartert mit wachen, beten, lesen, und anderer Arbeit. Luther's Werke, ed. Walch, XIX. 2299. "Kleine Antwort auf Herzog Georgen's zu Sachsen nächstes Buch."

[1] Myconius: Hist. Reformationis, p. 33.
[2] Luther's Briefe, ed. De Wette, 132 to Joh. Lange, I. 255.
[3] Vid. a letter from Glareanus to Zwingli, quoted by Hagen, II. 97.

in Europe, already the equal of Erasmus in influence, and soon to surpass him. It is almost a rival Papacy which he sets up in Wittenberg, though a Papacy the authority of which is based on his own strength of character, his own clearness of intellectual insight: on the one hand, Melancthon obediently holds the pen which he guides; on the other, Carlstadt pays the penalty of individual thought by exclusion from the charmed circle. When, in 1529, it is plain that union among Protestants is above all things necessary to the safety of the cause, and Philip of Hesse lends all the weight of his rank and character to effect an agreement between the theologians of Wittenberg and of Zürich, it is Luther who breaks up the Conference of Marburg by his determination to yield nothing. As long as he lives, he *is* the Saxon Reformation: one of the strongest, bravest, ruggedest of mortal men, who unhesitatingly identifies truth with his own view of it, and will not yield a hair's breadth, though Emperor and Pope, devils and men, be arrayed against him.

Naturally, he had the defects of his great qualities. He saw religious truth too clearly, and with outlines too sharp, to be indulgent to what he thought to be errors of conception and inaccuracies of statement: if he refrained from setting up against the religious system of the schoolmen another as elaborate, as detailed, as minute (as indeed his followers did afterwards), it was only that his characteristic doctrine, as he conceived it, was too spiritual to lend itself readily to that kind of treatment. In his confident moods, no one was ever so confident. He spoke as magisterially as if he sat in the fisherman's chair. He had the rough tongue of the Saxon peasant, made rougher still by many a theological affray, and he called names with a burly vehemence which modern ears find it hard to endure. When he is dealing with Pope or heretic, Clement VII. or Münzer, he either forgets all rules of Christian mildness and courtesy, or thinks that in such extreme cases they do not apply. I dare not quote illustrative passages, for then, to mitigate the effect which they would undoubtedly produce, I should have to bring parallels from the works of his opponents, and try to estimate the relation in which he stood to the practice of the times. Certain it is that, if most men scolded, few could scold with such blusterous bitterness as he. But we must not forget that his friends loved him as affectionately as his foes hated him heartily. He kept open house at Wittenberg, with what hospitality, what generosity, what unrestrained kindliness of intercourse, his Table-talk remains to tell. There was a perpetual coming and going of grave theologians, curious students, travellers from every country in Europe, young Protestant princes anxious to see the great leader, royal and noble ladies seeking consolation and advice; and all had their tale to tell of his accessibility, his frank and pleasant bearing, his cheerful acceptance of the burthens laid upon him. His letters to his children are among the most charming of their kind; while his half-fond, half-jesting references to the domestic masterfulness of his Käthe, unconsciously reveal the light of love with which his home was flooded. When I think of these things, I am not disposed to lay too much stress on an unrestrained loudness of speech, which in part belongs to the age, in part to the circumstances, and only for the rest to the man; and without which, after all, it might have been hard for him to have done his work. It is on a lower moral level, I know, than the sweet reasonableness which once before conquered the world; but will mankind ever again see that strange commingling of the mildest gentleness with the most resolved strength? Courage was the universal note of the Reformers' character: when the Regent Morton said at John Knox's grave,[1] "There lies one who never feared the face of man!" he was uttering Luther's epitaph too.

Luther had that directness and clearness of insight which come of assured religious conviction, and make every great religious teacher what he is. God and Christ, heaven and hell, were very near and real to him. He prayed much, with a profound belief in the answer to prayer; telling God what he wanted in the simplest, most straightforward way, and not scrupling to press for a favourable reply. When, after the unhappy affair of the Landgrave's double marriage, Melancthon, utterly beaten down by the reproaches of his own conscience and the shame of exposure, took to his bed at Weimar in despair and disgust of life, Luther went to him, and looking at his worn and wasted form, exclaimed to his companions, "God keep us! how has the devil brought me to shame this creature!" Then he turned to the window and prayed, after a fashion which he must be left to describe in his own words: "Then indeed our Lord God had to pay me for it, for I threw the sack before the door, and rubbed His ears with all the promises that He would listen

---

[1] Mr. J. Hill Burton (History of Scotland, V. 87) will not allow that this story, in the common form given in the text, is true. His version of it is that Morton said of Knox "that he neither feared nor flattered any flesh." Either saying is equally applicable to Luther.

to prayer that I could recount out of Holy Scripture, so that He must hear me, if ever I was to put faith in His promises again." Thereupon he took Philip by the hand and said, "Be of good cheer, Philip, thou shalt not die; although God have reason to slay, yet desireth He not the death of a sinner, but rather that he should turn from his wickedness and live."[1] And indeed, under the influence of these and other such comforting words, Melancthon roused himself to life and hope once more. Again, when Luther was at Coburg in 1530, waiting for news from the Diet of Augsburg, his companion, Veit Dietrich, writes thus to Melancthon:[2]

"No day passes that he does not give three hours, and those the fittest for study, to prayer. Once it happened to me to hear him praying. Good God! how great a spirit, how great a faith, was in his very words! With such reverence did he ask, as if he felt that he was speaking with God; with such hope and faith, as with a Father and a Friend. 'I know,' he said, 'that Thou art our Father and our God. I am certain, therefore, that Thou art about to destroy the persecutors of Thy children. If Thou doest this not, then our danger is Thine too. This business is wholly Thine—we come to it under compulsion: Thou, therefore, defend'—and so forth. In almost these words, I, standing afar off, heard him praying with a clear voice. And my mind burned within me with a singular emotion when he spoke in so friendly a fashion, so weightily, so reverently with God."

At the same time, this was only one side of Luther's religiousness, though the side which his biographers most love to display. It would not have been as deep and as genuine as it was if it had not had

---

[1] Ratzeberger's MS., ed. Neudecker, pp. 103, 104.
[2] June 30, 1530: Corp. Ref. II. 159.

another. Whenever this distinctness of religious insight is real, men pay for it by days and hours when a great heaviness settles on the soul, when all that once seemed clear and vivid is shrouded in blinding mist, and faith is exchanged for an unbelief that is itself a hell. In another connection I shall have to return to these times of trial, which recur in much the same form throughout Luther's life, and to show what was their intellectual relation to his more abiding moods. A mythology has grown up around them, taking them out of the class of sober psychological fact; and instead of watching the death-struggle of a strong soul with unbelief and distrust, we are invited to see the ink-stain upon the wall of the Wartburg which records the repulse of a visible Satan. But these temptations, too, were in their way a part of his strength. They gave him a knowledge of that valley of the shadow which enters into all Christian experience; and if, when the dark hour was passed, they did not abate the confidence of his dogmatic asseverations, they did something to make him tender as well as strong.

Even in the briefest enumeration of the worthies of the Reformation, a place beside Martin Luther must be kept for Philip Melancthon. Usually the two are compared and contrasted only in regard to vigour and mildness; and Melancthon's function is supposed to be shut up in the moderating influence which he exerted over his more vehement colleague. But this is only a very superficial view of the matter. That Melancthon was far less courageous, both mentally and morally, than Luther, is quite true; but I doubt whether, unless it be very carefully limited and explained, mild is the right epithet to apply to him. His advocacy of stern repression in the Peasants' War was as uncompromising as Luther's, if also less violent;[1] while whenever heretics of any kind were to be dealt with, he was much readier to recommend fire and sword.[2] I am sure that the stronger man of the two was also the tenderer: nor am I prepared to confound readiness of intellectual concession with gentleness of heart. Both friends and enemies of his own age understood Melancthon better; and while acknowledging his abounding merits, his patient industry, his untiring obligingness, his reckless generosity, gave him no credit for qualities which he did not possess. He represented Protestantism at the crisis of the Diet of Augsburg; and but for the fatuity of the Catholics, who thought that, as he had conceded so much, those for whom he spoke would concede everything, would have succeeded in betraying the cause which he was set to serve. Twice he was invited by Catholic princes, Francis I. and Henry VIII., to effect a reconciliation in their respective countries between old and new religion, and twice the cautious wisdom of the Elector of Saxony kept him at home. No sooner was Luther dead, than the sceptre of authority fell from his feeble hands: his last years were years of Protestant dissension, in the treatment of which he calls out our pity rather than compels our admiration. He was a timid and an anxious man, painfully feeling the weight of responsibility, easily

---

[1] Letter to Camerarius, Corp. Ref. I. 747. "Confutatio Articulorum Rusticanorum," Corp. Ref. XX. 641 et seq.

[2] Letter to F. Myconius, Corp. Ref. II. 17; to the Elector of Hesse, "de puniendis Anabaptistis," Corp. Ref. III. 195; to Calvin, approving the execution of Servetus, Corp. Ref. VIII. 362.

moved to resentment and as easily placated. He was by nature and preference a humanist, not a theologian. When in 1518 his kinsman Reuchlin sent him, then only nineteen, to Wittenberg to teach Greek, he was the rising hope of German scholarship. He never took orders: he married early: though he caught the prevailing enthusiasm of the place, he was always to some extent a theologian against his will. It is true that his *Loci Communes*, originally a Commentary on the Epistle to the Romans, became, as enlarged in successive editions, the systematic exposition of Lutheran theology; but he was the presenter of another's thoughts; he lent to Luther the services of a more elegant style, a purer Latinity, a more methodical mind than his own. He lamented the way in which at Wittenberg theology swallowed up all the other sciences: he complained that he had to give theological lectures when he would willingly be expounding the classics: Homer, he said, went a begging, Demosthenes could get no hearers.[1] I do not mean that he did not play an important and in some respects an individual part in the drama of the Reformation: he was its scholar, its systematizing theologian, its doctor, its diplomatist. But I think I can see that if he had not been overpowered by the more vigorous personality of Luther, his own inclination would have made him a Protestant

---

[1] "Nunc tantus est contemptus optimarum rerum, ut nisi gratis offerantur, et quidem præleguntur a peritis, mendicare Homerus auditores cogatur. . . . . Speravi, me suavitate secundæ Olynthiacæ invitaturum esse auditores ad Demosthenem cognoscendum. Quid enim dulcius aut melius ea oratione cogitari potest? Sed ut video, surda est hæc ætas ad hos autores audiendos. Vix enim paucos retinui auditores, qui mei honoris causa deserere me noluerunt, quibus propter suum erga me officium habeo gratiam." Quoted by Hagen, III. 199.

Erasmus, more pious perhaps, but certainly without the wit. It was a turbulent sea upon which he had ventured, and only with many faintings of heart did he reach the haven at last. Among his papers were found some reasons why he should not stand in terror of death. Is it not pathetic that, after a life spent in the service of theology, Melancthon should enumerate among these, "Thou wilt be set free from misery and the rage of theologians"?[1]

The intellectual centre from which Luther worked was the University of Wittenberg. Founded by Frederick the Wise in 1502, while Luther was still an undergraduate at Erfurt, it had at first no feature which distinguished it from the other High Schools of Germany. Frederick was a prince of renowned piety: at a time when such acts of faith had gone out of fashion, he had made a pilgrimage to the Holy Land, and it was his pride to enrich with abundant relics of saints the church which he had built at Wittenberg.[2] But the destiny of the new University was fixed when Luther, at the prompting of Staupitz, went there in 1508. The degrees which he afterwards took of Bachelor and Doctor of Theology were to him no formal academical honours: they bound him, as he thought, to the eager and per-

---

[1] Meurer: Melancthon's Leben, p. 176.

[2] These relics, which were 5000 in number, were exposed once a year, on the Sunday called *Misericordias*, to the gaze of the faithful, who were induced to attend the show by the promise of indulgences. It was calculated that an indulgence of 1443 years was thus placed within the reach of pious zeal. Something like 10,000 masses were celebrated in the same church every year. It is curious to read of these things in a church at Wittenberg built in Luther's lifetime. Köstlin: Luther, I. 92.

sistent study of the Bible: for it, he deserted first the schoolmen, then Aristotle. When in 1518 Melancthon came to Wittenberg to teach Greek, Luther's impetuous zeal bore off the young humanist in the same direction; and though classical and legal studies were still pursued with some success, the bent of the new University was henceforth theological, and indeed chiefly Biblical. The number of students, which in the first year had been 416, gradually sunk to 127; and in 1508, the year of Luther's coming, was still only 179. Under the new influences, however, this state of things was soon changed. Young men from every part of central Europe, and of every rank in life, flocked to Wittenberg to sit at Luther's feet as he preached or lectured upon various books of Scripture. The Reformer himself compares the activity of the place to that of an ant-hill.[1] Says Frederic Myconius, a contemporary witness: "Up to this time Wittenberg was a poor, insignificant town: little, old, ugly, low wooden houses: more like an old village than a town. But now came thither people from the whole world, desiring to hear, to see, and some to study."[2] In 1521, a student writes:

"There are more than 1500 students here, nearly all of whom, walking or standing, carry their Bibles about with them. All go unarmed, and complete concord obtains among them, as among brothers who are brought together in Christ..... There are here Saxons, Prussians, Poles, Bohemians, Suabians, Swiss, Franconians, Thuringians, Misnians, and many from other regions; and yet, as I have said, all live in the finest unity..... The

---

[1] Briefe, ed. De Wette, I. 193.
[2] Myconius, Hist. Reformat. p. 27.

whole city is, as it were, taken possession of and held by students."[1]

As it was to Wittenberg that men came to be indoctrinated in the theology of the Reformation, so from Wittenberg they were sent out, not only to preach it, but to introduce the new ecclesiastical organization which it rendered necessary. It was naturally the centre from which was made the visitation of the Saxon churches. From it, Bugenhagen started on many journeys of reformation in Northern Germany. The new gymnasium at Nürnberg, under Camerarius, owed its organization to Melancthon. Till Philip of Hesse founded the University of Marburg in 1527, Wittenberg was the only High School in which the new learning was taught. But for many years more, until the death of Melancthon in 1560, it continued to be the heart of Protestant Germany.

Over against Luther, as protagonists in this great drama, stand Charles V. and the contemporary Popes, Julius II., Leo X., Adrian VI., Clement VII. and Paul III. Of these I must attempt to draw some picture before I proceed to indicate the way in which events worked themselves out.

Charles V. was the issue of the two most splendid marriages which the House of Hapsburg, always for-

---

[1] Baum: Capito und Butzer, p. 55. Melancthon on one occasion writes to Justus Menius: "At my table to-day were spoken eleven languages: Latin, Greek, Hebrew, German, Magyar, Venetian, Turkish, Arabic, Romaic, Indian and Spanish." Meurer: Melancthon, p. 19. A lively picture of university life in Wittenberg in its best time, from the pen of an eye-witness, will be found in Mathesius' Life of Luther, Sermon viii.

tunate in wedlock,[1] ever made. His grandfather, the Emperor Maximilian, married Mary of Burgundy, the sole child and heiress of Duke Charles the Bold, who fell at Nancy, in battle against the Swiss, in 1477. Upon his death, Louis XI. of France seized the opportunity of incorporating with his own dominions that region which we now call Burgundy, leaving to the heiress, however, the still ample inheritance of the undivided Low Countries, then the richest and most flourishing part of Europe. Maximilian's only son, Philip (who died before his father), married Joanna, the daughter and heiress of Ferdinand and Isabella of Spain, whose dowry was the whole of the Iberian peninsula, except Portugal, the southern half of Italy, with Sicily and Sardinia, and the wealth which newly-discovered America began to pour in ever accelerating flood upon the Old World. When, therefore, in 1519, Charles, the eldest son of this marriage, was elected Emperor, in succession to his grandfather Maximilian, his position and prospects were such as no European prince had ever before or has since inherited. Emperor of the Romans, and as such, not only holding the world's supreme place open to a lay ruler, but wielding the whole force of the German Confederacy, he succeeded to imperial claims upon northern Italy,—Italy of which the southern half was already his own. His hereditary States, Austrian on the south-east, Burgundian on the north-west, embraced Germany, as it were, between

---

[1] The epigram, ascribed to Matthias Corvinus, King of Hungary, is almost too well known to quote:

Bella gerant alii, tu, felix Austria, nubes,
Nam quæ Mars aliis, dat tibi regna Venus.

them. He had old claims to pursue and old enmities to gratify against France. Spain, which he ruled in the name of his mad mother, gave him the finest troops in the world: American treasure helped to equip them: the fleets of the Netherlands transported them beyond sea. In 1526, Bohemia, in 1527, Hungary, fell to the House of Austria in the person of his brother Ferdinand. The circumstances of his birth so placed him in a position of preponderating influence in Europe, as to render it almost inevitable that he should try to make that preponderance absolute and complete. Why should not he and the Pope divide the world between them, one wielding the temporal, the other the spiritual sword? Some more or less distinctly conceived scheme of this kind seems to have floated before his eyes all his life, and, had fortune favoured him, might possibly, from the patient astuteness, the unscrupulous persistence, which he brought to bear upon it, have been carried to completion. But the Reformation divided Germany against him: Francis I., as ambitious and as unscrupulous as himself, was eager and obstinate in asserting French claims upon Italy: successive Popes had their own purposes to serve, their own families to endow: all through his reign, the Turks were a standing danger to eastern Germany, and once had to be beaten back from the very gates of Vienna. It is no wonder that a man who was sustained by no higher an ambition than that of the aggrandizement of himself and his house, succumbed at last to such a combination of enemies. Charles V., at Juste, taking refuge in the cloister, yet unable to detach himself from the world—rehearsing his own funeral rites, while eagerly expecting despatches from Vienna and Brussels and

Madrid—repenting of the gluttony from which he could not wean himself—complaining of the ingratitude of those to whom he had given everything—furnishes the moralist with a too obvious occasion for reflecting on the vanity of human wishes.

Perhaps Charles V. was more of a Fleming than either a German or a Spaniard. Something of the black blood which made his mother one of the unhappiest of women, and condemned the last Austrian Kings of Spain to melancholy idiocy, lurked in his veins, subtly poisoning his temper, while leaving his intellectual powers untouched. He never learned to speak German fluently: what German he had was the "Platt Deutsch" of the Low Countries: to the last he communicated with his German subjects either in Latin or by the mouth of his brother Ferdinand. All the magic of Titian's pencil could not invest his homely face and figure with an imperial grace: even in the equestrial portrait which represents him triumphing over the Protestants on the battle-field of Mühlberg, he does not sit his horse like an Emperor. He was slow of speech, meditative, cold; with a German homeliness among Castilians, with a Castilian haughtiness among Germans. He had many able ministers and servants: Gattinara, the two Granvellas, Pescara, De Guasto, Alva: but he kept the final decision of all important matters in his own hands. He pursued his ends with quiet persistence, could wait long for a favourable opportunity of striking, concealing all the while his intention to strike; was moved by no foolish scruples as to faith and honour, nor was easily accessible to pity. It was not in the nature of things that he should in the least understand the Protestant rebellion. When, at Worms in 1521, he for the first and only time saw Luther, the resolved yet modest bearing of the Reformer made no impression upon him: all he said was, "This man will never make a heretic of me." Adrian of Utrecht had carefully brought him up in the Catholic faith, and the rigidity of Castilian doctrine and practice completed the process. Like all Princes of the time, he had his grievances against the Pope: his grandmother's and his own great minister, Cardinal Ximenes, had remonstrated against indulgences as firmly, if not as bitterly, as Luther:[1] he felt the necessity of a disciplinary reform of the Church, and a Council to effect it. But the Council of Trent, when at last it met, fairly satisfied him: nor did he see why the Protestants should not submit themselves to its decisions. With the doctrinal demands of Protestantism—still more with the changes which it sought to introduce into the practice of the Church, the communion in both kinds, the marriage of the clergy, the curtailment of Papal and Episcopal power—he had no sympathy whatever: they offended at once his autocratic disposition and his conservative habits of mind. It is quite touching to see how, after years of adverse experience, Luther and Melancthon continue to believe in him: they cannot bring themselves to think that a young German Emperor can be really opposed to the wishes and aspirations of the German people: they are sure that if only they can counteract the influence of bad advisers, and make their appeal to his own native sense of truth and right, he will take their side. Never was there a greater delusion: at first, intent upon what he thought matters of more importance, he despised the

---

[1] Ranke, I. 303.

whole movement; once aware of what it was, he never wavered in his intention of stamping it out, utterly and remorselessly, as soon as the favourable moment should arrive.

The external history of the Reformation in Germany can be understood only by keeping steadily in view the fact that the centre of gravity of Charles's policy was not German or even Spanish, but Burgundian. What he cared for was the aggrandizement of the House of Austria as enriched by the great marriages of which I have spoken. He rarely visited that part of his dominions which had given him his highest title: the consolidation of German power, the settlement of German disputes, the welfare of the German people, were with him quite secondary to the grasp which he tried to get of Milan, or the possibility of compelling France to restore the lost provinces of Burgundy. Later in his life this passion took a meaner and more selfish form. At first it was so completely a part of his policy that his brother Ferdinand should succeed him in the empire, that he procured his election as King of the Romans: afterwards he attempted, though in vain, to induce him to abdicate, that the double inheritance of Spain and the empire might fall upon his own son Philip. This dynastic selfishness on the part of Charles was the safety of the Reformation. An Emperor whose attention was confined to German affairs alone, would have utterly crushed it out before it had had time to gather strength and permanence. One who was invading France, seizing Milan, sacking Rome, chastising African pirates, thrusting back the Turks from Vienna, and for these purposes always weaving the changeful web of treaties, truces, alliances, intrigues, could hardly be expected to understand the nature and the importance of the religious phenomena which occasionally invited his attention in a part of his dominions over which he had no personal control. He never had but one opinion of Protestantism; namely, that it was a mischievous revolt against authority, which he intended to put down whenever a favourable opportunity offered. But when the occasion came, he found that it was too late.

The peculiar political constitution of Germany had much to do, if not with the origin, at least with the protection and maintenance, of Protestantism during those early years in which it might not have been difficult to suppress it. It was a loose confederation of States, ecclesiastical and civil, varying in size and importance from the seven great Electorates to the tiny territory of the robber noble, who claimed right of war against his neighbours, and the free city, which was independent so long as its walls were strong enough to withstand assault. These States met in Diet almost every year, under the presidency of the Emperor or his deputy, to declare war and to make peace, to raise money for imperial purposes, to settle disputes among themselves, to take measures for securing general order. But the authority of the Emperor depended largely upon his position as an independent Prince and his personal qualities as a ruler, while the decisions of the Diet were often impossible of enforcement against a recalcitrant minority or even a single stiff-necked member. It might not be impracticable to put even the most powerful Elector, clerical or lay, under the ban of the empire, but who was to execute the decree and reduce the offender to submission? Whatever the rivalries and dissensions which separated the Estates, to protect the independence of each against the central authority was always more or less the interest of all: nor was this motive practically outweighed, except in cases where the execution of an imperial decree coincided with the grasp of personal ambition or the wreaking of private vengeance. When, therefore, Protestantism established itself under the protection of the Ernestine line of Saxon Princes, and from Saxony not only spread into the neighbouring states of Hesse and Lüneburg, but made its way into all the free cities that were not dominated by ecclesiastical influence, what could be done to dislodge it? If Frederick of Saxony would not execute the Edict of Worms in his own dominions, who was to compel him to do so? To march troops to force Nürnberg or Strasburg, Constanz or Ulm, to send away the preachers and to restore the Mass, would be to kindle the flame of civil war in Germany, after a fashion for which only a fanatical Papalist here and there was ready. After events showed that within any single State it was not impossible to put down the Reformation by a steady system of persecution. Austria and Bavaria were once almost as completely penetrated by the new spirit as Hesse and Brandenburg. Alva and the Inquisition won back Flanders to the Church, when it was hardly less lost in heresy than Holland. England under Henry VIII., France under Francis I., show how in a homogeneous State the fate of the Reformation was overpoweringly affected by the character and caprice of a monarch. It was the fact, that in a divided Germany the new teaching was able to avail itself of the various dispositions of rulers and the democratic independence of the free cities that gave the Reformation the breathing time it needed.

Critics who think that they discern in the first stirrings of reform the promise of a great national movement towards German unity and German liberty, have expressed their deep disappointment that the Reformation afterwards fell so completely into the hands of Princes. Luther and Melancthon are politically the most devoted subjects of rulers, to whom nevertheless they do not scruple to speak their minds freely: Bucer propounds a theory of civil obedience as servile as that defended by the Church of England in the days of Charles II. But whatever truth there may be in this complaint should not blind us to the fact that some at least of the Reforming Princes were men of singularly pure and noble character, who at certain crises of the story show to advantage by the side of the theologians themselves. What the Reformation would have been without the three Saxon Electors, Frederick the Wise, John the Steadfast, and John Frederick the Magnanimous, it is impossible to say. The first was the most powerful Prince of the empire, though far less from the extent of his territory or the weight of his material resources, than from the universal respect paid to his character. There was even a moment at which he might have succeeded Maximilian as Emperor, with what effect of change upon the history of modern Europe who shall say? His relation to Luther was singular. He never spoke to him. His communications with him were chiefly carried on through Spalatin, his chaplain and historiographer. Beginning life as a devout Catholic, he never wholly broke with the Church. The most decisively Protestant thing he ever did was to receive the Communion in both kinds on his death-bed.[1] But he felt a sincere admiration for Luther's courageous honesty; and without committing himself to much that the Reformer said and did, was determined that he should have fair play, freedom to speak, room in which to act. His brother John well deserved his name of Steadfast. Of less powerful and individual mind than Frederick, he was a convinced Lutheran, and resolved to stand by his convictions, cost what it might. It was characteristic of him that he went to the Diet of Speier in 1526 with the letters V.D.M.I.Æ. conspicuous upon all his ensigns and liveries: *Verbum Dei manet in æternum.* His was the first name to the immortal Protest of 1529. When at Augsburg, in 1530, his theologians, afraid of the possible political consequences, proposed that they alone should sign the Confession, he simply answered, "I, too, will confess my Christ with you." "Deny God, or the world," he said; "who could doubt which were better? God has made me an Elector of the empire, of which I was never worthy: for the rest, let Him make of me what He will."[2] His son John Frederick was a child of the Reformation, for his devotion to which he paid by the loss of his Electorate and the larger half of his hereditary dominions. He, too, though hardly an able, and certainly not a fortunate Prince, did not fall away from the religious and ethical standard of his predecessors. Misfortune neither deprived him of his cheerful imperturbability nor made him unfaithful to his creed. On the

---

[1] Spalatin: Friedrich der Weise, p. 65.
[2] Ranke, III. 274, 275.

character of Philip of Hesse rests a blot—such as indeed smirches the fair fame of almost all Princes—yet which the unscrupulous bitterness of Catholic controversialists has enlarged and blackened to the uttermost, in the hope of involving Luther and Melancthon in its shame. But apart from this, he is the most attractive of the Princes of the Reform. Young, eager, enthusiastic, struggling between his religious principles and the vices almost incident to his station, capable of swift decision, able to strike a sudden blow, he is far more a hero of romance than Wise Frederick, looking out with sad, dying eyes upon a world that seemed to be going to pieces all around him; or Steadfast John, too fat to mount his horse without the aid of machinery, and going to sleep under Luther's sermons, though all the while standing by his Reformer with unshaken firmness; or Magnanimous John Frederick, almost too patient in captivity, too resigned under dethronement. To Philip of Hesse also belongs the credit of discerning, with a liberal statesmanship far in advance of his times, the unimportance of doctrinal differences in comparison with the necessity of union among Protestants: it was he who called the Conference of Marburg, the effect of which, had not the obstinacy of the Wittenberg theologians stood in the way, would have been that Protestant Germany and Protestant Switzerland would have presented to the Emperor at Augsburg a united front. Could Philip have prevailed, the Church would have been built up from the first on a broader foundation; and the long dissensions between German and Swiss, between Lutheran and Reformed, perhaps even those between Lutheran and Lutheran—the bitterest of all—might have been avoided. When in a private audience before the opening of the Diet of Augsburg, Charles V. demanded of the Princes that they should silence the Protestant preachers who had taken possession of the churches, they answered that they could not with a good conscience comply with the request of his Majesty. Upon which Ferdinand of Austria, "That was what Imperial Majesty could not suffer." Philip of Hesse broke in, "Imperial Majesty's conscience was no lord and master over their conscience." The Margrave George of Brandenburg cried out, "Before I will suffer the word of God to be taken from me and deny my God, I will kneel down here and let my head be hewn off my shoulders." This outbreak seems to have startled even the saturnine Charles out of his coldness, for he raised up the kneeling prince, saying to him in his Flemish German, "Nit kopf ab, nit kopf ab, liever Fürst." "Not head off, not head off, dear Prince."[1] But these were brave and true men, worthy to be leaders in a religious revolution.

Many influences combined to give a character of worldliness to the Popes of this period, and to dye that worldliness with a stain of infamy. It was in Italy the age of the despots; a time when all the great republics except Venice had been robbed of their liberties by men who, both in the Greek and in the English sense of the word, were tyrants; that is to say, who had taken the government of the State into their own hands, and who administered it with arbitrary cruelty. The Medici at Florence, the Visconti and the Sforzas at Milan, the Scaligeri at Verona, the Baglioni at Perugia, were all families of

---

[1] Letter from Brenz to Isenmann, June 19, 1530, Corp. Ref. II. 115.

this kind, who conspired and intrigued and poisoned and slew with the single object of confirming and increasing their own power at home and abroad. Over most of them the breath of the Renaissance culture passed, bidding them fill their lives with luxurious splendour: they built castles, palaces, villas, and, in their moments of remorse, churches: they were liberal customers of the painters and the goldsmiths: they pensioned and protected scholars: they collected libraries: some of them really loved literature and fostered art with a discerning taste. But they were unscrupulous, faithless, cruel, lascivious; men who had lost the very conception of virtue, and in its place, as the rule of life, had set up a remorseless selfishness, varnished over with a certain stately courtesy. Out of this class of men came, with this class of men lived, the Popes of the Reformation, not superior in character, using the power of the Church to serve a dynastic ambition, all the more feverish for the brief period during which it could work its will, and displaying an unscrupulous worldliness, which to us shows the more revolting from the contrast, which they never felt, between their office and their ends. The Papacy was to them a mere political engine; the Church, a weight which they could throw into this or that scale of political intrigue; the Papal territory, that out of which appanages might be carved for nephews or sons. These Popes began to build St. Peter's; collected the treasures of the Vatican; employed Raffaelle and Michael Angelo, Sebastian del Piombo and Giulio Romano; drew to Rome the great men whom, of all Italian cities, she was most chary in producing; but all, as worldly potentates might have done, without a touch of religious awe upon their own souls, or even a sense of administrative responsibility as Vicars of Christ. The Pontiff who was reigning when Luther came to Rome in 1510 was Julius II., a terrible old man, of whose nostrils the life-breath was war, and who deluged Italy with blood that he might enlarge and cement the Papal territory into a solid sovereignty. He was followed by Leo X.,[1] Giovanni de Medici, son of Lorenzo the Magnificent, a coarse sensualist, whose name has wrongfully become associated with a period of literary and artistic splendour which was already passing away. "Since God has given us the Papacy, let us enjoy it," was his remark to a kinsman when he assumed his dignity: and he enjoyed it to the full, if by enjoyment be meant delicate meats, rare wines, splendid pageants, the homage of painters, the flatteries of poets, never embittered by a moment's fear of the storm that was gathering in the North. For Leo was a pagan in grain, almost a pagan in outward contempt of Christianity: his heart was with neither the past glories of the Church nor its present dangers, but with the last discovered fragment of ancient sculpture, the newest offering of classically turned flattery. Then for a little while came the Cardinal of Tortosa, Adrian VI., the son of a ship-carpenter of Utrecht, once a Professor at Louvain, and the preceptor of Charles V.,

---

[1] When Leo became Pope, the banker Agostino Chigi publicly exhibited the following epigram:

Olim habuit Cypria sua tempora, tempora Mavors
Olim habuit, sua nunc tempora Pallas habet.

To which the goldsmith Antonio di San Marco replied in a single line, which speaks volumes as to what Rome thought of her Popes:

Mars fuit : est Pallas : Cypria semper ero.

Symonds : Italian Renaissance, Age of the Despots, pp. 369, 370.

a simple and austere old man, who had never been in Rome till he entered it as Pope, fully conscious of the sins and miseries of the Church, and dreaming the vain dream that his feeble hand could sweep out this worse than Augean stable of abuse. But he reigned barely a year; and when he died, the people of Rome wrote over his physician's door the words, "The Roman Senate and People to the Liberator of his country."[1] Him followed Clement VII., again a Medici, though in defiance of canonical law an illegitimate one; the most unhappy of all Popes, who, himself a prisoner in the Castle of St. Angelo, saw Rome sacked and all but destroyed by the Constable Bourbon and his army of German lanzknechts. He had brought it on himself: he had striven to hold the balance in Italy between Charles V. and Francis I.; marrying a Medici to the Emperor's natural daughter; binding himself to Francis by the woful gift of his own niece Catharine; for yet another Medici seizing Urbino. Then, last of all, came Alessandro Farnese, Paul III., he who summoned at Trent the long-promised Council: born before Luther, and therefore an old man when he mounted the fisherman's chair, but intriguing, marrying, clutching for the Farnesi, just as Leo X. and Clement VII. had done for the Medici, and with as little care for the cause of religion and the welfare of the Church. The Popes, it is not too much to say, never discerned the danger that lay in Protestantism till it was too late either to combat or to avert it. They had a thousand things in hand which to them were infinitely more important. When at last they were aroused, their only chance was

---

[1] Symonds: Age of the Despots, p. 378.

to set Loyola against Luther, and to begin the Counter Reformation.

All this may help to explain why Protestantism was, in face of such tremendous forces of opposition, suffered to grow and gather strength. Pope and Emperor, Francis I. and Henry VIII., the armies of the Turk and the pirates of Algiers, unconsciously fought for it in turn. Charles was never wanting in the will to crush it: it was always an article of his numerous treaties with the Pope and Francis I. that their joint arms were to be turned against the heretic and the Turk. But just when the blow was about to descend, some exigency of politics always intervened to prevent or to turn it aside. When in 1521 the Edict of Worms was adopted by the Diet, Charles betook himself to his Italian wars, not to re-appear in Germany till in 1530 he came to Augsburg, to find himself confronted, no longer by a solitary monk, but by Electors and Princes, nobles and free cities, who had already at Speier announced the new and startling doctrine, that in matters of conscience they, the minority, could submit themselves to no majority, but only to the Word of God. During these nine years his own hand had never been free to strike, and his policy towards the Lutherans had varied, as he hoped to be able to execute speedy justice upon them, or felt that the day of suppression must be again postponed. The Pope had been against him, or Francis had broken the Treaty of Madrid, or the Turk had appeared before Vienna. At Augsburg, it seemed as if the decisive moment had at last come: the Protestants recorded their Confession: the Emperor and the Pope replied with a futile document, which they called a refutation, and in which they refused to give way even a hair's-breadth. But still war does not break out. The Emperor needs the help of a united Germany, now against France, now against the Turk, and cannot afford to quarrel with the Protestant Princes. All the while Protestantism is spreading and gathering strength: Catholic princes die to make way for Protestant heirs: city after city adopts the new faith: in many parts of Germany the goods of the Church receive fresh appropriation, more or less worthy: there is even a report that the Archbishop Elector of Cologne is bringing over his diocese to the Lutheran side. At last, in 1545, the war actually begins. Leagues and counter-leagues have been formed long ago: but the Protestant theologians have doubts as to the lawfulness of war even in defence of the faith, and their leaders quarrel for the post of command. It is personal ambition which after all applies the torch: Maurice, the Protestant nephew and successor of Duke George of Saxony, coveting the lands and dignities of his Electoral cousins, lends the Emperor the aid of his astute statesmanship and his military genius, and after a brief campaign the Protestant cause goes down upon the field of Mühlberg. For a time it seems as if all were lost. An oppressive ecclesiastical rule, under the title of the Interim, which is intended to keep Protestantism within strict bounds till the Council of Trent shall speak with a voice of authority, is imposed upon Lutheran Germany. The Elector of Saxony and the Landgrave of Hesse languish in a captivity from which they have no prospect of escape but by the scaffold. Maurice receives from the Emperor, as the price of his help, the Electorate and the larger part of the dominions hitherto attached to it.

Everywhere Charles's Spanish soldiery, under the command of Alva, give German cities a foretaste of that brutal repression which in Philip II.'s time was to whet its sharpest edge in the Netherlands. Then, goaded by the general discontent, and unable any longer to bear the reproaches which the captivity of his cousin and father-in-law drew down upon him, Maurice again changed sides, as secretly, as astutely, as successfully as before; and the Emperor, utterly unprepared for the blow, hurried, a helpless fugitive, up the passes of the Tyrol. "I have no cage big enough to hold such a bird," answered Maurice, when he was urged to finish the war at a stroke by taking Charles prisoner: he preferred to treat. So in 1552 was signed the Treaty of Passau, by which, Council or no Council, the position of Protestantism was assured, until the flame broke out with redoubled vehemence in the Thirty Years' War. It was but a maimed victory: *cujus regio, ejus religio*, was its principle: the subject follows the religion of the state. It vindicated Saxony, for instance, against Austria; but in Austria it offered no effectual protection to Protestants; in Saxony, none to Catholics. Yet a victory it undoubtedly was, such as no man hoped to see a year before, closing that act of the great drama with which alone we are at this moment concerned. Luther has gone to his rest before the outbreak of war: Calvin is now shaping French and Swiss Protestantism in the mould of his relentless logic and his iron will: the Lutheran theologians, under the nominal presidency of Melancthon, use the opportunity of peace to pursue dissensions which are as bitter as the subjects of them are obscure: the Council of Trent resumes discussions, henceforward important to Catholics alone; and Charles V. retires to Juste, worn out before his time, and weary of a power which he can resolve neither to retain nor to relinquish.

LECTURE IV.

THE PRINCIPLES OF THE REFORMATION.

IT has often been said that Catholicism is an objective, Protestantism a subjective form of religion, and that when the more obvious differences between them are traced to their root, they issue in this fundamental distinction. The statement, if only it be clearly understood and sufficiently guarded, is both true and suggestive. In one sense, indeed, all genuine religion is subjective; it is the meeting of God and man within the soul in awe, aspiration, affection. There is no distinction here between Tauler and Wesley, between Pascal and Channing: in proportion as chosen saints consciously penetrate into the secret of saintliness, they come to think that the things in which they differ are of infinite unimportance, compared with those in which they are at one. But on a lower level of discipleship these diversities become more accentuated, and religious men are seen to belong to either of two great Churches, one of which interposes a machinery of mediation—sacraments, priesthoods, discipline, ritual—between the soul and its infinite Object, while the other, denying the reality or the efficacy of these things, is content to leave the spirit face to face with God. The danger on the one hand is, we are told, that forms should stiffen into fetters, the shell be mistaken for the kernel, the means by which it was intended to lead the worshipper into the presence-chamber converted into a perpetual bar to his entrance; on the other, that ecstatic raptures should take the place of sober affection—fruitless emotion, of solid obedience—a succession of excited moods, of a steady growth in holiness. There is something formal, external, historical, dramatic, in one way of looking at the facts and truths of Christianity, while the other runs the risk of being merely emotional, lawless, individual. One principle preserves the unity of the Catholic Church, the other splits Protestantism into innumerable sects: Authority is the watchword there, and here Liberty. That bids a man keep his face steadfastly turned towards the past; this compels him, often against his will, to take into his account the future too. One is the spirit of rest—the other, of change and progress; this presents religion as one eternal truth, expressed in the same fixed forms—that owns truth one and eternal, but confesses it only half perceived as yet, and expects it to assume new forms as man grows and knowledge widens.

This statement, with whatever degree of accuracy it may represent the differences between Catholic and Protestant religion as now understood, would, I need hardly say, be far less true to the consciousness of Luther and Melancthon three centuries and a half ago. They understood neither the system which they attacked nor that which they founded, in its full relation to the long progress of the human mind. They worked in the twilight: only slowly and tentatively did they come to comprehend their own activity: more than once they turned their back on the logical development of their own principles: in many ways their work was greater than they knew. But I think that I can fairly state what was the religious change which the Reformation wrought in them and their contemporaries, and the means by which it was accomplished. This, then, will be the subject of the present Lecture. It will be at once understood that I approach the subject only from the standpoint of historical criticism, and that I have nothing to do with the abstract truth or error of the beliefs which will come within our view.

The devout Catholic believer before the Reformation found himself in presence of a vast and variously organized Christianity. Wherever he went, he was confronted with the visible church. The Greek church was far away and, moreover, defamed of heresy: beneath the surface of society there were secret religious communities, which to a pious son of the Church were not only disreputable but criminal. But externally there was one hierarchy, one faith, one ritual. Christendom was visibly one in its Papal head: Rome was the capital of a believing world. This actual unity was the result of organic growth. The Church of the fifteenth century was the Church of councils and schoolmen, of fathers and martyrs, of apostles and Christ himself. No voice which Europe had consented to hear had yet brought its historical claims to the test: it presented itself to every succeeding generation with the unbroken weight of the past at its back. But it did much more than thus impose itself upon the believer in the majesty of an unquestioned authority. It demanded his assent to a vast body of theological dogma, carefully reasoned out, with all its parts logically subordinated to one another and the whole, and that under penalties, temporal and eternal, of the most tremendous kind. There were, so to speak, no alternative means of theological knowledge: the Bible had disappeared from the general eye: the schoolmen had reduced Scripture, the Fathers, tradition, to a system upon which the Church had set the seal of its approval. And among the theological truths which a man was thus compelled to accept upon pain of not being a Christian at all, were, that the religious life could be nourished only by sacraments, and that sacraments could be administered only by a duly ordained body of priests. I will not waste time in trying to give an accurate definition of the word sacrament and the word priest: they stand for co-ordinated ideas: and the outcome of the system which they denote is, that what some would call a way of communication, others a wall of severance, is built between the soul and God. A man can no longer open his heart to the Divine grace, and be refreshed by the dew of benediction which falls upon it: he must be blessed by way of water or of oil, of bread or of wine; and these have no supernatural virtue if the priest's breath have not passed upon them. And it is unhappily a law of human nature that these hindrances between the soul and its Divine Object, once admitted, grow and multiply: the sacraments are accessible only on conditions of which the Church is the sole judge: the intercession of saints becomes desirable, if not necessary, to the weakness of humanity: the benignity of Mary wins all hearts, till at last the Saviour becomes an angry judge, whose avenging arm is averted from his people only by his Mother's gracious pleading.[1] Nor is the power of the Church confined to this life: she can bind and loose in purgatory as on earth: her favour and displeasure are as the favour and displeasure of God. Add to this the corruptions necessarily engendered in such a system by the ignorance, the coarseness, the love of rule, the moral callousness of those by whom it was often administered, and you will to some extent understand the sins and shortcomings of the Catholic Church before the Reformation. But neither with these, nor with its undoubted strength and merits, have we at this moment anything to do. The one point on which I desire to fix your attention is, that the believer found himself separated from God by a thousand barriers which he could not overleap, and which drew his attention on themselves as the proper objects of religious desire. For all good, he was the suppliant of the Church. She led him, she fed him, she imposed her own laws upon him, she rewarded him upon her own terms. He accepted her word for everything. She was the perpetual, the all-powerful mediator between earth and heaven. Without her there was no access to God, no spiritual life now, no salvation hereafter.

What, more than anything else, characterized Luther's attack upon this system, was his substitution of the authority of the Bible for the authority of the Church. This was not so much the result of closely-reasoned theological theory in his or any other mind, as the conse-

---

[1] See Michael Angelo's well-known picture of the Last Judgment, on the east wall of the Sistine Chapel, painted between 1533 and 1541.

IV. PRINCIPLES OF THE REFORMATION. 117

quence of facts, which could not be debarred from their natural operation. It is a well-known story that the first beginnings of change were produced in Luther himself by his discovery, when a student at Erfurt, that the Latin Bible contained much more than the lessons which he had been wont to hear read in church,[1] and by the eager study which he thenceforth gave to the book. At the moment when the abuses and oppressions of the Papal system weighed most heavily upon Germany, and at the same time the liveliest curiosity as to all the literary monuments of antiquity filled men's minds, the art of printing put the Bible into all hands. At first, of course, it was only the Vulgate, written in the language of Rome, and dating from a time when Roman religion was already being moulded into its characteristic shape. But the re-conquest of the human intellect by the Bible took place, so to speak, in two opposite directions at once: scholars penetrated beneath the Latin to the Hebrew and the Greek, while translations into the vernacular

---

[1] Mathesius: Luther, Sermon I. p. 3 b. Dr. S. R. Maitland, in his learned and lively Essays on "the Dark Ages" (pp. 468, 508 et seq.), pours contempt on Mathesius, and utterly refuses to believe his story. But what is to be made of Luther's own words (Tischreden, III. 229): "Vor dreissig Jahren war die Bibel umbekannt, die Propheten waren ungenannt und gehalten, als wären sie unmöglich zu verstehen. Da ich zwanzig Jahr alt war, hatte ich noch keine geschen. Ich meinete es wären kein Evangelia noch Episteln mehr denn die in den Postillen sind. Endlich fand ich in der Liberei zu Erfurt eine Bibel, die las ich oftmals mit grosser Verwunderung D. Staupitzen." On the other hand, it is curious that the University of Erfurt distinguished itself above other High Schools of Germany in the fifteenth century by its attention to Biblical exegesis, a fact to which the number of works on that subject in MS. still preserved in its libraries bears convincing testimony. Kampschulte: " Die Universität Erfurt," Part i. p. 22, note.

tongues restored the book to the people. A vivid illustration of the former process is supplied by the story of Luther's delighted astonishment[1] when he found that the *pœnitentia* of the Latin was the μετάνοια of the Greek; or, in other words, that what had always presented itself to him as *penance*, an external form, an ecclesiastical penalty, was really an inward and spiritual thing, repentance, change of mind: while, on the other hand, it is impossible to conceive what must have been the effect, especially at a time of freshly-aroused mental activity and deep religious commotion, of disinterring and making widely known the Biblical literature in all its antique vividness, with all its intellectual charm, in the plenitude of its moral persuasiveness, its spiritual force. I will say nothing here of what its power must have been over the individual heart and conscience: that is a fact which belongs to no age of the church in especial. But one thing must have been abundantly clear to the reader of the New Testament in the first years of the sixteenth century: that the church of Julius II. and Leo X. was in both form and spirit singularly unlike the church of Paul and John.

This result was quickened and enhanced by Luther's method of Biblical interpretation. In a very important sense he anticipated a well-known aphorism of our own day, namely, that the Bible is to be interpreted like any other book.[2] It was a mediæval maxim, which no one thought of questioning, that the language of the Bible

---

[1] Briefe, ed. De Wette, I. 116: letter to Staupitz.

[2] Essays and Reviews (Jowett on the Interpretation of Scripture), p. 377.

had four senses—the literal, the allegorical, the tropological, and the anagogical, of which the three last were mystical or spiritual, in contradistinction to the first. The literal sense preserves the record of facts; the allegorical teaches us what we are to believe; the tropological, what we are to do; the anagogical, what we are to hope.[1] If this is so, it is obvious that the meaning which lies on the surface is the least important of the four, and that the true gold of Scripture can be got only by digging—with this added difficulty, that in the absence of an infallible touchstone, each delver in the mine is apt to mistake whatever rubbish he comes across for the precious ore. Against this manifold sense of Scripture, which, it is plain, destroyed all certainty of interpretation and left the field open to the wildest absurdities, Luther set his face stoutly and on the whole consistently. "The Holy Ghost,"[2] he said, in controversy with Emser, "is the all simplest writer and speaker that is in heaven or on earth; therefore his words can have no more than one simplest sense, which we call the scriptural or literal meaning." But no declaration could possibly surpass this, which Luther repeats in a thousand different forms, in power of angering and alarming his opponents. It was the axe at the root of their dogmatic system. Poor Emser exclaimed in his rage, that if this were so, it was better to read a legend of Virgil's than the Bible.[3] But indeed Erasmus, standing with all his learning in the

---

[1] Litera gesta docet, quid credas Allegoria,
 Tropologia quid agas, quid speres Anagogia.

[2] Luther's Werke, ed. Walch, XVIII. 1602: Answer to Emser.

[3] Ibid. p. 1601.

full dawn of the new day, says much the same thing.[1] The story of Adam is not better worth reading than that of Prometheus, if you take it only in its literal sense. "What does it matter whether you read the Books of Kings or Judges, or Livy's History, if in neither you look to the allegory?" Of interpreters of Holy Scripture he says, in another place:[2] "Choose those in especial who depart as far as possible from the letter"—and then goes on in scornful disparagement of the innovators who uphold the grammatical sense. But this principle of the Reformation effected a greater change than is implied in the mere simplification of exegesis, by cutting away all that undergrowth of mystical teaching which hid the plain significance of the text. It converted the Scriptures from a dialectic armoury from which weapons of argument could be drawn in favour of any dogmatic subtlety or extravagance, into an historical record of God's dealings with mankind, full of life and inspiration and comfort. The soul had hitherto been nourished on sacraments alone: it was now to hold converse with the Spirit in the pages of the Bible. What God had done for faithful men of old, He would still do for the faithful: the words in which he had once spoken had an eternal and ever-present application. The Scriptures were no longer a closed treasury of truth and grace of which orthodox learning alone held the key, but an open garden, in which any devout soul might wander, plucking flowers and fruit.

There is no kind of hesitation in Luther's assertion of

---

[1] Erasmus: Opp. (Enchiridion), V. 29, B, C, D.
[2] Ibid. p. 8, D.

the authority of Scripture. He rises to its full height only by degrees: he makes the Bible the test, first of the scholastic theology, next of the Papacy, and only at last, when brought to bay by Eck at Leipzig, admits that even General Councils, tried by its standard, must be pronounced to have erred. But having once taken up this position, he never abandons it. It is unnecessary to quote illustrative passages from his writings: we might almost say that the authority of Scripture is their animating principle. But looking at the matter with nineteenth-century eyes, it is very curious to remark how absolutely unconscious the Reformers seem to be of the necessity of supporting this affirmation by any kind of proof, or even of defining the exact sense in which they make it. This is, no doubt, in part due to the fact that none of their opponents questioned it: it was an universal postulate of controversy. The debate with the Catholics was not as to whether Scripture was authoritative, but whether tradition and the Church were to be admitted to an equal position of influence: the quarrel with Protestant heretics was, again, one not of authority, but of interpretation. Still it is singular to find in Melancthon's *Loci Communes*,[1] the great repertory of Lutheran theology, absolutely no attempt to lay a surer

---

[1] Conf. the section, "De discrimine V. et N. Testamenti." "Quare cogitemus ingens Dei beneficium esse, quod certum librum Ecclesiæ tradidit et servat, et ad hunc alligat Ecclesiam. Tantum hic populus est Ecclesia qui hunc librum amplecitur, audit, discit, et retinet propriam ejus sententiam in invocatione Dei et in regendis moribus. Non igitur est Ecclesia Dei, ubi rejicitur hic liber, ut apud Mahometistas, aut ubi, extincta propria sententia, proponitur commenticia, ut apud hæreticos." Corp. Ref. XXI. 801.

foundation for the edifice of systematic dogma which he builds up than this assumption. It is like the Hindu cosmogony, with its tortoise resting upon nothing. Another curious fact, that the authority of Scripture is not expressly formulated in the Confession of Augsburg, is probably in part due to Melancthon's unwillingness to cut himself off from the ancient and mediæval Church by the implied denial of the authority of General Councils.[1] Calvin, as we might expect, both from the more logical and systematizing quality of his mind and the already changing character of controversy in his day, gives more attention to the subject, devoting to it three sections of the first book of his "Institution." But even he treats it with what we should now think a very inadequate apprehension of its importance. All rationalistic cavils he meets with lofty contempt, resting the authority of the Bible on its own inherent force and majesty, and the testimony of the Holy Spirit in the soul.[2]

"Read Demosthenes or Cicero, read Plato, Aristotle, or any other of all that sort: I grant they shall marvellously allure, delight, move and ravish thee. But if from them thou come to this holy reading of Scriptures, wilt thou or not, it shall so lively move thy affections, it shall so pierce thy heart, it shall so settle within thy bones, that, in comparison of the efficacy of this feeling, all that force of rhetoricians and philosophers shall in manner

---

[1] It is curious, in this connection, to note that the Confession of Augsburg begins by basing the doctrine of the Trinity on the decree of the Council of Nicæa. "Ecclesiæ magno consensu apud nos docent, decretum Nicenæ synodi, de unitate essentiæ divinæ, et de tribus personis, verum et sine ulla dubitatione credendum esse." Sylloge Confessionum (Oxford, 1827), p. 123.

[2] Calvin: Institution, Book i. chap. viii. I have used in the text the old English translation of Thomas Norton, 1634.

vanish away: so that it is easy to perceive that the Scriptures which do far excel all gifts and graces of man's industry, do indeed breathe out a certain divinity."

And again:[1]

"Let this therefore stand for a certainly persuaded truth, that they whom the Holy Ghost hath inwardly taught do wholly rest upon the Scripture, and that the same Scripture is to be credited for itself sake, and ought not to be made subject to demonstration and reason: but yet the certainty which it getteth among us, it attaineth by the witness of the Holy Ghost. For though by the only majesty of itself it procureth reverence to be given to it, yet then only it thoroughly pierceth our affections when it is sealed in our hearts by the Holy Ghost. So, being lightened by his virtue, we do then believe, not by our own judgment or other men's, that the Scripture is from God: but above all man's judgment we hold it most certainly determined, even as if we beheld the majesty of God Himself there present, that by the ministry of men it came to us from the very mouth of God."

This, then, in the most precise form in which I am able to give it, is the theory of the Reformation as to the authority of Scripture. It is based upon the concurrent witness of the Holy Spirit in the written word and in the believer's soul. And beyond doubt it expresses a spiritual truth, deeper than which no subsequent age has been able to penetrate: the only question is, to what kind of scriptural statement does this authentication extend, and what is its precise value? Does it cover historical, scientific, philosophical affirmations, or is it confined to the region of the theological and the moral? But the Reformers did not ask themselves these questions,

---

[1] Calvin: Institution, Book i. ch. vii.

and would have thought it a concession to blasphemy to answer them if asked by others.[1]

It is logically involved in the substitution of the authority of the Bible for the authority of the Church, that every believer has the right of interpreting Scripture for himself. Luther has said some clear and decisive words on this subject. He maintains, in the first place, that Scripture is easy of interpretation.[2] "The Bible belongs to all, and so far as is necessary for salvation is clear enough, but also dark enough for souls that pry and seek to know more." And again, in controversy with Erasmus:[3] "I say that no part of Holy Scripture is dark.... Christ hath not so enlightened us that any part of his doctrine and his word which he bids us regard and follow should be left dark." Once more: "It belongs to each and every Christian to know and to judge of doctrine, and belongs in such wise that he is *anathema* who shall have diminished this right by a single hair."[4] I shall

---

[1] Conf. Luther's Tischreden, I. 28. "Wer nachgiebet, dass der Evangelisten Schriften Gottes Wort sein, dem wollen wir mit Disputiren wol begegnen: wer es aber verneinet, mit dem will ich nicht ein Wort handeln. Denn mit dem soll man nicht disputiren, der da *prima principia*, dass ist die ersten Gründe und das Häuptfundament verneinet und verwirft."

[2] Werke, ed. Walch, XVIII. 1416. Melancthon is equally explicit. "Verbum Dei non est obscurum aut ambiguum, quia lex est perspicua et clara." And again: "Scribebat quidem, nullum vocabulum esse in Scriptura quod non varie possit exponi. Hæc est mera petulantia et diabolica sophistica..... In principalibus capitibus pertinentibus ad legem et Evangelium, Scriptura est aperta, et sine obscuritate. Sed certamina et rixæ tribuendæ sunt pravitati et malitiæ ingeniorum quæ corrumpunt Scripturam." Corp. Ref. XXV. 225, 226.

[3] Werke, ed. Walch, XVIII. 2163, 2164.

[4] Quoted by Köstlin, Luther's Theologie, II. 61.

IV. PRINCIPLES OF THE REFORMATION. 125

have to qualify the full breadth of this statement presently by mentioning certain laws of interpretation which Luther laid down; but even then it will be broader than the practice of the Reformers. For they soon felt the difficulty that the authority of the Scriptures could not be used for authoritative purposes in the same way and to produce the same results as the voice of the Church. The Bible once thrown open to private interpretation, it was impossible to provide that everybody should deduce from it the same doctrinal results as those contained in Melancthon's *Loci Communes*. All the Swiss Reformers held their own theory of the Eucharist, which was not Luther's. The general body of heretics, comprised under one name of infamy as Anabaptists, wandered into innumerable byeways of belief. Campanus, Denck, Hetzer, early struck the path which Servetus and the Socini followed. What was to be done? Melancthon[1] seems to have indulged the dream of a consensus of pious and learned opinion, though how this was to be imposed upon recalcitrant heretics he does not tell us. Calvin[2] went so far as to say that the written oracles of God were not of private interpretation, yet without showing how this statement was consistent with the maintenance of his Protestant position. Luther held on his way stoutly, not obscurely intimating in the general tone of his dogmatic

---

[1] Huc accedat et pia communicatio, conferant inter se pii de doctrina et audiantur etiam aliorum peritiorum sententiæ, et hi benigne et candide suam sententiam exponant et vicissim etiam alios comiter audiant. Talis sit consensus piorum, qui pio studio quærentes veritatem et cum timore Dei secundum Scripturam pronuntient. Hoc concilium audiatur! Melancthon, quoted by Schenkel, Wesen des Protestantismus, I. 93.

[2] Schenkel, I. 94.

affirmations, that if other people did not see things as he did, it was their own fault. But difference of opinion seems to have taught no one the lesson of tolerance. The making and branding of heretics went on as actively on one side of the great controversy as on the other.

Luther, and Melancthon, who may be taken in the general as the systematizer of Luther's thoughts, in part evaded this difficulty by their conception of the Bible as an organic whole, containing in all its several parts, from first to last, the development of a single divine purpose. It was, in Old and New Testament alike, a gospel, a revelation of God's grace to man. But as this idea could hardly be made to cover the Law, the Mosaic legislation was held to have been temporary and local, and even its moral element, as for instance the Decalogue, only binding upon Christians in so far as it agreed with the law of nature. It will at once suggest itself to those whose eyes have been opened by the literary criticism of modern times, that Luther could hardly trace the gospel through the very various regions of Old Testament history, prophecy, philosophy, without a copious use of that figurative method of interpretation which he had theoretically abandoned. But there is no reason to suppose that he was at all conscious of this inconsistency. "The gospel,"[1] he says, "according to Paul in the first chapter of his Epistle to the Romans, is a proclamation of the Son of God, who became man, and, without any desert of our own, is given to us for blessedness and for peace." This gospel was antecedent to any written promise or record. "Look at Adam and Eve;[2] they are full of sin and death: yet because they hear the promise of the seed of the woman, who shall bruise the serpent's head, they hope for the same things as we, namely, that death will be done away, and sin wiped off, and righteousness, life and peace, restored." Noah and Shem were preachers of the promise.[1] Jacob[2] "lived in faith in Christ," wherefore his works, however contemptible in themselves, were well-pleasing to God. Abraham and Moses were "two good Christians,"[3] Abraham especially "a right, yea a perfect Christian, who lived in the most evangelical fashion possible, in the spirit of God and in faith."[4] These instances may suffice to prepare us for the abstract rule which Luther lays down, namely, that the Scriptures are to be interpreted by the gospel, not the gospel by the Scriptures.[5] And this rule is not only applicable to the Old Testament, but supplies a test by which the differing values of the New Testament writings may be judged.

---

[1] Werke, ed. Walch, I. 700, II. 131. [2] Ibid. II. 2574.
[3] Ibid. III. 997.   [4] Ibid. III. 410.

[5] Wir erleuchten die alte heilige Schrift durch das Evangelium, und nicht wiederum, und vergleichen oder halten zusammen die Meynung des Alten Testaments mit der Meynung des Neuen Testaments. Ibid. IV. 1728. Und darinne stimmen alle rechtschaffene heilige Bücher überein, dass sie allesamt Christum predigen und treiben. Auch ist das der rechte Prüfestein alle Bücher zu tadeln, wenn man siehet ob sie Christum treiben oder nicht, sintemal alle Schrift Christum zeiget (Rom. iii. 21) und St. Paulus nichts denn Christum wissen will (1 Cor. ii. 2). Was Christum nicht lehret, das ist noch nicht apostolisch, wenn es gleich St. Petrus oder St. Paulus lehrete. Wiederum, was Christum prediget, das wäre apostolisch, wenns gleich Judas, Hannas, Pilatus und Herodes thät. Preface to the Epp. of James and Jude, ibid. XIV. 149.

"Those Apostles,"[1] says Luther, "who treat oftenest and highest of how faith in Christ alone justifies, are the best Evangelists. Therefore are St. Paul's Epistles more a Gospel than Matthew, Mark and Luke. For these do not set down much more than the story of the works and miracles of Christ; but the grace which we receive through Christ, no one so boldly extols as St. Paul, especially in his letter to the Romans."

Again:[2]

"John's Gospel, St. Paul's Epistles, especially that to the Romans, and St. Peter's First Epistle, are the right kernel and marrow of all books.... for in them thou findest written down not many works and miracles of Christ, but in a quite masterly way expounded how faith in Christ overcomes sin and death and hell, and gives life, righteousness and peace. Which is, as thou hast heard, the right kind of gospel."

After this it is quite consistent that he should add:[3]

"Therefore is St. James' Epistle, in comparison with these, a mere letter of straw, for it has nothing evangelical about it."

How far this theory may contain in it a secret implication of what would now be called rationalism, I must leave to be discussed at another time. At present it serves as a natural transition to the characteristic Lutheran doctrine of justification by faith alone. This doctrine, as Luther found it expounded in St. Paul's Epistles, furnished the standard to which all other scriptural statements of the method of salvation were brought to be judged, and to which they were made to conform.

---

[1] Preface to the Exposition of 1 Peter: Werke, ed. Walch, IX. 626.
[2] Preface to the New Testament, 1524: ibid. XIV. 104.
[3] Ibid. XIV. 105.

Let us take it in the words of the fourth Article of the Confession of Augsburg :[1]

"We teach that men cannot be justified before God by their own strength, merit or works, but that they are freely justified, because of Christ, by faith, when they believe that they are received into grace, and that their sins are remitted because of Christ, who by his own death has given satisfaction for our sins. This faith God reckons for righteousness before Him."

In order to give this doctrine its true place in a spiritual system of religion, we must not forget the belief, and still more the practice, to which it was opposed. When the greatest value was being set on mere ritual observance—when the inner pains of repentance were being hidden behind the ecclesiastical form of penance which too often took their place—when benefactions to the Church were accepted in atonement for flagrant sin, and escape from purgatory was to be bought of wandering indulgence-mongers in any market-place—it was a great thing to recal men's minds to the fact that religion is an invisible frame of mind, from which alone can spring actions acceptable to God. This was indeed the antithesis of the New Testament over again, in a shape but slightly altered. Once more there was a ceremonial law, a religion of ritual acts, an intolerable burthen of formal obedience laid upon the conscience of the believer, in opposing to which a spiritual gospel, a consecration of the affections, a service of the heart, Luther might well think that he was following in the footsteps of Paul. Nor, so long as the doctrine of justification by faith was preached

---

[1] Sylloge Confessionum, p. 124.

by Luther himself, could there be any pretext for asserting that he was indifferent to the sanctity of moral law, or that the good works on which he poured scorn and contempt were those without which the manly or the Christian character cannot be conceived. Only those critics who have utterly failed to understand both the great Reformer and his characteristic position, can accuse him of a personal tendency to Antinomian heresy. It is true that the heat of controversy, and his own power of paradoxical statement, sometimes led him to make affirmations which will not bear to be taken literally: it is true that after he was gone, men of a harder logic than his, and a less vigorous moral instinct, developed his doctrine into forms which are ethically repulsive. But he delighted in preaching moral sermons. He expounded the Decalogue more than once: he returned again and again for the material of teaching to the Lord's Prayer and the Apostles' Creed. He was uneasy lest the constant preaching of justification by faith alone, by men whose enthusiasm for righteousness was cooler than his own, should lead to consequences of which he could not approve. That note of a great religious teacher—a passionate conviction that holiness is the one thing needful—is almost as conspicuous in him as in his master, Paul.

At the same time, he would hear of no modifications of his central doctrine. It was faith alone, not even faith working by love, that justified. He was too jealous of the operative power of his great principle to admit any other to even a subordinate partnership with it. But then with him, at least in his better moments, faith was no mere intellectual acceptance of Christ and his atoning death, even if that acceptance were of a strictly personal kind:[1] it was such a spiritual incorporation of the soul with its Saviour as involved a changed individuality, a renewed and strengthened nature, out of which all the fruits of righteousness naturally grew. For the Christian so transmuted, it was no longer a question of doing good works in obedience to an external law and, so to speak, to order; they were the natural expression of the new man, as inevitable as breathing and speaking.[2] The doctrine so stated has the advantage of being true to two well-known and indisputable facts of human nature: first, that the motive power of character lies in the affections, and that to produce a cleansed, strengthened, renewed man, there is no other way than to inspire into the heart a passionate love and trust of some worthy object: next, that actions do not so much determine character as are determined by it, and that, to go back to the familiar phrase of the New Testament, if you would have good fruit, you must make the tree good. But the difficulty is, that this doctrine is peculiarly liable both to ambiguous statement and practical abuse. All the words to which "faith" answers—$\pi i\sigma\tau\iota s$, *fides*, *glaube*—have, in different proportions, an intellectual and a moral side. On one they rise into "trust," and imply a personal affection; on the other they sink into "belief," and may mean no more than an intellectual assent. But unhappily "glaube" alone covers the whole ground. It is faith and belief too. There is no other word in common use for either. Of what a shock are we conscious when for "justification by faith" we substitute "justification by

---

[1] Vid. Luther's Sermon, "Von der Freyheit eines Christenmenschen," Werke, ed. Walch, XIX. 1206, especially p. 1215 et seq.

[2] Ibid. XIX. 1223.

belief"! yet for Luther the two phrases were and must have been identical. There is a dynamic force in faith, especially if it be conceived of as inseparable from love; but what strength of change and renewal in mere belief? And it cannot be denied that, as Luther grew older, his conception of faith became more and more intellectual, till at last it comprised little beyond the assent of the mind to certain articles of an orthodox creed.[1] But, once more, what is to prevent the practical abuse of this doctrine by men who accept it on authority, without being conscious of its efficacy in their own hearts, or discerning its justification in facts of human nature? It is a doctrine which fires and fortifies great saints, but is terribly apt to delude common men with a show of religion. What guarantee can there be in any particular case that faith is that transforming passion of the soul which really makes it one with Christ, and not a cool adherence of the intellect, or a passing spasm of excitement, either quite unable to produce such an effect? While if, on the one hand, faith have worked no spiritual change—if, on the other, the moral law have been systematically disparaged—into what hideous mockery of true religion may not men fall who are cherishing all the while the conviction of their most perfect orthodoxy!

But whatever the merits or the dangers of this doctrine, it was admirably adapted to work the great change of which I have spoken. For it led the soul straight to its Divine Object. It made religion a matter only for the believer and Christ. The promise of the gospel was made known everywhere, from the pulpit and in the pages

---

[1] Werke, ed. Walch, X. 1314, 1341, VIII. 2623 et seq., especially VIII. 2660 et seq.

of the Bible: when once it was accepted, what more was necessary? The need of a priesthood, of a visible church, even of sacraments, fell away. The whole fabric of the Catholic Church crumbled to pieces under the operation of this powerful solvent. Christianity was once more a personal thing, a power within the soul placing it in direct relation to God.

Closely connected with this is the doctrine which Luther held, in common with the Waldenses, with Wiclif, and with Huss, of the priesthood of every Christian believer. He will admit of no distinction between clergy and laity except one of office only.[1]

"For all Christians," he says, "are truly of the clergy, and there is among them no difference, save of office alone, as Paul says, that we are all one body, yet has each member its own office, that it may serve the others. This is the all-important thing, that we have one baptism, one gospel, one faith, and are all alike Christians. For baptism, gospel and faith—these alone make men clerical and Christian."

He explicitly denies all efficacy to Papal or Episcopal ordination. Baptism makes a man a priest.[2]

"A Bishop's ordination is no more than this, that in place of the entire congregation he takes one out of the whole body of those who possess equal power, and commits to him the exercise of that same power for the rest..... And that I may put it still more clearly, if a little body of pious Christian laymen were taken, and placed in a desert, who had not among them an episcopally ordained priest, and being there agreed, were to choose one among their own number, married or not, and were to commit to him the office of baptizing, saying mass, absolving, preaching— he would be as truly a priest as if all Bishops and Popes had ordained him."

---

[1] Werke, ed. Walch, X. 302.   [2] Ibid. X. 303.

He thinks that the spiritual dignity conferred upon the Christian by baptism is so high that nothing can be added to it. Whoever is baptized, needs only to be chosen by his fellows to be fit to fill the highest place.[1]

"What is common to all," he says, "may no one take to himself without the will and command of the congregation. And whenever it happens that any one chosen to such an office is deposed for misconduct, then is he straightway what he was before. Therefore the priestly status among Christian people should be only that of a public officer, who, so long as he holds his office, has precedence, but when he is deposed is a peasant or a citizen like another. Thus, truly, is a deposed priest a priest no longer. But now have they invented *characteres indelibiles*, and prate that a deposed priest is nevertheless something other than a bad layman .... all of which are laws and talk invented of men."

I have given this trenchant doctrine in Luther's own words, as they are found in one of his most characteristic works, his "Address to the Christian Nobility of the German Nation," published in 1520. For this is the centre point of his opposition to the Catholic system. In regard to every other matter of dispute with the Reformers, it is possible to conceive that a church sincerely desirous of reform should have met them at least half-way. The abuses of the Roman Curia might have been removed, and the Pope's autocracy modified into a constitutional rule. The history of French Jansenism shows into how close a likeness to Calvinism Catholic doctrine may develope. Even the tenet of justification by faith has been held within the Church in forms which it needs some ingenuity to distinguish from that of Wittenberg. The

---

[1] Werke, ed. Walch, X. 304.

present attitude of Catholicism towards the Scriptures is quite different from that against which Luther protested. The Counter Reformation removed many practical abuses, and might have proceeded to legalize even the marriage of the clergy, without touching the essential principle of Catholic Christianity. That principle is the nourishing of the religious life by sacraments, which can be duly administered only by a sacerdotal order. Whatever church says and means "priest," is on the Catholic side of the great controversy of Christianity; whatever church says and means "minister," in that act proclaims itself Protestant. The one in effect declares its belief that Divine grace and help can descend upon human nature only by certain fixed channels, of which a supernaturally endowed class of men have the control; the other asserts that the intercourse between the Eternal and the human spirit is absolutely free, and that all its conditions are fulfilled in Infinite Love on the one hand, and on the other in awful aspiration and the passionate desire of holiness. Neither can free itself from the necessity of defining the visible Church; but in one case it is simply the assembly of the faithful, united by common beliefs, hopes, purposes; in the other it is a mystic communion, inheriting authority from the past, wielding supernatural power by organized instruments, and standing permanently between the soul and God. It was from one of these entrenched heights of Christian theory to the other that Luther made the irrevocable transition.

Sacraments and priests commonly stand or fall together; but they are not united by any logical bond that cannot be broken. If a sacrament be a divinely-appointed means by which grace is imparted to the soul, it may as well accord with the purpose of God to entrust its administration to a minister duly elected by a Christian community, as to a priest who claims succession from the Apostles by the channel of episcopal ordination. Luther's theory of the universal priesthood of the believer does not therefore necessarily conflict with the conception of a sacrament even in its severer form. But this is not the case with his general idea of the relation of the faithful disciple to Christ. If all that is necessary to secure salvation, both in its narrow and its spiritual sense, is to have faith, and if faith must be taken to mean that mystic incorporation with Christ in which all strength and holiness and blessing are shut up, what is there left for the sacrament to do? Push the conception of faith to the uttermost, and it is recognized as all-powerful: without faith, the sacraments are only empty forms; while with it, they are at best occasions of recollection, spurs to effort, opportunities of devotion. This is in fact Zwingli's doctrine of sacraments: deriving the word from *sacramentum*, the military oath of fidelity, he looked upon them as visible marks of allegiance, which the Christian puts on, and which therefore draw their efficacy from the faith of the receiver. And, at first, this was to a large extent Luther's view also. He is so possessed by his central principle of justification by faith alone, as to feel little inclination to spend time and thought upon the modification, in a Protestant sense, of this part of traditional theology. He does not know how many sacraments there are: he is uncertain as to the definition of a sacrament: it is only by degrees that, with Melancthon, he settles down to the affirmation of two.[1] But as he grows older, and especially as he sees to what excesses, as he thinks, Carlstadt and the radical enthusiasts of the party are dragging him, his conception of a sacrament stiffens and becomes more external. But the two opposing principles always remain in conflict in Luther's mind, and will not be reconciled. Are we to suppose that an ordinance instituted by direct command of God can fail, and must there not be something given which is independent of the receiver's state of mind? And yet, again, how can spiritual changes be produced by other than spiritual causes, or what effect upon the soul can water or wine have *without* faith? So Luther is very hard put to it to reconcile his subjective principle with any sacramental conception of baptism: he shrinks from acknowledging a purely supernatural effect of the water and the words upon the unconscious child: on the one hand, he declares that the water is not mere water, but water deified by the Word, so as to have become something quite other than its natural self:[2] on the other, he falls back upon a theory which would be ludicrous but for the perplexity of mind which it betrays, that the representative faith of sponsors somehow stands in the place of the genuine spiritual affection in the subject of the sacrament.[3] But the illogical character of Luther's sacramental theory is still more manifest in the case of the Eucharist. He denied its validity as a sacrifice, representative and repetitive of that on Calvary: he would not look upon it as an *opus operatum*, a spiritual benefit

---

[1] Von der Babylonischen Gefängniss der Kirchen: Werke, ed. Walch, XIX. 13, 14.

[2] Werke, ed. Walch, X. 2539.   [3] Ibid. XIX. 88, 1625.

conferred irrespective of the frame of mind of celebrant or receiver. But still he could not shake off the influence of that Catholic doctrine of sacraments which I can only call the magical. He insisted on the Real Presence. If he denied Transubstantiation, he substituted the still more cumbrous and less intelligible doctrine of Consubstantiation for it. He decisively took his stand on the magical rather than the spiritual side of the sacramental controversy, in the declaration that the body and blood of Christ were eaten, not merely by the faithful, but by the ungodly recipient.[1] At the Conference of Marburg, called by Philip of Hesse, in the hope of reconciling the German and the Swiss Reformers upon this vital point, he wrote with a piece of chalk upon the tablecloth before him the words, "*Hoc est corpus meum*," and pressed their literal interpretation whenever any concession was asked

---

[1] Brenz, who after Luther's death was among the most active opponents of union with the Reformed theologians, put the doctrine in a form more vivid than reverent by asking what would be the consequence if, by any accident, the consecrated bread were eaten by a mouse. He decides that the mouse would have eaten the true body of Christ. "Soll man aber sprechen, das Brod, so die Maus gessen, sei der Leib Christi, so will es sich nicht reimen oder schicken, dass die Mäuse sollen den Leib Christi essen. Wohlan! es schick' sich oder reim' sich vor der menschlichen Vernunft wie es woll', so müssen wir eher etwas Ungereimtes und vor der Welt Ungeschicktes zulassen, ehe wir wollten dem wahrhaftigen und ewig beständigen Wort Gottes eine Unwahrheit und Lüge aufbürden. Es mussen eher alle Menschen Lügner sein und die Mäuse Leibesser, ehe unser lieber Herr Christus ein Lügner sollte erfunden werden. . . . . Demnach dieweil Gottes Wort stärker ist denn eine Maus und das Brod einmal durch das Wort Gottes zu dem Leib Christi verordnet ist, eine Maus aber verzehrt dasselbe : so muss bekannt werden, dass das Brod auch der Leib Christi sei, wenn es schon von einer Maus gegessen würde." Quoted by Schenkel, Wesen d. Prot. I. 563.

of him.[1] He did not shrink from the most perverse exegesis of other apparently plain passages of Scripture, in order to justify his literal acceptance of this.[2] Something of this stubbornness was perhaps due to Luther's high conception of the authority of Scripture, and his determination to subject to what he considered to be its plain deliverance the hesitations and difficulties of human reason; but something more, too, to his inability or unwillingness to follow out his spiritual conception of Christianity to its just issues, and to break, if necessary, with old forms of worship. But to any critic of the present day who has quite passed beyond the influence of sacramental ideas, it is strange and sad to see how the Reformation was wrecked upon this rock. It made an irreparable breach between Luther and Zwingli, who agreed upon so much else, and who, in face of a united and an implacable enemy, had so much reason to draw together. It defied the reconciling efforts of Bucer and the attempt of Calvin to find a mediating theory. When Luther was gone, his followers wandered away into deserts of Protestant scholasticism in search of a defi-

---

[1] Zuinglii Opp. IV. 175.

[2] Luther declares that we might as well interpret the words, "In the beginning God made heaven and earth," "In the beginning the cuckoo eat the hedge-sparrows, feathers and all," as take the words of institution in other than the literal sense. Walch, XX. 971. Being pressed with the words, Gen. xli. 26, "The seven good kine are seven years," &c., he actually says: "Denn die sieben Ochsen bedeuten nicht sieben Jahre, sondern sie sind selbst wesentlich und wahrhaftig die sieben Jahre: denn es sind nicht natürliche Ochsen, die da Gras fressen auf der Weide, welche wol durch alte gemeine Worte (sieben Ochsen) genennet werden. Aber hie ists ein neu Wort, und sind sieben Ochsen des Hungers und der Fülle, das ist, sieben Jahre des Hungers und der Fülle." Walch, XX. 1137.

nition of the essentially undefinable, and spent their strength in sectarian hatreds and internecine wars. On his own theory of Christianity, the Catholic is justified in attaching the utmost importance to what is at once the central act of worship and the fountain from which the spiritual life is fed; but once the doctrine of faith, and with it that of the soul's immediate relation to God, is formulated, the Eucharist sinks, or ought to sink, into a secondary place. But experience shows that, in religion at least, it is always the lesser differences which engender the bitterest animosities.

It must not be forgotten, in the last place, that the movement of human thought of which the Reformation was the first manifestation on the ground of religion, was a reaction against Mediævalism, not merely intellectual but ethical. I do not mean by this that we can set the sixteenth century on a moral pedestal as compared with any that had preceded it—every age has its own strength and weakness—but that it rejected the ethical ideal which it found in vogue, and set up another. That ideal had been ascetic. The monastic was the highest life. Celibacy was better than marriage, virginity than chastity. The way to the perfection of the spirit was through the subjugation of the flesh. Long fasts, daily scourgings, to wear coarse clothing, to sleep on a hard bed, to rise thrice in the night for prayer, were at once things acceptable to God and a discipline that would purge the eyesight of the soul. But unfortunately this method had signally broken down. It had produced many saints after its own fashion of saintliness, some famous, more without a name; but apart from them, a fearful mass of deliberate licentiousness and open-eyed sin. The long struggle of the Popes to enforce the celibacy of the clergy had ended in an external compliance with the rule of the Church; but almost every parish priest had in his house an unacknowledged wife and family, whose position was in some sort assured by a dispensation which any bishop would sell. But this was far from being the worst feature of the case. Without going the full length of Protestant polemics to the assertion that every monastery was a sink of iniquity, we may safely affirm that monastic scandals were frequent and grievous. From the eleventh century downwards, before the Poor Men of Lyons had lifted up their protest, or Wiclif anticipated the doctrine of Luther, one perpetual cry of moral remonstrance, expressed in every variety of tone, grave, satiric, carelessly humorous, is being uttered in all literature. The vices of the clergy are at once the complaint of the theologian and the motive of the novelist. What the Popes of the Renaissance were in this respect we know; few of them but were notoriously foul livers: but as Agamemnon was taller by the head than any of his confederates, so Alexander VI. towers over his predecessors and followers in magnificence of infamy. I do not suppose, from anything I know of them, that our good Saxon Reformers, princes or theologians, were men of a fastidious refinement or a singular niceness of moral discernment; but their consciences rose up in hot rebellion against this frightful state of things, and with a reformation in theology they desired a return to decent and natural life.

In the language of our own day, we should call this a reversion to Hellenism. In a sense perhaps this may be so, but yet not consciously. I have already pointed out the fact that the German, were animated by a severer ethical spirit than the Italian humanists; and I can imagine that Agricola and Reuchlin, still more Luther and Melancthon, looked with deep disgust at the Hellenism of a man like Filelfo, who, great scholar as he was, emulated, as far as his opportunities would allow, the naked vices of his aristocratic patrons. And it is too much forgotten, in speaking of this matter, that the domestic life of Israel, as recorded in the Bible, is on the whole singularly healthy and beautiful; while whatever germs of asceticism there may be in the New Testament, did not develope into baneful growth until Europe was within sight of the ages of darkness. And it was therefore to the same scriptural source from which he drew so much other inspiration, that Luther turned for the justification of the universal instincts of the human heart. Perhaps in this respect he did not so much direct events as was carried away by them. The time was ripe for this revolution. When he appeared before Charles V. at Worms in 1521, he still wore a cowl. It was while he was in his Patmos in the Wartburg that the Augustinian monks of his own convent at Wittenberg began to break their bonds and to go out into common life. Nor can I so truly say that the infection spread, as that the disease, if disease it were, manifested itself everywhere: vows were renounced, monasteries dissolved. So in regard to the marriage of the clergy. First one or two obscure men took unto themselves wives, scandals rather than examples: next, in 1522, Carlstadt, Archdeacon of the Stiftskirche at Wittenberg, yet already regarded as an adventurous, if not dangerous spirit, married Anna Mochau: at last, in 1525, Martin Luther, the Augustinian monk, espoused Catharine von Bora, the runaway nun of Niemtsch. The outcry was prodigious: that a monk should marry at all was bad enough; that he should marry a nun, an unutterable portent: Catholic controversialists predicted diabolical offspring from such a union. When, two years afterwards, Œcolampadius also took a wife, Erasmus, with bitter wit, declared that the Lutheran tragedy was nothing better than a comedy, and ended in weddings.[1] But the marriage of Wittenberg was well and wisely as well as boldly done; and when the pair plighted their troth, in the house in which they were to live, and in the presence of their friends, they secured the purity and the happiness of innumerable homes.

It would be difficult to understand how Luther "the monk, who, if ever any, would have got to heaven by monkery," became the loving husband, the tender father, the cheerful friend, who loved music and kindly talk with his fellows, and held out a frank hand to all the lawful enjoyments of life, were it not that we recognize in him one of those strong and many-sided natures who try many extremes before they arrive at an equilibrium, and throw an equal energy into every experiment of life. He frankly trusted nature, and would hear of no scruples. "If our Lord God,"[2] he said once, "may make excellent large pike and good Rhenish wine, I may very well venture to eat and to drink. Thou mayest enjoy every pleasure in the world that is not sinful: that, thy God forbids thee not, but much rather wills it. And it is pleasing to the dear God whenever thou rejoicest or

---

[1] Ep. 951, Opp. III. p. 1071 E.
[2] Quoted by Hagen, II. 232.

laughest from the bottom of thy heart." I freely admit that his theory of the relation between the sexes, if pursued into its details, is not untinged with coarseness; but we must recollect that those relations find their guarantee of refinement in unconsciousness; and unconscious in that regard was precisely what Luther and his age could not be. Mr. Galton has lately asked, in his book on "Hereditary Genius," what loss has been inflicted on the race by the monastic system, in the extinction without offspring, generation after generation, of the lives best fitted to hand down a refined and strengthened humanity. The merit of Luther in counteracting this evil was recognized more than a century ago. "Justus Möser," says Ranke,[1] "reckoned, in the year 1750, that from ten to fifteen millions of human beings, in all lands, owed their existence to Luther and his example, and declared that a statue ought to be erected to him, as the sustainer of the human race." This is, after all, only an arithmetical way of looking at it: some may even say, that as weal and woe are meted out, it is not an unmixed good to be born. But to have lifted the load of sin from many consciences—to have reconciled nature and duty, purity and passion—to have made woman once more the faithful helpmeet of God's servants as of other men—to have been the founder of countless sweet and peaceful homes—is no small part of Luther's true glory. And he has this appropriate reward, that while it is possible to arraign his intellectual methods of inconsistency and incompleteness, to convict him of passionate self-will and unchecked vehemence of controversy, to show that

---

[1] Ranke, II. 465.

he was sometimes bitter to his enemies and arrogant to
his friends, no shadow of criticism can rest upon him in
that simple home at Wittenberg, where he was as a little
child among his own little children, and bravely bore,
with his true yokefellow, the daily burden of his life.

NOTE TO LECTURE IV.

A question has been raised, and in some quarters very eagerly discussed, as to the moral effects of the Reformation. Dr. v. Döllinger, in especial, in his book, "Die Reformation, ihre innere Entwicklung und ihre Wirkungen im Umfange des Lutherischen Bekenntnisses," has accumulated a vast mass of evidence to show that the immediate result of the Reformation was a dissolution of morals; that the restraints of religion were relaxed; on the one hand that the characters of the Protestant preachers were by no means without stain, on the other that they were treated with indifference and almost contempt by the people. Part of this evidence is drawn from the works of Catholic theologians, who were altogether out of harmony with the Reformation; part from those humanists, who, like Mutian and Pirkheimer, grew dissatisfied with it before they died; part from the utterances of such men as George Wizel, who retreated from the Protestant into the Catholic ranks, and pursued their old faith with.the bitterness of deserters. In the case of all these, one thing is eminently noticeable: they lay the blame of the neglect of morals, which they deplore, upon the doctrine of justification by faith alone, denouncing it as utterly subversive of old impulses and sanctions of duty. Evidence proceeding from such sources might fairly be taken with more than a grain of salt; but there remain a painful series of confessions of disappointment with the moral results of their work on the part of the Reformers themselves, and especially of Luther. It is difficult to give an idea of the weight of this evidence, except by such an accumulation of quotations as is impossible in this place. In passage after passage Luther declares that the last state of things was worse than the first; that vice of every kind had increased since the Reformation; that the nobles were greedy, the peasants brutal; that the corruption of morals in Wittenberg itself was so great that he contemplated shaking off the dust of his feet against it; that Christian liberality had altogether

L

ceased to flow; and that the preachers were neither held in respect nor supported by the people. Towards the close of his life, these complaints became more bitter and more frequent. Sometimes the Devil is called in to account for so painful and perplexing a state of things; always Luther and Melancthon are sure that they have fallen upon the last days, when the temporary triumph of evil is permitted to precede the final victory of good. But it is significant that Luther himself does not altogether acquit the doctrine of justification—though in his view misapprehended—of blame in this matter. .

On the other side, it must be remembered that the Reformation, in introducing a new ideal and fresh types of goodness, excited bitter criticism in all who adhered to the old; that such facts as the abandonment of monastic vows and the marriage of monks and nuns were regarded with a moral loathing of which it is now hard to form a conception. Again, in a certain way, the Reformation inherited the sins of the preceding age. It arose in part out of the dissolution of morals in which mediæval Christianity had ended, and with which it had, more or less successfully, to cope. May not the worst that can be truly said of it be, that it had to deal with a corrupt generation, and left it little better than it found it? The monasteries were full of monks and nuns, without vocation, who embraced Protestantism for the sake of the liberty which it offered them, and were afterwards its disgrace. Something, too, in the case of such men as Luther and Melancthon, we may put down to a kind of "divine despair," the disappointment which comes of a high ideal confronted with ordinary facts of life. Still, when all these allowances have been made, I am afraid that we must admit that, whatever its after effects (and certainly no grave moral charges can be justly made against English and Scottish Puritanism), the Reformation did not at first carry with it much cleansing force of moral enthusiasm. The question is only indirectly connected with my main subject; but it will require much more careful treatment at the hands of any future historian of the Reformation than it has yet received.

LECTURE V.

THE REFORMATION IN RELATION TO REASON AND LIBERTY.

It is now, after the lapse of four centuries, possible to state with something like accuracy the nature of that movement of the human mind which began with the Revival of Letters, and has gone on with accelerating rapidity to the present moment. It has been, in the first place, an effort to bring both traditional and new knowledge to the test of reason, rejecting as untrue whatever will not stand it, and building up all that it approves into a compact system of fact and inference; in the second, a slow struggle towards a state of society in which every man is permitted to think and speak as he will, without incurring legal penalty or social disability. I use the word reason here, in its largest sense, as denoting the faculties of the human mind in their collective application to all problems of science and of life, and without wishing to imply that methods of inquiry are absolutely the same in all branches of knowledge. There are degrees of certainty in truth; and the severe procedure of mathematics is not applicable to history, to morals, to religion. But the period of which I have spoken has been marked throughout by the development of the scientific method. Men have learned the folly of making large assumptions, and then trying to force facts into agreement with them: it is an accepted principle that the collection, the comparison, the classification of facts must precede and justify generalization. Every science in turn has abandoned the principle of authority, and now expects belief only for what it can prove. And liberty of thought, speech and life, is the practical corollary of the scientific method. Nothing can be less logical than to subject everything to inquiry and yet to annex penalty to the result. First, toleration—next, equality before the law—last of all, social equality—are stages of progress in the art of life necessarily involved in the development of the scientific spirit. The final consummation will be reached when all belief rests upon adequate evidence, and none affects a man's relations to his neighbours.

Perhaps it is only of late years that the scientific method has become sufficiently self-conscious to be thus defined. It certainly was very far from being so in the first half of the sixteenth century. Then, a greater force than they knew was urging men on to issues which they could not foresee. We shall hear presently that Luther speaks of human reason in the most disrespectful terms; and that the sins of the Reformers against religious toleration were only less heinous than those of their Catholic adversaries. Yet the Reformation was, however unconsciously, both the first great triumph of the scientific spirit and a very effectual assertion of human liberty. It was brought about by the application of certain keen and independent minds to the study of theology: the

Reformers, at the very moment that they were denouncing reason and proclaiming their unconditional submission to Scripture, were, in a very true sense, rationalists without knowing it. They had broken away from tradition, the schoolmen, the Church, and, with an audacity the extent of which we are now hardly able to realize, had taken their religious fate into their own hands. Nor does the fact that in their intellectual career they stopped short at a certain point, that they failed to draw what seem to us plain inferences from plain facts, or to follow out their principles to their legitimate issue, at all militate against this view. How can the substitution of Calvin's Institution for Aquinas' *Summa* be otherwise described than as the consequence of a *rational* revolt? So, too, the Reformation undeniably made for liberty. It broke the overwhelming force of a Church that would allow no difference with itself. Even though the new churches very imperfectly understood the principles and the practice of religious liberty, it was a step in advance to have substituted three intolerant communions for one. In spite of persecutions, exclusions, disabilities, men breathed the intellectual air more freely. The sects which the Reformation could not put down, proved how real had been its liberating power.

The rationalism of the Renaissance on the field of theology cannot be better exhibited than by returning for a moment to Erasmus, its characteristic representative in Germany. Luther and Melancthon looked upon him as a doubter, a scoffer, an Epicurus, a Lucian. His reputation among devout Catholic theologians was not much better. His fertile pen was constantly employed in defending a position which adversaries on opposite sides agreed in thinking quite untenable. But the editor of so many Fathers, the scholar who made the first attempt to form a critical text of the New Testament, could not possibly accept many of the conclusions to which orthodox Catholics and orthodox Protestants alike bound themselves. His "Annotations on the New Testament," and the defences of them which various opponents afterwards drew from him, are full of sound observations, which often anticipate the results of modern criticism. His omission from the New Testament of 1516 of the verses 1 John v. 7, known as the Three Heavenly Witnesses, and his subsequent insertion of them in his third edition, when a Greek manuscript containing the words had been brought under his notice, form a well-known episode in the history of the Biblical text.[1] He gives the textual evidence against the story of the woman taken in adultery quite fairly, remarking that it was absent from most Greek manuscripts. At the same time he retains it in the text as found in one, which he had himself seen, and as being universally received.[2] He enters largely into the discussion as to the right way of punctuating Romans ix. 5, alleging that in any case the text is not an effectual refutation of Arianism.[3] He admits lapses of memory and failures of judgment in the apostles: Christ alone is called the Truth, and is wholly free

---

[1] His note on the passage (Opp. VI. 1080 D) is, however, couched in terms which show how little he was convinced. "Verumtamen, ne quid dissimulem, repertus est apud Anglos Græcus codex unus, in quo habetur quod in vulgatis deest. . . . . Ex hoc igitur codice Britannico reposuimus, quod in nostris dicebatur deesse, ne cui sit ansa calumniandi. Tametsi suspicor codicem illum ad nostros esse correctum."

[2] Note to John viii. 1 : Opp. VI. 373 E.

[3] Note to Romans ix. 5 : Opp. VI. 610 B.

from error.¹ He thinks that the Gospel of Mark is an abridgment of that of Matthew,² and calls attention to the fact that Luke is not an eye-witness of the things that he relates.³ He repeats the opinion of Jerome, that Clement of Rome was very likely the author of the Epistle to the Hebrews:⁴ in his own cautious way he casts doubt on the Johannine authorship of the Apocalypse, going so far as to say that he could easily believe that the heretic Cerinthus had written the book as a means of spreading his poison through the world.⁵ Nor is he less hardy in regard to doctrine. Accused of unsoundness on the subject of the Trinity, he adduces eighty passages from his writings in which he had expressed himself in the true orthodox way;⁶ but not the less he points out how very seldom Christ is called God in the New Testament,⁷ and declares that the Holy Ghost is never so denominated.⁸ In his dialogue, "The Shipwreck," he does not scruple to treat the Virgin as the successor of Venus, once the peculiar goddess of unhappy mariners.⁹ He was not too orthodox as to the Sacraments. In regard to Baptism, he made a distinction,

---

¹ Note to Matthew ii. 7 : Opp. VI. 13 E.
² Note to Mark i. 1 : Opp. VI. 151 E. Luke i. 2 : Opp. VI. 217 C.
³ Note to Luke i. 4, 5 : Opp. VI. 218 D.
⁴ Note to Hebrews xiii. 18 : Opp. VI. 1023, 1024.
⁵ Note to Apoc. sub fine : Opp. VI. 1124 F. It is only fair to say that Erasmus adds : "At rursum mihi non potest persuaderi Deum passurum fuisse, ut Diaboli techna tot seculis impune deluderet populum Christianum."
⁶ Adversus Monachos quosdam Hispanos : Opp. IX. 1023 et seq.
⁷ Ibid.: Opp. IX. 1040 B.   ⁸ Ibid.: Opp. IX. 1050 D.
⁹ Colloquia : Opp. I. 713 B.

which is certainly inconsistent with Catholic doctrine, between those who receive the sacrament without its accompanying grace, and the true Christians who answer to it with newness of life.[1] If it were not for the general opinion of the Church, he says that he should adopt Œcolampadius' opinion as to the Lord's Supper;[2] while Melancthon boldly declares that the whole Eucharistic strife took its origin from Erasmus.[3] Upon Eternal Punishment he was still more hopelessly rationalistic. "There is no other flame," he said, "in which the sinner is plagued, and no other punishment of hell, than the perpetual anguish of mind which accompanies habitual sin."[4] These statements, which might be made much more numerous, may suffice to show that the Renaissance, in the hands of serious men, was prepared to bring Scripture and the Creeds to the test of sound reason, and that, but for the action of other and opposing forces, many of the questions which we are apt to think exclusively characteristic of our own age, might have taken shape and received at least a tentative answer three centuries ago.

At first it seemed as if Luther might be about to apply, with a more fiery earnestness and a deeper dogmatic

---

[1] Adversus Monachos quosdam Hispanos: Opp. IX. 1061 A.

[2] Ep. to Pirkheimer: Opp. III. Ep. 723, p. 941 A.

[3] Letter of Melancthon to Camerarius: Corp. Ref. I. 1083. Conf. letter to Aquila: ibid. IV. 970.

[4] Enchiridion: Opp. V. 56 C. "Nec alia est flamma, in qua cruciatur dives ille comessator evangelicus. Nec alia supplicia inferorum, de quibus multa scripsere Poetæ, quam perpetua mentis anxietas, quæ peccandi consuetudinem comitatur. Tollat igitur qui velit futuri seculi tam diversa præmia: habet annexum sibi virtus propter quod abunde debeat expeti: habet adjunctum peccatum, cujus causa debeat horreri."

purpose, the method of Erasmus to theology. His intellectual history, from his first attack upon indulgences to the consummation of his revolt against Rome at the Diet of Worms, is one of gradually rising discord between his own mind and accepted opinions. Had I time, I might enumerate its stages and trace its method, showing how he was forced, as it were against his will, to abandon Popes, schoolmen, tradition, fathers, councils, until at last he entrenched himself behind the inexpugnable authority of Scripture. And he knew both what he was doing and on what principle he did it. When at the supreme moment of his life he was asked, in the presence of the Emperor and the assembled States, whether he would retract what he had written, he replied that he could not do so unless he was refuted by appeal to Scripture or by cogent reasons.[1] A few days later, before a Commission presided over by the Elector Archbishop of Trier, he made the same reply in the same terms to the Margrave Joachim of Brandenburg. It is impossible to doubt that he here assigns to reason an independent position by the side of Scripture: the words will bear no other interpretation: while the repetition of them, after some days had passed, forbids us to suppose that they had been lightly uttered. But I know of no later word of Luther's that can be fairly quoted in the same sense.

---

[1] Sleidan's phrase is (p. 37 b), "Quod nisi Scripturæ sacræ testimoniis vel evidenti ratione convictus fuero." The second passage (p. 39 a) is even a little more emphatic: "Tum Brandeburgicus, Num hoc, inquit, vis, te non cessurum nisi convictum sacrâ scripturâ? Plane, inquit Lutherus, aut evidentissimis rationibus." The German original seems to have been, "oder durch helle Gründe." Sleidani De Statu Religionis et Reipublicæ Carolo Quinto Cæsare, Commentarii.

From Worms he passed to his Patmos on the Wartburg, whence he emerged only to quell the tumult which the so-called Prophets of Zwickau had raised at Wittenberg. And this was the beginning of reaction. First Carlstadt, who had caught the infection of independent thought from the men of Zwickau, seceded from the main body of the Reformers; next Thomas Münzer fanned that flame of social discontent which kindled the widespread conflagration of the Peasants' War; then the various forms of free thought and moral revolt which are all comprised in the one word Anabaptism began to perplex and discredit the Reformation. All these things were, in Luther's view, only so many manifestations of presumptuous human reason intruding itself into the region of faith: it was reason that denied the necessity of baptism; it was reason that would not accept, in their plain literal meaning, the words, "This is my body;" and against reason, therefore, he set himself, with a hardness and a bitterness which grew harder and more bitter to the day of his death.

It is possible, I know, to quote passages from Luther's works which at first sight do not seem to agree with this account of his position. But on further examination they will all be found so limited by the context as really to fall in with it. For instance, he writes in 1522:[1] "What then is contrary to reason is certainly much more contrary to God. For how should not that be against divine truth which is against reason and human truth?" But then, only a few lines before, he had said that the monas-

---

[1] Werke, ed. Walch, XIX. 1940: Von den Gelübden der Mönche und Nonnen, § 246. Conf. Auslegung des Propheten Jonä, § 43, 44, et seq.: ibid. VI. 2618, 2619.

tic vows of which he is speaking were "contrary to natural reason, that is, to the dark and gross light of nature. For although," he goes on, "the same can neither understand nor of itself attain to the light and the works of God, so that *in affirmativis* its judgment is quite gross and uncertain, yet *in negativis*, that is, in what a thing is not, its judgment and understanding are certain. For reason does not comprehend what God is; yet it comprehends in the most certain way what God is not." So in certain articles of disputation, of the date of 1536, he says:[1] "It is admitted that reason is the chief of all things, and among all that belongs to this life the best, yea, a something divine." She is the inventress and queen of all arts, of all wisdom, power, virtue, honour, which men possess in this life: that which distinguishes man from all other creatures: a sun, and as it were a god, which is set for the ruling of these things in this life. But, again, he proceeds to say that reason knows her own majesty and excellence not of herself, but only from Scripture, and that the moment she sets herself against Scripture her ignorance is manifest. In 1544, he calls reason a very great and priceless gift of God, yet goes on to qualify it as a light that is only darkness;[2] while in 1546, the last year of his life, he acknowledges it to be a light, and a beautiful light too, yet which cannot find the way out of sin and death into righteousness and life, but abideth in darkness.[3] So that, even taken alone, the passages in which Luther is supposed to sound the

---

[1] Werke, ed. Walch, XIX. 1777 et seq.

[2] Ibid. VI. 181, 182: Kurze Auslegung über den Propheten Jesaiam, § 51, 52.

[3] Ibid. IX. 1382: on Psalm cxix. 105.

praises of human reason would justify the assertion that he assigned to it only a narrow place and a low function in relation to the highest subjects of thought. He allows it none but a negative efficacy: he strictly limits its action to the things of this life. But there are other passages again in which, especially when angered by rationalistic objections to the doctrines which were the foundation of his system, he vituperates it with all the energy of which he is capable. "The more subtle and acute is reason, without knowledge of divine grace," he says in his Exposition of the Epistle to the Galatians,[1] "the more poisonous a beast, with many dragons' heads, is it, against God and all His works;" while a few lines further on he calls it "an ugly Devil's bride" and "God's bitterest enemy." "There is a speculative theology," he is reported to have said in his Table-talk,[2] "which men regulate according to reason and their own speculations of things. Such a speculative theology belongs to the Devil in hell." But it was in a sermon of the date of 1546,[3] the last he ever preached at Wittenberg, that Luther, now upon the verge of the grave, gives full vent, in language that is too gross to be quoted, to his

---

[1] Werke, ed. Walch, VIII. 2048, § 152.   [2] Tischreden, I. 9.

[3] Predigt über die Epistel am andern Sonntage nach Epiphaniä: Werke, ed. Walch, XII. 1521. One or two extracts may suffice. "Wucherey, Saüferey, Ehebruch, Mord, Todtschlag, &c., die kann man merken, und verstehet auch die Welt, dass sie Sünde seyn: aber des Teufels Braut, Ratio, die schöne Metze, führet herein, und will klug seyn, und was sie saget, meinet sie, es sey der Heilige Geist; wer will da helfen? Weder Jurist, Medicus, noch König, oder Käyser. Denn es ist die höchste Hure die der Teufel hat" (p. 1530). Further on, he addresses Reason, "Hörest du es, du schäbichte, aussätzige Hure, du heilige Vernunft?" (p. 1533); and again, "Höre auf, du verfluchte Hure" (p. 1537).

hatred and contempt of reason in the domain of theology. It seems now as if the very utterance of the word were enough to throw wide open the flood-gates of his abuse.

At the same time, nothing can well be more marked than the inconsistency between Luther's theory and his practice in this matter, especially in regard to Biblical criticism. It is quite true that he had little or no conception of Biblical criticism as a science, and was very far indeed from working on the lines which Erasmus had begun to lay down. But he formed independent judgments as to both the authorship and the contents of Biblical books which are not easy to reconcile with that unconditional submission to the authority of Scripture which he exacted of others. And these judgments he often expressed in very trenchant phrase. I have already, in my last Lecture, quoted passages in which he measures the worth of the various books of the New Testament by the prominence which they give to his peculiar conception of the gospel: strongly preferring the Fourth to the Synoptical Gospels: elevating the Epistle to the Romans to the highest, depressing the Epistle of James to the lowest place. For this he might plead the principle of the *analogia fidei*, although it must be confessed that his application of it was not only uncompromising, but rude. But he looked at the Scriptures with an individual eye, and was not restrained by any superstitious reverence from reporting what he thought he saw. He asked, what it mattered even if Moses were not the author of Genesis?[1] He saw the essential superiority of the Books of Kings over those of Chronicles as an historical

---

[1] Tischreden, I. 28.

record, and did not hesitate to pronounce the former the more credible. He discerned the dramatic character of the Book of Job, and compared its structure to that of the Comedies of Terence.[1] The Book of Ecclesiastes, he thought, was not the production of Solomon, but of Sirach, and belonged to the time of the Maccabees.[2] He wished that the Second Book of Maccabees and that of Esther did not exist, partly for their too Jewish tendency, partly because they contain much heathen folly.[3] He points out that the prophecies of Jeremiah, as we have them, are not in chronological order, and hence infers that they were made into a book, not by the prophet himself, but by a compiler.[4] The story of Jonah he stigmatizes in the strongest terms as absolutely incredible, "more lying and more absurd than any fable of the poets; and if it did not stand in the Bible, I should laugh at it as a lie."[5] He declares the Epistle to the Hebrews to be the work neither of Paul nor of any other apostle, and rightly appeals to chap. ii. 3 to prove that the author must have belonged to another generation than the apostolic. "Who wrote it," he says, "is unknown, but also it does not matter."[6] He did worse than call the Epistle of James a letter of straw: he did not believe it to be the production of an apostle at all,[7] and would not admit that it was possible to reconcile its doctrine with that of Paul.

---

[1] Tischreden, IV. 405, 406.   [2] Ibid. IV. 400.   [3] Ibid. IV. 403.

[4] Werke, ed. Walch, XIV. 50: Vorreden zu der Deutschen Bibelübersetzung, Jeremiah.

[5] Tischreden, IV. 418.

[6] Werke, ed. Walch, XIV. 146, 147: Vorrede auf die Ep. an die Ebräer.

[7] Ibid. XIV. 148: Vorrede auf die Epp. St. Jacobi und St. Judä.

"Many have laboured and sweated over the Epistle of St. James to reconcile it with St. Paul. As also Philip Melancthon has somewhat treated of the matter in his Apologia, but not earnestly: for that faith justifies and faith does not justify are clean contrary the one to the other. Whoso can make them accord, upon his head will I set my doctor's cap, and allow myself to be reproved for a fool."[1]

The Epistle of Jude he clearly saw to be an extract from or a copy of 2 Peter, and to be post-apostolic.[2] Last of all, the figurative character of the Apocalypse offended him: he found nothing like it in any prophet either in the Old or the New Testament, and in a Preface, which was afterwards suppressed, he declared that he held it as neither prophetic nor apostolic.[3]

Nor did he apply this freedom of treatment only to questions of authenticity or genuineness. He criticised the matter as well as the form of Scripture. He disparaged, for instance, the predictive function of prophecy, appealing for support of his view to the authority of Paul.[4] Such prophecy is in the New Testament unnecessary, "for it neither teaches nor augments Christian faith. Wherefore it is almost one of the least gifts of God, and sometimes even comes from the Devil."[5] He had no great opinion of the efficacy of miracles in producing conviction. What, he asked,[6] without faith, is the use of all miracles? What good to the Jews were the miracles of Christ and his apostles? He did not

---

[1] Tischreden, IV. 399.   [2] Werke, ed. Walch, XIV. 150.
[3] Ibid. XIV., Preface, p. 13.   [4] Romans xii. 6, 7.
[5] Werke, ed. Walch, XII. 451, 452: Auslegung der Ep. am andern Sonntage nach Epiphaniä.
[6] Ibid. X. 2308: Vom Gebet des Herrn.

care to be able to work miracles himself; for signs, he thought, would not move them who did not of themselves turn to that Word against which the whole world can object nothing.¹ Besides, as he said over and over again, miracles may deceive: the Devil can and does work wonders when he chooses.² If a saint, after his death, works miracles at his tomb, who knows that God is not thereby tempting us?³ He compares the physical with the moral miracles of Christ, greatly to the disadvantage of the former, which he calls "trifling and almost foolish wonders in comparison with the right lofty miracles which Christ performs in Christendom, without intermission, by his divine almighty power."⁴ He recognized the existence of discrepancies in Scripture, but thought them of little consequence if the main facts of faith were fully grasped.⁵

"There are and remain questions which I will not resolve: nor are they of any great matter, except that there are many people who are so sharp and subtle, and bring up all manner of questions whereof they will have exact speech and answer..... When a contradiction occurs in Holy Scripture, and it cannot be reconciled, so let it go."

He takes a strong view on the contention of Paul with Peter,⁶ being very unwilling to let the latter off as

---

¹ Werke, ed. Walch, IX. 574: Lection wider die Rottengeister.

² Ibid. X. 363: An den Christlichen Adel.

³ Ibid. XV. 2787: Wider den neuen Abgott und alten Teufel der zu Meissen soll erhaben werden.

⁴ Ibid. XI. 1339: Kirchen Postill. Am Tage der Himmelfahrt Christi.

⁵ Ibid. VII. 1730, 1731: Auslegung des ersten und andern Capitels Johannis.

⁶ Ibid. VIII. 1774: Erklärung der Ep. an die Galater.

easily as Jerome does: on the contrary, he declares the apostle not only to have made a mistake, but to have sinned grossly and grievously. "Foolish" is a word which he applies both to James[1] and to Moses:[2] to the former, certainly in sad earnest; to the latter, usually, if not always, with a tacit reference to that "foolishness of God which is wiser than men," and in not dishonourable contrast to human reason.

In one sense, the fact that the Bible was a fresh phenomenon in Luther's eyes helped him to see it as it was; nor did his perception of its literary peculiarities at all impair his sense of its wonderful spiritual worth and efficacy. It was an after-thought of less original and courageous minds to make no distinction between different parts of the Bible, to regard it all with the same dull and superstitious reverence, and to force the most reluctant facts into the mould of this belief. But if it was a necessity of Luther's nature and intellectual position thus to look at Scripture with rationalistic eyes, his whole theory of the relation of faith to reason shows that if he were not a rationalist—but indeed the logical opposite of one— it was in virtue of a rigorous process of self-suppression. With him, reason and faith were mortal enemies. He almost seems to glory in the "*credo quia impossibile.*" He does not shrink from stating in the most uncompromising way that what Scripture imposes upon us is precisely what reason would bid us reject.

"All the articles of our Christian faith," he says in his Exposition of the Epistle to the Galatians,[3] " which God has revealed to us in His Word, are in presence of reason sheerly impossible,

---

[1] Werke, ed. Walch, I. 2303: Auslegung des ersten Buch Mosis.
[2] Ibid. III. 518, 700, 1137.   [3] Ibid. VIII. 2042.

absurd, false. What, thinks that cunning little fool, can be more absurd and impossible than that Christ should give us in the Supper his body and his blood to eat and to drink? Item, that Baptism should be a bath of regeneration and renewal of the Holy Ghost? That the dead should rise again at the last day? That Christ the Son of God should be conceived and borne in the womb of the Virgin Mary, should become man, suffer, die a shameful death upon the cross, sit at the right hand of the Father, and have all power and might in heaven and on earth?"

He repeats this thought in a variety of forms. Speaking of the Trinity, he says:[1]

"It is only Christians who believe what reason cunningly concludes to be such foolish things..... For reason will never be able to reconcile itself to this, that three should be one, and one three; that God should be man; that we, when we are dipped in the font, are cleansed from our sins by the blood of Christ; that in bread we eat the body of Christ, in wine drink his blood, and thus receive forgiveness of sins. Such articles of faith are held by the worldly wise to be pure foolishness. But whoso believes shall be blessed."

He describes Paul's teaching of the derivation of human sin from Adam as "a laughable doctrine,"[2] and asks what can be more ridiculous than that the fact that Adam took a bite of an apple should have the tremendous result of putting all men, to the very end of the world, into the power of death?

"For he had committed," he goes on to say, "neither murder nor adultery; he had robbed no one, nor blasphemed God, nor committed any of the horrible sins of which the world is now full; but only eaten the apple, over-persuaded and deceived by

---

[1] Werke, ed. Walch, XIII. 1528: Die dritte Predigt am Tage der Heiligen Dreifaltigkeit.
[2] Ibid. VIII. 1240, 1241: Auslegung 1 Cor. xv. § 136.

the Devil, through the woman. Must we then, says reason, make this single apple of so much account that the whole world must pay for it, and so many fine, excellent, wise folk, yea, God's Son himself, with all Prophets, Fathers and Saints, must die?"

To all this, and much more of the same kind, there is but one answer; let me give it in Luther's own vigorous words:[1]

"It is a quality of faith that it wrings the neck of reason and strangles the beast, which else the whole world, with all creatures, could not strangle. But how? It holds to God's Word: lets it be right and true, no matter how foolish and impossible it sounds. So did Abraham take his reason captive and slay it, inasmuch as he believed God's Word, wherein was promised him that from his unfruitful and as it were dead wife, Sarah, God would give him seed..... There is no doubt faith and reason mightily fell out in Abraham's heart about this matter, yet at last did faith get the better, and overcame and strangled reason, that all-cruellest and most fatal enemy of God. So, too, do all other faithful men who enter with Abraham the gloom and hidden darkness of faith: they strangle reason,.... and thereby offer to God the all-acceptablest sacrifice and service that can ever be brought to Him."

But to a mind of the force and vivacity of Luther's—a mind, too, which had measured its individual strength against the prescriptions of centuries, and held its own against a world in arms—the strangling of reason was not an act to be lightly committed, or to be regarded afterwards without at least passing pangs of remorse. Under certain mythological forms, with which no Christianity in the sixteenth century could dispense, we discern the fact of a perpetual struggle going on in Luther's mind. When his natural reason rebelled against the

---

[1] Werke, ed. Walch, VIII. 2043: Erklärung der Ep. an die Galater.

violence which orthodox faith offered to it, the revolt was ascribed to the direct agency of the Devil, and was contended against as a suggestion from hell. And, as we might infer from the vivid way in which he puts the contrast between reason and the fundamental articles of dogmatic Christianity, Luther felt that his only safety was in clinging to the clear declarations of Scripture. If he lost that hold, he was lost indeed.

"Experience," he says,[1] "has taught me this only too often: when the Devil attacks me outside the Scripture, and I begin to wander with my own thoughts, and even to flutter up towards heaven, then he brings me to this, that I know not either where God is or I myself am."

Again:[2]

"I am myself also a doctor, and have read the Scripture; yet it comes upon me daily, that if I do not stand straight in my armour, and therewith be well equipped, such thoughts attack me as would make me lose Christ and the gospel: and I must therefore always hold to the Scriptures, that I may continue to stand."

Once more:[3]

"All the articles of the Creed are very difficult and high, so that no man can comprehend them without the grace and gift of the Holy Spirit. I speak and witness thereof as one who has had no little experience: wilt thou also gain only a little experience, take any article of the Creed which thou wilt—the incarnation of Christ, the resurrection—so wilt thou keep hold of none if thou graspest it with reason. It has indeed happened to myself that when I have let the Word go, I have lost God and Christ

---

[1] Werke, ed Walch, VIII. 571: Auslegung des xiv. xv. and xvi. Capitels Johannis.

[2] Ibid. VIII. 1181: Auslegung 1 Cor. xv.

[3] Ibid. XII. 2070: Predigt über das Evangelium am Ostermontage.

and all together..... There is no easier way to lose all articles of the faith than to think of them apart from Scripture."

And in 1524 he confesses, in a very remarkable passage too long to quote,[1] that if, five years before, Dr. Carlstadt or any one else could have convinced him that the Eucharist was nothing but bread and wine, he would have done him the greatest service. He had suffered the severest temptation in regard to this matter: even now the old Adam in him was inclined to the rationalistic view: and what a blow could he not have struck against the Papacy with the simpler doctrine!

The Devil plays a large part in Luther's life. His faith in Satanic temptation and possession was not only very real and deep, but of a childish simplicity and credulity. Side by side with passages in his published works and familiar letters where he clothes his spiritual throes and temptations with this mythological form, should be placed the chapter in the Table-talk which shows that his belief in the perpetual and all-pervading energy of Satan was a precise counterpart to his faith in the omnipresent activity of God. But Luther's use of this kind of language at once misleads us as to facts of his life, and tends to hide their real meaning. When we look into it minutely, his personal acquaintance with the Devil, if I may use such a phrase, turns out to have been very slight. He heard noises in his solitary cell in the Wartburg[2] which he could not explain, and an unaccountable scratching behind the stove in his room at Wittenberg.[3] Twice he saw the

---

[1] Werke, ed. Walch, XV. 2448: Warnungsschreiben an alle Christen zu Strassburg, &c.

[2] Tischreden, III. 37.   [3] Ibid. III. 93.

Evil One in the shape of a great hound.[1] He ascribed to Satanic agency a vision of Christ with the five wounds.[2] The fact is, that to whatever excesses of credulity his theories of diabolic activity might push him, his intellect was too robust, his common sense too sound, to make him desire or put faith in visions and apparitions. At the same time, he was subject all his life to *Anfechtungen*, conflicts, temptations, tribulations, in which the Devil was a chief actor. The years from 1527 to 1530 were particularly disturbed in this way. Again and again we find the Reformer, usually so full of a courageous cheerfulness, and a perennial spring of comfort to other tried and tempted souls, sunk in the depths of despondency, pitifully asking for the prayers of his friends, and only painfully and slowly struggling towards a return of light and peace. Nor are these the throes and agonies which, on a system such as his, naturally precede conversion; or even the after-pains which come to remind the soul of what it has gone through, and to suggest circumspection. They were struggles in which the whole peace of his life was at stake: storms which shook the very foundations of his faith. I do not believe that we can say we understand Luther so long as these dark and bitter hours remain unexplained.

Of one of the worst of these *Anfechtungen*, which occurred in July 1527, we have an elaborate account by Bugenhagen and Justus Jonas, who were called in to help.[3] But it tells us nothing except the visible symp-

---

[1] Myconius: Historia Reformationis, p. 42.
[2] Tischreden, I. 400.
[3] Keil: D. Martin Luther's merkwürdige Lebensumstände, II. 187.

toms of the case. The word Satan stands in place of an explanation. It is only when we turn to Luther's own letters about this period, that a gleam of light begins to break in upon us. At the time of his seclusion in the Wartburg, he complains in strong terms of temptations of the flesh: but there is nothing of that kind now: the trouble is partly spiritual, partly intellectual.

"For more than a week,"[1] he writes to Melancthon, "I have been tossed about in death and hell: so that, hurt in all my body, I still tremble in every limb. For having almost wholly lost Christ, I was driven about by storms and tempests of despair and blasphemy against God. But God, moved by the prayers of the saints, begins to have pity upon me, and has drawn my soul out of the lower hell."

Again, a few months afterwards, to Nicholas Hausmann:[2]

"I truly think that no common devil, but the very prince of the devils, has risen up against me, so great and so equipped in knowledge of the Scriptures is his power against me: so that unless I held to the word of another, my own knowledge of Scripture would not suffice."

He asks Brenz for the prayers of the church in Halle:[3] "for Satan, let loose against me, seeks by his devices to rob me of Christ in secret, since he sees that publicly, and in the confession of my faith, he can snatch nothing from me." He is still in the valley of the shadow when the new year comes. On the 1st of January, 1528,[4] he writes, that with this kind of conflict he had been familiar

---

[1] Briefe, ed. De Wette, III. 189.   [2] Ibid. III. 222.
[3] Ibid. III. 230.
[4] Ibid. III. 254, to Gerard Viscamp.

from his youth, but had never thought that it would become so sharp.

"Christ nevertheless has triumphed so far, though holding me up by ever so little. I commend myself to your prayers, and to those of the brethren. I have saved others, myself I cannot save. Blessed be my Christ, even in the midst of despair, death and blasphemy; and may he give us to behold one another in his kingdom!"

I cannot resist the conclusion that the explanation of these things is to be largely found in such passages of Luther's works as I have already quoted — and they might be multiplied to almost any extent — in which he places faith and reason in vivid and irreconcilable opposition.[1] I do not deny the existence in his tribulation of a purely spiritual element: all deeply religious men have their times of darkness and despondency; nor was Luther likely to escape the common lot. But he has expressed the difficulties of reason in regard to the orthodox creed in terms far too clear and strong to permit us to doubt, not only that he had himself stood in the rationalist's position, but that it was, in a sense, natural to him. The other position was natural too; for it was that into which he finally settled down; but after what a struggle! If a man who has looked at faith and unfaith

---

[1] It may be worth while in this connection to notice the words used by his contemporary, Hieronymus Weller, in a letter to Wolfgang Hebold, "von den Wundergabe Lutheri," 1561. "Es haben auch seine vielfältigen und mancherley Anfectungen, Streit und Kampf, ihn oft dahin bewogen, dass er vom Herzen begehret von hinnen zu scheiden, und bey Christo zu seyn, auch oft gesagt, er wollte lieber um Christus willen sein Blut vergiessen denn mit solchen tödtlichen Gedanken, des Teufels feurigen und giftigen Pfeilen, geplaget werden." Quoted by Keil, Preface.

with clear eyes says to himself, I will believe, he may succeed in believing; but there will be times at which the tension of his will will suddenly relax, and he will find himself at the mercy of the doubts which he thought he had fought down for ever. I take it that the *Anfechtungen* of 1527 were a turning-point in Luther's life, and therefore in the history of the Reformation. Up to his return from the Wartburg in 1522, to allay the disturbances at Wittenberg created by the Prophets of Zwickau, his intellectual history had been one of continual progress. He was not in 1517, the year of the indulgence theses, the finished Protestant champion which some conceive him: then, and long afterwards, he was quickly working his way forward to a completer apprehension of his characteristic principles and a larger sense of their application. But while his mind kept moving in answer to Papal opposition, it crystallized under the influence of division and excess among Reformers. First came the Zwickau Prophets, then Carlstadt claiming to better his instruction. The Peasants' War, with the cruelties committed in its suppression, gravely endangered his work. The Swiss Reformers not only denied his doctrine of the Eucharist, but threatened to draw South Germany away after them. Everywhere Anabaptism was developing into various forms of heresy. In a word, the application of reason to religion was bearing its necessary fruits of difference and division: what was there to oppose to the unbroken front of Papal authority, except the uncompromising assertion of the authority of Scripture? But the adoption of this position was the result, not of any calculation of ecclesiastical expediencies on Luther's part, not even of a calm intellectual estimate of conflicting evidence, but of a terrible struggle in the depths of his fiery soul between two principles, each of which was rooted in his very nature. He saw whither the free working of his own mind would take him, and he dared not make the adventure. He used the weapons of faith to slay reason, lest perchance reason should lure faith to her destruction. But who can tell what might have been the effect upon the Reformation, and the subsequent development of the intellectual life of Europe, had Luther put himself boldly at the head of the larger and freer thought of his time, instead of using all the force of his genius, all the weight of his authority, to crush it?

To turn to the second half of our subject, we find the early documents of the Reformation full of brilliant declarations of the rights of conscience. It could not well be otherwise. Only by an appeal to those rights could the Reformers justify their own attitude towards a religious system which, until they attacked it, had commanded the assent of Europe. To insist upon liberty of thought and speech in matters of religion, apart alike from ecclesiastical censure and civil disability, was no more than a measure of necessary self-defence. We cannot be surprised, therefore, to find Luther, in 1519, distinguishing, in his "Sermon on Excommunication," between inward and outward church communion, and declaring that of the first none can be deprived "by any man, be he Bishop or Pope, yea, not by angels or any creature, but only by God Himself."[1] On the other hand, he defends the rights of conscience as stoutly

---

[1] Werke, ed. Walch, XIX. 1100: Sermon vom Bann.

against Kings and Princes. From many passages which illustrate this, I select one or two from his book "On Temporal Authority, and how far Obedience is due to it," which bears the date of 1523.

"Worldly rule," he says,[1] "has laws which do not extend further than over body and goods, and what is external upon earth. For over souls God can and will suffer no one to rule, save Himself alone.".... "Beloved, we are not baptized into the name of Kings, Princes or Mobs, but into the name of Christ and God only: we are not called after Kings, Princes or Mobs; we are called Christians. No one can or ought to command the soul, except he who can show it the way to heaven. But that can no man do, but God only. Therefore, in matters which concern the salvation of souls, nothing but God's Word ought to be taught or received."[2]

Again:[3]

"A tribunal, when it pronounces judgment, must and ought to be quite certain, and have everything in a clear light. But the thoughts and mind of man can be open to no one but God; wherefore it is futile and impossible to command, or by force to compel, any one to believe so, or so. There wants another grip for that: force avails nothing."...."It is at a man's own risk what he believes, and he must see for himself that he believes rightly. For just as little as another can go for me to hell or heaven, can he for me believe or disbelieve: and just as little as he can open or shut heaven or hell for me, can he drive me to belief or unbelief. .... For belief is a free work; thereto can no man be compelled."

In the same way Luther had fully grasped the idea that force can produce only an external conformity.[4]

"For the miserable blind people do not see what a quite futile and impossible thing they undertake. For however straitly they

---

[1] Werke, ed. Walch, X. 452: Von weltlicher Obrigkeit, wie weit man ihr Gehorsam schuldig sey?

[2] Ibid. X. 453.   [3] Ibid. X. 455.   [4] Ibid. X. 456.

command, however stoutly they rage, they cannot bring people further than to follow them with mouth and hand: the heart they cannot compel, should they even tear at it. For true is the proverb, 'Thoughts are toll-free.'"

And last of all :[1]

"But thou sayest once more, 'Yea, worldly power cannot compel to belief, but is only an external protection against the people being misled by false doctrine: how else can heretics be kept at bay?' Answer: That is the business of Bishops, to whom the office is entrusted, and not of Princes. For heresy can never be kept off by force: another grip is wanted for that: this is another quarrel and conflict than that of the sword. God's Word must contend here: if that avails nothing, temporal power will never settle the matter, though it fill the world with blood. Heresy is a spiritual thing, which no iron can hew down, no fire burn, no water drown."

Nothing can be clearer or more satisfactory than these declarations, which, it will be observed, cover almost the whole theoretical ground of religious liberty. But it is unhappily one thing to claim liberty for oneself, another to accord it to others; much easier to lay down a general principle than to follow it faithfully into its various practical applications. As we certainly, after the lapse of so many years, have not yet learned either of these lessons thoroughly, we need not wonder that Luther and Melancthon repeated them with stammering tongues. Their position was in many respects difficult and painful. They could not confine Protestantism to their own protest. All round about them sprang up a crop of heresies with which they had little or no sympathy, yet for which their Catholic opponents held them responsible. These heresies,

---

[1] Werke, ed. Walch, X. 461, 462.

from the opinions of Zwingli on the Eucharist, which were shared by all Switzerland and a large part of South Germany, on the one hand, to the Antitrinitarian views of Denck and Campanus, and the wild excesses of the Münster Anabaptists, on the other, were in every way a hindrance to their successful maintenance of their own position. They did not permit them to show to Catholicism a united front; they embroiled them with Princes naturally jealous of their own authority. I do not wonder that the Reformers of Wittenberg fell into the trap which lies in wait for all earnestly believing men, in the distinction set up between heresy and blasphemy. Is there not a point at which the expression of misbelief becomes an insult to the majesty of God, and so an offence against laws of man? And is not all heresy, in proportion as it is bold and outspoken, likely to be interpreted and punished as blasphemy? Then again, granting that difference of belief is to be tolerated, to what lengths ought toleration to go? Does it include full right of citizenship, with liberty to preach and print? Or are heretics to be allowed to live side by side with orthodox believers only on condition that they hold their tongues? Is it in any case right to co-operate with them for political or religious purposes? Lastly, it is often difficult to draw Luther's theoretical line between temporal and spiritual things, and to decide to which half of human life—and therefore to which jurisdiction—belong certain opinions, and with them the action in which they necessarily issue. The Peasants' War was a social and political revolt, but it justified itself upon religious grounds: Anabaptism was a system of theological opinion, which often encroached upon accepted principles of social life. It is easy to see that these things necessarily gave occasion to a series of practical questions, which even yet receive various answer from men who profess an equal allegiance to the principle of religious liberty.

I have already alluded more than once to Philip of Hesse's well-meaning attempt to bring Lutherans and Zwinglians together, at the moment when the near approach of the Diet of Augsburg made a reconciliation among Protestants in the highest degree expedient. Theologically, the Conference of Marburg was a failure: Luther would not consent to modify the Eucharistic doctrine, which was the chief matter in dispute. But it was just as much a failure from the point of view of toleration. When it was plain that no theological agreement could be arrived at, Philip asked the Wittenberg doctors that they would at least recognize the Swiss Reformers as brothers, a request which Zwingli met with tears in his eyes and outstretched hand. "There were no people on earth," he said, "with whom he would more willingly be at one than with those of Wittenberg." But Luther rudely rejected the offer of friendship: "You are of another spirit," he said, "than ours."[1] Melancthon and Brenz, each in his own way and with different terms of insult, supported the intolerance of their chief.[2] The whole concession to which Luther could be moved he

---

[1] Briefe, ed. De Wette, Letter to Jacob Probst, IV. 28.

[2] To an earlier letter of Luther's addressed to Agricola, Melancthon added the characteristic postscript: "Valde contenderunt, ut a nobis fratres nominarentur. Vide eorum stultitiam cum damnent nos, cupiunt tamen a nobis fratres haberi. Nos noluimus eis in hac re assentiri." Ibid. III. 514. For Brenz's account of the transaction, see his letter to Schradinus and the other clergy of Reutlingen. Zuinglii Opp. IV. 203.

himself expressed in the words, "that the Zwinglians, unless they yielded on the Eucharist, might indeed claim their charity, but could not be regarded by them as brethren and members of Christ."[1] This grudging friendliness the Swiss, greatly to their credit, accepted as far as it went, and a kind of reconciliation was patched up on this narrow and insecure basis. But as soon as the conference of Marburg was over, a meeting of Protestant Princes and Cities was held at Schwabach, soon followed by another at Schmalkalden. At each of these doctrinal articles were drawn up, subscription to which was exacted as a condition of political alliance. Not even the cost and risk of resisting, peaceably or in arms, the House of Austria and its confederates could be shared by men who were unsound on the Real Presence, or who did not see eye to eye with the Wittenberg Reformers in the matter of predestination.[2] There was no common action at the Diet of Augsburg: in addition to the Confession drawn up and defended by Melancthon, the Swiss Reformers presented their own; while a third, known as the *Confessio Tetrapolitana*, was put forward by the four cities, Strasburg, Constanz, Memmingen and Lindau. And when the Diet had come to an end, the policy was deliberately adopted of narrowing the political basis of Protestantism to the ground covered by the Confession; for the Lutheran States agreed that, until the General Council which was to settle everything had met, they would tolerate no other form of it than their own. Under these

---

[1] Briefe, ed. De Wette, III. 511, to Gerbellius.
[2] Corp. Ref. II. 386: Letter of ambassadors of Nürnberg to the Senate. Ranke, III. 182 et seq.

circumstances, we need not wonder that the only religious toleration provided for by the Convention of Passau was the maimed and ineffectual form expressed in the maxim, *cujus regio, ejus religio*—the subject follows the religion of the State.

The result of the Peasants' War and its suppression was to throw the Reformation very much into the hands of the Princes. From a popular it became largely a political movement. On the one hand, the Princes saw that its effect must be the secularization, to a large extent, of Church property, a process of which they wished to secure the control; on the other, the Reformers, from very dread of being confounded with noisy and seditious heretics, propounded theories of submission to temporal authority which in some cases, as for instance in that of Bucer, assumed the most servile form. This was not inconsistent with the freest speech on Luther's part about and to worldly rulers:[1] his openly expressed contempt of Duke George finds a parallel in the frank, not to say the rough, way in which he constantly offered his advice to his own Prince, the Elector John. But it is important to note in this connection the fact, that the reorganization of the Church, which the Reformation rendered necessary, was in almost every case undertaken by the State, and conducted on principles laid down by its head, whoever he might

---

[1] The following passage from Luther's "Schrift vom Weltlicher Obrigkeit," 1523, dedicated to Duke John, is characteristic: "Und sollt wissen, dass von Anbeginn der Welt gar ein seltsam Vogel ist um einen klugen Fürsten: noch viel seltsamer um einen frommen Fürsten. Sie sind gemeiniglich die grösten Narren oder die ärgsten Buben auf Erden: darum man sich allzeit bey ihnen des ärgsten versehen, und wenig Guts von ihnen gewarten muss, sonderlich in göttlichen Sachen, die der Seelen Heil belangen." Werke, ed. Walch, X. 460, conf. p. 464.

be. We may take as an instance the famous Visitation of the Saxon Churches in 1528, made by Melancthon, with other commissioners, lay and clerical, under instructions given to them by the Elector. It was naturally unavoidable that, in the course of a reorganization the object of which was to Protestantize what had been the Catholic Church of Saxony, offences against the religious liberties of those who still adhered to the old faith should be committed. Revolutions require and justify revolutionary methods. But the Elector's instructions go a good deal beyond this.[1] Not only were priests who would not conform to lose their benefices, but recalcitrant laymen, who after instruction were still obstinate, had a time allowed them within which they were to sell their property and then leave the country. "For although," said the Elector, "it is not our intention to bind any one to what he is to believe and hold, yet will we, for the prevention of mischievous tumult and other inconveniences, suffer neither sect nor separation in our territory." So the year before this, we find Melancthon writing to the Landgrave of Hesse,[2] asking him to decide controversies among preachers by his own authority, and to put down dissensions by the secular arm. The pretext of danger to the public peace was never wanting whenever it was desired to crush a nascent sect or to silence an inconvenient opponent. Nor was this a lesson which arbitrary rulers were at all loth to learn from their favourite theologians.

But the word by which, above all others, the theolo-

---

[1] Seckendorf, Bk. ii. Sect. 13, § 36. Comp. Köstlin: M. Luther, II. 29.

[2] Corp. Ref. I. 819, Sept. 1526.

gians justified attack upon the liberty and sometimes
the lives of heretics was blasphemy. I shall not attempt
to define blasphemy, or even inquire if it have a definition: it is enough to say that it is the word by which
the religious opinions of a minority, if sufficiently unpo-
pular, have always been designated. And in the intellectual tumult to which the Reformation gave rise, many
convictions were expressed which would not square with
orthodox Protestantism, whether of the Lutheran or the
Zwinglian type. Presently we shall have to look a little
more closely into the nature of the religious movements
which all went under the generic name of Anabaptism:
now we have only to ask, what was the bearing of the
four great Reformers to the men who boldly excluded
themselves from the Church as they strove to define it?
Luther was by far the mildest and most tolerant. I
think that, stern and violent as he often was, the tender-
ness of strength was a part of his character; and I have
given in this Lecture reason enough for believing that
he was not without a deep personal sympathy with men
who could not bring themselves to stifle reason by the
hands of faith. It is true that he writes to the Elector
John,[1] begging him to silence a certain Hans Mohr, who
was spreading Zwinglian opinions in Coburg; while, in
another place,[2] he lays down as a rule for the treatment
of unbelievers in an evangelical state, that if after instruction they still persist, they are to be made to hold
their tongues. But his intolerance chiefly spends itself
in violent words. He draws back in horror from inflict-

---

[1] Briefe, ed. De Wette, III. 256.
[2] Ibid. III. 498, to J. L. Metzsch.

ing capital punishment in cases of heresy. He writes, in 1528, in reference to Anabaptists:[1]

"Yet it is not right, and I think it great pity, that such wretched people should be so miserably slain, burned, cruelly put to death: every one should be allowed to believe what he will. If he believes wrongly, he will have punishment enough in the eternal fire of hell. Why should they be tortured in this life too?—provided always that it is a case of mistaken belief only, and that they are not also unruly and oppose themselves to the temporal power. Dear God! how soon it happens that one goes astray and falls into the Devil's net! These men should be fought off and withstood with Scripture and God's Word: fire will do very little good."

"I am slow to adopt the judgment of blood," he says to Link, "even where it is abundantly deserved." Such a precedent would be eagerly caught up and abused by the Papists. "I can in no way," he goes on, "admit that false teachers should be put to death: it is enough that they should be banished."[2] Zwingli, who is in some respects the largest-minded of the Reformers—Zwingli, who speaks of a heaven in which Christians may hope to meet the wise and good of heathen antiquity—had no such scruples.[3] The Anabaptists of Zürich were numerous and stiff-necked, poor and untaught men who could not hold their own in debate against the leaders of the Swiss reform. They were not convinced—what heretic ever is?—by successive disputations, and persisted in both teaching and practising their characteristic doctrine; till in 1529 their leader, Felix Mantz, was solemnly and

---

[1] Werke, ed. Walch, XVII. 2644, 2645: Brief an zwei Pfarrherren von der Wiedertaufe.

[2] Briefe, ed. De Wette, III. 347.

[3] Zuinglii Opp.: Fidei Christianæ Expositio, IV. 65.

judicially drowned for his heresy in the Lake of Zürich, dying with the steadfastness of a true martyr.[1] Two others, Jacob Falck and Heinj Reyman, suffered the same fate not long afterwards, with the same courage and constancy.[2] In 1530,[3] Melancthon, writing to his friend Frederick Myconius, expresses his opinion on the proper treatment of obstinate heretics in sufficiently clear terms. At the beginning, when he first became acquainted with Storch and his faction, from whom the Anabaptists took their origin, he was, he says, "foolishly merciful." But that mood is long past. Sedition ought to be suppressed by the sword. Blasphemers, even if not seditious, should be put to death by the civil magistrate. There were precedents for this course in the Law of Moses. The Christian Emperors employed capital punishment against the Arians: Augustine permitted armed force to be used against the Donatists. What Calvin thought in regard to the duty of repressing heresy by the sharpest methods, he let the world know in the most signal way when, in 1553, he arrested Servetus, who was only a wayfarer in Geneva, and over whom neither he nor the magistrates of that city had a shadow of jurisdiction, and condemned

---

[1] Bullinger: Reformationsgeschichte, I. 382.

[2] Ibid. II. 14.

[3] Corp. Ref. II. 17, 18. Another letter, also to Myconius (Oct. 31, 1531), is worth quoting, as showing that this was Melancthon's habitual mood towards Anabaptists. "De Anabaptistis tulimus hic in genere sententiam : quia constat sectam diabolicam esse, non esse tolerandam : dissipari enim ecclesias per eos, cum ipsi nullam habeant certam doctrinam. Nihil igitur est ea secta, nisi confusio et dissipatio publicarum ecclesiarum : praesertim cum aperte ministerium verbi damnent. Ideo in capita factionum in singulis locis ultima supplicia constituenda esse judicavimus." Corp. Ref. II. 549.

him to the flames. Of this act the "mild" Melancthon did not hesitate to express his entire approval.[1]

"I have read your work," he writes to Calvin on the 14th of October, 1554, "in which you have lucidly refuted the horrible blasphemies of Servetus, and I thank the Son of God, who has been the arbiter of this your contest. The Church, both now and in all generations, owes and will owe you a debt of gratitude. I entirely assent to your judgment. And I say, too, that your magistrates did right in that, after solemn trial, they put the blasphemer to death."[2]

But I think we are justified in saying that Luther, who when Servetus paid the penalty of free thought had been seven years in his grave, would never have written a letter like this.

Things grow far worse in the second generation. I shall speak in another connection of the Protestant inquisition which Calvin set up in Geneva, the peculiarity of which was that it visited with impartial severity laxity of conduct and error of opinion. But it would not be easy to find a parallel to the hatreds of theologians, constantly appealing to, and constantly supported by the civil power, which divided the Protestant churches of Germany from the death of Luther to the breaking out of the Thirty Years' War. Controversy after controversy

---

[1] Corp. Ref. VIII. 362.

[2] He wrote a very similar letter on the same subject to Bullinger on Aug. 20, 1555: Corp. Ref. VIII. 523. A week or two before this, he had made it a question for disputation in the University of Wittenberg, "An politica potestas debeat tollere hæreticos?" Corp. Ref. X. 851. The declamation, though very short, contains the germ of almost every bad argument in favour of relentless persecution. Again, in 1557, in a warning which he issued to the world at large against the errors of Theobald Thamer, he calls the execution of Servetus, "pium et memorabile ad omnem posteritatem exemplum." Corp. Ref. IX. 133.

arose on comparatively minute points of doctrine, and each gave rise to a literature unequalled in polemical bitterness and vulgarity. It may be doubted whether Lutherans most hated and abused Calvinists or their own dissidents. Little by little these animosities almost took the place of the old hostility to Catholics and Anabaptists. The Flacianists raged againts the Philippists: Jena thundered against Wittenberg: whoever would not subscribe every article of ultra-Lutheran orthodoxy was a crypto-Calvinist and therefore a traitor. It is a painful task to watch the bright flame of religious enthusiasm which once lighted all Europe, quickly dying down into these obscene embers of theological strife; and when I have told one sad and shameful story, I will gladly turn away from it. Among the foreign theologians who found refuge in England during the reign of Edward VI. was John a Lasco, a Pole of noble birth, who had been the friend of Erasmus, who had travelled in Italy, and who had been destined to high ecclesiastical office in his own country. Under the patronage of Cranmer, he had gathered together in London, in that church of Austin Friars which, having happily escaped the Great Fire, still stands, a congregation of foreigners, whom he was permitted to organize on the Presbyterian type, and who adopted the Genevese theology. With the accession of Mary, all this came to an end, and a Lasco, with a large part of his congregation, fled beyond sea. They embarked for Denmark in two small Danish ships which they found lying in the Thames, and to that zealously Lutheran country confidently looked for refuge and welcome. Late in the autumn they arrived, but were warned that they might not so much as land unless they would repeat the

Lutheran shibboleths. It did not matter that they were flying from Catholic intolerance: Lutheran hearts were shut against Calvinist sufferers. All appeals were fruitless: the people of Copenhagen were friendly enough; it was the King and the preachers who would have none of them. So during almost the whole of a stormy northern winter, these poor creatures, among whom were many women and children, were driven from port to port: Rostock expelled them; Wismar allowed them a brief respite, making them the while the object of abusive preaching; Lübeck turned them out; Hamburg raged against them with special bitterness; at last in Emden they found a little rest. The very seas and storms were kinder to them than those who ought to have been their brethren. Calvin, who was at this very moment burning Servetus, raised a loud voice of protest, for the sufferers were his fellow-believers; but I cannot find that any word of remonstrance came from Wittenberg. It was but in 1553: so soon had died away even the faintest echo of that claim of liberty of conscience in which the Reformation took its birth: so soon had new and more savage theological hatreds replaced the old.[1]

---

[1] H. Dalton: Johannes a Lasco, pp. 427 et seq. Henry: Leben Calvins, III. 303, note.

LECTURE VI.

THE SECTS OF THE REFORMATION.

MANY forces combined to produce the Reformation, some of which, when once it had assumed its permanent shape, gradually disengaged themselves and began to manifest a separate activity. The phase of the movement which finally prevailed may be called the biblically orthodox. It set up against the old forms of doctrine and practice a new one, regarded as exclusively true, deviations from which were to be discouraged, or, if sufficiently wide, suppressed and punished. This was, further, based upon the authority of Scripture, assumed to be final, and substituted for the rejected authority of the Church. In these terms we may succinctly describe the Lutheran Reformation, expounded by Melancthon in his *Loci Communes*, and reduced to practice by the Saxon Visitation and similar measures of organization in other Protestant States. The same general description applies to the Reformation of Zwingli in German Switzerland, as well as to the later activity of Calvin in Geneva. Each set up a strict standard of orthodoxy. Each deduced that standard from Scripture, more or less rigorously interpreted.

According to the common view, this constitutes the Reformation. It was simply the substitution of one form of theological authority for another, and the consequent replacement of a false and corrupt by a true and pure body of doctrine. And on the same theory, the process was accomplished once for all: after ages have had nothing to add to or to take away from it. On the other hand, we have been learning to look at the Reformation as only a partial manifestation of forces which were of wide and prolonged operation, the activity of which, in other men and other religious movements than were acceptable at Wittenberg, it will be necessary for us to trace, if we are to give any completeness to our picture of the period. There was the pure humanistic impulse, the form taken in that age by the simple love of knowledge for its own sake. There were the mystic desires and aspirations which the history of the fourteenth and fifteenth centuries shows to belong to the very essence of Teutonic religion. There was the deep social dissatisfaction, and the desire for an immediate fulfilment of the promise of the kingdom of God, which always follow upon a fresh and vivid presentation of the gospel. There was the critical and rationalistic spirit, which desired to dig down to the basis of all religious authority, and rejecting not only the Church and the Schoolmen, but the Creeds, accepted Christianity, if at all, in quite another than the orthodox form. But though these currents of opinion may be accurately discriminated, we must beware of thinking that it is possible to divide men or sects into corresponding classes. Many tendencies of thought unite in one thinker. Your mystic often has in him something of the revolutionary: the line between mysticism and rationalism is easy to draw in theory, but also easy to overpass by a soul of apt constitution. If much that I shall say appears indistinct, by reason of its necessary brevity, I must beg you to remember that rigid outlines and sharp contrasts of colour are always untrue to the shifting lights, the changeful glooms, the subtly shaded hues of the natural landscape.

The sects of the Reformation are usually regarded as the opprobrium of a great and beneficial religious movement. The attempt which the Prophets of Zwickau made in 1522 to take the management of the Reform into their own hands—an attempt the later stages of which are associated with the better-known names of Carlstadt and Münzer—was directly connected with the Peasants' War of 1525-26, which shook the whole fabric of German society to its base, and not only gravely endangered Luther's work, but did much to change its character. Again, the seizure of Münster by the Anabaptists in 1535, the wild and wicked parody of the kingdom of God which they there set up, and the blood in which the fire of their fanaticism was finally quenched, made the very name of Anabaptist a by-word in every country of Europe where the new thought was wrestling with the old. But no philosophical historian can afford to pass by these and many other allied phenomena as mere blots upon the face of human affairs, which he may regret, but for which he is not called upon to account. Some good Protestants would have us believe that as, on the Aristotelian principle, virtue is the mean between two extremes of vice, so the Reformation of Luther and Calvin stands, in the equilibrium of eternal truth and right, between reprehensible excesses of Catholicism on the one side, of Anabaptism and Rationalism on the other. Those who see somewhat deeper into the facts, attempt to purge the Reformation of complicity with its own abnormal manifestations, by tracing them to their origin in peculiarities of German religious thought in the fourteenth and fifteenth centuries. But a little closer inspection will show that this is only a part of the truth. These sects of the Reformation represent tendencies of the human mind in dealing with the mysteries and difficulties of religion, which are peculiar to no century, but appear, under different shapes, in almost all. They pushed, it may be, their principles to one-sided excess; they lost sight of other guiding and controlling forces; they had in them little possibility of organization and continuance; but their leaders were not always wrong, nor Luther, in his opposition to them, always right. In a crude and undisciplined way—unavoidable in that age of half-knowledge and undetermined methods of thinking —they had a grasp of principles which, as time advances, are destined to play an ever greater part in the development of religious thought and life. Theirs were the truths which the Reformation neglected and cast out, but which it must again reconcile with itself if it is ever to complete its work.

The old Christian mysticism of Germany, which Tauler and the author of the *Theologia Germanica* may be taken to represent, had a considerable share in the development of Luther's religious opinions. Justification by faith, at least in its earliest, its deepest, its most spiritual form, is really a mystical doctrine; that is to say, it brings the soul into immediate contact with its Divine Object, and from that contact expects all the fruits of the religious life. But it does not furnish any basis on which an organized church can be built up. It is a matter for the individual soul. It is an invisible thing, which eludes tests and cannot be made into a criterion of fellowship. Accordingly the mystics of the Reformation are usually at one with Luther here: it is when he attempts to erect the edifice of a church on the foundation of sacraments, to insist on the importance of the external, to establish visible tests of discipleship, that they begin to part company with him. But, again, mysticism has comparatively little to object to the Eucharist; on the contrary, it rejoices in signs and symbols which, under the interpretation of faith, help to express that which is essentially ineffable: it may indeed put its own meaning on the Lord's Supper, but it does not feel the temptation to reject it. The contrary is the case with baptism as usually administered to infants. Here there can be no living faith to appropriate the divine grace of the sacrament.[1] If the child is benefited at all, it must be by a quasi-magical process which is repugnant to the fundamental principles of mystical religion. Adult baptism, the conscious assumption by a Christian man or woman of the obligations of discipleship, is evidently a very different thing. Here once more the conditions of a true sacrament are fulfilled: the grace of God, the outward sign, the operative faith, are all present. When this distinction is clearly seen, it at once helps to liberate the mind from the influence of ecclesiastical usage, and to reveal the scriptural justification for infant baptism in its

---

[1] Vid. Lecture IV. p. 137, and the references there given for Luther's perplexities on this subject, and his theory of the representative faith of sponsors.

VI. SECTS OF THE REFORMATION. 189

real weakness and insufficiency. It was, therefore, no dogmatic accident which made the mysticism of the Reformation assume the Anabaptist form. The word Anabaptist, as I have already pointed out, is used to cover very various phases of religious belief. But this one peculiarity was common to all Anabaptists.

The Anabaptists were the individualists of the Reformation. They took up the protest against ecclesiastical authority, and pushed it to the furthest point. The more thoughtful among them, or the men who, without being of them, gave the tone to their religious thought, clearly saw the distinction between the Word of God in Scripture, and Scripture as the Word of God, and were not slow to carry it to its logical issue. If Luther not only denied to human reason the right of criticising Scripture, but demanded that it should be strangled and slain by the hands of faith, he still based the authority of the Bible on the conjoint testimony of the Holy Spirit in the mind of the believer, and of the Holy Spirit in the written book. But why stop at precisely this point? Why limit the function of the Spirit in man to establishing the authority and interpreting the deliverances of the Bible? Why may not God speak to man now, as He did to holy men of old? In other words, the Anabaptists, beginning with the Prophets of Zwickau, had imperfectly and half-consciously grasped the principle of the continuity of revelation, and were coming to see that revelation as recorded in Scripture, and the results of present religious experience, were different phases of one and the same divine phenomenon. Even such a man as Münzer says:[1]

---

[1] Quoted by Keller: Geschichte der Wiedertäufer, p. 19.

"The Scripture is only a dead letter: man must hear the voice of the Father speaking within him. God still speaks with His own to-day, as once He spake with Abraham, Isaac and Jacob." I cannot help thinking that this position was logically very difficult of assault. It was a first feeble attempt to work out that problem of the basis of scriptural authority which the Reformers systematically neglected. Again, I find Münzer saying:[1]

"The Wittenbergers say that we should begin with Scripture, which will bring faith; but we cannot give the godless any certain reason why Scripture is to be accepted and not thrown away, except that it comes from antiquity and has been received by many men. But this is Jewish and Turkish. True faith needs a clearer light than that of the Word: it follows only the moving of the Spirit. And the Spirit a man receives by longing and waiting for enlightenment."

At the same time, this principle was not worked out into any philosophical coherence, and it manifestly opened the door to every kind of fanatical extravagance and abuse. When, in December 1521, Claus Storch, the weaver of Zwickau, came to Wittenberg with two companions, one as enthusiastic and ignorant as himself, the other with some pretensions to scholarship, Melancthon and Carlstadt, in the absence of Luther on the Wartburg, represented the Reform. Carlstadt, with all the ill-regulated impulsiveness of his nature, threw himself into the new movement. Melancthon at first wavered: the pretensions of the men imposed upon him:

---

[1] Quoted by Dorner: Geschichte der Protestantischen Theologie in Deutschland, p. 130. For other passages of a similar kind, see Franck's Geschicht Bibel, Part iii. fol. 160.

he thought them "prophetic and apostolic."[1] "How much I am moved by them," he writes to the Elector Frederick, "I cannot easily tell." His youth, and the deference which he had already learned to pay to Luther, alone saved him. "Of the spirit that is in them," he said, "only Martin can easily form a judgment." Even Luther, when he came to Wittenberg to calm the tumult which Carlstadt and the men from Zwickau had raised in town and University, was for a moment shaken. But it was only for a moment: and with a "God rebuke thee, Satan!" he dismissed the Prophets from his presence.[2] From that time his course was taken, and it led him more and more in the direction of a rigid and arbitrary scripturalism, for which he did not even attempt to find a theoretical justification.

The position of the Anabaptists in regard to Scripture cannot be defined in a word. Some, to whom the name is commonly if not altogether justly applied, were feeling their way towards a deeper and more spiritual theory of inspiration than any which is indicated in the works of the orthodox Reformers. But the majority deviated from a crude literalness only to wander through the maze of a lawless allegorical interpretation. These two appa-

---

[1] Corp. Ref. I. 513 : Letter of Melancthon to the Elector, St. John's-day, 1522. "Ex horum motuum auctoribus huc advolarunt tres viri, duo lanifices, literarum rudes, literatus tertius est. Audivi eos. Mira sunt, quæ de sese prædicant : missos se clara voce dei ad docendum esse sibi cum deo familiaria colloquia : videre futura ; breviter, viros esse propheticos et apostolicos. Quibus ego quomodo commovear, non facile dixerim. Magnis rationibus adducor certe, ut contemni eos nolim. Nam esse in eis spiritus quosdam multis argumentis adparet, sed de quibus judicare præter Martinum nemo facile possit."

[2] Camerarius : Vita Melancthoni, p. 52.

rently opposite principles, in practice mingle and cross one another in a most perplexing way. Yet it is the experience of all Christian centuries that men only need to bring to the Bible sufficiently strong prepossessions, sufficiently fixed opinions, to have them reflected back in all the glamour of infallible authority. So there is, if I may use the expression, a flavour of Scripture in all Anabaptist extravagances. Nicholas Storch chose for himself twelve apostles and seventy disciples. Carlstadt gave up his archdeaconry, his professorship, his scholastic philosophy, and, putting on a peasant's coat, tilled the soil as Neighbour Andrew. One of the results of the troubles at Wittenberg in 1522 was that 200 students, convinced of the uselessness of all carnal learning, left the University. Some of the later developments of Anabaptism were stranger still, and at the same time permanent. Bullinger, in his contemporary history, says of certain Anabaptists:

"They looked to the mere letter of Scripture. Wherefore they roamed about the country, without staff, shoes, wallet or money, boasting of their heavenly call to the work of preaching. And because the Lord said, 'What ye hear in the ear, that preach ye on the house-tops,' they went up to the house-tops and preached thence. They washed one another's feet; said that with children it was necessary to become children, and behaved therefore in a childish way, which is foolish enough. Item: because the Lord says that whoever does not forsake house and home and all that he has cannot be his disciple, they left wife and child, house and trade, wandering about the country, quartering themselves upon the brethren, and eating them up."[1]

---

[1] Quoted by Erbkam, p. 559.

VI. SECTS OF THE REFORMATION. 193

Some adopted a peculiar dress and manner of life, as if they would found a new monastic order; others gave themselves up to trances and ecstacies, in which they claimed to receive direct inspiration from Heaven; some spent their days in silence, some in prayer, some in perpetual groaning and tears. Under this various surface lived and moved darker impulses, such as are rarely absent in times of fierce religious excitement. The Anabaptist theory of marriage pointed not indistinctly to excesses which, as they can hardly be proved, it is not expedient to describe. The Chiliastic predictions of the Apocalypse, floating before the minds of men who found themselves at deadly war with Church and State, encouraged the frightful idea of a universal blood-bath, which could alone usher in the final reign of the Saints. In a word, Anabaptism ranged over the whole gamut of human passions and possibilities, from the pure and pious enthusiasm of a Balthasar Hubmaier, to the licentious and cruel fanaticism of a John of Leiden.

Religious individualism is always inapt to organize itself, and when it reaches its highest pitch becomes a dividing force. While Lutheran Protestantism, under the protection of Electors, Princes, Free Cities, crystallized itself into a church, taking parochial possession of the country, appropriating what it could of ecclesiastical revenue, and marking its boundaries by confessions and sacraments, Anabaptism also spread with great rapidity through Germany, Switzerland, Holland, but always in isolated communities, more or less secret conventicles, bound together by brotherly ties, but not organized for mutual help and protection. There was no attempt to set up a common standard of faith. Doctrine and prac-

o

tice varied from city to city. But there were certain notes of Anabaptism which may serve to explain the dislike with which Anabaptists were regarded by authorities in Church and State, even before the catastrophe of Münster had thrown a lurid light upon the possibilities which lay hid in their theories. They stood outside all Church organizations, the uselessness of which they loudly proclaimed. They did not baptize their children. They thought it sinful to take an oath. They refused military service. They would not admit the duty of obedience to a civil power which was not, in their own sense of the word, Christian. They held that a marriage between a believing husband and an unbelieving wife was *ipso facto* invalid, and that either was at liberty to contract a fresh union. Modern Protestantism, in some of its more eccentric forms, has accustomed us to nearly all these things, and we have come to think it possible that a man may be under the influence of such scruples and yet fairly discharge his civic duty. But German rulers, in the first half of the sixteenth century, were of a very different opinion, and their theologians for the most part encouraged them in the work of persecution. An Anabaptist was not only a heretic, but a bad subject, and in either capacity deserved the severest treatment. Naturally, Catholic Princes had no mercy upon them: in Austria and the Tyrol, they were slain by the thousand: said Duke William of Bavaria,[1] "Behead those who recant; those who will not recant, burn." We have seen what was done at Zürich with Zwingli's concurrence: Bern, Basel, Schaffhausen, St. Gall, followed the

---

[1] Keller, p. 42 et seq.

evil example. In 1527, at Rothenburg on the Neckar, Michael Sattler had his tongue cut out, and was then committed to the flames. Balthasar Hubmaier, a man not only of genuine piety, but of undoubted learning and a fine and liberal spirit, was executed at Vienna in 1528. Elsewhere, all through these years, Anabaptists go to the scaffold or the fire, a dozen at a time, yet always with unshaken constancy, as men who have heaven full in view. Luther cannot account for their steadfastness, except on the hypothesis of Satanic inspiration:[1] Capito, in a spirit at once more Christian and more philosophical, says: "I testify before God that I cannot say that the Baptists despised this present life more out of unreason than a Divine Spirit. They show neither madness, nor folly, nor excitement; but in self-possession and astonishing patience they go to death, as confessors of the Christian name."[2]

I have found among Melancthon's letters a *Narratio de Anabaptistis*, some parts of which I will venture to lay before you, in the belief that any real glimpse we can get of living men and their troubles is more instructive than many general statements.[3] At the end of the year 1535, the plague was raging in Wittenberg, and Melancthon was in Jena. Here certain Anabaptists lay in prison, who, at the request of the Burgomaster and Council, were examined by a clerical commission, consisting of two Wittenberg professors, Melancthon and Caspar Cruciger, and Antonius Musa, the pastor of the town. What were the circumstances under which they were arrested

---

[1] To Link, May 12, 1528: Briefe, ed. De Wette, III. 311.
[2] Keller, p. 44.   [3] Corp. Ref. II. 997 et seq.

we are not informed; but the scandal at Münster had just come to a violent end, and all Germany was in a fever of excitement and horror. They were Heintz Krauth, Jobst Moller, Hans Peissker, all of the simple village sort, who with one accord protested that they had never been at Münster, and had neither good nor bad to say about it. Interrogated as to the Trinity, they had little that was heretical to confess: "they were not learned men, and could not speak much of this high article of faith." As to forgiveness of sins, they thought it was heartily to be desired, being of opinion that it consisted in perseverance in righteousness, belief and trust in God's Word, following of Christ, and doing the will of the Father. Their idea of community of goods was, that a Christian ought to stand free and indifferent to all his property, ready to share with a brother in his need, so that if any had a room full of money, he could not say that a single coin of it was his own. They denied the lawfulness of oaths. Christians were all brothers, and therefore none had authority over other. Of the sacrament of baptism, they said that—

"Baptism of children was not enjoined, and that all children were saved, whether of Christians, Heathens or Turks. God was not such a God as would damn a little child for the sake of a drop of water, for all His creatures were good. And they denied original sin in children; for such have never consented to it; but when a man grows up and consents to sin, then for the first time original sin has power."

When to this Melancthon replied with appropriate texts from David and Paul, they answered, first, that they did not care a farthing for all the Scriptures in the world; next, with texts on their own side, as, for instance,

"Of such is the kingdom of God;" and thirdly, with the principle that in all cases belief must go before baptism. On a second day's examination, Melancthon pressed them with the same texts—"Behold, I was shapen in iniquity, and in sin did my mother conceive me;" and, "We were by nature the children of wrath."

"Magister Philippus asks, whether the children also must be saved through Christ. Answers Heintz Krauth, Yes. Thereupon Magister Philippus, 'If they have no sin, they need not the sufferings of Christ,' and asks of him Scripture. Whereupon he answers, 'It stands written in his heart as God had taught it him. The Devil too can write.'"

Hans Krauth further thought that that was no true marriage where husband and wife were not one in the faith; but in that case he would have patience with his wife, and pray God for her that she would betake herself to the Word. The question of obedience to civil authorities was much pressed. These poor men said that they wanted no lord and master: One they had to whom they would cleave, God alone. Worldly government was only for the wicked, nor in that respect would they condemn it. All that were his own, Christ had made free. At the same time, if the civil power had let them alone in their faith, they would willingly have paid taxes and done as they were bid. Jobst Moller said that he could neither read nor write. But what God had written in his heart, of that he had been instructed by a man sent of God. Afterwards he had prayed to God, who had given it him into his heart. Not unnaturally this confessor, in the simplicity of what he regarded as his direct intercourse with Heaven, added that "he did not believe in a Lord God made of bread." Upon all this, and much more of the same kind, Melancthon makes a report, setting forth, without passion and, so far as I can judge, without exaggeration, the tenets held by these poor men, and concluding thus:

"After a friendly and Christian fashion have we prayed and warned them, that they should suffer themselves to be persuaded and have regard to the Scriptures, which we have laid before them; in time God would enlighten them, if they would set His Word before them and diligently consider it. But they say that they will abide by what God has taught them."[1]

So in truth they did; for on the 27th of January, 1536, they sealed their faith with their blood. A few days after, Melancthon despatched to the Elector John Frederick a quite conclusive refutation,[2] from his own point of view, of their crude and ignorant heresies, which nevertheless he was able to silence only by the same rough logic of axe and faggot as the Catholic Church was at any moment ready to apply to himself. Since that time the world has threshed out many of the questions which were in dispute between Jobst Moller, who could neither read nor write, and the first Christian scholar of Germany; and the result is not in all respects what the theologians of Wittenberg would have expected.

It would, however, be unjust to the leaders of the Reformation to omit to mention the connection of Anabaptism with revolutionary politics. In some of its manifestations, at least, it was much more than a theological opinion. Carlstadt and the men of Zwickau stood in close alliance with Thomas Münzer, the fanatical prophet, and not the least miserable victim of the Peasants'

---

[1] Corp. Ref. II. 1003.   [2] Ibid. III. 28.

War. It must not be forgotten that though Luther at an after time carefully disengaged himself from national politics, and, by throwing himself on the support of the Princes, signified his acquiescence in things as they were, a distinctly political element mingled in the earliest movement of the Reformation. The age was excited on every side. Men knew not what might result from the new stirring of intellectual and religious life. Hopes, at once wild and vague, were entertained of the young Emperor, who, no German himself, was yet supposed to impersonate the aspirations of Germany. Ulrich von Hutten, in whom the religious was distinctly subordinate to the political purpose, sought to draw Luther into the enterprize of Franz von Sickingen, and for a moment it seemed as if he had succeeded. Next, in 1525, the teachings of the early Anabaptists, and especially of Münzer, blew into a flame, which soon spread over all Germany, the smouldering embers of the Peasants' revolt. It was no new thing: they had risen many a time before, and in Switzerland had conquered their liberty and their rights. The cry of "Bundschuh," the peasants' clog, which they carried before them as a standard, was only too familiar in men's ears; for it meant, first, the excesses in which the sense of intolerable wrong always seeks revenge, and next, sanguinary and remorseless repression. This revolt ended as all previous ones had done: at first successful, it startled the German Princes into union, and then maddened them by cruelties which indeed admit of no excuse, but were nevertheless such as they themselves inflicted with absolute callousness on men of no condition. The process of repression was frightful. Such encounters as that at Frankenhausen were not battles, but massacres.

VI. SECTS OF THE REFORMATION.

The crowds of undisciplined peasants, armed with little more than their implements of husbandry, were simply slaughtered by the mail-clad knights and their well-drilled and well-equipped retainers.[1] Germany was delivered from a great social danger, but at what a cost! Serfdom still oppressed the people: a wider gulf than ever, filled with blood and tears, yawned between the owners and the tillers of the soil. Perhaps the most lamentable result, because the most permanent in its effect, was the divorce of the Reformation from popular sympathies, and its delivery into the hands of the Princes. Luther, himself "a peasant and a peasant's son," at first took the side of the class from which he sprang. But their appeal to force alienated him for ever. He was compelled to choose a side decisively, and he declared for the powers that were. In a pamphlet[2] which all his honest admirers must wish had remained unwritten, he exhorted the Princes to slay, and slay, and slay: the peasants were no better than mad dogs, and to be hunted down as such: whoever fell with a good conscience on the side of authority was a true martyr. And from those years 1525-27 a change came over him. He, and the Reformation with him, became harder, more dogmatic, less spiritual, less universal. He is no longer

---

[1] Luther says in a letter to Amsdorf, June 21, 1525 (Briefe, ed. De Wette, III. 13): "Certa res est in Franconia cæsa esse XI millia rusticorum in tribus locis divisa, captæ LXI bombardæ bonæ, arx Wirtenbergensis liberata. Casimirus Marchio vehementer sævit in suos, ob fidem bis violatam. In Wirtenbergensi ducatu VI millia cæsa sunt, alibi in Suevia X millia diversis locis: fertur Ducem Lotharingiæ in Alsatia XX millia cecidisse. Sic ubique cæduntur miseri rustici."

[2] Wider die räuberischen und mörderischen Bauern. Werke, ed. Walch, XVI. 90 et seq.

a leader of thought, but the builder up of a church, and that within limits and on conditions prescribed by the existing political constitution of Germany.

When I look at this story a little more closely, I find something inexpressibly pathetic in it. This is no common Jacquerie; though I think that Jacqueries, in which miserable people, maddened by intolerable wrong, throw themselves upon their oppressors in despair, and are crushed back into a last state worse than the first, are among the saddest of human phenomena. The old story,[1] that the revolt began with the peasants of Count von Lupfen, who on holidays and in harvest time were ordered to turn out to collect snail-shells to wind yarn upon, may be taken as sufficient proof that the German peasants had grievances of the most irritating kind; but in that, this revolt did not differ from many others. The characteristic of it which concerns us is the glimpse which these poor people had caught, as they imagined, of a coming kingdom of God, in which, among other crooked things that were to be made straight, were their own wrongs and woes. They formulated their demands in twelve most temperately worded articles;[2] to which was prefixed a

---

[1] "Unter vielen Stücken durch die sie gedrängt seien, klagten im Jahre 1524 die Bauern der Grafen von Lupfen und Fürstenberg 'dass sie weder Feyer noch Ruh möchten haben, vielmehr am Feiertag und mitten in der Erndte müssten sie der Gräfin Schneckenhäuslein suchen, Garn darauf zu winden, und für sie Erdbeer, Kriesen und Schlehen gewinnen, und anderes dergleichen thun, den Herren und Frauen werken bei gutem Wetter, ihnen selber im Unwetter, und das Gejägd und die Hunde liefen ohne Achtung eigenes Schadens.'" Zimmermann: Allgemeine Geschichte des grossen Bauernkrieges, II. 10, quoting from Anshelm, Bern. Chronik. VI. 298.

[2] Werke, ed. Walch, XVI. 24 et seq.

preamble formally declaring that they sought nothing that the gospel did not justify, while the last article provided that all the rest should be brought to the test of Scripture, and stand or fall accordingly. The majority of the articles relate to compulsory service, excessive rents, common lands and forests, feudal incidents and the like. But it is noticeable that the first demands that the whole congregation shall have the right of choosing a minister, whose duty shall be to preach to them the pure gospel, and, if necessary, of dismissing him. The obligation of tithe is to be regulated by the Levitical Law: game laws, and especially the consumption by wild animals of the fruits of the earth intended for man's use, are declared to be contrary to God's will: all bondage and serfdom are put in striking opposition to the fact that "Christ bought and redeemed us all by his precious blood, the shepherd as well as the noblest, none being excepted"—wherefore, they go on to say, "it accords with Scripture that we are and will be free." Of course it is easy to say, in reference to all this, that the promises of the New Testament were not intended to be of literal fulfilment; that, for instance, freedom, as Luther and Melancthon abundantly proved, signifies spiritual freedom, and is quite consistent with bodily slavery; that what Christ meant by the kingdom of God was the gradual separation, by a process of individual conversion, of the church from the world; and that, so far from the reign of "righteousness and peace and joy in a holy spirit" being possible here and now, all that lies before society is to go on from bad to worse, till it draws down on itself the consuming anger of the Eternal Judge. At the same time, there is another reading of the gospel which goes upon the supposition that Christ meant what he said, and in their crude and imperfect way these peasants seem to have made it their own.

The same aspiration reappears in a shape of the grossest and most repulsive caricature in the Anabaptist kingdom of Münster. But ten years of restless thought and excited religious feeling have elapsed since the Peasants' War, and what was then a vague sense that social ills were all to be remedied by a return to the precepts of the New Testament, has become an ecclesiastical theory which many strange forces have helped to mould. There is the Puritan notion that all true believers must be a peculiar people, not only distinguished from the outer world by invisible states of mind, but fenced off from it by visible tokens. There are the wild millennial expectations which always lend themselves so readily to the impulses of revolutionary fanaticism. But, above all, there is the Antinomianism which lies in wait for enthusiastic Christianity on more than one line of its possible development. It follows logically, though, I am prompt to acknowledge, in practice very rarely, from a hard and external interpretation of the doctrine of justification by faith alone, especially when held, as it often is, in conjunction with a belief in predestination. Once identify faith with belief—empty out of it the moral element and leave only the intellectual—make it, *not* the soul's passionate devotion to its Saviour, but a mental assent to certain historical and theological facts—and you have already done much to degrade morals into a subordinate place. But when you assure a nature that has thus never known the transforming glow of spiritual affection, but rests in a purely intellectual self-satisfaction, that, come what will, its eternal salvation is beyond question, and that by no transgression of law it can finally fall out of a state of grace, it is possible that you may obliterate moral distinctions altogether, and make the divorce between religion and ethics complete. And, strange to say, the same result may be arrived at by that path of mystic speculation which claims to lead the soul into the very presence of God. For if once the fortress of individual personality is given up, the control of the will abandoned, and the soul suffered to fall as an indistinguishable drop into the infinite ocean of divine existence, man's action becomes God's action, and, whatever its apparent relation to human laws of morality, spiritually right and good. In the Münster Anabaptists both these tendencies to Antinomianism coincided, and the result was the most hideous parody of the City of God which the world has ever seen.

We shall not, however, do justice to the dissidents of the Reformation unless we select for special description some of the men who stood out above their fellows in individuality of thought and character. I take three: Johann Denck, Caspar Schwenkfeld, Sebastian Franck. These men cannot, without inaccuracy, be made the representatives of classes; the activity of each must speak for itself.

The date and place of Denck's birth are unknown. When he died in 1527, he was described as still a young man—from which we may conclude with some certainty that he was born in the last years of the fifteenth century. He first appears at Basel, where he graduated, and was afterwards employed as a corrector of the press. Even then he was a friend of Œcolampadius—as, indeed, he

continued to be throughout the whole of his brief life—
and attended the lectures on Isaiah in which the Reformer of Basel put forward the characteristic ideas of
the Reformation. It was on the recommendation of Œcolampadius that, in the autumn of 1523, Denck went to
Nürnberg, to fill the post of school-rector at St. Sebald's.
Here the humanist became the theologian; the orthodox
Protestant—if, indeed, he ever were one—a heretic. The
old and famous free city was, throughout all these years,
the centre of a vivid and many-coloured religious life:
here lived Pirkheimer, the representative lay scholar of
his day, surrounded by a circle of theologians and artists
and literary men: here, too, Osiander, the chief pastor
of the city, a man of harsh and unlovely character, who
anticipated the narrow and rigid Lutheranism of the
next generation: while in less conspicuous social regions,
every variety of theological speculation developed itself,
in reliance upon the free institutions of Nürnberg and the
known forbearance of its Council. But Denck had been
only a year and a half in Nürnberg when he had a difference with Osiander on the subject of the Eucharist.
The result was, that he was called upon to make a confession of his faith; and when this proved unsatisfactory,
was expelled from the city, and forbidden on peril of
his life to return within ten miles of it. After this, he
was a wanderer for the brief remnant of his days. We
hear of him at St. Gall, Augsburg, Worms, Strasburg;
and if one tradition be true, in spite of the sentence
against him, at Nürnberg once more. At Augsburg,
he becomes the head of an Anabaptist community; at
Strasburg, he engages in a public disputation with the
Lutheran preachers: from both cities he is compelled

to flee. In Worms he published, in conjunction with Ludwig Hetzer, a translation of the Prophets, which remains to bear witness to the solid and impartial scholarship of its authors. Osiander procured the prohibition of its sale in Nürnberg; but not the less was it reprinted thirteen times within three years, after which we may conclude that Luther's version took its place. Everywhere, not only theological controversy and ecclesiastical unsettlement, but religious revival, followed Denck's steps. There is a great concurrence of testimony both to the depth of the influence which he exerted and the integrity and sweetness of character which justified it. Sebastian Franck calls him "a quiet, withdrawn, pious man, the leader and Bishop of the Anabaptists."[1] Another contemporary chronicler, Johann Kessler, describes him as learned, eloquent, humble. Capito, who, as one of the preachers of Strasburg, was only half a friend, speaks of his great gifts and exemplary life.[2] He belonged to that best age of Anabaptism, when it was at once a deeply religious and a truly ethical movement, before the relentless rage of stupid persecution had deprived it of its natural leaders, and handed it over to extravagance and license. Men gathered eagerly about Denck, hung upon his lips, adopted his principles, and were afterwards not afraid to suffer for their faith. He showed himself, in the three years within which all his activity was comprised, a great religious leader, and might possibly, had his life been prolonged, have developed into a philosophical theologian too. In a quite

---

[1] S. Franck: Chronica, Zeytbuch und Geschichtbibel, III. 135.
[2] Keller: Ein Apostel der Wiedertäufer, p. 6.

singular way he united the qualities which kindle religious enthusiasm in others with a sweet reasonableness, such as belongs to hardly any other theologian, orthodox or heretical, of the age of the Reformation. In 1527, expelled from city after city and worn out with persecution, he took refuge in Basel once more, asking Œcolampadius, in a very pathetic letter, for a little peace before he died. It was granted, and before many weeks had passed the end came. In the hands of Œcolampadius he left a so-called recantation, which is really only a re-statement, in careful and measured terms, of his peculiar opinions.[1] I do not know whether, if he had lived, the disruptive forces of Anabaptism would not have been too strong for Denck; but in him radical Protestantism lost a leader whose place no Spanish or Italian rationalist could supply. But is it not a little unjust to class as a sectary one among whose last words were these: "God is my witness that I desire that things may go well with me only for the sake of one sect, the Communion of Saints, let it be where it will"?[2]

In some respects Denck occupied the ordinary Anabaptist position. He drew the familiar distinction between the outer and the inner Word, that written in the Bible and that inscribed on the fleshly tables of the heart—a distinction which at once undermines the exclusive authority of Scripture and provides for the continuity of revelation. "I esteem Holy Scripture," he says, "above all human treasures, but not so highly as

---

[1] See passages quoted by Heberle in his article in the Theol. Studien und Kritiken, 1851, "Johann Denck und sein Büchlein vom Gesetz," p. 154.

[2] Letter to Œcolampadius, quoted by Keller, "Ein Apostel," p. 252.

the Word of God which is living, powerful, eternal, free and independent of all elements of this world: for as it is God Himself, so is it spirit and not letter, and written without pen and paper, so that it can never more be blotted out."[1] He took the side of his sect as to adult baptism, but it was a matter on which he laid no stress. "It harms no faithful man," he said, "to have been baptized in his childhood; and God asks no other baptism, so he observes the order which becomes a Christian community."[2] He had grasped the idea that in a truly spiritual theory of Christianity sacraments have no authoritative place. They are but signs and reminders of love, which is the one thing needful. Whoso has love is above rules and ceremonies. "Love is God Himself: whoso has not God, him cannot all creatures help, though he were already lord of them all. But who has God, has all creatures."[3] But he went much further than this: he abandoned the ground of Reformation theology in his rejection of its entire scheme of salvation. He denied Luther's fundamental assumption of the slavery of the will, asserting, on the contrary, the existence in every soul of a divine spark, the Christ within, which the charm of the personal Christ fanned into a flame of goodness. The imitation of Christ was one of his characteristic ideas: without formally denying that Christ suffered for us, he insisted much more upon the thought that we are to suffer with him, and held him up as an example

---

[1] From Denck's so-called recantation, quoted by G. Arnold, "Kirchen und Ketzer Historie," Part iv. Sec. ii. § 31, p. 533.

[2] Quoted by Heberle, Theol. Studien und Kritiken, 1855, p. 882.

[3] Ibid. 1851, p. 185.

VI. SECTS OF THE REFORMATION. 209

rather than pleaded him as a sacrifice. With these views, it is not wonderful that Denck should have been widely accused of holding the Antitrinitarian opinions which were notoriously entertained by his friend and fellow-worker Hetzer.[1] So far as I can judge, it would not be easy to produce any direct evidence of the fact from his writings. None of them touch upon metaphysical mysteries of the Divine Nature. They approach Christianity from the spiritual and the ethical side, and are interested in questions of Divine personality only so far as they affect the practical life. Still there are passages in them which the trained theologian will recognize as belonging to quite another region of thought than the Athanasian. Speaking of the inner light, he says: "If now a carpenter's son, who had never gone to school, should come and

---

[1] When and where Denck and Hetzer first met is a difficult point, which I shall not attempt to decide. The lives of these half-forgotten heretics have to be reconstructed out of the scantiest and most scattered materials, the right interpretation of which is often very difficult. Hetzer was a scholar of some accomplishment, and a thinker of much speculative daring; unhappily, also, a man of many sins and repentances, who died upon the scaffold at Constanz in 1529 for breaches of the moral law, which might have been visited upon him less harshly had his heresy not been so notorious. The following rude verses, preserved by Franck, Chronica, III. 139 b, are decisive as to Hetzer's opinions:

  Ich bin allein der Einig Gott
  Der ohne Hülf all Ding beschaffen hat.
  Fragst du, wie viel meiner sei?
  Ich bin's allein, meiner sind nicht drei.
  Sag' auch darbei ohn allen Wohn
  Dass ich glat weiss von keiner Person.
  Bin auch weder diess noch das
  Wem ich's nicht sag, der weiss nicht was.

P

rebuke the lies of the learned, where should he have learned it?"[1] And again:

"Therefore hath it pleased the Eternal Love that the man in whom love hath been manifested in the highest should be called the Saviour of his people: not as though it were possible to humanity to save any one, but that God was so completely united in love with him, that every act of God was this man's act, and all this man's suffering is to be regarded as God's suffering. This man is Jesus of Nazareth, who was promised in Scripture by the true God, and manifested in his season."[2]

Still Denck's heresy, such as it was, was not developed on these lines. The affection of the soul which Luther calls faith and makes all-important, he declares to be love, self-forgetfulness, trust in the promises of God. And God on the moral side is Love, and Love only. So Denck, anticipating in a very remarkable way the course of the newest thought, could not be brought to believe

---

[1] Quoted by Keller, p. 191.

[2] Quoted by Arnold, Part iv. Sec. ii. § 31, p. 532. Denck's latest biographer, Dr. L. Keller, "Ein Apostel der Wiedertäufer," Leipzig, 1882, who has most industriously acquainted himself with Denck's very rare and scattered works, strangely says nothing about the Antitrinitarian opinions which have been so commonly attributed to him. He refrains from investigating the connection with Hetzer, which was certainly very close; and while instructing his readers about everything else nearly or remotely connected with Denck's career, does not mention the notorious heresy of his friend and literary fellow-worker. In this connection I must think it strange that he translates the passage (see below) in Denck's last letter to Œcolampadius, "quam ut quam plurimi uno corde et ore Deum et Patrem Domini nostri Jesu Christi glorificarent"—"als dass recht Viele eines Herzens und Mundes Gott, den Vater unseres Herrn Jesu Christi, rühmen" (p. 229). This disingenuousness is a blot upon an otherwise meritorious book.

in an endless hell. The omnipotent love of God must be victorious, and not only all men, but all devils, be saved at last.[1] Critics, indeed, differ as to whether he believed in any material hell at all, or conceived of it as other than the torment of conscience and the conscious sense of God's justice.[1] Texts in support of eternal punishment he answered in part by other texts; but the necessary and unchangeable love of God was his mainstay. It is plain that we have here a religious phenomenon of quite another kind from those which have hitherto occupied our attention. This theology is as strongly opposed to Wittenberg, to Zürich, to Geneva, as to Rome. In the letter to Œcolampadius, written near the end of his life, of which I have already spoken, Denck says:

"I ask no other result, God knows, than that as many men as possible should with one heart and voice glorify the God and Father of our Lord Jesus Christ, whether they be circumcised, or baptized, or neither; for I greatly differ from those, whoever

---

[1] Keller (p. 76) denies that any proof of Denck's belief in the salvability of Satan can be adduced from his works, and goes on to say that it is very doubtful whether he believed in a personal Devil at all. Franck is, however, explicit on the point. "Diser hat under andern gehalten die Meynung Origenis, dass sich Gott werd endtlich aller erbarmen, Gott werd und mög nit ewig zürnen noch verstossen, und werd in summa endtlich alles selig, auch die verstossnen Geister und Teuffel." Chronica, III. 135. Denck was here only following the true path of German mysticism. The "Theologia Germanica" says (ch. xvi.): "If the Evil Spirit himself could come into true obedience, he would become an angel again, and all his sin and wickedness would be healed and blotted out and forgiven at once." Again (ch. li.): "But in hell every one will have self-will; therefore there is all manner of sin and wretchedness. So is it also here on earth. But if there were one in hell who should get rid of his self-will, and call nothing his own, he would come out of hell into heaven." Theol. Germ., transl. Winkworth.

they may be, who too much bind down the kingdom of God to ceremonies and elements of the world."[1]

Ought not the fact that a man like this was regarded all over Upper Germany as the leader of the Anabaptists, to go some way to relieve Anabaptism of the heavy load of opprobrium which ecclesiastical historians have laid upon it?[2]

Caspar Schwenkfeld fills a much larger place than Denck in the church history of the time, partly, perhaps, because he gave his name to a sect which long lingered in Germany and still survives in America.[3] He was a Silesian nobleman who, having had the best education of his time at Cologne and elsewhere, passed the early years of his manhood in service at some of the petty courts of his own province. Born in 1490, he received the first fresh impressions of the Lutheran Reformation, with which, for a time, he felt himself in full accord. But he had too individual a mind to follow any master blindly, while the fact that he was a born mystic placed him more and more, as years went on, in opposition to the later developments of Lutheran theology. I have no

---

[1] Keller, p. 252.

[2] For Denck, vid. Hagen, III. 275 et seq. Trechsel: Die Protestantischen Antitrinitarier vor Faustus Socin. I. 13 et seq. G. Arnold: Kirchen und Ketzer Historie, I. 735, II. 530. Keller: Geschichte der Wiedertäufer, p. 33 et seq. Heberle: Two Essays in the Theologische Studien und Kritiken, 1851, 1855; and especially Keller, "Ein Apostel der Wiedertäufer."

[3] A letter addressed in 1875 to Mr. Robert Barclay, author of "The Inner Life of the Religious Societies of the Commonwealth," by the authorities of the Schwenkfeldian church at Colebrookdale, Pennsylvania, states that at that date they had three hundred families comprising eight hundred persons and two churches. Barclay: Inner Life, &c., p. 243.

time to tell his story in detail. His religious position which in the eyes of partizans was neither Protestant nor Catholic, drew down upon him dislike and persecution from both sides. King Ferdinand of Bohemia, the brother of Charles V. and his successor in the Empire, brought pressure to bear upon his Prince, the Duke of Liegnitz, to dismiss him from his service, and in 1529 Schwenkfeld betook himself to Strasburg. Here he found an asylum for five years, which were the prelude to many more of wandering and trouble. He was always faithful with a kind of free allegiance to Luther; but Luther repulsed him with the bitterest reproaches, and Melancthon fulminated a decree of excommunication against both him and Franck, from the half-political, half-religious assembly of Schmalkalden. The much-enduring man took up his abode first in one city of Southern Germany, then in another, always collecting about him a little circle of adherents whom he organized into a congregation apart, always writing books which were proscribed and burnt, always opposing to persecution a mild persistence which it was impossible to overcome. His gentle birth and courtly manners won him a class of converts whom no plebeian Reformer could have approached, while at the same time they attracted to him the hostile attention of Princes who might have let plebeian Reformers alone. He was no Anabaptist, though he associated much with them: on the one hand, they listened to him patiently; on the other, he had too large a soul to believe that piety was peculiar to any church. "The Anabaptists,"[1] he said, "are all the dearer to me that they care about divine

---

[1] Quoted by Erbkam, p. 382.

truth somewhat more than many of the learned ones. For whoso seeks God in earnest will find Him." This, like almost everything else in Schwenkfeld, belongs to the character of the mystic. Even while collecting his little conventicles, the only bond of which was the consciousness of a common spiritual inheritance, he was careless of church organization. He was not so much heretical in regard to the doctrines of the Reformation, as felt that he had penetrated beneath them to something more real and stable. The older he grew and the more the spiritual element faded out of Lutheranism, the greater was his insistance that the spirit was the one thing needful. When men made, first the sacraments, then preaching, mere matters of external administration, declaring that, so the truths were preached, it mattered not how or by whom, and defining faith as no more than an intellectual assent to a creed, it was well that Schwenkfeld should reiterate the distinction between the outer and the inner Word, and insist on the direct communication between God and every soul. The peculiarly Protestant character of his mysticism was shown in his doctrine of the deification of the flesh of Jesus, which was his way of explaining the difficulty of the Real Presence in the Eucharist. Jesus, sitting at the right hand of God, was in his heavenly humanity truly Lord and God, and the puzzle of the ubiquity of his body in the bread and wine upon the altar fell away of itself. This deified humanity of Jesus was a great point with Schwenkfeld: his followers called themselves "confessors of the glory of Christ." But notwithstanding he thus put forward a peculiar doctrine of the Eucharist, it was a necessity of his spiritual theory that he should sit loose to all rites and sacraments. The mystic who aims to possess God and believes that he has attained his end, is quite careless of minor matters, and not least of the wings with which less daring souls attempt to fly. That Schwenkfeld, in spite of his long activity and the persecution which pushed him into notoriety, left little permanent result behind, will surprise no one who reflects that mysticism does not easily propagate itself, and can grow only in fit spiritual soil. Still the meditative, patient, persistent man, always striving to sound the depths of religious experience, always endeavouring to draw for others the distinction between the formal and the real, not heterodox except out of the necessity of his spiritual nature, and finding brethren everywhere in all true seekers after God, is one of the most characteristic figures of the Reformation, and not the least amiable. He died at Ulm in 1562.[1]

Sebastian Franck's life resembles in many respects those of Denck and Schwenkfeld: there is the same untiring allegiance to theological opinions, the same wandering and harassed existence, the same result of contemporary fame and speedy forgetfulness. He was a native of Donauwörth in Swabia, born probably in the last decade of the fifteenth century, though neither the year of his birth nor that of his death is precisely known. We find him about 1527 in Nürnberg, the Nürnberg of Willibald Pirkheimer, of Albrecht Dürer, of Hans Sachs, and, only a year or two before, of Johann Denck and possibly Ludwig Hetzer. His first work was a translation into German of the *Diallage* of Althammer, the attempt

---

[1] For Schwenkfeld, see especially Erbkam, Bk. I. ch. iv. pp. 357— 475. Conf. also Barclay: The Inner Life of the Religious Societies of the Commonwealth, p. 227 et seq.

of a Lutheran minister to reconcile inconsistencies of Scripture; his next, also a translation of that famous tract, the "Supplication of the Beggars," which played a part in the English Reformation. From that time, for about fifteen years, his literary activity is incessant and very varied. Popular history and mystical theology divide him between them. He writes a great *Geschicht Bibel*, or Bible of History, the ecclesiastical part of which characteristically includes a catalogue of heretics, a History of Germany, a Chronicle of the Franks, a *Welt Buch*, or system of Cosmography. He is the author of a book against the national vice of drunkenness; he translates Erasmus' "Praise of Folly;" he makes a collection of German Proverbs. Then there are his Paradoxes, two hundred and eighty in number, dealing in a startling but suggestive way with all deep theological questions; his "Golden Ark," a collection of wise sayings, gathered from Scripture, the Fathers, and heathen sages; and his "Book sealed with Seven Seals," which treats of the contrariety between the written and the inner Word of God, in the spirit and with something of the form of the Paradoxes. During the fifteen or sixteen years in which Franck was producing these voluminous works—and there are more than I have enumerated—he was driven from city to city of Southern Germany, supporting himself sometimes by soap-boiling, sometimes by printing, but always having his heart in his literary work. Banished from Strasburg for publishing his *Geschicht Bibel*, he settled in Ulm, where he boiled soap for a while, but afterwards, when he had won his citizenship, turned to book-making again. Here he met with his worst enemy, Martin Frecht, the Lutheran pastor of Ulm, who not only after a long struggle procured his expulsion from the city, but stirred up Melancthon—nothing loth—to prevent, by his widely extended influence, the hunted man from finding rest for the sole of his foot in any German city. I have already spoken of the denunciation which the humanist of Wittenberg directed from the assembly of Princes and Divines at Schmalkalden against Franck and Schwenkfeld, friends and brothers in misfortune, a document which the latter not inaptly described as a "Papal Bull." Then there is another expulsion from Strasburg; and in 1542 we find Franck pursuing the business of a printer in Basel. Soon after, though how and when we do not know, came the end, and Franck's restless pen no longer provoked the relentless animosity of orthodox Lutherans.

Franck was not a learned man: he wrote in German for Germans, making no pretensions to exact scholarship. His historical works are largely compilations: except in flashes of insight now and then, they show little trace of the critical spirit. In regard to matters beyond his personal observation, he is as credulous as Sir John Mandeville: "gorgons, and hydras, and chimeras dire," to say nothing of "men whose heads do grow beneath their shoulders," figure in his pages; and, like Milton after him, he goes for the beginnings of native history to the Trojan War. At the same time he had read widely, if not critically: he pours out upon his pages all the wealth of ancient learning, while his accounts of contemporary events are vivid and exact. Melancthon, we are told, was never tired of lavishing contempt upon him in his character of historian; but modern opinion has not ratified the judgment. Men who know comparatively little of Franck as a theologian or a philosopher, declare him to have been the father of German history. There is a fine national spirit about him: he appealed, not to the learned, but to the people, and the people rewarded him by buying edition after edition of his books. Had he been less popular, he might have been less persecuted; but this half printer, half soap-boiler, who had never had a university education, and would not, perhaps could not, write in Latin, was a maker of public opinion such as the new orthodoxy could not afford to despise. But what on this side of his activity is chiefly interesting to us is the religious spirit in which he wrote history. The common distinction between sacred and profane would have been abhorrent to him. He inscribes upon the first page of his *Geschicht Bibel*—the very title of which implies a theory—" Come and behold the works of the Lord." History, with him, is the continued exemplification in human life of what Scripture enjoins, teaches, forbids. It is the peculiar advantage, thinks Franck, of those who live in the last days that so large and various an experience of humanity lies behind them. We might call him a humanist for the interest he takes in manifestations of life and thought which are neither Hebrew nor Christian, did he not deserve the name in its nobler sense of one upon whom everything that is human makes an equal claim.

This could hardly have been the case with a theologian like Luther, to whom mankind since the fall lay in moral bondage and corruption, and who could save patriarch and prophet from the general sentence only by attributing to them a kind of Christianity before Christ. From this view of things Franck was saved by his doctrine of the Word. Like the Anabaptists, with whom he is often unjustly classed, he distinguished between the written and the unwritten, the outer and the inner Word. This distinction is indeed the key to all his theology. The written Word—that which the Reformers of Wittenberg made their idol—often deceived and led astray, as indeed was sufficiently shown by the various and contradictory doctrines which men drew from it. But there is an inner Word, which lives and moves in every man, Jew, Christian, Heathen, Turk, to which the outer is only a witness:[1] in one sense the light of nature, in another the Christ in men's souls, the only true Christ. Franck has indeed very little to say of the historical Christ: it is, so to speak, the universal Christ who engages his attention. It was in the strength of the inner divine Word that not only the prophets spake, but all wise and virtuous heathens, Plato not less than Isaiah. Adam and Christ, the bad seed and the good, are in every man's soul: it lies with each to choose to which he will conform himself. But without that inward conformity which involves the putting away of sin and the cleansing of the conscience, the sufferings of Christ are a dead letter to us, just as much as any heathen history. Closely connected with this idea of the unwritten Word is Franck's conception of nature, which is far more modern than any other that I find in the speculations of this age.

---

[1] "Dies Licht der Natur, so durch die Latern des Fleisches nicht kann leuchten, ist allen Menschen gemein, dass ein Jeglicher das Urtheil in seinem Busen stecken hat, und dies Licht heisst die Schrift das eingepflanzte Wort, Gesetz und Willen Gottes. Aus diesem Licht und Grund haben geschrieben Plotinus, Plato, Diogenes, Trismegistus, Seneca, Hiob und alle erleuchtete Heiden." Quoted by Hase: S. Franck, p. 215.

"The whole world,"[1] he says, "and all creatures are only an open book and living Bible, in which, without guidance, thou mayest study the art of God and learn His will. For all creatures preach to a man who is considerate and instructed of God. .... To the devout all is an open book, wherein he learns more from the creatures and works of God, than a godless man out of all Bibles and words of God. For whoso does not understand God's work, does not apprehend His Word also."

What is this but that Hellenism made Christian which it is the object of our best religious thought to-day to define and expound?

Franck was a Reformer of the Reformers in his hatred of the Papacy, and the sharp criticisms of the Papal system, in which his historical works abound. But his attitude of opposition to Lutheranism was hardly less stiff. If any doctrine more than another cut athwart his deepest convictions, it was that of the authority of the letter of Scripture. He accused the Lutherans of deposing a human, to set up a paper Pope.

---

[1] Quoted by Hase: S. Franck, p. 30. It is, however, worth while to cite in this connection a passage from Theobald Thamer, a divine who, driven from Lutheranism by disgust at the hard and immoral interpretation of the doctrine of justification by faith, found refuge at last in the Catholic Church. He graduated at Wittenberg in 1539, and died in 1569. "Es ist eine grosse Gotteslästerung zu sagen, die Kreaturen seyen um des menschlichen Bauches Willen geschaffen: sondern vielmehr seyen sie geschaffen zu Gottes Ehre, dass der Mensch durch sie Gott in seiner Herrlichkeit erkenne und an ihnen Gott verherrlichen lerne. Es ist nichts auf Erden, das nicht ein Element und Anleitung zum wahren Glauben ist und predigt Gottes Ehre. Die Kreaturen sind dem Menschen zu einen sichtbaren, wie die heilige Schrift zu einem hörlichen Worte vorgestellt: denn wenn die Kreaturen uns nicht lehrten zur Seligkeit, sondern nur zu diesem Leben, wie ihr vorgeht, so wären sie nicht allein unnütz, sondern auch der Sünde unterworfen, und mehreten das Reich des Teufels." Quoted by A. Neander: Th. Thamer, p. 31.

"Antichrist,"[1] he said, "who is now tired of the Pope, and has well-nigh used him up, will put on another disguise, and set himself in the midst of the letter of Scripture .... and be more learned in Scripture than we. Thus many are now making an idol of Scripture, not even asking God to explain His secret to us; for nevertheless Scripture can change no bad heart, else were the most learned in Scripture the most pious too."

Again:[2]

"With many, Scripture and Gospel have now become such an art that no one can understand them who does not know four or five languages. I set much more store upon a quiet, self-denied heart, wherein God may shine and mirror Himself; for this is what Christ thinks alone necessary to his method and secret."

So, in like manner, he is indifferent to sacraments. To lose oneself in God, to live in communion with the Divine Word within, is everything; external signs and rites, nothing.

"Temples,"[3] he says, "pictures, festivals, sacrifices, ceremonies, have no place in the New Testament. For this is nothing but the Holy Ghost, a good conscience, love unfeigned, a pure spirit, an innocent life, the righteousness of the heart, proceeding from genuine faith."

Franck was thus no Anabaptist, for he looked upon baptism as an indifferent thing. And he was profoundly averse, too, to the sectarian spirit of the Anabaptists. He was that strangest of religious phenomena, which the world has not yet learned to understand, a deeply religious man who cared nothing about churches or church organizations. It was not that he wished to stand alone,

---

[1] Quoted by Hase: S. Franck, p. 78.   [2] Ibid. pp. 79, 80.
[3] Franck: Paradoxa, No. lxxxix. p. 116 b.

but that no external exclusions could shut him out from the consciousness of universal brotherhood. He was content to be a Christian only; and he interpreted that word in so wide a sense, as to make it include the wise and good of every age.[1]

---

[1] "Weil nun bis ans Ende Gut und Bös in einem Netz und Acker dieser Welt bei einander sein werden und Jerusalem mitten unter den Heiden zerstreuet soll liegen, halt ich von keiner Sonderung und Secte nichts. Ein Jeder kann für sich selbst wohl fromm sein, wo er ist, darf nicht eben hin und her laufen, eine sondere Secte Tauf, Kirchen suchen, anrichten, und auf einen Haufen sehen und seinem Anhang zu lieb glauben, fromm sein und zu Dienst heucheln." Paradoxa, Preface, p. 7 b.

"Paulus will nicht leiden, dass sich Jemand nach ihm paulisch nennt: also hoffe ich, begehre auch keiner von uns armen Erdwürmern dass ich nach ihm Papistisch, Lutherisch, Zwinglisch, oder Taüferisch genannt werde, weil ich sammt ihnen auf Christum getauft bin, und Christo nach werde genannt. Ich halte aber mit Petro für meine Brüder alle, die unter allen Völkern Gott suchen." Quoted by Hase: S. Franck, p. 247.

"Nun sind gewiss alle Secten aus dem Teufel, und ein Frucht des Fleisches, an Zeit, Statt, Person, Gesetz, und Element gebunden, allein das freie, ohn sectisch, unparteiisch Christenthum, das an der Dinge keins gebunden ist, sondern frei in Geist auf Gottes Wort steht und mit Glauben und nicht mit Augen begriffen und gesehen kann werde, ist aus Gott. .... Die Kirche nicht etwa ein sonderer Hauf und fingerzeig Sect ist, an Elementen, Zeit, Person und Statt gebunden, sondern .... die Versammlung und Gemeinde aller recht gottfrommen und gutherzigen neuer Menschen, in aller Welt durch den heiligen Geist in dem Frieden Gottes mit dem Band der Liebe zusammengegürtet, ausser dem kein Heil, Christus, Gott, Verstand der Schrift, heiliger Geist, noch Evangelium ist. In und bei dieser Kirche bin ich, zu der sehne ich mich in meinem Geist, wo sie zerstreuet unter den Heiden und Unkraut umfähret, und glaube diese Gemeinschaft der Heiligen, kann's aber nicht zeigen, bin aber gewiss, dass ich in der Kirche bin, sei, wo ich wolle." Paradoxa, Preface, pp. 7, 8.

For Sebastian Franck, vid. Hagen, III. 314—396, who in modern times first called attention to his merits as a philosophic and religious

Perhaps some acute hearer may already have divined that, to describe Franck exactly, we must use not only the word Mystic, but one of worse repute, Pantheist. I might possibly, by invoking the aid of subtle philosophical distinctions, deny the charge, but I am not greatly concerned to do so: he saw God in all things, all things in God: and when he tried to define Deity, found it hard to do so in terms which should include personality. But I notice that this is a difficulty into which many profoundly religious men are apt to fall; and I can at least plead for Franck that he held to free-will, and so saved, in his own view, the citadel of human morality. There were more dangerous heresies afloat in that orthodox age —yes, and in some of its most orthodox places too—than that which discerned the presence of the Living God in all history and in all nature.

It is a significant thing that Franck, who during the period of his brief literary activity had been so popular, was soon forgotten, and has only within the last few years been restored to the light of human memory. His books ceased to be reprinted: he fell into the general crowd of those Anabaptists who were looked upon as the shame of the Reformation, and of whom men chiefly thought in connection with the catastrophe of Münster. If, now that he lives again, he is found to be strangely modern, the fact may account both for his own fate and that of many of the sectaries, learned and unlearned, whom I have tried to describe. They were half-blindly reaching forward to something better and more stable

thinker; Erbkam, pp. 286—357; and particularly the excellent monograph of K. A. Hase, "Sebastian Franck, von Wörd, der Schwarmgeist."

than they knew or could firmly grasp. Those seem to us to have succeeded best who stood on the ground of that pure spiritual intuition which is the same in all ages, and not essentially affected by intellectual change; but in proportion as they succeeded, were they out of tune with their own age and that which came after. These ideas of the continuity of revelation, of the Divine in nature and in history, of the inner, which must in the last resort interpret the outer Word, of the unimportance of sacraments compared with the consecration of the life, even of the kingdom of God as a realizable ideal of human society, are only now, after the lapse of so many years, working themselves clear, and winning recognition as the result of a just interpretation of Scripture, of history, of nature. It is impossible to deny the presence in Anabaptism of an element, coarse, fanatical, immoral; though we must recollect that the Anabaptists have been chiefly described by their enemies, and may predict that history will be gentler to them in the future than in the past. Nor do I compare Denck, Schwenkfeld, Franck, with Luther, Zwingli, Calvin: each did a necessary work, and each in his own way. But the men whom the world has almost forgotten, and whom it remembers only to blame, saw, though perhaps dimly, truths and principles which the men who have reaped their full harvest of fame as leaders and benefactors of humanity contemptuously neglected. But time brings its revenges: and though men be forgotten, truth cannot die.

LECTURE VII.
THE REFORMATION IN SWITZERLAND.

The force of the Reformation has been transmitted to modern times in two great currents, that of the Lutheran and that of the Reformed Church. But these have run a very different course. At first, the centre and turning-point of Protestantism was undeniably Wittenberg. It is Luther who stands in uncompromising opposition to Pope and Emperor, a new Athanasius against the world. He appears before Diets: Cardinals are sent to negotiate with him and those who support him: he is the mark of all Catholic controversialists: a King takes up the pen to refute him: a special bull places him under the ban of the Church. Movements similar to his, but independent of it, are going on all over Europe, a significant testimony at once to the tendency and the ripeness of the time; but they attract comparatively little attention. Colet and his friends strove to give a new direction to the studies of Oxford before Luther had taken his vows at Erfurt: it has been claimed for France that in the person of Lefevre d'Etaples she led the way in the van of reformation: when the theses against indulgences were nailed to the church door of Wittenberg, Zwingli was already preaching against pilgrimages to the pilgrims at Einsiedeln. Still it was a wise instinct which concentrated the attention of Rome and Europe upon Saxony. Luther is indisputably the chief figure of the Reformation, and the Saxon movement that in which we still rightly study the principles and motives of the great religious uprising of Europe. But as time went on, all this was changed, and the primacy of the Reformation was transferred from Wittenberg to Geneva. The Scandinavian kingdoms were the only permanent conquest which, beyond the limits of Germany, the Lutheran Reform won for Protestantism: from whatever footing it gained in the east of Europe, it was gradually expelled by the Counter Reformation. In truth, it was far too much occupied with arid controversies and ignoble divisions to have the self-forgetting energy necessary for successful missionary effort. Not even in Germany did it hold its own: on the one hand, Calvinism soon penetrated into the Palatinate; on the other, the Catholic Princes of the south, under the astute direction of the Society of Jesus, crushed out Protestantism by slow and persistent persecution. But the Protestant churches of France, Holland, Scotland, were distinctly Calvinistic. The foreign theologians whom the advisers of Edward VI. invited to their aid, either belonged to the Reformed Church or were largely under its influence: the Marian exiles breathed the air and imbibed the principles of Zürich: while the same spiritual succession has been continued in Puritanism, in English Dissent, in the prevailing character of American religion. I do not mean that there are no traces of Lutheran influence upon the history of the English Church, but they are comparatively few and mostly beneath the surface. It is Calvinism which has furnished the missionary enterprize of Protestantism.

The history of Swiss Protestantism is peculiar in the fact that it follows a double line of development. It boasts two names of the first rank, Zwingli and Calvin: it had two centres, Zürich and Geneva. And it is obvious to remark that one of these is German, the other French; that standing in close relation to the Rhineland, this to France, Italy, Savoy. The movement in Switzerland divides itself into two parts, chronologically as well as geographically. Zwingli was born on the 1st of January, 1484, and was therefore less than two months younger than Luther. He was at work in his own way— a way which I shall try to describe presently—as early as Luther was. The scene of his activity was the northern and German-speaking Cantons of Switzerland, Glarus, Zürich, St. Gall, Schaffhausen, and afterwards Basel and Bern; while many of the free cities on the German side of the frontier, Strasburg, Constanz, Ulm, Augsburg, Reutlingen, adopted with more or less unanimity his opinions on the Eucharist. But when in 1531 he fell in the Battle of Cappel, in which Zürich was defeated by the five Forest Cantons, and his friend and helper Œcolampadius died a few weeks after, it seemed as if the cause of Swiss Protestantism would fall from the comparatively feeble hands of their successors. It was at this moment of crisis that a young refugee from northern France, John Calvin, stepped into the breach and held it victoriously. He was a full generation younger than Zwingli and Luther: born in 1509, the first edition of his "Institution" was published in 1536, five years after Zwingli's death: the period of his theocratic sway at

Geneva extended from 1541 to his death in 1564. Henceforth the little free city on Lake Leman is the centre of Swiss, I had almost said of European Protestantism. Here were gradually developed that scheme of theological thought, that method of ecclesiastical organization, those principles of church discipline, which, in more or less modified form, were destined to so wide a prevalence. There is little direct intellectual relation to be traced between Calvin and Zwingli; indeed, the great systematizer was wont to speak in higher terms of the Saxon Reformer than of his own immediate forerunner. But not the less was his work a continuation of Zwingli's. The leading ideas of Calvinism are ideas which Zwingli had already put forward in a less precise and systematic form. There is a well-marked sense in which the Swiss theology as a whole can be compared and contrasted with the German. It would serve no good purpose were I to attempt in this place to define the shades of difference which in the middle years of the sixteenth century separated the Swiss churches from one another, and all from the Saxon Reformers. They led to many controversies; they are embodied in many confessions. But the final result was that the Calvinistic type of doctrine prevailed, especially in the foreign churches. The Confession of La Rochelle, the Decrees of the Synod of Dordt, the Westminster Confession, have nothing in them which can be called distinctively Zwinglian. But it is at least an allowable speculation that the milder, more rational, humaner spirit of the great Reformer of Zürich reappeared in the Arminian theology which in the seventeenth century was so powerful a factor of European thought.

The doctrine of Zwingli was Lutheranism with a difference. Like Luther, he substituted the authority of the Bible for the authority of the Church; like Luther, he preached justification by faith alone; like Luther, he maintained the true priesthood of every Christian man. Under the influence of the same forces, the Reformation, all over Europe, assumed the same forms: Lutheranism, Zwinglianism, Calvinism, even when the most is made of their differences, resemble each other much more than any of them the faith of the Church to which they were all opposed. And we should miss a significant fact if we failed to note that Zwingli was a religious phenomenon parallel with Luther, but not dependent on him. While the Reformer of Zürich speaks in admiring language of the Reformer of Wittenberg, he will not be called a Lutheran: he drew his doctrine, he said, from the Scriptures; he had preached it before ever he heard the name of Luther:[1] why should he not rather be called by the

---

[1] "Es habend die grossen und gwaltigen diser welt angehebt die leer Christi under dem namen des Luters ze durächten und verhasst ze machen, also dass sy alle leer Christi, von wem sy uf erdrych gepredjget wirt, luterisch nennend. Und ob einer schon des Luters handel nit gelesen hätte, und sich allein des worts gottes hielte, dennoch gdörend sy jn luterisch schelten: der gstalt mir beschicht. Ich hab vor und ee dhein mensch in unserer gegne üts von des Luters namen gwüsst hat, angehebt das evangelion Christi zu predgen im jar MDXVI; also dass ich an dhein canzel gegangen bin, dass ich nit die wort, so am selben morgen in der mess zu eim evangelio gelesen werdend, für mich näme, und die allein us biblischer gschrift usleite." Uslegen und gründ der Schlussreden oder Artikel: Zwingli. Opp., ed. Schuler und Schulthess, I. 253.

"Denn wer hat mich ufgerüft das evangelion ze predgen und einen ganzen evangelisten von einet ze predgen? Hat das der Luter gethon? Nun hab ichs doch angehebt ze predgen, ee ich den Luter je hab ghört

name of Paul or of Christ? At the same time there were differences in the original constitutions of the men, as well as in the training which they had received, which influenced their apprehension and presentation of what was substantially the same group of truths. We can find in Zwingli no trace of the mysticism which Luther had learned from Tauler and the *Theologia Germanica*. There is nothing in his life-history at all answering to the spiritual crisis which drove Luther into the monastery at Erfurt, and there left him to his almost solitary struggle for deliverance and peace. He bears about with him no marks of conflict. He does not, as Luther did, retire into the darkness for a season, coming back trembling and chastened. There is an admirable and cheerful good sense about him, a keen apprehension of the simplicities

nennen, und hab zu sölichem bruch vor 10 jaren angehebt griechisch lernen, damit ich die leer Christi us jrem eignen ursprung erlernen möchte. Wie wol ich das ergriffen hab, lass ich andre um urteilen, jedoch hat mich Luter nit angewisen, dess namen mir noch in zweyen jaren unbekannt ist gsyn, nachdem ich mich allein der biblischen gschrift gehalten hab. Aber die päpstler beladend mich und ander mit sölichen namen us alefanz, wie vor gemeldt, und sprechend: Du müst wol luterisch syn: du predgest doch glych wie der Luter schrybt. Antwurt ich jnen: Ich predige doch glych als wol wie Paulus schrybt: warum nämst du mich nit als mär einen paulischen? Ja, ich predge das wort Christi, warum nämst du mich mit als mär einen christen? Darum ist es nüt dann ein alefanz. Luter ist, als mich bedunkt, so ein treffenlicher stryter Gottes, der da mit so grossem ernst die gschrift durchfündelet, als dheiner in tusand jaren uf erden je gsyn ist (ich acht hie nit, dass mich die päpstler mit jm einen ketzer schelten werdend) und mit dem mannlichen unbewegten gmüt, damit er den papst von Rom angegriffen hat, ist jm dheiner nie glych worden, als lang das papsttum gwäret hat, doch alle andren ungescholten. Wess ist aber sölliche that? gottes oder Luters? Frag den Luter selbs: weiss ich wol, er spricht, gottes. Warum schrybst du denn anderer menschen leer dem Luter zu, so er sy selbs gott zuschrybt?" Ibid, pp. 254, 255.

of piety, a firm grasp of religion on the ethical and practical side. But the sense of mystery does not weigh upon him: the contemplation of divine things neither excites him to paradox nor awakens him to rapture.

The fact is that, much more than Luther, Zwingli was a humanist. First at school, at Basel and at Bern, next for two years at the University of Vienna, then for four years more again at Basel, he gave himself up to the studies of the day. It was at Basel, already a centre of busy literary activity, that he fell under the influence of Thomas Wyttenbach,[1] one of those grave scholars of the Rhineland who found the keenest admiration of ancient literature not inconsistent with an earnest Christian faith, and who directed his pupil to the study of the Scriptures apart from scholastic commentary. At a later period he learned for this purpose first Greek and then Hebrew, copying out with his own hand all the Epistles of Paul, that he might know them through and through. But he was not on this account untrue to his first classical preferences. He learned Valerius Maximus off by heart. Thucydides and Aristotle, Plutarch and Lucian, were familiar to him. He thought Plato had drunk at the fountain of Divine Wisdom; he extolled the piety of Pindar;[2] he gave the great heroes and poets of pagan

---

[1] In connection with the passage above quoted, Zwingli says that it was from Wyttenbach, and not from Luther, that he learned the true character of indulgences: "dann ich vorhin von dem ablass bericht was, wie es ein betrug und farbe wär, us einer disputation die doctor Thomas Wytembach von Biel, min herr und geliebter trüwer leerer, vor etwas zyten ze Basel gehalten hatte, wie wol in minem abwesen." Opp. I. p. 254.

[2] Vid. Zwingli's preface to an edition of Pindar, edited by Cœporinus: Opp. IV. 159.

antiquity a place in the Christian heaven. When Luther, in the first ardour of his Biblical zeal, was forswearing all philosophy, Zwingli was burying himself in the speculations of Pico della Mirandola. In relation to these and similar facts, the word Switzerland is apt to lead us astray. What we have really to do with are not the narrow valleys, the lofty pastures, the sparse population of the Forest Cantons, so much as the wide and fertile Rhineland, a great highway of nations, having on either side a broad belt of cities, free, wealthy, enlightened, the region of central Europe where civilization had reached its highest point, the chosen home of the German revival of letters. Here were the oldest Universities, the most celebrated schools: here had taught the mystics: here the mediæval sects had honeycombed society: here art went hand in hand with letters: here the citizens of many little republics had learned the secret of a life in loosest dependence on the Church. On the other hand, the learning and civilization of Saxony, and of North Germany in general, were of later origin, and had penetrated the popular life less deeply: society was constituted on more aristocratic principles: the prince went for more, the burgher for less. It would be difficult to think of Erasmus at Wittenberg, nor had Luther ever a firm hold on the Rhineland.

In this connection I must point out that the republican constitution of Switzerland gave direction and colour to all Zwingli's activity. He was born only seven years after the Confederates had vindicated their independence in leaving Charles the Bold dead under the walls of Nancy; and the patriotic glow which that marvellous event had kindled in men's hearts must have been fresh

VII. THE REFORMATION IN SWITZERLAND. 233

as he grew up to manhood. But this victory and those which preceded it taught the Swiss a fatal lesson, in making them acquainted with the strength of their right arms and the force of their disciplined onset: they were brave and they were poor: what more natural than that they should sell their swords? So a system grew up pregnant with national demoralization: now the Pope, now the King of France, recruited in the mountains an army of lanzknechts, whose courage decided many a battle: the spoils of war corrupted the simplicity of republican life: rival potentates bound their friends to their cause by pensions and gratuities: foreign and interested influences turned the currents of Confederate politics. Against this system Zwingli set his face at the very beginning of his career. He had been required as army chaplain to attend more than one expedition into Italy; he had been present at the Battle of Marignano, and as patriot and reformer he deplored the evils which he could not choose but see in their true colours. These things provided him with a policy which the forms of republican life enabled him to carry out. He aimed at concentrating the life of the Confederacy within its own frontiers, at detaching its several members from foreign alliances, at raising the chief citizens of its republics to a sense of national dignity, and its incompatibility with royal pensions and mercenary service. His friend and biographer Myconius describes his object as the restoration of ancient virtue.[1] After the Battle of Pavia in 1525,

---

[1] "Congredi cœpit juxta Christi normam cum flagitiis quibusque perniciosissimis, ante omnia tamen cum pensionibus (sic appellamus munera principum quæ certis, milites parundi bellique conficiendi gratia dabantur hominibus) eo quod eas extirpare et patriam reformare ad

in which the Swiss soldiers suffered severely, Zwingli, standing in the Minster pulpit of Zürich, drew from the misfortune a trenchant political moral.[1] He told his hearers that when, of old time, their life had been simple and pious, God had given them great victories, and that unless they returned to their former way, there was nothing before them but Divine wrath and utter ruin. All his life long he had a double purpose, the reformation of the Church and the reformation of the State, which were indeed in his view but one. You may say, if you will, that he took religion more on the social, Luther more on the personal side; that while the latter thought of individual salvation and the soul's union with God, the former had before him the ideal of a well-ordered state, a righteous and peaceful community. But this is the answer to the reproach sometimes directed against Zwingli that he was a politician, and as such degraded religion by bringing it down to the level of earthly intrigue and passion. It is not easy to see what else he could be. He was the first citizen of Zürich, as Calvin afterwards of Geneva; and in that capacity endeavoured to guide the policy of the Republic to the advantage of righteousness and the interests of the Protestant Church. Would he not have been justly open to the imputation of cowardice if, sheltering himself behind his clerical

---

sanctitatem pristinam prorsus haberet in votis." O. Myconius, "De D. Huldrichi Zuinglii vitâ et obitu," prefixed to D. D. Jo. Œcolampadii et Huld. Zuinglii Epistolarum libri quatuor: Basel, 1536. In a similar passage (quoted by Hundeshagen, Theol. Studien u. Kritiken, 1862, p. 665, but which I am unable to verify), Myconius says: "Cœpit igitur huc omne conferre studium, si qua ratione res tam pestilens aboleri, majorum probitas restitui posset."

[1] Bullinger: Reformationsgeschichte, I. 259.

character, he had always worked by others' hands and others' voices, and so thrown on his colleagues the responsibility of measures which were really his own? It is impossible now to say that he did not sometimes succumb to the peculiar temptations of politics, and give himself to widely-reaching schemes of European alliance and attack: let the statesman bear the blame of the statesman's errors. Had Zürich conquered on that field of Cappel where Zwingli left his life, had the tide of Swiss Reformation in consequence risen over the whole land, her Reformer might have escaped heavy censure and much invidious comparison with Luther.

These facts stand in close relation, on the one hand, with the popular character of ecclesiastical government in the Reformed Churches; on the other, with the ethical type of Zwinglian religion. Calvin in Geneva worked under substantially the same political conditions as Zwingli in Zürich, and the result is that the organization of the churches which descend from him is neither Episcopal nor Consistorial, but Presbyterian. To take the instance with which we are most familiar, it is easy to trace a likeness between the Presbyteries, Synods and Assembly of the Church of Scotland, and the greater and lesser Councils of Zürich or Bern, deriving their power from the citizens at large. I do not mean that one set of institutions is the direct copy of the other, or that the Presbyterian organization of the Church does not sincerely claim for itself the authority of scriptural precedent and primitive example. But men are unconsciously swayed by the circumstances in which they have been brought up, and easily find in the Bible what they go there to look for. On the other hand, Zwingli's application of religion to the reform and guidance of the State, partly shows how ethical his conception of it was, partly made it more ethical still. One of the distinctions that may be drawn between Lutheran and Zwinglian religion is, that the former is more than anything else a justification of the sinner effected by faith; the latter, a law of God which asks obedience of all believers. And in accordance with this, we find in Zwingli's works many ethical definitions of religion in which an experienced ear will detect the absence of any Lutheran ring.

"Piety," he says, "is a fact and an experience, not a doctrine or a science."[1] "The Christian life is innocence.... But no soil produces innocence more richly than contempt of oneself."[2] "All the writings of the apostles are full of this opinion, namely that the Christian life is none other than a firm hope in God through Jesus Christ, and an innocent life after Christ's pattern."[3]

There is a little work of Zwingli's, covering only a few pages, "*Quo pacto adolescentes formandi*," addressed to his step-son, Gerald Meyer, in which he depicts a noble ideal of active manliness:

"For God, as He is an Energy, which, itself unmoved, turns and moves all things, will not suffer to be slothful one whose heart He hath drawn to Himself. And the truth of this is approved, not by reasoning, but by experience, for only the faithful know how Christ allows no ease to his own, and how cheerfully and joyfully they engage in toil."[4]

Again

"An ingenuous mind will in the first place think thus with

---

[1] De Vera et falsa religione: Opp. III. 202.
[2] Ibid. III. 285.   [3] Ibid. III. 201.
[4] Quo pacto adolescentes formandi: ibid. IV. 152.

itself, that as Christ offered himself for us and is made ours, so it behoves thee to be offered for all, to think thyself not thine own but another's; for we are not born that we may live to ourselves, but that we may be all things to all men. These things alone, justice, fidelity, constancy, will it meditate from its tender years, in what things it may profit the Christian commonwealth, in what its native country, in what all mankind, one by one. Those are languid minds which look only to the attainment of a quiet life; nor are they so like God as those who study, even at their own risk, to do good to all."[1]

And once more:

"It is the part of a Christian man not to talk magnificently of doctrines, but always, with God, to do great and hard things."[2]

In Zwingli's view, the church and the state were practically one body under different aspects. How the realization of this idea is facilitated by republican institutions is clear at first sight. In Germany it was a necessity of the case that the subject should follow the religion of his ruler: but for the succession of three devoutly Protestant Electors, the Reformation could not have subsisted in Saxony. When Duke Henry succeeded Duke George, his people abandoned Catholicism at once: with the best will in the world, Protestantism was unable to maintain itself in Austria and Bavaria. But in Zürich, in Basel, in Bern, the church and the state were administered through the same institutions by the same persons. Each step in the process of revolt against Catholicism, of the adoption of Protestantism, was marked by a public debate, and a solemn decision arrived at by the authorities of the city. The change in religion, with all

---

[1] Quo pacto adolescentes formandi: Opp. IV. 155.
[2] Ibid. IV. 158.

that it involved, was the will of the people, and therefore held to be binding upon the people, in the same way as any regularly enacted law, any legally concluded alliance. It is in this light that we have to look at that persecution of Anabaptists which throws a dark shadow upon this phase of religious administration. They were held to be offenders against the expressed will of the commonwealth, and therefore justly liable to be treated like any other criminals. They were fined, they were banished, they were imprisoned; and it was only upon their repeated and impenitent obstinacy that at least some of their leaders were made to pay the forfeit of their lives. And from the same idea of the identity of church and state follows that conception of ecclesiastical discipline as a thing to be enforced by the secular arm, which was afterwards worked out with such relentless logic by Calvin in Geneva. Here, as in so many instances more, the beginnings of Calvinism are to be traced back to Zwingli. If the citizens of a particular state are also members of the church of Christ, what more natural and expedient than that the laws of the church should be enforced in the same way and by the same means as the laws of the state? Nor if it is true that the prosperity of the state is built upon the righteousness of the people, is the attainment of the political, possible except in the attainment of the moral and religious ideal. In this connection, the Proclamation which was issued on the 26th of March, 1530, by the Burgomaster, in conjunction with the greater and lesser Councils of the city of Zürich, is a curious and significant document.[1] It prescribes that all

---

[1] Bullinger: Reformationsgeschichte, II. 277.

VII. THE REFORMATION IN SWITZERLAND. 239

the people shall go to church, remain there till the sermon is over, and refrain from talking against the preacher. The number of taverns is to be diminished. All kinds of games—not cards and dice only, but others which lead less directly to gambling—are forbidden. Profane swearing is made an offence against the law. All these moral delinquencies are punished by fines of greater or less amount. In some cases the culprits are to be excluded from their guild, or forbidden the exercise of their trade or calling within the city. These things, as we shall presently see, were carried much further in Geneva, but the principle of Calvinistic discipline is already conceded in Zürich.

Zwingli adopted to the full the Reformation principle of the authority of Scripture. In the public disputations or conferences, which were the republican way of settling all controversies approved at Zürich, the Bible was solemnly put forward as the rule of faith and practice. Each of these disputations, as, for instance, that in which Zwingli defended his doctrine against the Pope's Vicar,[1] those against the Anabaptists,[2] that which secured the alliance of Bern,[3] was therefore a public re-assertion of this fundamental principle. But a distinction has been drawn between Luther's attitude to Scripture and Zwingli's, which, if not easy to support by specific quotations from their writings, is, I think, a legitimate deduction from their practice. Luther, it is said, was willing to abide by any existing doctrine or usage which he did not find expressly forbidden in Scripture, while Zwingli

---

[1] January 29, 1523.   [2] January 17, March 20, 1525.
[3] January 6, 1528.

demanded distinct warrant of Scripture for whatever he was willing to allow. It is easy to see that the latter rule is of much more sweeping application than the former, and to trace to its operation the more rigid severity of worship in the Reformed than in the Lutheran Church. But if Zwingli was more precise than Luther in bringing all matters of faith and practice to the test of Scripture, he also took a wider view of what Scripture was. He was more Biblical than Pauline. While in the main agreeing with Luther in his conception of spiritual religion, he did not so exclusively take his gospel from the Pauline Epistles and then read it into the whole Bible. He had a scheme of scriptural instruction, which he explains more than once, as if its use were habitual to him.[1] It began with the Gospel of Matthew, which was succeeded first by the Acts of the Apostles and then by the two letters to Timothy. Only when he had laid this foundation of gospel teaching and primitive practice, did he proceed to explain the Epistle to the Galatians, followed by the Epistles of Peter and that to the Hebrews. It is significant that the Epistle to the Romans finds no place in this series. This method, which makes a selection from the New Testament in which most of the varied elements of its teaching are fairly represented, would evidently lead to a different result than that which begins and almost ends with Paul.

The religious faith which Zwingli was engaged in establishing—and it must not be forgotten that we are criticising an incomplete and violently interrupted work—

---

[1] Apologeticus Archeteles adpellatus: Opp. III. 48. Conf. I. 151, 485, for slightly differing forms of the same statement.

has frequently been charged with containing a rationalizing element. If the word rationalism be used in the definite sense now attached to it, this is no more true of Zwinglianism than of the other great presentations of Reformation theology. Zwingli neither declaims against reason like Luther, nor, like Luther, erects his own theological preferences, his own untaught insight, into a rule of Biblical criticism. What he might have done had he lived longer, we cannot tell; but as a fact he did not call in the aid of human reason, as did Calvin, to pour the fluid and indeterminate elements of his thought into the rigid mould of a system. But at the same time there is a breezy atmosphere of good sense about his religion. It was meant for every-day use among the affairs of men. Its ultimate object was practical: if it aspired to soar on wings of faith into the heavenly abyss of the Divine decrees, it always came back to earth with a message of innocence and purity and justice between man and man. Zwingli's sympathy with Erasmus and the scholars of the Rhineland, which never failed him, both prevented him from becoming narrowly ecclesiastical and helped to keep him human. His conception of baptism, as a pledge of fidelity on the part of the recipient rather than as a mystical channel of grace—that explanation, in the words of institution, of "is" by "signifies," which so vexed the soul of Luther—his designation of original sin as a disease (*morbus*) rather than as an offence (*peccatum*)—his substitution of a mere figure of rhetoric for the mysterious transference of qualities from the divine to the human nature of Christ, which the Lutherans knew as the *communicatio idiomatum*—are all instances of what we may call his religious common sense. To this answered the character of the man, strong, kindly, sincere. He was of untiring energy both in study and in affairs, taking delight in simple pleasures, a musician like Luther, and a performer upon several instruments.[1] His disposition and habits were social: his campaigns, no less than his active participation in politics, had given him a large knowledge of men: he mingled with the citizens in their guilds, with the peasants at their merry-makings, and had an acceptable word for all. What would have been the course of events had he lived— whether he would have been drawn more and more into the whirlpool of Confederate or European politics—whether he would have thrown his thought into a more systematic form, or worked out his principles of faith to further consequences—who can say? When Œcolampadius died, no man of originating power was left to take Zwingli's place: Bullinger, Myconius, Leo Jud, fell naturally into the second rank; and after a few years of wrangling controversy on their part, with Geneva on the one side, with Germany on the other, it was clearly seen that the task of moulding and guiding Swiss Protestantism henceforth belonged to Calvin.[2]

It is, however, impossible to understand Calvin's place and work in the church, until we clearly apprehend that he belongs to a later stage in the development of the Reformation than Luther and Zwingli. The period of

[1] Bullinger: Reformationsgeschichte, I. 31.

[2] I may refer here to an excellent essay in the Theologische Studien und Kritiken for 1862, p. 631, by Hundeshagen, "Zur Charakteristik Ulrich Zwingli's und seines Reformationswerkes unter Vergleichung mit Luther und Calvin." Another essay in the same periodical, to which I am under obligation throughout this Lecture, is one by Ullmann, "Zur Charakteristik der Reformirten Kirche," 1843, p. 749.

his commanding influence in Geneva stretches from 1541 to his death in 1564. The epoch of creative religious thought is now past. But the process of doctrinal development is still going on: systems are being built up and shaped into symmetry: the churches are only just entering upon a period of arid and minute and bitter controversy. The conflict with Rome is without remedy or recall, and the line of battle, from which after ages have found it difficult to depart, is determined. Nor is the Reformation any longer a merely national thing, Saxon or Swiss: in France, in Holland, in England, in Scotland, in the Northern kingdoms, everywhere indeed, the struggle is going on with more or less violence, and the time is rapidly coming at which Europe will find itself divided into two camps, a Protestant and a Catholic, owning the force of neither alliances nor enmities but such as spring from this distinction. Think now of the movements and changes of fortune in the religious world upon which Calvin looked out from his fortress under the shadow of the Alps! The twenty-three years of his rule at Geneva comprehended in Germany the death of Luther, the Schmalkaldic War, the defeat of Mühlberg, the melancholy period of the Interim, the abdication of Charles V., and the settlement of Passau. Just as it closed, Philip II. and the Duchess Margaret were making ready for Alva in the Netherlands; while in Scotland, Mary Stuart was contending with John Knox, and in all the insolence of power and beauty preparing the tragedy of her own downfall. During these years the first generation of Huguenots in France are maintaining an unequal fight with Catharine de Medici and the Guises, and the day of St. Bartholomew is soon to follow. They cover in English history almost exactly the interval between the Six Articles of Henry VIII. and the Thirty-nine of Elizabeth: what a time of hope, and feverish expectation, and wild terror, and good cheer renewed, lies between! The Council of Trent met for the first time in 1545, and was finally dissolved in December, 1563: to it, the Church of Geneva and the "Institution of the Christian Religion" were the most resolute and the most complete answer of the Reformation. When Calvin's theocratic rule began, Paul III., a Farnese, the last of the old line of Popes who founded families and clutched their own advantage in utter disregard of the interests of Christendom, sat in the fisherman's chair: when it ended, Pius IV. had succeeded Paul IV., both, by comparison, grave and austere Pontiffs, the Inquisition had been re-founded, and the Counter Reformation had begun. For already in 1540, Paul III. had sanctioned the incorporation of the Society of Jesus; and in command of these new and splendid soldiers of the faith, the Church of Rome, stunned and perplexed for the moment by the brilliant onset of Luther, had recovered her courage and advanced once more to the attack.

During these years, then, Calvin gradually grew to the height of a commanding figure in Europe. He is the only one of the great Reformers who can justly be called international. Though he never re-entered France after his first flight from it, he is the director of the French Reformation, dictating, as it were, to the Huguenots, both their theology and their church government. During the reign of Edward VI. he is the adviser to whom Somerset and Cranmer listen with the deepest respect, while it is from Geneva that John Knox goes out to mould and to teach Scotland. Among the Swiss Reformers he is something more than *primus inter pares*: when Luther is gone, and Melancthon is more and more the mark for the rage of theologians, he represents the Reformation in the eye of Pope and Emperor. And I do not think that we shall do him justice unless we look upon Geneva as a fortified post of the Reform, to be held against all comers, and within whose walls, always open to attack, the sternest discipline is necessary. When Calvin took it and made it his own, it was just struggling into independent political life. Originally a free city, subject to its Bishop, it had fallen under the dominating influence of the House of Savoy, which it shook off only after many struggles. The Reformation introduced a new line of division among its citizens: the partizans of Genevese independence were mostly Protestant; the friends of Savoy clung to the old faith; while there were many who, without any faith at all, disliked the new austerity of manners, the stern restraint of license. Calvin failed in his first attempt to impose his theocracy on the mixed and mobile population of Geneva: I am not sure that if he had had to deal with it alone, he would ever have succeeded. But Geneva soon became a city of refuge. From France especially, and from Italy, men fled for their lives to this secure haven, where they could worship God in their own way (so long as it happened to be Calvin's way too), and bring up their children in the saving knowledge of the gospel. And these men naturally gathered round Calvin, and upheld him in all his measures. His convictions were their convictions, and they found it no hardship to submit to his ecclesiastical rule, however sharp it might seem to be to those who remembered and loved the easy days of old. Between them, they made Geneva at once a city of God after their own pattern, and a frontier fortress of the Reformation. I suppose that, little by little, cruel persecution and stern, steady repression crushed out the rebellious elements of Genevese life: the partizans of the old régime; the sect of the Libertines, in whom wild Pantheistic speculation is said to have undermined all moral conviction; the genuine lovers of freedom, who rebelled against the tyranny of preachers and an inquisition disguised under the name and forms of a consistory. But whatever Geneva became, Calvin must have the credit or the shame of it. It is a mistake to suppose, as some seem to do, that he held the reins of power in his own hands and openly wielded the authority of a dictator. It is equally a mistake to attempt to lift from his shoulders the responsibility of what was done at Geneva, by pointing to the civil institutions of the place. His was the kind of influence, the most powerful, the most pervading of all, which bends independent minds to itself, and works by the hands of others. There were councils of various kinds, syndics, a consistory; but from 1541 to 1564, Geneva was John Calvin.

Of Calvin as a systematizing theologian I shall have to speak at another time: we are concerned with him now as the founder and governor of a church. It has been said, with as much truth as such antitheses usually contain, that Catholicism is a religion of priests, Lutheranism of theologians, Calvinism of the believing congregation. And it is obvious at first sight that Calvin availed himself of the republican constitution of Geneva to establish a religious community as distinct in its outline, as definite in its faith, as rigid in its administration, as the Papal system itself had been in its palmiest days. It is not, with Luther, "the freedom of the Christian man" on which he insists; much more he delights to magnify the office and authority of the church. With him, the individual depends on the community; the unit is part of a well-ordered whole. Have not the following words, which stand at the beginning of his exposition of the theory of the church, more of a Catholic than a Protestant sound?[1]

"But because our rudeness and slothfulness, yea, and vanity of wit, do need outward helps, whereby faith in us may both be engendered and grow and increase in proceeding towards the mark whereunto it tendeth, God hath also added them thereby to provide for our weakness. And that the preaching of the gospel might flourish, He hath left this treasure with the church. He hath appointed pastors and teachers, by whose merits He might teach them that be His: He hath furnished them with authority: finally, He hath left nothing undone that might avail to the holy consent of faith and right order. . . . . I will begin at the church, into whose bosom God will have His children to be gathered together, not only that they should by her help and ministry be nourished while they are infants and young children, but also be ruled by her motherly care till they grow to riper age and at length come to the mark of faith. For it is not lawful that those things be severed which God hath conjoined; that to whom He is a Father, the church be also their mother; and *that*, not only under the Law, but also since the coming of Christ, as Paul witnesseth, which teacheth that we are the children of the new and heavenly Hierusalem."

This is a very different tone from that of the Saxon Reformers, who were satisfied with an ecclesiastical con-

---

[1] Instit. Christ. Rel. IV. 1. I have adopted Norton's translation.

stitution which had shaped itself according to circumstances, or even of Hooker, who strove to penetrate, and as it were to interpret by his own theory, one which had just weathered the storm of reformation. It is the utterance of the self-confident legislator who rejoices to be able to go back to first principles and to apply them upon new ground. And not only was Calvin's theory of the relation between church and state definite enough, but he was prepared to carry it out by the use of a discipline which did not yield for weight and edge to any weapon that Catholic Bishop or Inquisitor ever wielded.

Discipline is the constant dream of churchmen of every kind. Give them but power enough, they say, and they will cleanse the church of all heresies and unfaithfulnesses, transforming her into the likeness of the pure Bride of Christ, without blemish and without taint. In their rage against error, they forget the wheat and the tares that are to grow together till the final harvest. In their anger against open manifestations of vice, they overlook the subtler sins which no inquisition can detect, which no severity can cast out, but which not the less canker the Christian life at its core. But Europe, in the sixteenth century, had had enough of discipline as administered by clerics; and when the whole system by whose terrors it had been enforced crumbled into ruins, there was no basis on which to erect another. Princes would not, and churchmen could not, take up again the rod that had fallen from Papal hands. Error indeed might be repressed, but vice was perforce left to itself. So deeply, however, is this passion for moral judgment engrained in the hearts of theologians, that I doubt not Luther and Melancthon would gladly have set up, if they could, a discipline analogous to that of Rome, if perchance milder: fortunately for themselves and the church, they were compelled to rely upon moral and religious influence alone. Still the Reformation had everywhere to contend against a relaxation of morals which its enemies put down to its own account, which its friends declared to be a legacy of the past: perhaps in Geneva, with its mixed population, with its southern blood, with the turbulence of its recent history, things were worse than elsewhere. However this may have been, reformation of morals was henceforth a matter of life and death struggle between the Genevese and their new pastor. He had come to Geneva for the first time in 1536, and had been expelled from it, on this very quarrel, in 1538: when in 1541 he was recalled, it was on the understanding that the life of the city was to be controlled and organized as he would have it.

I cannot here enter into the particulars of the ecclesiastical constitution which Calvin established, or define with accuracy the different functions of the Councils and the Consistory. He calmly lays it down in the "Institution" that the church knows of no punishment save exclusion from the Lord's Supper. "For the church hath not the power of the sword to punish or restrain, no empire to command, no prison, no other pains which the magistrate is wont to lay upon men."[1] But what if the state, penetrated through and through with the spirit of the church, acts upon its information, makes crimes of its offences, and is prompt to inflict the severest punishments upon its criminals? Two things are especially to be noticed

---

[1] Instit. Christ. Rel. IV. 11, § 3.

in the holy reign of terror which Calvin established and left behind him as a legacy to Geneva: first, the vast extension given to the idea of crime, and next, the worse than Draconian severity of the punishments inflicted. Adultery was repeatedly punished with death. A child was beheaded for having struck father and mother. Banishment, imprisonment, in some cases drowning, were penalties inflicted on unchastity. To sing or even to have in one's possession lewd songs was a crime: to laugh at Calvin's sermons, or to have spoken hot words of him in the street, was a crime: to wear clothes of forbidden stuff or make was a crime: to give a feast to too many guests or of too many dishes was a crime: to dance at a wedding was a crime:—to all of which, with many others of like sort, appropriate punishments were meted out. Everybody was obliged to attend public worship: everybody was required to partake of the Lord's Supper: no sick man might lie in bed for three days without sending for the minister of the parish. Do not let it be thought that these penalties were of infrequent enforcement, unwelcome breaks in a smooth current of civic life: in the years 1558 and 1559 alone, there were in the little city four hundred and fourteen of such prosecutions.[1] Now and then, as might be expected, there

---

[1] I lay no stress upon the fact that the registers of the city of Geneva show that within the space of sixty years a hundred and fifty poor wretches were burned for witchcraft; that the application of the torture was an incident of almost all criminal trials; that thirty-one persons were burned at one time for the fantastic offence of spreading the plague. These cruelties, these popular terrors, were common to all Europe, and cannot be specially laid to the charge of either Calvin or Geneva. Yet they belong to the delineation of this City of God,

was a sharp spasm of rebellion against so grinding a tyranny. The Libertines were not wholly suppressed. The old spirit of Genevese freedom was not quite dead. Some man, or as often some woman, was goaded into open revolt, which almost inevitably took such a form as gave a plausible pretext for fresh severity on the part of the guardians of faith and order. Then the prison, the pillory, the scaffold, did their work, and the reign of repressive holiness was resumed.

Did this method of church government succeed or fail? This question will be answered differently according to the side from which it is approached. It must not be forgotten that its story has been chiefly told by Calvin and his friends; and, in particular, that his book against the Libertines is still quoted as the best, and indeed almost the only authority for their false and immoral doctrines. But it is never safe to accept against heretics the testimony of the orthodox doctor who glories in having put them down: heresy, in the common judgment, always involves a taint of immorality, and is only too easily associated with it. The Genevese must have been either more or less than human if the rigid and minute discipline of the Consistory had not now driven sin beneath the surface, and again excited it to bravado: an over-strained severity of criminal jurisprudence is quite as much provocative as remedial. In opposition to the writers who hold up the Geneva of Calvin and Beza as a model community, there are others who, relying on the irrefragable evidence of public records, assert that at no period was its immorality

---

upon which so much strange admiration has been spent, and must be suffered to remain and to darken the picture.

fouler or more deeply seated than when it was covered over with the thickest varnish of religious observance.[1] On the other hand, there can be no doubt that in some respects Calvin largely succeeded in reaching his own ideal. Geneva was to all external appearance sound in the faith. The majority of the inhabitants submitted willingly to the new discipline, while those who hated it maintained, with occasional outbreaks, a sullen silence. Refugees, if only they reached the standard of Genevese orthodoxy, were safe beneath the shelter of the city walls. A flourishing University became the centre from which the Calvinistic theology was diffused. Geneva was, as it were, the High Change of Protestant thought and action: hither came missionaries to be instructed and inspired: hence they issued, to preach all over Europe the gospel of the Divine decrees. But in spite of the admiration which this polity still continues to excite in some minds, we must pronounce the Geneva which Calvin created but a poor and mechanical imitation of the City

---

[1] "Je montrerois à ceux qui s'imaginent que Calvin n'a fait que du bien, nos régistres couverts d'inscriptions d'enfans illégitimes—on en exposait dans tous les coins de la ville et de la campagne,—des procès hideux d'obscénités, des testamens, où les pères et mères accusent leurs enfans non pas d'erreurs seulement, mais des crimes—des transactions par devant notaire entre des demoiselles et leurs amans, qui leur donnoient en présence de leurs parens de quoi élever leurs bâtards, des multitudes de mariages forcés ou les délinquans étoient conduits de la prison au temple, des mères qui abandonnoient leurs enfans à l'hôpital pendant qu'elles vivoient dans l'abondance avec leur second mari, des liasses de procès entre frères, des tas des dénonciations secrètes, des hommes et femmes brûlés par sortilège—sentences de mort en effrayable quantité. Tout cela parmi la génération nourrie de la manne mystique de Calvin." Galiffe: Notices généalogiques sur les familles Genevoises; quoted by Henry, Leben Calvin's, II. 78.

of God. The true holiness is that which men live and grow into in the strength of high principles and noble affections, not that which is bolstered up by regulations and protected by penalties. I do not even discuss the question whether the ideal of life was in itself a lofty one: the polity by which it was sought to be promoted condemns itself.

Calvin's principles of church government led straight to persecution. In this respect he was neither before nor behind his age: he differed from other Reformers, if at all, in the calm and logical outspokenness with which he defended his position. If sins and crimes are obnoxious to the same kind of judgment—if adultery is punishable with death, reading loose books with imprisonment, neglect of divine ordinances with a fine—why should not heresy, the immoral character of which orthodoxy is always ready to assume, receive the same treatment? Who can be a greater offender in a theocratic state than the heresiarch who is active in the propagation of his soul-destroying errors? Then there is that distinction between heresy and blasphemy of which I have already spoken, and the duty, as to the obligation of which Calvin never entertained a doubt, of being jealous for the honour of God. The chief victims of this theory of upholding religious truth and repressing religious error were Gruet and Servetus. No doubt Gruet was a scoffing unbeliever of a very coarse type; but the evidence on which this fact rests was not discovered till three years after long torture had crushed out of him a confession which led him to the scaffold:[1] while the crime for which he actually

---

[1] Gruet was executed in July, 1547: it was not until April, 1550, that a MS. book of his handwriting was discovered under the roof of

suffered was that of having affixed to Calvin's pulpit at St. Peter's a scurrilous and threatening placard. The case of Servetus I shall not re-open. All the world, except the few persons who are determined to clear Calvin's fame by any means, is agreed about it. His only defence lies in the proof afforded by the approval of Melancthon and the Swiss churches, that the act was not out of accord with the spirit of the age. He wanted to give the world at large, and the Papacy in especial, an assurance of the fact that such heresy as that of Servetus was no more tolerable in Geneva than in Rome, and bade men read his witness in the smoke that went up to heaven from the faggots of Champmel. Two damning facts, neither of which can be denied or explained away, blacken the deed with special infamy: first, that terrible phrase in Calvin's letter to Farel of February, 1546, seven years before its threat was fulfilled, "*nam si venerit, modo valeat mea auctoritas, vivum exire nunquam patiar;*" and next, that Servetus was only a stranger in Geneva, taking it as one temporary resting-place on his flight into Italy, over whom therefore neither Consistory nor Council had any pretence of jurisdiction. But the lurid light which surrounds the death of Servetus, and the controversy which it continues to excite, have done much to draw away attention from the fact that it was only part of a system and the logical outcome of a theory. In a long letter to the Protector Somerset, written in the name and with assumption of the authority of Christ, Calvin

---

his house, severely characterized by Calvin in a still extant document, and ordered to be burned by the Syndics. Henry: Leben Calvin's, II. 439 et seq.; Beilage 16, p. 120.

lays down with great distinctness the duty of repressing heresy by force:[1]

"From what I understand, my Lord, you have two kinds of rebels who have risen up against the King and the State of the realm. The one are fantastic people, who under colour of the gospel would cast all into confusion; the other, obstinate adherents to the superstitions of the Roman Antichrist. Both alike well deserve to be repressed by the sword which is committed to you, seeing that they attack not the King only, but God who has seated him upon the throne, and has entrusted to you the protection as well of his person as of his majesty."

In the latter part of the same letter, the Protector is exhorted for the honour of God "to punish the crimes which men are not accustomed to hold in much account," adultery, unchastity, blasphemy, drunkenness. The state, however theoretically independent of or even superior to the church, is practically to be its instrument in enforcing a scheme of doctrine, in carrying out a method of polity, which are assumed to be in complete accordance with the mind and purpose of God.

To turn to considerations of a more general kind, the Calvinistic type of theology differs from the Lutheran, not so much in the doctrines which it includes, as in the relative importance which it gives to such as are common to both. Its centre of gravity is not the same. Both are Augustinian in their origin and essence: both assume the absolute foreknowledge and determining power of God, the servitude of the human will, the corruption and incapacity of man's nature. But while Lutheranism crystallizes round the idea of justification by faith, and

---

[1] The letter is dated October 22, 1548. Henry: Leben Calvin's, II.; Beilage 4, p. 26 et seq.

is, so to speak, anthropological, Calvinism, beginning and ending with the supremacy of God, is theological. Another side of this distinction has been expressed in the statement, that while Lutheranism chiefly opposed itself to the Judaizing element in the Papal system by cutting at the root of ceremonial piety, Calvinism stood in stronger contrast to its Paganism by merging all forms of idolatry in the awe of the Supreme. In the one, the main thing is the sinner's personal relation to Christ, his appropriation of the Saviour's work, his resurrection from sin and death to holiness and life; in the other, the majesty of God, who is over all and in all, and the awful omnipotence of the Divine decree fixing the unalterable succession of events, and rigidly determining the eternal fate of men from a period before time was. And when we come to look a little more closely at the constituents of Calvinistic theology, we see how this master-thought runs through it all. In the process of salvation, it at once shuts out all co-operation of the human will, and assures the final perseverance of the elect: shall not God begin, round off, complete His own work? We have no doctrine here of a *communicatio idiomatum:* the attributes of the deity of Christ cannot be transferred to his manhood. The sacraments may be signs or seals or what you will; a veil of words may be drawn over the too naked simplicity of the Zwinglian conception; but no true Calvinist could admit an actual presence of the Living God under the species of bread and wine. To the same source may be traced the bareness of Calvinistic worship and its unwillingness to charm the soul through the senses: God, the Omnipotent and the Omnipresent, will choose and occupy and mould His own, without the vain help of audible and visible things. The one thought of God dominates, almost engulfs, all others; and it is a God whose will binds the world and men in bonds of adamant.

It would seem at first sight as if such a conception of religion must be fatal to morals. If the essence of Calvinism be, as John Wesley put it, that the elect shall be saved, do what they will, and the reprobate damned, do what they can, what motive is left for self-restraint in the one, for effort in the other? In what does the convinced Calvinist differ from the Moslem fatalist who resigns himself with *Allah Ackbar*, to be a counter in the hands of Omnipotence? Yet so far is Calvinism from producing slackness of will and feebleness of character, that Calvinists have been among the most strenuous of men: Calvin himself, John Knox, William of Nassau, Oliver Cromwell. The secret lies in that communication between earth and heaven for which Mohammedanism makes no provision, except in the case of the world's great prophets. No true Calvinist, save one perhaps here and there, ever believes that he is finally reprobate: as in the case of Cowper, "that way madness lies:" on the contrary, he feels himself to be an instrument of the Omnipotent Will, and bends to whatever toil he undertakes in the unshakable conviction that he is on the side of God. How copious a spring of energy lies in this thought I need not tell you; nor is it without a power of moral consecration too. It is customary to say that Calvinism is a more distinctively ethical form of religion than Lutheranism: that while the latter represents it as a grace that is imparted, the former holds it up as a law to be obeyed. But does not the ethical efficacy of Calvinism take a direction of its own, and act within limits? There are specific moral dangers in the absolute identification of God's will with our own conception of it, from which, it seems to me, neither Calvin nor some of the most eminent of his followers have been able to escape. Nothing is more difficult than to be jealous for the Divine honour and to abate all personal pretension. To hate the enemies of God and to love one's own, are practically incompatible precepts.

The relations of Calvinist and Lutheran theology to the Bible are in theory the same. Luther and Calvin alike appealed from the authority of Pope, Church, Schoolmen, Tradition, to that of the Scriptures themselves. The Genevese Reformer, as I have already pointed out, true to his systematizing instinct, developed the theory of Biblical authority into a somewhat more definite form; but in the general both stand upon the same ground. Yet Calvin, it must be confessed, was the more consistent scripturalist of the two. He was a not less industrious expositor of Scripture than Luther, and probably more acute and systematic; while the literary and theological difficulties which the latter found in the Bible, and cut asunder rather than solved by his trenchant good sense, did not trouble him. He believed that all Scripture was written under the direct dictation of the Holy Spirit, and was to be received by the church as a living voice from heaven. So given to men, it could not possibly contain discrepancy or contradiction: to question its genuineness, was simple rebellion against God. Calvin went to the New Testament for his theory of church government, and claimed a Divine sanction for Presbyterianism; while Luther in setting up his Consistories did not look beyond the practical necessities of the case and the prejudices of his pious Electors. And, like Zwingli, Calvin took the Bible much more as a whole than Luther did. He was full of a Hebrew spirit: he went back willingly to Jewish precedents, and used them to modify the too great humanity of the gospel. The apologists for some of his questionable actions defend him on this line: "Whoso ventures to judge him," says a late biographer, "judges the Hebrew Prophets too." When the Duchess Réné of Ferrara alleges that the example of David in hating his enemies is not applicable to those who live under the milder dispensation of the gospel, he sternly replies[1] that "such a gloss would upset all Scripture," and alleges that the Holy Ghost has in this respect set David before us as a pattern. "And, in fact," so he continues, "it is declared to us that in this ardour he is the type of our Lord Jesus Christ. Now, if we assume to surpass in sweetness and humanity him who is the fountain of piety and compassion, woe be unto us!" What of this kind the English Puritans thought and said is known to all, and how in the seventeenth century the Old Testament, the Mosaic legislation, the Jewish kingdom and church, assumed a place in religious thought and practice to which the earlier history of Christianity offers little that is like. This particular phase of Calvinistic thought has in the main passed away; nor do fanatical politicians or wild social reformers now, as under the Commonwealth, borrow the language of the Old Testament. But Calvin's way of looking at Scripture still survives in much uncritical

---

[1] Henry: Calvin's Leben, I. 452, 453.

apprehension of the relation between the Old Testament and the New, and a method of exposition which takes little account of differences of age and authorship.

To conclude: Calvinism is the last word of what may be called the orthodox Protestant Reformation. It stands further from Rome than Lutheranism, and is at the same time a compacter system, a more reasoned protest, a more pronounced antithesis. In its appeal to the authority of Scripture over the whole ground of faith and practice, it breaks more decisively with tradition. Whatever we may think of Calvin's attempt to find a middle place between Luther and Zwingli for his doctrine of sacraments, Calvinistic, in a very different way from Lutheran churches, have always been opposed to Rome in that great and critical controversy. Partly in the line of natural development, partly in that of reaction, the process of doctrinal decay in the Reformed Church has often led to rationalism. Calvinism is an intellectual system, proceeding by logical method from premiss to conclusion, having all its parts duly subordinated to the whole, and held together by the strongest argumentative cement. But when thought is once encouraged to activity, who shall prescribe limits? And, on the other hand, there are demands upon belief of such a kind as to provoke unqualified rejection, if they do not meet with submissive assent. From the beginning, Calvinism has been at the opposite pole from Rome in the application of art to the service of religion: it rejects all symbolism, it sets up no cross, it lights no candles, it has inspired no architecture, it distrusts even music. Lutheran hymnology began with Luther, and from the first put forth a strong and sweet luxuriance; but it was only in the eighteenth century that Calvinism learned how to write hymns, the help of which Scottish piety does not even yet value. But while it is almost Papal in its theory of the church, and would, if it could, exercise as rigid a rule as Rome over men's minds and actions, it stands in long historical opposition to Papal politics. "No Bishop, no King,"[1] said James I. at the Hampton Court Conference; and, on the other hand, your true Calvinist is always on the side of freedom and national independence. He has not been as tender of others' rights as strenuous to maintain his own: the children of the Dutchmen who had withstood Alva, exiled the Remonstrants: the Puritans, who had fled for freedom of worship to New England, banished Baptists and branded Quakers. But in the incidental mention of these names, I have done enough to vindicate for Calvinism an honourable place in history. It was the form of faith in the strength of which the Dutch Republic was sustained and the American Republic was founded: to propagate which, Tyndale gave to the English people the Bible in their own tongue, and with it his life: which formed the royal intellect of Cromwell, and inspired the majestic verse of Milton. Shall I say more, or is not this enough?

---

[1] Fuller: Church History of Britain, III. 180.

Lecture VIII.

THE RISE OF PROTESTANT SCHOLASTICISM.

Church systems which formally reject the use of reason are nevertheless moulded and developed by rational processes; nor is it in the power of authority either to display or to defend itself. Its advocates may go so far as to admit, first, that the principle itself requires intellectual justification, and next, that the claims of rival authorities can be settled only by an appeal to reason. But this by no means exhausts the facts of the case. The system which imposes itself as authoritative, either on the bare word of a Church or its own alleged accord with Scripture, still requires and always receives exposition, co-ordination, development; and these are rational processes conducted under rational rules. This is not less true of Catholic than of Protestant systems. The scholastic theology—the form of Christianity universally accepted in the middle ages—was, if not rationalistic in the sense in which we now use the word, at least a result of the application of reason to religion. A series of very able and acute thinkers took up theology at the point at which the Fathers had left it, and applied themselves through many centuries to the task of moulding it into a complete system of belief. Their materials were of three kinds—Scripture, Tradition, the writings of the Fathers—all accepted, though as having different degrees of certitude, on the authority of the Church. Their object was to show that the Christian religion, thus conceived, was identical with the results of sound knowledge and right thinking; in other words, to make religion philosophical, and philosophy religious. And the philosophical method by which they sought to execute their task was the Aristotelian dialectic. Plato, and still more some of the later masters of Greek speculation, made a not unimportant contribution to the matter of scholastic thought, but its form was certainly Aristotelian. To the syllogistic method of the Schoolmen much exception has been taken: they used it with tiresome persistence: it led by necessary process to much unprofitable debate, to many needless distinctions, to many oppositions of words which had little or no counterpart in the reality of things. But when all these defects have been fully taken account of, the scholastic theology must be recognized as a masterpiece of the systematizing intellect. It subjected its materials to no critical analysis. It combined and developed them according to rules of its own. But admit its premisses and allow its method, and the force of its conclusions is very difficult to evade. The reasoning powers of the human mind are substantially the same in one century as in another: the difference in the worth and permanence of the results which they attain, chiefly depends upon the matter in which they work. To reason upon assumptions, ends in scholasticism; to reason upon ascertained facts, issues in science.

It was against Catholic scholasticism, pleading at once and wielding the authority of the Church, with its system of dogma equally symmetrical and minute, covering the whole ground of speculation, yet with a constant practical reference to the supremacy of the Pope and the maintenance of the Roman polity, that Luther rebelled. Nor can he be said to have been ever personally unfaithful to the spirit of that rebellion. He was not the creed-maker of the Reformation. He left to Melancthon and Calvin the work of consolidating the new truth into a system. His favourite method was that of Biblical translation and exposition. There were certain points of Christian doctrine on which he laid the greatest stress—the Real Presence in the Eucharist, justification by faith alone, the true priesthood of every believer; but there were others, as, for instance, the Trinity, and all metaphysical questions as to the nature of God, on which he accepted the statements of the creeds, unless when he preferred even to these the statements of Scripture. Nevertheless, the course of events and the intellectual habit of the time, coupled with the view entertained by the Reformers as to the authority of Scripture, gradually led to the formation of a Protestant scholasticism, the effects of which we have not wholly thrown off even yet. I do not say that the Protestant system was as complete, as coherent, as minute, as the Catholic, or weighed as heavily upon the mind of Europe. But it was animated by the same spirit and followed a similar method. The difference was, that while the mediæval Schoolmen endeavoured to construct their edifice from the three-fold material offered by the Bible, the Fathers, Tradition—their Protestant imitators used for this purpose the Bible, and the Bible only.

The growth and characteristics of Protestant Scholasticism form the subject of the present Lecture.

The use which a systematizing Protestant theology has made of the Bible involves more than one very large assumption. I have already pointed out that the Reformers, with the exception, as we shall presently see, of Faustus Socinus, practically took for granted the authority of the Bible, the substitution of which for the authority of the Church was a central point of their system. But they also, one and all, assumed that the Scriptures of the Old and New Testament contain a complete, self-consistent and symmetrical system of doctrine, which can be extracted from them by the use of ordinary methods of reasoning; that this system is susceptible of logical statement and amplification; and that rational inferences from the language of Scripture are of co-ordinate authority with Scripture itself. I do not mean that the Reformers said this. They did not think it necessary to say it. But it is involved in their very method. Though the conclusions of Socinus differ so widely from those of Melancthon and Calvin, he deduces them from Scripture on precisely the same principle and in precisely the same way. All three construct systems of religious belief which have a logical coherence, which go into minute detail, which cover the whole ground of theological fact, which aim at leaving no mystery unexplained, which are in reality the translation of the Bible into the forms of contemporary dialectic. All claim that there is nothing in their systems which is not explicitly or implicitly contained in Scripture and logically derived from it. It does not occur to any of them that they may be putting the Bible to a use for which its obvious literary peculiarities show it to be unfit. In spite of the emancipation from tradition of which they make their boast, it is still too strong for them. Christianity had always been presented to them by the mediæval Church as a system of reasoned religious truth, complete in all its parts, and they cannot conceive of it in any other way. So they proceed, with less various material and under greater difficulties, to repeat the labour of the Schoolmen, and to construct systems which in process of time not only superimpose themselves on the plain declarations of Scripture, but actually tend to prevent, except for purely controversial purposes, that free and general resort to the Bible which it was one of the first objects of the Reformation to vindicate and to secure.

In a subsequent Lecture it will be my duty to show how one of the results of a scientific literary criticism has been to bring men face to face with the undeniable facts of Scripture, and to prove that the complete logical accord assumed to exist between all parts of the Old and New Testament is a figment of the theological imagination. To-day, I have only to exhibit the conception of the relation of Scripture to religious truth which was the common starting-point of all the systematic developments of theology which had their origin in the Reformation. These were three—the Lutheran, the Calvinistic and the Socinian—of each of which I shall have something to say. The last was latest in date; but as it sprang full-grown from the brain of its author and suffered little subsequent change, it may engage our earliest attention—the more as it will introduce us to a chapter of Reformation history which we have not yet studied.

The criticism which the Reformers directed against

VIII. RISE OF PROTESTANT SCHOLASTICISM. 267

the mediæval Church was at first kept within well-defined limits. The greater part of what was regarded as primitive truth was accepted, so to speak, as it stood. The theory of the sacraments was profoundly modified: all the body of doctrine which is crystallized about the idea of salvation suffered change, greater or less; but there was no desire to touch the doctrine of the Trinity, or to question the authority of the three Creeds. The Confession of Augsburg,[1] in its first Article, "Of God," begins by accepting the Nicene Creed and anathematizing all heretics, Arian, Unitarian and Mohammedan. It returns to the subject in the third Article, "Of the Son of God," which is little more than the Apostles' Creed in a more theologically dogmatic form, and thenceforth is wholly occupied with the points of difference between the old Catholicism and the new Protestantism. Still there is more than this to be said. At first, the Reformers manifested a distinct repulsion to scholastic speculations upon the nature of God. They preferred to leave this mysterious subject in the obscurity of scriptural statement. Luther[2] says that the best of the Fathers disliked the word "Homoousion," which Jerome would willingly have done away with, nor will he allow that any one who is reluctant to use it should on that account be deemed a heretic. "For the simplicity of Scripture," he continues, "is to be preserved: nor let men presume to speak more clearly or more simply than God Himself has spoken." He notes[3] that the word Trinity is nowhere to be found

[1] Sylloge Confessionum, pp. 123, 124.
[2] Werke, ed. Walch, XVIII. 1455, 1456: "Dr. M. Luther's Widerlegung der Ursachen Làtomi," &c.
[3] Ibid. XI. 1549: "Kirchenpostill. Sonntag der Heil. Dreyfaltigkeit." Ibid. XII. 830: "Auslegung der Epistel am Sonntage Trinitatis."

in Scripture, and does not like the sound of it either in Latin or in German. In his earliest unpublished sketch of the *Loci Communes*, Melancthon[1] introduces the words, "*Deus, unus, trinus,*" into the list of topics to be treated, but then passes them by without further amplification. The first edition[2] follows the same course, justifying it, however, by the example of Paul and the evil practical result of "the foolish disputations of the Schoolmen." But as time went on, and the necessity of definition was pressed upon him by the rise of various heresies, Melancthon became more explicitly orthodox, and dedicated distinct chapters of his book to God, to the Trinity, to the Son, and to the Holy Ghost.[3] Still, even as late as 1533, he strongly condemns controversy as to the nature of God, declaring that he is content to base the invocation of Christ upon the authority of Scripture.[4] It is only the heresy and the fate of Servetus which repel him at last into full and precise orthodoxy.

But it was not possible that speculation, once permitted to employ itself upon the creed of the Church, should be confined to any single group of doctrines. We have seen already that Hetzer, Denck, Franck, were not deterred by the sacredness of any article of Christian belief

---

[1] Corp. Ref. XXI. 11.   [2] Ibid. XXI. 84, 85.
[3] Ibid. XXI. 607 et seq.
[4] Ibid. II. 630: Letter to Camerarius, Feb. 9, 1533. "De Serveto rogas quid sentiam. . . . . περὶ τῆς τριάδος scis me semper veritum esse, fore ut hæc aliquando erumperent. Bone Deus, quales tragœdias excitabit hæc quæstio ad posteros εἰ ἐστὶν ὑπόστασις ὁ λόγος, εἰ ἐστὶν ὑπόστασις τὸ πνεῦμα. Ego me refero ad illas scripturæ voces quæ jubent invocare Christum, quod est, ei honorem divinitatis tribuere, et plenum consolationis est. τὰς δὲ ἰδέας τῶν ὑποστάσεων, καὶ διαφορὰς ἀκριβῶς ζητεῖν, οὐ πάνυ συμφέρει."

from allowing their rationalizing intellect free play upon it. Still it remains true that the moral and practical problems of religion were those which chiefly engaged the Teutonic mind. The current of hardy rationalism which directed itself against the metaphysical forms into which the Schoolmen had thrown the mysteries of Christianity, set in from the South. Servetus was a Spaniard. Ochino and the Sozzini were natives of Sienna. Biandrata and Gentile fled northwards in search of a freer air, the one from Cosenza, the other from Saluzzo. We need not speculate on the intellectual peculiarities of the Latin race, or the efficacy of a dominant Catholicism in engendering an all-daring scepticism: the Protestantism which claims to have found a defensible position between Catholic orthodoxy and blank unbelief, still leads only a precarious life in Italy and in Spain. From 1530 onwards, we meet with these Southern refugees everywhere in Switzerland and Germany, seeking a resting-place, but not finding it. No sooner is it discovered that their revolt against the Church does not take the usual doctrinal form, than city after city bids them depart. Geneva and Wittenberg are the chief centres of attraction: they have a great desire to measure dialectical swords with Calvin and Melancthon, but they neither convert nor are converted. In the case of Servetus, Calvin appeals to the secular arm, and one pestilent heretic is silenced: in 1566, Gentile meets a similar though a less cruel fate at Bern. Neither was a citizen of any Swiss Republic or amenable to its laws: there never were more signal cases of usurped jurisdiction. But in those days men killed a heretic as they would set their foot upon a noxious insect: and what Christian state would interfere on behalf of a self-convicted blasphemer? All these men tended to Poland, which, for many reasons, was at that time the general refuge of free-thinkers. Thither the doctrines of John Huss had early made their way from Bohemia, with the effect, not merely of turning men's minds in the direction of ecclesiastical reform, but of putting the nobility into permanent opposition to the clergy. These nobles were numerous, wealthy, independent: if stained with the vices, yet not without the characteristic virtues, of an aristocracy. They had received the best education of the time in foreign and especially in German Universities: they had caught the spirit of the Humanists, and, when the signal was given from Wittenberg, ranged themselves eagerly on the side of reform. They lived on their vast estates, surrounded by dependents over whom they exercised a patriarchal authority. To their King they owed only a loose allegiance; while the *liberum veto*, the right of every member to stop by his single vote the action of the States of the realm, helped to maintain them in a condition of careless independence of each other and all central control. They welcomed the Italian refugees as men of learning and refinement; afforded them the protection which the free cities of Germany and Switzerland had refused; allowed them to preach and to print what they would. Side by side with the Catholic Church, Protestantism of both the Lutheran and the Calvinistic type already existed in an organized form in Poland. To these was now added what its enemies afterwards called a Unitarian or Socinian Church, in which the rationalism of the Reformation for the first time took a definite shape. Its existence was brief, its fortunes troubled; but it was too peculiar a thing, and has exercised too large an influence upon the subsequent development of Christian thought, to be passed over without due description.

The name inseparably connected with this Church is that of Socinus. Of this family, two are inscribed in the catalogue of heretics, Lælius and Faustus, uncle and nephew, both born at Sienna, and belonging to the nobility of the robe.[1] The intellectual relation between them, long misunderstood, has been cleared up only by recent researches. Lælius, who was born in 1525, left Italy at an early age, in part, at least, to avoid persecution: travelled in an easy patrician way in search of a religion: made the friendship of Calvin in Geneva: studied for almost a year in Wittenberg: extended his wanderings westwards to Holland and England, eastwards to Krakau and Vienna. But the death of his father, and an exile attended by so many circumstances of theological suspicion, threw him into pecuniary difficulties, and he died at Zürich in 1562, at the early age of thirty-seven, poor and, in comparison with his brighter years, almost neglected. He was not known during his lifetime as an Antitrinitarian. He was simply a theological inquirer, to whose essentially sceptical mind new doubts and difficulties perpetually presented themselves. He is always putting questions to Calvin, to Bullinger, to Melancthon,

---

[1] The chief authority on the subject of Lælius Socinus is F. Trechsel : Die Protestantischen Antitrinitarier vor Faustus Socin. Zweites Buch. Lelio Sozini und die Antitrinitarier seiner Zeit. Heidelberg, 1844. But for both Lælius and Faustus Socinus, I may also refer to two learned and accurate articles in the Theological Review, Vol. XVI. 1879, by Alexander Gordon, M.A., "The Sozzini and their School," which contain in a lucid and interesting form the results of the latest research.

who all mingle careful reply with rebukes, sometimes gentle, sometimes stern, of the itch of inquiry which afflicts him. But it is quite plain that everybody loves him. There is a fascination not to be resisted in his patrician breeding and his candid temper. Nature did not mean him for an heresiarch, and he never tried to play the part. Faustus Socinus went to Zürich to take possession of his uncle's papers, and the story has long been current that he was so deeply impressed by the religious opinions which he found in them, as afterwards to have devoted his life to their propagation. But uncle and nephew hardly ever met in the flesh: the papers were few and fragmentary: and all that we certainly know of the two men reveals much more their intellectual dissimilarity than their likeness.

Faustus Socinus, whose life extends from 1539 to 1604, passed eleven of the best years of his manhood in the service of Duke Cosmo de Medici,[1] by whom he was much trusted as minister and diplomatist. At the death of that Prince in 1574, he threw off the cloak of conformity, which he had hitherto loosely worn, and left Italy for ever. With the opinions which he entertained, he was naturally attracted to the East of Europe; and, after a brief sojourn in Transylvania, settled in Poland, where, chiefly in Krakau or the neighbourhood, he passed the last twenty-five years of his life. He found there an Antitrinitarian church, on the one hand slowly growing

---

[1] This is Cosmo I., sometimes called the Great, who, after the murder of Alessandro—the last, though illegitimate, scion of the old Medici—became Duke of Florence, and afterwards of Sienna. He was the founder of the Ducal dynasty of the Medici, reigning from 1537 to 1574.

into an organized existence; on the other, vexed with the kind of dissension which always troubles "left wings," political or religious. These dissensions he made it the business of his life to allay, and in some considerable degree succeeded. Curiously enough, he never became a member of the church over which his influence was so great; for it demanded re-baptism, and Socinus would not submit to a repetition of the rite. He had neither the inspiring force of Luther, nor the complete learning of Melancthon: he approached religion from the intellectual and ethical sides alone: the deep things of the Spirit were a sealed book to him: while, again, he had never undergone the scholastic training of the age, and the years which some men devote to enlarging and correcting the acquirements of their youth, had been spent by him in the service of Florentine diplomacy. But he had the advantage of knowing precisely what he believed, and what he wanted other people to believe: his thought was a middle way between extremes: he was a disputant of imperturbable temper and unwearied perseverance: his dialectic was cold, clear, acute, convincing even when not persuasive. Before his death the tide of Jesuit reaction set in in Poland, and he suffered the fate of Priestley two centuries later, in having his books burned and his life endangered by a fanatical mob. Still a church was founded. It had an organization which we should now call Presbyterian. It possessed flourishing schools, one of which, at Racow, almost rose to the rank of a university. It exercised a strong moral discipline over its members, whom it restrained as far as possible from recourse to the courts of law, or indeed any parti-

T

cipation in political life. Its chief preachers and writers were partly Polish, partly German. In the German Universities the Socinian leaven was always working, detaching to the service of the Polish church such men as Ostorodt, Crell, Ruarus, Wollzogen, and many more who were not ashamed to be enrolled among the "*Fratres Poloni.*"[1] That this church finally succumbed to persistent persecution, no one needs to be told. The Jesuits took possession of successive Kings of Poland, whom they educated to be the tools of their purposes, and the internecine hatreds of Protestants gave them all the opportunity they needed. The final blow fell on the 10th of July, 1660, when the Unitarians were compelled either to become Catholic or to leave a kingdom which still affected to tolerate Mohammedans and Jews. One body of them found their way to Transylvania, where they maintained a corporate existence apart from their Tran-

---

[1] This was particularly the case at the beginning of the seventeenth century at Altorf, a little University not far from Nürnberg, in the territory and under the influence of the Free City. Here one Ernst Soner was Professor of Medicine, a man who had studied at Leiden, and there, through intercourse with Ostorodt and Woidowski, had been converted to Socinianism. He seems to have devoted his energy at Altorf much more to the propagation of his religious views than to the teaching proper to his chair; but he worked in strict secrecy, and died in 1612 in the odour of unsuspected orthodoxy. After his death his disciples were less cautious: the scandal broke out, and in the subsequent investigations, dismissals, burnings of books, it is impossible to say how much blame was cast upon Soner which might have been more properly borne by his living successors. The story of the affair, which made a great noise in Germany, is told by G. G. Zeltner, in two bulky quartos: "Historia Crypto-Socinismi Altorfinæ quondam Academiæ infesti arcana," &c., Leipzig, 1729. Conf. Fock: Der Socinianismus, I. 235.

sylvanian co-religionists[1] till almost the end of the last century. Prussia received some, Holland others, who, theoretically discountenanced but really tolerated, gradually lost themselves in the ranks of the Remonstrants. But all through the years during which the scattered Socinians were gradually losing ecclesiastical cohesion—while the tradition was feebly kept alive in the remote valleys of Transylvania, and before English Presbyterianism had begun to suffer the process of doctrinal decay—Socinianism, both in England and on the Continent, was the readiest and the bitterest reproach which confident orthodoxy could throw at rational or latitudinarian thought. It was the "red spectre" of Protestantism; the *reductio ad damnabile* of rationalism. Hales of Eton, Falkland, Chillingworth, were all in turn accused of it, and all unjustly. "No man can tell you truth," says Andrew Marvel,[2] "but he must presently be a Socinian." And under the cloud of angry prejudice thus

---

[1] The Unitarian church in Transylvania, which has subsisted ever since the Reformation, and still enjoys a modest degree of prosperity, was distinct in origin and history from the church of Poland. Its first name is also that of an Italian refugee, Giorgio Biandrata, a physician of great worldly skill and address, but of worse than doubtful character, who went back to the Catholic Church, to meet a miserable death at the hands of a kinsman. But its true illustration in the age of the Reformation is Franz David, a noble and pious man, who, refusing to give to Christ the title of God and the honour of invocation, was, at the instigation of Biandrata, tried, condemned, and ended his days in prison. It was in connection with this controversy that Faustus Socinus paid his only visit to Transylvania; but there is no justification for associating his name with the church. Transylvanian Unitarianism is a religious phenomenon parallel to, but not identical with, Polish Socinianism.

[2] The Rehearsal Transposed: the Second Part, p. 307.

raised, the real features of a very remarkable system of religious thought have almost disappeared from view.[1]

With the doctrinal details of Socinianism, however, I have now nothing to do, except in so far as they stand related to the general movement of human thought which I have been trying to describe. I shall not attempt to distinguish the doctrine of Socinus from that of Servetus, or to re-open the controversy, which was to the former so vital, as to the "invocation" and the "adoration" of Christ. It is more in accord with my present purpose to point out the intellectual hardihood of the method of religious thought which in Poland and Transylvania was made the basis of an ecclesiastical organization. Here was a reaction against Rome which, whatever its logical and historical justification, was at least thorough.[2] I do not think, though I speak with diffidence upon this point, that Socinus adopted the historical method at all, or went back to the ante-Nicene Fathers, to justify himself against the great doctors of the fourth and fifth centuries. Their enemies indeed accused the Socinians of having revived the heresies of Artemon and Paul of Samosata; but this calling of names, which is so common a device of theologians, does not at all indicate the real lines of attack and defence. Socinus' method consisted simply in the application of reason to Scripture. He did not believe in the possibility of natural religion: religion is revelation only,

---

[1] My principal authority for the history of Socinianism is Otto Fock: Der Socinianismus, Kiel, 1847, 2 vols. 8vo. I may also refer once more to Mr. Gordon's excellent articles, "The Sozzini and their School."

[2] The epigram is well known, but may be once more quoted:
Alta ruit Babylon: destruxit tecta Lutherus,
Muros Calvinus, sed fundamenta Socinus.

and, in the case of godly men before Christ, must be referred to the fact that in the beginning God made Himself known to Adam. There is no real distinction between law and gospel: Christianity is only a better and more explicit law, to the performance of which the promise of eternal life is attached. And the truths, the precepts, the promises of Christianity are to be extracted from Scripture by the use of human reason, which, however, has not merely an interpretative but a critical faculty. Many things, indeed, in Scripture are to be believed which are above, but none that are contrary to reason; though the line between what is above and what is contrary was drawn in what to modern apprehension appears a sufficiently arbitrary way. And the application of this method by Socinus to the body of commonly-accepted Christian dogma led to startling results. The doctrine of the Trinity disappeared, and its place was taken by those of the Unity of God and the simple humanity of Christ. The centre-point of Christ's mission is not his death upon the cross, in which he made satisfaction for the sins of the world, but his resurrection, in which he brought life and immortality to light. The whole fabric of a vicarious atonement, its key-stone being thus taken out, crumbled into ruin: the literary antithesis of Anselm's "*Cur Deus Homo?*" is Faustus Socinus' "*De Jesu Christo Servatore,*" a book in which is to be found every rational and moral argument since directed against the theory of satisfaction. Christianity thus becomes, after a fashion, a rational religion: God speaks: reason listens and accepts. But as God speaks by human voices and through human instruments, it is necessary that reason should also interpret, criticise, discriminate.

The result is a doctrinal system which rejects ecclesiastical Christianity in all its stages as a corruption of primitive truth, and represents itself as alone the mirror of apostolical tradition.

Socinus, therefore, accepted to the full the Reformation principle of the supreme authority of Scripture. But it was characteristic of his clear, cold, questioning intellect that he was not content to assume that authority with as little attempt as Luther and Calvin made to prove it. His book "*De Sacræ Scripturæ Auctoritate*" is extremely interesting and valuable, not only as being the first attempt to solve a problem, upon the answer to which depends the whole intellectual justification of the Reform, but as the fountain-head of a method of Scripture apologetics upon which some reliance is yet placed. The New Testament—in comparison with which the Old, in Socinus' view, holds only a subordinate position—was written under the immediate dictation of the Holy Spirit, and is therefore, subject to a distinction between the essential and the non-essential, infallible in matters of doctrine. But how is this to be proved? Not by the authority of the Church, as was the teaching of Rome; not by the conjoint witness of the Spirit in Scripture and in the mind of the believer, as Calvin asserted; but by obvious reasons, level to ordinary comprehension. The books are the production of the authors to whom they are assigned: there is no reason to suppose that they have been corrupted: the apostles were men who had abundant opportunity of becoming acquainted with the facts which they recorded: they were honest witnesses who sealed their faith with their blood: in everything that is essential they are in full accord with one another—and so forth. It is not my object to draw out the argument in its complete form, much less to criticise it: it is sufficient to have indicated its character, which was a few years ago, and perhaps still is, familiar enough. This book is the precursor of what we may call the literature of "credibility," and in the honesty and thoroughness of its attempt, if not for the measure of its success, deserves our respect. But it is plain that the superstructure is far too massive for the foundation on which it is erected. No mere literary reasoning of this kind will reach as far as the dictation of the Spirit, and the infallible authority of the word dictated. It is the only way in which the credibility of a Thucydides or a Tacitus can be established; but it does not touch the intellectual region which lies between the general credence which we give to their statements of fact, and the submission with which we are expected to receive authoritative utterances of doctrine from men who are the mouthpieces of God. Nor, again, can anything be more obvious than that Socinus starts from the large assumption as to the literary character of the Bible of which I have spoken. He declares that such discrepancies as exist in the New Testament are of small account, and relate only to historical fact. So far from there being any doctrinal diversity in its statements, its extraordinary agreement and consistency with itself are such as of themselves to put it in a position of greater authority than any other book of doctrine. It would be difficult to find an example in which the writings of any one man, however few and brief, manifest this quality to the same extent as these books,[1] the production of

---

[1] "Dico igitur, quod attinet ad repugnantias aut diversitates quæ in N. T. scriptis inveniantur, nullam esse, quæ aut non videatur quidem

many writers. In so saying, the arch-rationalist of the Reformation is less true to fact than the Reformer who called upon his disciples to strangle reason like a dangerous beast. Luther at least saw that no dialectic ingenuity would reconcile Paul and James.

We are at the opposite pole of thought now from the mysticism of Tauler, of the *Theologia Germanica*, of Sebastian Franck. And whatever there is of truth in mysticism, the system of Socinus altogether neglects. It separates God and man, making the relation between them purely intellectual. It leaves no room for a doctrine of the Spirit. There is much meaning in the fact that its characteristic phrase is not *inspiratio*, but *patefactio divina*. God does not enter into men's souls, moulding them to Himself, but declares His will and promises a reward of obedience. There is no opportunity for the manifestation of a divine passion, as in the spiritual form of the doctrine of justification by faith, but only the calm apprehension by the intellect of certain abstract and practical truths of great and eternal importance. But even as a system of avowed rationalism, Socinianism was born prematurely. Had

---

vera, sed tamen non sit, aut non in re sit parvi, seu potius nullius momenti. Quæ videri tantum possunt, nec tamen sunt revera, ea sunt, quæ ad doctrinam spectant: in qua non modo nulla vera in scriptis illis repugnantia aut diversitas invenitur, sed tanta est concordia et convenientia, ut vel hoc satis esse deberet ad conciliandam libro illi auctoritatem majorem, quam quivis alius liber habeat, ubi doctrina aliqua tradatur. Vix enim, aut ne vix quidem, in scriptis unius tantum hominis, licet brevibus et paucis, tanta unquam doctrinæ ubique concordia et convenientia, reperietur, quanta in eo libro, qui ex tot diversis multorum scriptis constat. Repugnantiæ porro aut diversitates seu veræ, seu quæ videri tantum possint, quæ in rebus sunt parvi momenti, eæ sunt, quæ pertinent ad historiam." F. Socini Opp. I. 267, "De Auctoritate S. Scripturæ.'

Socinus possessed all the learning of Melancthon, his method would still have been in advance of his knowledge. Rationalism could not have its perfect work till Biblical, following in the track of all other literary criticism, had accumulated such a store of indisputable facts as would warrant settled inferences. But even when the knowledge is accumulated and the inferences drawn, the rationalists will still have to go to the mystics if they would learn the whole secret of Christianity.[1]

Socinianism, as a dogmatic system, hardly has a history. The doctrine of the Racovian Catechism is substantially that of Socinus; and though the Unitarians of the second generation did not in every respect agree with their predecessors, their theory of confessional obligation left the way open to growth and change.[2] In Lutheranism, on the contrary, we find going on, for at least two generations, a process of dogmatic development kept as far as possible within the limits of authoritative state-

---

[1] The Antitrinitarians of Poland, at first organized as a church under the title of "ecclesia minor," had many names applied to them, mostly descriptive, but some that with lapse of time have become almost opprobrious. They certainly never wished to be called Socinians. They preferred the simple designation of Christians. The great collection of Socinian divinity, published at Amsterdam in the middle of the seventeenth century, bears the general title, "Bibliotheca Fratrum Polonorum, *quos Unitarios vocant.*" The Transylvanian church finally took the name Unitarian. But in 1762, the church of Polish exiles at Kolozsvar published a " Confessio Fidei exulum Christi, qui ab ejus sanctissimo nomine, Christiani tantum appellari amant." Possibly this desire on the part of the Polish Unitarians to be called by no other name than that of Christian, stands in some relation to the determination of their orthodox opponents to deny it them altogether. A. Gordon: Theol. Review, XVI. 568.

[2] See Preface to the Racovian Catechism (ed. Rees, 1818), by Andrew Wissowatius and Joachim Stegman the Younger, p. xcv et seq.

ments, dissent from which is the sure mark of heresy, and usually attended by pains and penalties. Of these statements, the first in point of date is contained in the fifteen Articles of Marburg, which Luther and the other theologians of Wittenberg drew up in 1529, with a view of defining their position as against Zwingli and the Swiss Reformers. These were reproduced, after the lapse of a few weeks, in the seventeen Articles of Schwabach, which were made the basis of alliance between the Lutheran States of Germany. And both these documents led up to and were superseded by the Confession of Augsburg, which, in opposition to the Confession presented to the Emperor by Zwingli, and that of the four cities, Strasburg, Constanz, Lindau and Memmingen, known as the *Confessio Tetrapolitana*, was adopted by the Lutheran Princes and Cities, and is still the central symbolic document of the German Reformation. Much might be said of this famous Confession which I cannot pause to say now: how it was the work of the temporizing and reconciling genius of Melancthon, who, but for the opposition of the Protestant Princes, would have gone to far greater lengths of concession than are represented in the actual settlement: how it marks not the maximum but the minimum of Protestant revolt against Rome: and how, therefore, while quite useless as a measure of conciliation towards Emperor and Pope, it has greatly tended to impress upon Lutheranism its peculiar character of narrow and rigid orthodoxy. But two things may be said of it. First, it was the introduction to the Christian world of a new kind of creed. It is conceived and executed on quite a different scale from that of the ancient symbols of the Church. It occupies many pages; it covers a large theological area. And next, the selection of the points which it chiefly elaborates was determined by the exigencies of controversy. It has not the scientific symmetry of a general confession of faith. It is anthropological rather than theological. It takes for granted the old creeds, which define the nature of God; while, in regard to matters which touch the relation of men to God—faith, works, grace, justification—it is full and explicit.

The Confession of Augsburg, and the Apology for it which soon followed, were Melancthon's work. The next contribution to confessional literature, the Articles of Schmalkalden, came from Luther's pen, and were signed by Melancthon only under protest. Their date is February, 1537: they were the confession of faith of the Lutheran States, which had drawn together for mutual defence in what was known as the Schmalkaldic League, and were intended, not only for their own instruction and encouragement, but for the information of the Pope, the Emperor and the coming Council. Upon the Articles of Schmalkalden followed a long succession of similar documents. The Confessions of the German and Swiss churches fill more than one portly volume. One series of them took its origin in the differences between the Lutheran, and first the Zwinglian, next the Calvinistic, doctrine of the Eucharist. Bucer, who as the Reformer of Strasburg held both geographically and theologically a middle position between Wittenberg and Zürich, interposed, after the Diet of Augsburg, with proposals of a reconciling kind; and in 1536 an agreement, more verbal than real, was formulated in what is known as the Concord of Wittenberg. But in 1544, two years before he died, Luther renewed the wordy warfare,[1] and the breach between the two churches became absolute. I will not enumerate the long and elaborate confessions of faith in which the various niceties of this embittered controversy found expression: it would be a mere catalogue of titles, to which hours of patient theological exposition would hardly restore the faintest breath of living interest. But it is curious to remark how the doctrine chiefly in question, that of the Real Presence in the Eucharist, led back the Protestant churches to precisely those scholastic subtleties of speculation which Luther and Melancthon were at first so anxious to avoid. Said the Zwinglians, How could the human nature of Christ be present in the bread and wine, when the man Christ Jesus was in heaven, sitting at the right hand of God? Could a body be at once in more places than one? Could two bodies be at the same time in the same place? The answer to these questions was afforded by the peculiarly Lutheran doctrine of the ubiquity of Christ's body. But how is this ubiquity, in itself contrary to the conditions of physical existence, to be accounted for? Again, the answer comes in the still more abstruse doctrine of the *communicatio idiomatum*, according to which the divine nature of Christ imparts its mysterious faculties and properties to the human. Whether this doctrine really explains in a satisfactory way the relation between the two natures in Christ, which has so exercised the most speculative minds of the church from the Council of Nicæa downwards, I must leave to acuter theologians to decide; but it is certainly one which the Doctor Subtilissimus among the

---

[1] In his "Kurzes Bekenntniss vom heiligen Sacrament," Werke, ed. Walch, XX. 2195

VIII. RISE OF PROTESTANT SCHOLASTICISM. 285

Schoolmen need not have been ashamed to father. It was stated at great length in that Formula of Concord of 1580, in which at last the rigid Lutherans recorded their agreement among themselves, and their disagreement with all Calvinists and crypto-Calvinists. I find, however, that even this did not satisfy the rage for definition, and that the dogmatic theologians proceeded to discuss three separate kinds of *communicatio*—the *genus idiomaticum*, the *genus apotelesmaticum*, and the *genus majestaticum*, phrases which I shall not attempt to explain.[1] But here, too, was found fresh opportunity for further distinction and subdivision; while a quite new line of heated and bitter controversy was opened out at the beginning of the seventeenth century by the application of these ideas to the earthly life of Christ. It was conceived of as a voluntary self-humiliation, or, as the technical phrase was, an "exinanition." But what during that period became of the divine attributes, the omnipresence, the omnipotence, which, in virtue of the *communicatio*, belonged to his human nature? A distinction was made between their κτῆσις or possession, and their χρῆσις or use; while as to the χρῆσις there were two theories—one, that Christ secretly exercised his divine powers, κρύψις; the other, that he, so to speak, emptied himself of them, κένωσις. Upon this subtle issue a furious dispute arose between the theologians of Tübingen on the one side, those of Marburg and Giessen on the other. But here I pause. We are a very long way now from the

---

[1] Baur: Lehre von der Dreieinigkeit, Vol. III. Part i. chap. 8. Bretschneider: Dogmatik, pp. 575—578.

point at which Luther objected to the words Trinity and Homoousion that they were not to be found in Scripture.[1]

Other controversies, more in number and not less bitter than those which separated it from the Swiss Protestants, arose in the bosom of the Lutheran Church itself. I have already said that its dogmatic theologian was Melancthon, and its symbolic book his *Loci Communes*.[2] It is a fact very characteristic of the theology of the Reformation, that this famous book had its origin in a course of lectures on the Epistle to the Romans, which were given by Melancthon very soon after his arrival in Wittenberg. In its earliest form it was a collection of Heads, or *Loci*— topics for further systematic exposition, which received oral amplification from the Professor at his desk. Nor in the first edition, which was published at Wittenberg in 1521, was it much more than this. The book was received with unbounded applause in Lutheran circles: between 1521 and 1523, seventeen editions were issued: George Spalatin, the chaplain and friend of the Elector Frederick, translated it into German: and in a famous phrase of commendation, which soon found its way on to the title-page of the book, Luther said of it " that it was worthy not only of immortality, but of a place in the

---

[1] Baur: Dreieinigkeit, III. 450. Gass: Geschichte der Protestantischen Dogmatik, I. 277.

[2] The full title of the first edition was " Loci Communes rerum theologicarum, seu Hypotyposes Theologicæ. Auctore Philippo Melanchthone. Wittembergæ, an. MDXXI." In its last form, " Loci Theologici recens recogniti. Autore Philip. Melanthone. Wittebergæ, anno 1543."

Canon of Scripture."[1] On the other hand, Cochlæus, the champion of Rome, called it the Alkoran[2] of Lutheranism, while Eck set to work to produce *Loci Communes* of Catholic theology. But the book had a curious and significant history. Its last learned editor[3] distinguishes three periods of its development within its author's lifetime: the first, from 1521 to 1525; the second, from 1535 to 1541; the third, from 1542 to 1559. In each of these, the number of *Loci* was increased and their treatment made more elaborate. The work, from a systematic commentary on the most systematic of Paul's letters, became a compendium of Christian doctrine. To citations from Scripture were gradually added quotations from the Fathers. The Schoolmen, once mentioned only in terms of contempt, were adduced as authoritative. The necessities of system-making were laid upon Melancthon, and the longer he lived, the more he yielded to them.

The Lutheran Church was not absolutely at one, even while the commanding genius of its founder was still able to assert itself. Reformation doctrine was on many important points fluid and indeterminate: on the subtleties which clustered round the theory of grace and predestination, in especial, it was easy for men of independent minds to take different sides. In 1537, Johann Agricola, of Eisleben, a friend and fellow-worker of both the great Reformers, started a theory of the relation of the law to the gospel, which, but for his own uncertainty

---

[1] Selnecker, an early Lutheran divine, was content to call it "the best book *after* the Bible." Calvin edited, possibly himself executed a translation of it into French, published in 1546.

[2] Corp. Ref. XXI. 79.

[3] H. E. Bindseil, in the 21st and 22nd vols. of the Corp. Ref.

of theological grasp and want of moral steadfastness, might have produced disunion. But when Luther died in 1546, the storm broke from many quarters of the theological sky in succession. Melancthon, it must be owned, had declined from the full rigidity of Lutheran doctrine. He had gradually introduced into his *Loci* the theory that man's will co-operates with God's in the work of salvation. He had laid down the fine distinction that of salvation good works were not a *causa efficiens*, and yet a *causa sine quâ non*. On the one hand, Flacius Illyricus, a hard and reckless dogmatist, flew at him with the assertion of a doctrine of human corruption which out-Luthered Luther; on the other, Amsdorf advanced the paradoxical thesis that to salvation good works were an absolute hindrance. A fourth controversy arose out of a theory of justification peculiar to Osiander: a fifth, as to the extent to which the Church might lawfully submit itself in things indifferent (*adiaphora*) to unfriendly compulsion. Till 1560, when death delivered Melancthon from "the rage of theologians," these debates, conducted with an incredible arrogance and bitterness, assailed his reputation and destroyed his peace. New names came up: men were no longer Protestants, but Lutherans and Philippists : Melancthon was called a crypto-Calvinist, and accused of having traitorously transferred his allegiance from Wittenberg to Geneva. Princes as well as divines were bitten by the gadfly of orthodoxy, and spared no pains, shrank from hardly any severity, to enforce a rule of dogmatic soundness in their dominions. At first, Wittenberg was the stronghold of the Philippists; Jena, with its University newly founded in the interest of the severest Lutheranism, of their opponents; while Philippists and Lutherans alike pursued with a hearty hatred the Calvinism which had now established itself in more than one German State. But professors were invited and dismissed, sometimes even proscribed and imprisoned, as the fortunes of the theological war changed. Possibly the Christian life and spirit may have survived in some of the obscure places of which the dignified Muse of History takes no cognizance; but I know no epoch of Christianity to which I could more confidently point in illustration of the fact, that where there is most theology there is often least religion.

It need not be said that such a state of things as this produced a very plentiful crop of creeds and symbolical books. Some of these are truly portentous documents. The fashion grew up that every Protestant State should have its *Corpus Doctrinæ*, or body of doctrine, expressive of its own precise shade of orthodoxy, and rigidly enforced upon all its subjects. When we recollect the very slender dimensions of the Apostles' or the Nicene Creed, we are struck with unpleasing astonishment to find that each of these was a folio volume, containing several independent expositions of doctrine, all of great length and precision. The first, the authorship of which is due to Melancthon himself, was published in 1559, under the title of *Corpus Doctrinæ Philippicum* or *Misnicum*. It contained—I give its table of contents as a sample of the rest—the Confession of Augsburg and Melancthon's Apology for it, the *Loci Communes*, the *Examen Ordinandorum*, the *Responsio ad articulos Bavaricæ Inquisitionis*, and the *Responsio Serveti*. Such was, in 1560, the standard of Saxon orthodoxy. The cities of Hamburg and Brunswick each had a *Corpus* not less ample. There was the *Corpus Pomeranicum*—of a distinctly Lutheran cast—for Pomerania; a *Corpus Prutenicum* for Prussia; a *Corpus Brandeburgicum* for Brandenburg. Others were loyally named after reigning Princes: as the *Corpus Wilhelminum* of Lüneburg, and the *Corpus Julium* of Brunswick-Wolfenbüttel. All these, and others which I have not named, were superseded in 1580—fifty years after the presentation of the Confession of Augsburg—by the *Formula Concordiæ*, which remains the standard of Lutheran orthodoxy. This document adopts, so to speak, into itself the three Creeds, the Confession of Augsburg in its original form with the Apology, the Schmalkaldic Articles, Luther's two Catechisms, and adds twelve Articles, dealing at great length with the controversies of which I have spoken, in a Lutheran sense. Though not quite universally adopted, the *Formula Concordiæ* was in effect the triumph of rigid Lutheranism over Melancthon and Calvin alike. But while Protestants had thus been spending their strength in ignoble internecine strife, the Counter Reformation had been actively at work, Catholic Germany had gathered up its strength for one more desperate contest, and before long the Thirty Years' War involved them in a struggle for very life.

That struggle, however, interposed no hindrance in the way of the all-powerful dogmatizing impulse. In the very midst of cruel war and reckless devastation, Johann Gerhard of Jena, who is held in honour as the chief of Lutheran dogmatists, quietly toiled at the construction of his vast theological system, which filled nine quarto volumes, and, in an edition published a century and a half afterwards, was expanded to twenty of the same goodly dimensions. The work was framed on the

Melancthonian pattern, and bore almost the same title as Melancthon's—*Loci Theologici*.[1] As characteristic a figure as Gerhard is Abraham Calov, who a generation later represented at Wittenberg, in opposition to George Calixt, the uncompromising Lutheranism of his day. Calixt, who was the chief ornament of the University of Helmstädt, was a man of large and liberal mind, which he had cultivated not only by comprehensive study, but by foreign travel. But he had conceived the dangerous idea that the essentials of Christianity consisted in the doctrines which are held by all churches alike, and that their peculiar and characteristic tenets are only of secondary importance: need it be said that the accusation of Romanism was hurled at him from one side, of Atheism from the other? Against him, Calov, the very type of a rigid and narrow dogmatist, maintained a life-long war, one ponderous engine of which was his *Systema Locorum Theologicorum*, in twelve quarto volumes.[2] What little excuse can be alleged for these extravagant exaggerations of dogmatic system, is to be derived from the fact that Lutheranism was put on its defence against the subtleties of Jesuit polemic on the one side, of Calvinist controversy on the other; that it was pressed here

---

[1] Joh. Gerhard, "Loci Communes Theologici cum pro adstruenda veritate tum pro destruenda quorumvis contradicentium falsitate solide et copiose explicati inque novem tomos divisi," Jena, 1610—1622. J. F. Cotta's edition in twenty volumes was published at Tübingen, 1762—1781.

[2] Ab. Calov, "Systema locorum theologicorum e sacra potissimum Scriptura et antiquitate nec non adversariorum confessione doctrinam, praxin et controversiarum fidei cum veterum tum in primis recentiorum pertractationem luculentam exhibens," Wittembergæ, 1655—1677, XII. tomi.

by Syncretistic liberality, there by Socinian rationalism, and so became absorbed in the single task of theological self-development. But the religious, and in some degree even the intellectual life of the Church was cankered at the core. The philological studies which had given its first impulse to the Reformation were neglected. Fanatics were found to assert that philosophy was an invention of the devil, and that what approved itself to the natural reason could not be theologically true. The only philosophy which found any favour was precisely that Aristotelian dialectic which had determined the form of the scholastic theology, and now served the Lutheran system-makers as the basis of their endless definitions and distinctions. Calov, who belonged to the generation between Kepler and Newton, denied on scriptural grounds the possibility of the earth's revolution round the sun.[1] The Bible was still the highest authority in matters of faith; but the sole object of interpretation was to bring it into accordance with the Lutheran symbols, a task which was much facilitated by a free use of the *analogia fidei*. The systematic study of Scripture almost disappeared from the Universities. Spener,[2] the famous founder of the Pietistic school and the leader of a Biblical reaction, has left it on record that preaching was to a large extent

---

[1] Gass, I. 343.

[2] Spener's "Pia Desideria," quoted by Hossbach, "Philipp Jakob Spener und seine Zeit," I. 96. The following distich from a poet of the time, shows the connection in the popular mind between Pietism and revived interest in the Scriptures:

    Was ist ein Pietist? der Gottes Wort studirt
    Und nach demselben auch ein heilig Leben führt.

Hossbach, I. 235.

VIII. RISE OF PROTESTANT SCHOLASTICISM. 293

confined to texts taken from the lessons of the day (*Perikopen*), to the exclusion of continuous exposition. The study of dogma, in and for itself, reigned supreme. There was once more a scholastic system of theology, developed in scholastic form by scholastic methods, which, hardly less than that against which the Reformers had rebelled, hid the Scriptures and crushed out the life of the Church.

The doctrinal development of the Reformed Church ran a similar course. It starts from Calvin's great work, the "Institution of the Christian Religion," which in its relation to its author has a history not unlike that of Melancthon's *Loci*. The first extant edition was published at Basel, in the Latin language, in 1536.[1] The general supposition is, that this was preceded in 1535 by a French edition; if so, the book has entirely disappeared. But the "Institution" of 1536 was only a skeleton of what it afterwards became. Here, too, there are three well-marked epochs in the history of the work, reckoning from the time of its first publication to the date at which it finally left its author's hands. The Basel edition of 1536 contained only six chapters; that of Strasburg in 1539 was enlarged to seventeen; while the final and authoritative issue of Geneva in 1559 contained no fewer than eighty. The form of the book, too, underwent

---

[1] Henry: Joh. Calvin, I. 102 et seq. Conf. Beilage, Literatur der Schriften Calvins, Vol. III. No. 3, p. 177. Paulus Thurius, an Hungarian scholar, is the author of the following distich on the "Institution:"

Præter apostolicas post Christi tempora chartas,
Huic peperere libro sæcula nulla parem.

But this hardly equals in weight Luther's commendation of Melancthon's *Loci*.

important changes. Originally it began with an exposition of the Decalogue, followed by similar expositions of the Apostles' Creed and the Lord's Prayer. The other three chapters treated of True and False Sacraments respectively, and of Christian Liberty, including the relation of the Church to the State. The final form of the work, however, is that of four Books, divided into eighty chapters. The first treats of the knowledge of God the Creator; the second, of the knowledge of God the Redeemer in Christ; the third, of the manner how to receive (*percipiendæ*) the grace of Christ, what fruits come thereof to us, and what effects follow of it: the last, of the outward means and helps whereby God calleth us into the fellowship of Christ and holdeth us in it. To the first edition and to every subsequent one is prefixed a Dedication to Francis I., stating that the object of the work is to set forth the doctrine which in the author's native land is persecuted with fire and sword. But the changes of form in this celebrated book, of which I have spoken, were accompanied by no change of doctrinal statement. Calvin was only twenty-seven when he wrote it; but he never afterwards found occasion to withdraw or modify anything. The theology of the edition of 1536 is in every respect the same as that of the edition of 1559. The scheme of Calvinistic theology came *totus teres, atque rotundus*, from the mind of its author.[1]

---

[1] I copy the full title of this celebrated work from an edition published at Geneva in 1585. "D. Joannis Calvini vigilantissimi pastoris et fidelissimi doctoris ecclesiæ Genevensis Institutio Christianæ religionis, ab ipso authore anno 1559 et in libros quatuor digesta, certisque distincta capitibus ad aptissimum methodum: et tum aucta tam magna accessione ut propemodum opus novum haberi posset."

VIII. RISE OF PROTESTANT SCHOLASTICISM. 295

The "Institution" occupies a very different position in theological literature from the *Loci Communes*. So long as Calvinism retains its attraction for any large part of Christendom, it can never become obsolete. The complete occupation of the ground of religious belief, the systematic exposition of doctrine, the logical subordination of point to point, the acute interpretation of Scripture, the deep insight into human nature, all make it difficult, if once its premisses be accepted, to resist its conclusions. I am only expressing the opinion of friend and foe alike, when I say that Christianity has never before or since been so completely cast into the mould of a system. For Luther's brilliant attack, now on this, now on that critical point of the Roman entrenchments, is substituted the careful selection of the Protestant position, and the scientific construction of works of defence on every side. There was no secret desire in Calvin's mind, as there was in Melancthon's, to explain away differences and to find a reconciliation with Rome: he better knew the enemy with whom he had to contend, and the utter uselessness of concession. The "Institution" was the last, formal, complete answer of the Reformation to the claims of the Papacy. It gathered up all the diverse threads of the new thought, and wove them into homogeneous strength. Against a system, it set up a system, as completely thought out, based on adequate authority, stern in its demands upon the believer, rigid in its application to life. I have already alluded to the fact, that the theology of Calvin supplied and directed the missionary energy of the Reformation. In Switzerland, the influence of Zwingli paled before that of the Genevese Reformer. Lutheranism did not hold its own even in Germany, where Calvinism, especially in the Palatinate, soon found and kept a footing. In France, the Huguenots were Calvin's children, and the Confession of La Rochelle an echo of his teaching. It was in the heroic self-devotion which the doctrine of the absolute supremacy of God is well fitted to call out, that William the Silent and his Dutchmen defended Holland against Philip II. Calvinism in part turned the current of the English Reformation in the direction of Puritanism—with what practical results for political and religious liberty you well know—and has made Scotland, for good and for evil, what she is. I frankly and fully admit all that this form of faith has done for modern Europe, especially in deepening the sense of the grandeur of human destiny, and introducing a manlier spirit into politics. But I gravely doubt whether the sum of good which it has effected is not outweighed by the prevalence which the mighty genius of Calvin has given to the idea that Christianity can be presented in dialectical form; that its aspirations, its affections, its insight into divine things, its half-apprehensions of realities too great for finite grasp, can be stated with scholastic accuracy and tied together by bonds of logic.

It might have seemed as if Calvin had done once for all the work which the inadequacy of Melancthon's *Loci Communes* left to the later Lutheran dogmatists. But it was not so. The passion for dogmatic system, once it has laid hold of a church or an age, is insatiable, and can never want material on which to work. As characteristic as the *communicatio idiomatum* of Lutheran dogmatics is, in the Calvinistic churches, that debate as to the Divine decrees which is conducted by Supralapsarians on one side, by Sublapsarians on the other. When men undertake on such scant evidence as is afforded by Scripture—if, indeed, on such a point it can be called evidence at all—to decide whether God, when He framed the decree of predestination, had in His mind man fallen or man unfallen, it is plain that nothing is too sacred for the dogmatic passion to touch, or too difficult for it to attempt to resolve. But a keener edge was given to definition by the fact that within the bosom of the Reformed Church itself a reaction soon took place. Arminius was a student under Beza at the University of Geneva : it was from the very heart of Calvinism that Arminianism developed itself. I cannot pause to tell the story of the controversies which distracted the Church of Holland, and which were for a time settled at the Synod of Dordt, where in 1618-19 the doctrine of the "Institution" was defined with more uncompromising rigidity than ever. In Switzerland and in Holland, the men who are admiringly called by their Scottish disciples and imitators "the great Calvinistic systematic divines of the seventeenth century"—Turretine, Heidegger, Witsius, Van Mastricht,[1] and many more whose ponderous folios now sleep the sleep of dusty forgetfulness on college shelves—pursued their patient toil.

"Their works," says Dr. Cunningham,[2] "are based wholly upon the theology of the Reformation ; but they carry it out to its completion, and may be said to form the crown and the copestone of theological science, viewed as an accurate, comprehensive and systematic exposition and defence of the doctrine

---

[1] The Reformers and the Theology of the Reformation, by W. Cunningham, D.D., p. 411.
[2] Ibid.

revealed in the Word of God. We believe that these men have given us an exposition of the doctrines which are made known to us in the sacred Scriptures, and which all men are bound to understand and believe, because God has revealed them, such as, in point of clearness and fullness, accuracy and comprehensiveness, was never before equalled, and has never since been surpassed."

Once more the wheel has come full circle, and, by the side of a Lutheran, a Reformed scholasticism opposes itself to the scholasticism of mediæval Europe.

Was, then, the Reformation, from the intellectual point of view, a failure? Did it break one yoke, only to impose another? We are obliged to confess that, especially in Germany, it soon parted company with free learning; that it turned its back upon culture, that it lost itself in a maze of arid theological controversy, that it held out no hand of welcome to awakening science. Presently we shall see that the impulse to an enlightened study and criticism of the Scriptures came chiefly from heretical quarters; that the unbelieving Spinoza and the Arminian Le Clerc pointed the way to investigations which the great Protestant systematizers thought neither necessary nor useful. Even at a later time it has been the divines who have most loudly declared their allegiance to the theology of the Reformation who have also looked most askance at science, and claimed for their statements an entire independence of modern knowledge. I do not know how, on any ordinary theory of the Reformation, it is possible to answer the accusations implied in these facts. The most learned, the profoundest, the most tolerant of modern theologians would be the most reluctant to accept in their fullness the systems of Melancthon and of Calvin, much more those of Gerhard and of Turretine. They would be slow to pronounce Luther justified in every point of his polemic against Catholic theology, and would recognize in the teachings of the heretics whom he denounced seeds of truth which the influence of three centuries has slowly but surely developed. The fact is, that while the services which the Reformers rendered to truth and liberty by their revolt against the unbroken supremacy of mediæval Christianity cannot be over-estimated, it was impossible for them to settle the questions which they raised. Not merely did the necessary knowledge fail them, but they did not even see the scope of the controversies in which they were engaged. It was their part to open the flood-gates; and the stream, in spite of their well-meant efforts to check and confine it, has since rushed impetuously on, now destroying old landmarks, now fertilizing new fields, but always bringing with it life and refreshment. To look at the Reformation by itself, to judge it only by its theological and ecclesiastical development, is to pronounce it a failure: to consider it as part of a general movement of European thought, to show its essential connection with ripening scholarship and advancing science, to prove its necessary alliance with liberty, to illustrate its slow growth into toleration, is at once to vindicate its past and to promise it the future.

LECTURE IX.

THE REFORMATION IN ENGLAND.

It may have already excited some surprise in your minds that an English writer treating of the Reformation should not have selected the movement in his own country as typical, and arranged other manifestations of the same kind according to their various relations to it. Such a procedure would have had the obvious advantage of dealing at the outset with known personages and familiar controversies, and forces still in visible operation. But it would have been, in the first place, to reverse the order of history. The German and Swiss Reformations not only preceded the English, but exercised upon it definite attractions and repulsions. And, next, the English Reformation, both in its method and in its result, is a thing by itself, taking its place in no historical succession, and altogether refusing to be classified. When a laborious German compiler[1] enumerates the English among the Reformed Churches which own a Genevan origin, and puts the Thirty-nine Articles, under the name of the *Confessio Anglicana,* side by side with the Helvetic

---
[1] Collectio Confessionum in ecclesiis Reformatis publicatarum, ed. H. A. Niemeyer, Lipsiæ, 1840.

and Belgic Confessions, an Anglican churchman, who is not angry, can only be amused. And in truth such a procedure is conspicuously unfaithful to historical fact. Lutheran, Calvinistic, perhaps even Zwinglian lines of influence upon the English Reformation may be traced without difficulty; but there was a native element stronger than any of these which at once assimilated them and gave its own character to the result. That after the lapse of three centuries and a half it is still possible to discuss whether the English Church is Protestant or Catholic, that characteristic parties within her pale eagerly claim one name and angrily repudiate the other, sufficiently shows that the Reformation in England followed no precedents, and was obedient only to its own law of development.

At the same time it was due to the same general causes as the Reformation in Germany and Switzerland. Here, too, there had been a genuine though ineffectual movement of reform before the time of change had fully come. John Wiclif exercised a far wider influence upon the English nation than the isolated thinkers of whom I gave a brief account in my first Lecture, upon Germany: he was a popular teacher in a great University: he enjoyed the support of a party in the state: he was involved in public struggle with the hierarchy: his polemical works, as well as his translation of the Scriptures, had a wide circulation. He was a Reformer in the distinctest sense of the word, upholding the principles, in many cases preaching the precise doctrines, with which Luther afterwards shook the world. That he was suppressed, may be traced to a concurrence of causes not now necessary to be enumerated; but had England been ripe for reformation, the process of suppression would not have been as decisive as it was. It was the advent of the new learning that rekindled the flame. England caught the fire of classical enthusiasm from Italy almost as soon as Germany, and perhaps more eagerly. What can be more significant than the fact that it was to Oxford that Erasmus, unable to make the Italian pilgrimage on which he had set his heart, came to learn Greek? In the last years of the fifteenth, the first of the sixteenth century, his is the name which is a link between English and Continental scholarship: he enjoys the patronage of Henry VII. and Archbishop Warham: he is constantly going backwards and forwards between England and the Continent: he teaches at Cambridge the Greek which he has learned at Oxford: he knits friendships with the best scholars and most liberal thinkers of his time— Grocyn, Linacre, Colet, More: to his caustic pen we owe vivid descriptions of the great English shrines at the very moment when desecration was hanging over them: it is from England that he hastens to Basel to print the New Testament in Greek. Colet never left the Church of Rome: More died a martyr for its claim of supremacy: with reformation, as Luther preached it, Erasmus had no sympathy. But these men were not the less the precursors of the great coming change that they could not foresee it, and would willingly have made it other than it was.

I have pointed out how the Reformation in Germany and Switzerland was politically conditioned: how much in the former case depended upon the unstable equilibrium of the Empire; in the latter, on the free development possible under republican institutions. In both cases, however, there was a strong, steady tide of religious conviction, a popular enthusiasm which carried all before it. It is difficult to say what the course of reformation in Saxony might have been, had the successive Electors not been men who were able to understand the grandeur of Luther's aims, and yielded themselves to the fascination of his enthusiasm; but it is instructive to note that the moment Duke George died, his people fell joyfully and all but unanimously into the general current. But an unpleasant truth, which I think an impartial inquirer cannot help gathering from the records of the English Reformation, is, that its motive power was at least as much political as religious, and that the tone which it took and the rapidity of its progress depended more upon the caprices of a line of arbitrary princes than upon the serious convictions of the people. I do not mean that there were not at Oxford and Cambridge men who were earnestly studying the Scriptures for themselves; merchants in London, enlightened and steady friends of the new learning; a secret leaven of Wiclif's influence working beneath the surface; simple and devout souls upon whom light shone from Wittenberg, or directly from the pages of the New Testament. Without these, the Reformation in England would hardly deserve the name of a religious movement at all; and amid discouragements, persecutions, martyrdoms, the force which they exercised gathered energy and persistence as years passed on. But the story is sullied at the beginning by the scandal of the Divorce, and it takes a deeper dye when Ann Boleyn's head falls on the scaffold, and no man ventures to say that she is innocent. What a sad and shameful story is that of the suppression of the monasteries, and the wasteful distribution of Church lands, under Henry and Edward, to feed the necessities of the Crown and glut the greed of a crowd of hungry courtiers! All through these Tudor times the tide of Reformation ebbs and flows, as the Monarch wills: now Henry is the Defender of the Faith against Luther, and now is urgent that Melancthon should undertake the task of English Reformation: he is Protestant in the assertion of his own supremacy, Catholic in his adhesion to sacramental doctrine: the translation of the Bible is promoted or retarded as his royal caprice dictates: and when he has swept the wealth of the monasteries into his coffers, he issues the Six Articles, and burns the heretics who deny the Real Presence. I will not inflict upon you the familiar story of the fluctuations of religious policy under Edward, Mary, Elizabeth: the strange thing is, how little the nation counts for, how much the Prince. It is true that the tide was slowly rising all the time, and that each successive wave carried it higher on the shore; till Mary found that she could not burn heresy out of her people's hearts, and Elizabeth, that the surest way to their love was to put herself at the head of the Protestant coalition against Spain. But it is impossible not to feel that, had Edward lived, or Mary taken less counsel of her Spanish husband, the course of Reformation in England might have been very different. No wonder that when Mary's death extinguished the fires in Smithfield, the people threw up their caps for Elizabeth; but they had acclaimed the principle of legitimacy in her sister just as loudly, and preferred her Catholicism, which they had not yet convicted of cruelty, to the Protestantism of an amiable pretender.

IX. THE REFORMATION IN ENGLAND.

On this account it is that the English Reformation produced no great heroes of faith. It has no name to set beside those of Luther, Melancthon, Zwingli, Calvin, Knox. It called forth no commanding soul able to raise and rule the whirlwind of popular enthusiasm. I have sometimes thought that its noblest name is that of William Tyndale, the Gloucestershire scholar, who, after much study and many searchings of heart, resolved to give his life to the translation of the Bible into the vulgar tongue. Some theologian, disputing with him while he was yet young, said, "We were better without God's law than the Pope's." "If God spare me life," was the reply, "ere many years I will cause the boy that driveth the plough to know more of the Scripture than you do."[1] It was a pledge that could not be redeemed in England; but it was nobly redeemed amid perils and hair's-breadth 'scapes in Germany and the Low Countries, until the Reformer, who meanwhile had flooded his native country with New Testaments, was basely betrayed into the Emperor's hands, and in 1536, without a word of remonstrance from the England on which he had conferred so priceless a gift, strangled and burnt at Vilvoorde. There is no stain of base compliance upon that name: from the first moment of self-devotion to his great purpose to his last dying prayer, "Lord, ope the King of England's eyes," all is strong, constant, pious, pure. But it needs much special pleading to make a hero of Cranmer. His was the mind of an ecclesiastical lawyer rather than a divine: apt to find compromises and to abide in expediencies, rather than able to think out a principle, and to

---

[1] Bagster's English Hexapla, Introd. p. 43.

recognize it as a thing to be defended, if need be, at the cost of life. Who is not moved at the recollection of the old man's hand, stretched out in his last agony into the cleansing flame? But history sternly demands her due, and will not suffer the pathos of that hour to wipe out the recollection of many doubtful deeds, of many shameful acquiescences, of even the last fruitless attempt to buy life at the price of recantation. Recantation, it must be confessed, is a stain upon the garments of too many English Reformers. Some who were afterwards faithful—Garrett, Barnes, Bilney, Bainham—had borne the faggot in their hour of weakness. In his earlier days even Latimer had recanted. A short durance in the Fleet had persuaded Hooper of the lawfulness of episcopal vestments. We must in justice own that it was very difficult to move in step with a revolution which arbitrary Princes assumed the right to hasten or retard. To cross either Henry VIII. or any of his children was a dangerous thing, and their means of swift punishment were as effectual as their resentment was sudden and sharp. If we except some of the humbler sufferers for the new truth, whose fate history passes by with brief but compassionate record, I am not sure that the purest honours of martyrdom do not rest upon the heads of Fisher and of More.

What there was of Reformation under Henry VIII. chiefly consisted in the spoliation of the monasteries and the substitution of the Royal for the Papal supremacy. The former was so entirely a financial expedient, as to be altogether unworthy of notice in any religious connection: whatever may have been the sins and laxities of the monasteries, no one who looks at the character of the

King, the agents whom he employed, and the uses to which the proceeds were put, can believe that they were dissolved for that reason. But we shall altogether miss the peculiarity of the English Reformation if we regard the Royal supremacy as an arbitrary invention of Henry's, suggested to him, perhaps forced upon him, by the difficulties of the Divorce. From the Norman Conquest downward, the Pope had never taken tax and toll in England without more or less protest, and except under conditions. In virtue of its insular position—on the verge of the great European Commonwealth, yet only in part belonging to it—a certain quasi-imperial dignity attached to England, and the Archbishop of Canterbury was *alterius orbis Papa*. Throughout the whole mediæval period, there is a constant record of struggle between King and Pope, with the maintenance of which, whatever influence we may ascribe to the character of successive monarchs, the existence of free institutions had much to do. However self-willed the King, however caught in the necessities of foreign politics, it could not be without importance that the great Councils of the nation afforded opportunity for the formation and expression of public opinion on matters that concerned all citizens. The struggle of Rufus and Henry I. with Anselm, the struggle of Henry II. with Becket, the Constitutions of Clarendon, the Statute of Mortmain, the Statute of Provisors, the Statute of Præmunire, all mark as many epochs in this unintermitted warfare. The King established the right of investing Bishops with their temporalities; criminous clerks were compelled to submit themselves to the civil tribunals; the accumulation of wealth in the hands of the Church was checked;

appeals to Rome were restrained; Papal bulls might not be brought into England, nor Papal legates allowed to land, without permission. These statements probably express the maximum of national demand, rather than the actual amount of Papal concession at any given moment: on both sides rights were always reserved, claims always renewed; and Popes of high spirit and arbitrary temper knew how to avail themselves of the political necessities of Kings, as when Alexander III. absolved Henry II. of the murder of Becket, or Innocent III. sent Pandulf to restore England to John as a Papal fief. Nor, especially in the fight for patronage, was right always on the side of royalty: if the Pope sometimes thrust into English sees Italian ecclesiastics who unblushingly spent their revenues in Rome, the King often kept bishoprics vacant, that the income might find its way into his own coffers; while, between the two, the rights of chapters dwindled almost to nothing. Still the formal assumption of supremacy by Henry VIII. was but the last stage of a process which had been going on for almost five hundred years. It was an act that could be defended by many precedents, and was fully in accord with national feeling. When Henry dexterously turned the acceptance by the clergy of Wolsey's legatine authority into a pretext for inflicting the penalties of præmunire upon the whole English Church—a position from which it extricated itself only by the payment of an enormous fine—his conduct may have been criticised as arbitrary and even treacherous, but it was never impugned as illegal. And it is curious to note how Mary, when in the last year of her reign she was more than ever anxious to show her devotion to the Pope and to reconcile England with the Holy See, ordered the bearer of a red hat to her confessor William Peto to be stopped at Calais, because Paul IV. had also appointed him to supersede as legate her cousin and favourite, Reginald Pole.

Under Wolsey there had been some faint beginnings of disciplinary reform. He had received his legatine authority from Rome, with full acquiescence of the King and Archbishop Warham, in the intention of cleansing the Augean stable of the ecclesiastical courts. Perhaps we may take his application of monastic property to educational purposes in Oxford and Ipswich as a step in the same direction. But he was too much of an international politician, too intent on his own far-reaching schemes of ambition, to bend to the homelier task of reforming abuses which had become inveterate in the Church. On the other hand, Henry, in the latter part of his reign, was quite content with the confiscation of the monastic estates and the establishment of his own supremacy. In all the controversies which I have on a former occasion indicated as critical, he took the Catholic side. There are four documents, published during his reign, which set forth, with a clearness that left nothing to be desired, what his subjects were to believe: the Ten Articles of 1536; the "Institution of a Christian Man," or Bishops' Book, of the same year; the Six Articles of 1539; and "The necessary Doctrine and Erudition for any Christian Man," or King's Book, of 1544. And the colour of all these is decisively Catholic. The Six Articles, "the whip with six strings," as the Protestants called it, laid down as necessary matters of belief and practice the Real Presence, communion in one kind, the celibacy of the priesthood, the obligation of vows, the lawfulness of private masses, and the expediency of auricular confession. This was the doctrinal bond within which the nascent Protestantism of England groaned, until the accession of Edward gave it liberty of expansion. The same fact comes out in relation to certain friendly overtures which, for political reasons, Henry made to the Protestants of Germany. In 1538 and 1539 a German embassy was in England, conferring with Cranmer and other divines as to the possibility of a common basis of faith. But it was of no avail. The Germans stood by the Confession of Augsburg, between which and the doctrine of the "Institution of a Christian Man" there could be no reconciliation. England was still Catholic.

The reign of Edward VI. opened another era. The old learning all at once gave place to the new. The pent-up stream of Protestant doctrine and feeling burst its bounds and carried all before it. Communications were opened with the Reformed churches of the Continent, and Cranmer even entertained the dream of a federated Protestantism. The year of Edward's accession was that of the Battle of Mühlberg, and the consequent imposition upon Protestant Germany of the semi-Catholic régime known as the Interim, disposed many theologians of name to betake themselves to a country where the hope of reformation stood so high. Bucer and Fagius were invited from Strasburg to teach at Cambridge: Peter Martyr, Dryander, Tremellio, were active at Oxford: John a Lasco established in the city of London a Presbyterian community, rigid in doctrine, well organized in discipline: Calvin wrote long letters of advice and exhortation to the Protector Somerset, and after his fall, to the King. The refugees, the colour of whose theology was more Calvinistic than Lutheran, were Cranmer's trusted friends and counsellors: many of them lived with him at Lambeth, sitting at his table and sharing his secretest thoughts. And it was while this foreign influence—the influence, be it remembered, of trained dogmatic theologians—was at its height, that the English Prayer-book was shaped and the foundation laid of the Thirty-nine Articles.

At the same time, in order that we may not lay too much stress on these circumstances, we must take some pains to understand a fact which more than any other differentiates the English Reformation—I mean the continuity of the Anglican Church. There is no point at which it can be said, here the old Church ends, here the new begins. Are you inclined to take the Act of Supremacy as such a point? I have already shown that Henry's assumption of headship was but the last decisive act of a struggle which had been going on for almost five centuries. The retention of the Episcopate by the English Reformers at once helped to preserve this continuity and marked it in the distinctest way. I speak here as an historian, not as a theologian, and I have nothing to do with that doctrine of apostolical succession which many Churchmen hold, though the Articles do not teach and the Prayer-book only implies it. But it is an obvious historical fact that Parker was the successor of Augustine, just as clearly as Lanfranc and Becket. Warham, Cranmer, Pole, Parker—there is no break in the line, though the first and third are claimed as Catholic, the second and fourth as Protestant. The succession, from the spiritual point of view, was most carefully provided for when

Parker was consecrated: not even the most ignorant controversialist now believes in the Nag's-Head fable. The canons of the pre-Reformation Church, the statutes of the Plantagenets, are binding upon the Church of England to-day, except where they have been formally repealed. There has been no break, unless by what we may call private circumstances, in the devolution of Church property. The Church may be Protestant now, as it undoubtedly was Catholic once; but it is impossible to fix the point at which the transition was legally and publicly made.

A great force has been exerted in the same direction by the principles on which the Service-book was compiled. Something had been done in Henry's reign to provide the people with a form of worship in their own tongue; the Litany had been translated, a Scripture lesson every Sunday and holy-day ordered to be read in English. But when, on the accession of Edward, Cranmer set about the task of providing an English Prayer-book, it was to the ancient ritual of the country that he turned for his materials. The mediæval custom had not been uniform: there were many "Uses," as they were called: the Use of Bangor, the Use of Lincoln, the Use of York. But in the eleventh century, a great ritual reformer, Osmund, Bishop of Salisbury, had so improved the Use of Sarum as to have secured for it a preference over all others. And the Use of Sarum is the basis of the Prayer-book. The Breviary, its eight daily services compressed into two, furnished the order of Matins and Evensong; the Missal, with certain necessary alterations, of the Communion Service. Some guidance was afforded to the compilers by the Breviary of Cardinal Quignon, a bold attempt at reformation made, not without Papal sanction, in 1536, but superseded by the labours of the Council of Trent. On the other hand, in the very stronghold of the Catholic party in the Church are to be found traces of Protestant influence. Cranmer and his colleagues made considerable use of a work called the "Consultation" of Hermann von Wied,[1] that Elector Archbishop

---

[1] The copy of this book used by Cranmer is still preserved in the Library of Chichester Cathedral. Dean Hook (Lives of the Archbishops, N. S. II. 289) gives its full title as follows: Nostra Hermanni ex gratia Dei Archiepiscopi Coloniensis et Principis Electoris &c. simplex ac pia deliberatio, qua ratione Christiana et in verbo Dei fundata Reformatio Doctrinæ, administrationis divinorum Sacramentorum, Cæremoniarum, totiusque curæ animarum et aliorum ministeriorum ecclesiasticorum, apud eos qui nostræ Pastorali curæ commendati sunt, tantisper instituenda sit, donec Dominus dederit constitui meliorem vel per liberam et Christianam Synodum, sive Generalem, sive Nationalem vel per ordines Imperii Nationis Germanicæ, in Spiritu Sancto congregatos. Bonnæ, ex officina Laurentii, Typographi, anno MDXXXV. This was translated into English under the title, "A simple and religious consultation of us, Hermann, by the Grace of God," &c., and two editions were published, one in 1547, another in 1548. In Melancthon's letters (Corp. Ref. V.), the reader will find several which refer to the composition of this book. All the important facts of the case, however, are mentioned in the following extract from a letter to Casper Cruciger, written from Bonn on the 23rd of May, 1543 (Corp. Ref. V. 113): "Scripsi vobis antea, Episcopum secuturum esse formam Noribergensem, eratque ante meum adventum institutus liber ad exemplum Noribergense scribendus. Retinuit pleraque Osiandri Bucerus, quosdam articulos auxit, ut est copiosus. Mihi cum omnia religissem attribuit articulos περὶ τρίων ὑποστάσεων, de creatione, de peccato originis, de justitia fidei et operum, de Ecclesia, de pœnitentia. In his consumpsi tempus hactenus, et legi de cerimoniis baptismi et cœnæ domini, quæ ipse composuit." If, as is most probable, the "Consultation" was used in the compilation of the Articles also, this enumeration of Melancthon's contributions to it has a special interest. As Cranmer's wife was Osiander's niece, may not the fact that the "Kirchenordnung" of Nürnberg was largely the work of that Reformer,

of Cologne who all but succeeded in Protestantizing his diocese. This book contained, with other matter, a directory of public worship, which, as it was the work of Melancthon and Bucer, was distinctly framed upon a Lutheran model. In Edward VI.'s reign, however, events marched quickly. The set of the party of movement was away from ancient methods of belief and devotion. The doctrinal Protestants naturally thought that the new book retained too much of the Catholic leaven. The influence of the foreign refugees made itself felt: the opinion of Bucer and Peter Martyr, formally asked, was in favour of a still further departure from Catholic standards. The result was the Prayer-book of 1552, commonly known as the second of Edward VI. But this marks the highest flood-tide of Protestant feeling. The changes made in the Elizabethan Prayer-book of 1559 were intended to conciliate Anglo-Catholics; and the revision of 1662 worked, as far as it went, in the same direction.[1]

---

have something to do with the Archbishop's use of Hermann von Wied's "Consultation," which was framed upon its model?

[1] It is impossible to give the evidence for this statement within the compass of a note; but we may select as a fair illustration the words of administration in the Communion Service. The first Prayer-book of Edward VI. has, "The body of our Lord Jesus Christ, which was given for thee, preserve thy body and soul unto everlasting life." For this, the second substitutes, "Take and eat this, in remembrance that Christ died for thee, and feed on him in thy heart, by faith with thanksgiving." Between these two formulas there is a great theological gulf, which the Prayer-book of Elizabeth ineffectually endeavoured to bridge over by combining the two into one, without alteration of either. But it is noticeable that the rubric which Edward VI. had added to the Communion Service, by his own authority, after the publication of the second Prayer-book, declaring that in the kneeling posture of the communicant "no adoration was done or ought to be done to any

The history of the Articles runs parallel with that of the Prayer-book. The formation of both practically belongs to the reign of Edward; while both underwent a revision, by which no essential feature was altered, in that of Elizabeth. But while the materials of the Prayer-book were quarried in the mines of English mediæval piety, those of the Articles were largely derived from foreign sources. That the Thirty-nine Articles contain many points of likeness to the Confession of Augsburg, no one who is familiar with both can doubt: not only are the verbal resemblances many and striking, but the two evidently belong to the same class of document. The actual link of connection between them has recently been discovered in a copy of the Thirteen Articles drawn up by Cranmer when the German Embassy visited England in 1538 and 1539. Then it was impossible to come to any terms, and the Six Articles of 1539 sufficiently tell us why. In 1553, things were in a very different position. Protestantism, though not of the Lutheran type, was in the ascendant in England. Had a second attempt been made to treat with Wittenberg, it might have been the Saxon Reformers who would have held off. And by this time, too, Cranmer had given up his idea of a federated Protestantism, and was content to frame a national Confession for the use of his own Church. In 1553, therefore, were promulgated the Forty-two Articles, which, ten years later revised and reduced in number to Thirty-nine, were formally adopted by Queen and Church,

---

real or essential presence there being of Christ's natural flesh and blood," was expunged under Elizabeth. Cardwell: The Two Books of Common Prayer of Edward VI. compared, pp. 303—308; A History of Conferences on the Book of Common Prayer, pp. 34, 35.

and have ever since been subscribed by all clerics. The Confession as a whole resembles all similar documents, in bearing plain traces of contemporary controversies in which it was thought necessary to speak with decisive voice: of the suppressed Articles, seven in number, four referred to heresies of the Anabaptist type, which seem to have abated in virulence in the ten years intervening between the first and second form of the document.[1] And it is an additional proof of the foreign origin of the Articles, that much of the new matter added in 1563 was taken from the Confession of Würtemberg, a document presented to the Council of Trent in 1551, which is only the Confession of Augsburg in a slightly different form.[2]

The years of reaction under Mary may be dismissed with brief mention. It is true that they had a serious influence upon the temper of the nation. If it was a

---

[1] Setting aside minor changes, some of which were, however, doctrinally important, seven Articles were omitted from the forty-two, and four added. The seven omitted were the tenth, "Of grace;" the sixteenth, "Blasphemy against the Holy Ghost;" the nineteenth, "All men are bound to keep the moral commandments of the law;" the thirty-ninth, "The resurrection of the dead is not yet brought to pass;" the fortieth, "The souls of them that depart this life do neither die with the bodies nor sleep idly;" the forty-first, "Heretics called Millenarii;" and the forty-second, "All men shall not be saved at the length." The Articles added were the fifth of the present enumeration, "Of the Holy Ghost;" the twelfth, "Of good works;" the twenty-ninth, "Of the wicked who do not eat the Body of Christ in the use of the Lord's Supper;" and the thirtieth, "Of both kinds." Hardwick: History of the Articles of Religion, Appendix, III. p. 275 et seq.

[2] Hardwick, p. 127, note. The theologian chiefly answerable for the Confession of Würtemberg was Brenz, whose Lutheran orthodoxy was unimpeachable.

significant thing that Mary's well-known Catholicism was no bar to her almost unanimous and even enthusiastic acceptance by the people, it was equally significant that the measures of her Spanish and Papal advisers wore English loyalty threadbare. The result was that Elizabeth ascended the throne much more in the character of a Protestant champion than her own convictions and inclinations would have dictated. She was indeed the daughter of Ann Boleyn, whom by this time Protestants were beginning to regard as a martyr of the faith; but she was also the child of Henry VIII., and the heiress of his imperious will. Soon, however, she found herself Protestant almost in her own despite. The Papacy, in the first pride of successful reaction, offered her only the alternative of submission or excommunication, and she did not for a moment hesitate to choose the latter. Then commenced that long and close alliance between Catholicism and domestic treason which is so differently judged as it is approached from the religious or the political side. These seminary priests, who in every various disguise come to England, moving secretly about from manor-house to manor-house, celebrating the rites of the Church, confirming the wavering, consoling the dying, winning back the lapsed to the fold, too well acquainted with Elizabeth's prisons, and often finding their way to her scaffolds—what are they but the intrepid missionaries, the self-devoted heroes, of a proscribed faith? On the other hand, the Queen is excommunicate, an evil woman, with whom it is not necessary to keep faith, to depose whom would be the triumph of the Church, whose death, however compassed, its occasion: how easy to weave plots under the cloak of religious intercourse, and to make the unity of the faith a conspiracy of rebellion! The next heir to the throne, Mary of Scotland, was a Catholic, and, as long as she lived, a perpetual centre of domestic and European intrigue: plot succeeded plot, in which the traitorous subtlety was all Catholic—the keenness of discovery, the watchfulness of defence, all Protestant. Then, too, the shadow of Spanish supremacy began to cast itself broadly over Europe: the unequal struggle with Holland was still prolonged: it was known that Philip's dearest wish was to recover to his empire and the Church the island kingdom which had once unwillingly accepted his rule. It was thus the instinct of self-defence which placed Elizabeth at the head of the Protestant interest in Europe: she sent Philip Sidney to die at Zutphen: her sailor-buccaneers, whether there were peace at home or not, bit and tore at everything Spanish upon the southern main: till at last, in 1588, Philip gathered up all his naval strength and hurled the Armada at our shores. *Afflavit Deus, et dissipati sunt.* The valour of England did much; the storms of heaven the rest. Mary of Scotland had gone to her death the year before, and her son had been trained to hate his mother's faith. There could be no question any more of the fixed Protestantism of the English people.

It might seem, at first sight, as if the period of Reformation in England ceased at the beginning of Elizabeth's reign. The Prayer-book as then settled is, notwithstanding the revision of 1662, substantially the same as that which is used now. The Articles of 1563 have since undergone no alterations and are still binding. The peculiar churchmanship of Parker, who believed in the continuity of the Church of England, who maintained the right of a national communion to reform itself, who clung to historical and antiquarian precedents, who held little intercourse with foreign Protestants and distrusted what he called "Germanical natures," is a type of churchmanship much in vogue just now. But, in truth, the Reformation in England was a case of arrested development, and Elizabeth's settlement, a compromise which came too soon. The popular movement, that which inspired the enthusiasm of preachers and the constancy of martyrs, had always been eagerly Protestant, demanding doctrinal as well as disciplinary reform, adopting in earlier days the Lutheran, afterwards the Calvinistic type of belief, and not sparing of dislike and contempt of Catholic usage and worship. The men who belonged to this party had no sympathy with the reluctance of others in high places to break away from old precedents: to them, the continuity of the Church was a matter of indifference: what some called compliance with decent custom, they flatly qualified as idolatry: they asked that the new truth which God had given should be enthusiastically accepted and carried to its full issue in worship and practice. These were the theologians who in Edward's reign had been in closest intercourse with the Reformers of the Continent, and who, when Mary succeeded, knowing that they were compromised beyond recall, fled over seas till the storm should abate. They found refuge chiefly in Switzerland and the cities of the Rhineland which were under Swiss religious influence, and, after five years' exile, came back more Calvinistic than they went, more enamoured of Presbyterian discipline, more eager to continue the work of Reformation interrupted by the death of Edward. To these Marian exiles the

Elizabethan settlement was a deep discouragement. They submitted with but an ill grace to ceremonies which they looked upon as relics of Popery, and an episcopal rule which they did not think scriptural, and applied themselves to the task of changing from within a church the legal foundations of which they were unable to undermine.

Nothing can show so conclusively that the Anglican churchmanship of Parker and his associates was more the theory of a few learned men in high places than the serious conviction of the nation, as the gradual gathering of Puritan strength, and still more the growing prevalence of Calvinistic theology, during the long reign of Elizabeth. Notwithstanding the Queen's well-known Catholic preferences, and her determination to stand by the settlement of religion which she had made—notwithstanding the establishment of the Court of High Commission, the very purpose of which was to enforce uniformity, and which was sufficiently harsh and arbitrary in its methods—Puritanism spread in every diocese. In 1577, Grindal, Parker's successor in the Primacy, refused to suppress the "Prophesyings," or meetings for religious conference, which were the chief means of disseminating Puritan opinions, and was in consequence sequestrated from his see. Whitgift, who followed him, had no scruples as to putting down sectaries; but, on the other hand, it was he who devised the Nine Lambeth Articles of 1595, in which the five points of Calvinism were laid down with uncompromising rigidity. It is true that they were never imposed upon the English Church; but what a strange drawing together of Canterbury and Geneva was this! While Whitgift was still Archbishop, James I. succeeded Elizabeth. The Puritans, knowing his Pres-

byterian education, fondly thought that their hour was
come, and met him on his way from Edinburgh with
what is known as the Millenary Petition, asking for the
abolition of the usages against which they had so long
protested. But the Hampton Court Conference showed
that the King had learned to know Presbyterianism only
to hate it; and the ecclesiastical situation remained un-
changed, except that a foolish and obstinate pedant sat
in the seat of a woman who, if often wilful, loved her
people and received their love in return. Still Calvinism
was in the ascendant. James himself sent representatives
to the Synod of Dordt, who approved the rigidly Calvinistic confession which it enacted against Arminian heresy.
Abbot, who was Primate from 1611 to 1633, though he
used the powers of the Court of High Commission against
the Puritans, was in doctrinal sympathy with them, and
contended less for Catholic theory and usage than for the
general maintenance of authority. It was with Bishop
Andrewes, whom many men had wished to see in the
Primacy in Abbot's place, and with Laud, who actually
succeeded Abbot, that the reaction began. They were
Anglicans of a higher type than even Parker, men whom
modern Anglo-Catholics revere, the one as a saint, the
other as a martyr. Accusations of personal unfaithfulness to the Church of England were freely made against
Laud, and his ecclesiastical principles were attacked as
logically leading to Rome. But the fairer criticism
of modern times has decided that at least the former
charge was unfounded, and that Laud faithfully kept
that *via media* in which so many pious feet have of late
years learned to walk. In him there was a reversion to
the churchmanship of a time when foreign influence had

not yet made itself decisively felt on the English Reformation, and Puritanism was not; a churchmanship which learned its doctrine from the "Institution of a Christian Man," and drew its devotion from the Use of Sarum, and for the enforcement of uniformity, returned to the methods of the Tudors. For the moment, the reaction came too late: Laud died upon the scaffold; the Westminster Confession took the legal place of the Articles, the Directory, of the Prayer-book; till, after but an instant's partial prevalence, both were swept away by triumphant Independency. But such a victory bore in itself the seeds of defeat; and when 1661 came, the demands of the Presbyterians at the Savoy Conference were almost contemptuously rejected; the Act of Uniformity brought organized Dissent to the birth; and the Caroline Bishops trod in the footsteps, not of Whitgift or of Abbot, but of Laud.

I am not concerned to vindicate either the character or the aims of Puritanism; it is sufficient to have affiliated it on the true stock of the Reformation. Now, after two centuries and a half, historical students whose judgment is not disturbed by the fascination of old controversies in new forms, are beginning to discern that the roots of all that is noble in English life to-day go down to Roundhead and Cavalier alike, and that piety and learning were not the monopoly of either Churchman or Puritan. Let George Herbert the Anglican, Colonel Hutchinson the Independent, Lord Falkland the Latitudinarian, stand side by side as the best that that troubled time could produce, and let each of us leave it to the force of natural attraction to adjust the order of their precedence. One word only I would say as to the charge of pettiness in controversy often brought against the Puritan party. What they perpetually asked from Elizabeth and her Bishops, what they begged of James I. at the Hampton Court Conference, what they urged upon the triumphant Church of the Restoration, touched the same points: the kneeling posture at the Lord's Supper, the sign of the cross in baptism, the use of the surplice, the bowing at the name of Jesus, the reading of apocryphal lessons. All external things, it will be said; things indifferent to a man of robust conscience who can look below the surface into the essence of controversies; certainly not matters upon which to divide a church and rend a nation in twain. Nor am I prepared to deny that in the course of the hundred years during which these ceremonies were in dispute, they assumed the nature of shibboleths, became standards of bitter contention rather than matters of reasonable debate, and were eagerly defended or assailed by many who had no real conception of their significance. But a glance at the list which I have given sufficiently shows that these ceremonies had to the Puritan a very definite symbolic meaning. They stood for the old Church, for its authority over Scripture, for its doctrine of the Real Presence, for its theory of priests and sacraments. Looked at in this light, the external conformity which was asked of the Puritans involved a transition from the Protestant to the Catholic side of the Reformation. It meant the substitution of the authority of the Church for the authority of Scripture and Conscience.

From what has been said, it will be plain that from the first, two distinct elements have been present in the English Church, sometimes struggling for the mastery, sometimes living peacefully side by side, and that it is contrary to historical fact for either to assert itself in such a way as to exclude the other. Whether they can be brought into logical accord, is a question with which I do not presume to meddle. Evangelicals interpret, in a way satisfactory to themselves, the Ordinal and the Baptismal Service; while John Henry Newman, following in Tract 90 the steps of Sancta Clara, has sought to give the Articles a Catholic sense. I am only adopting the theological nomenclature of the day, and at the same time conforming to historical fact, when I call these elements Catholic and Protestant. It is the peculiarity of the Church of England that she is both. Apply to her the test which I laid down in a former Lecture, the belief in sacramental religion and the possession of a sacerdotal order, and she is Catholic. She has priests who in virtue of episcopal ordination exercise the mysterious power of forgiving sins, and sacraments which only duly ordained priests can administer. Yet in the Articles we find a confession of faith in closest relation with the Confession of Augsburg, and which in contents and in history alike takes its place among the symbolic documents of the Reformation. On one side we have the national character of the movement, the theoretical continuity of the Church of England, the uninterrupted episcopal succession, the Prayer-book drawn from mediæval sources, the Catholic preferences of Henry and Elizabeth, the Anglican churchmanship of Parker: on the other, the light kindled from Wittenberg, the popular revolt against Catholic superstition and abuse, the doctrinal Protestantism of the Universities, the influence of Cranmer's foreign advisers, the Calvinistic zeal of the Marian exiles, the enthusiasm of a newly acquired faith, which was careless of old usage, and did not fear to contemplate revolution. These were the two forces which Elizabeth sought to compel to live together on terms prescribed by the Prayer-book of 1559 and the Articles of 1563. How premature the compromise was, the history of every subsequent century sufficiently shows. The growth of Puritanism, the reaction under Andrewes and Laud, the triumph of Presbyterianism in the Westminster Assembly of Divines, and the usurpation of power by the Independents of the army, were only the first stages of the struggle. The Restoration re-established the Church on a footing which Laud would have heartily approved, and Puritanism could re-appear only in the form of persecuted Dissent. On the other hand, the Revolution settlement involved the High-church secession of the Non-jurors; while the Evangelical revival of almost a century later called forth, as its first strength began to wane, the Oxford movement, and that Anglo-Catholic fervour which has so greatly raised the present tone of Church doctrine and ritual. All this constitutes an historical phenomenon quite different from that presented by any of the Reformed Churches of the Continent. The development of Lutheranism, the development of Calvinism, have been simple and homogeneous. It is possible to speak of the Lutheran Church of Germany, of the Calvinistic Church of Scotland, in terms that shall be applicable to either as a whole. But only within narrow limits can we apply descriptive epithets to the Church of England, which will not be angrily repudiated by one of her two opposed yet equally characteristic parties.

I cannot speak in terms too strong of the efficacy of the

Prayer-book as a connecting link between the mediæval Church and the Church of to-day. It would not be true to say that all parties in the Church are equally attached to it; but its hold even upon those worshippers who are least in accord with its doctrinal implications is enormous; and recent events seem to show that the tenderest measure of revision is only a distant possibility. I have often heard churchmen confess that it supplies the only form in which they can happily worship; while those who have not been nurtured upon it freely admit the charm of its grave piety, its chastened ardour, the solemn harmony of its periods, the completeness of its adaptation to the daily needs of devotion. If we admit the propriety of making creeds in any case a constituent of worship, it is well that the Prayer-book should recite no national or local confession, but the symbols of the ancient Church. But it certainly has not been possible to draw from the fountains of mediæval devotion, without at the same time adopting to some extent a mediæval theology. Nothing short of complete remodelling could have made the Use of Sarum speak the language of Luther or of Calvin. The function of the priest is not that of the minister, and words descriptive of the one fail in applicability to the other. Luther formulates the Protestant principle when, in words which I have already quoted, he declares that whoever is qualified to administer the sacraments, becomes so in virtue of the congregation's choice, and when deposed is but as other men. With this, the idea of the priest, who receives an indelible priesthood at the hands of a Bishop, and to whom is committed the very power of Christ in the forgiveness of sins, cannot by any device of logic or rhetoric be reconciled. On the other hand, much pains have been bestowed to prove that the Articles are not Calvinistic. I do not now allude to Newman's attempt to put a Catholic meaning upon them: that was a logical *tour de force* which convinced only those who were waiting to be convinced. But men who desire to dissociate as far as possible the English from the German and the Swiss Reformations, have advanced the theory that the Articles, especially the seventeenth, are really Augustinian, and that their doctrinal origin is to be sought rather in the fifth century than in the sixteenth. In so far as this is a debate of names and epithets, I shall not try to settle it. It should not be forgotten that Augustine, Luther, Calvin, whatever their minor differences, were all doctors in the same school of theology, and that the Reformers exulted in sitting at the feet of the great African Father. I have already shown that, in regard to the characteristic points of what is called the Calvinistic scheme, Calvin differed from Luther chiefly in the relentless logical precision with which he had worked them out and co-ordinated them into a system. We may be thankful that the seventeenth Article is less minutely rigid in its tone, less cruelly inclusive in its scope, than it would have been if Calvin had dictated it. But nothing, it seems to me, can be doctrinally or historically plainer than that the theology of the Thirty-nine Articles is the theology of the Confession of Augsburg. What that was, and what possibilities of development lay within it, is plainly indicated by the Nine Lambeth Articles approved by Archbishop Whitgift. Happy was it for the Church of England that she was content to abide by the settlement of 1563!

It would, however, be much less than just to assume that the convinced and logical adherents of these two schools of thought together make up the Church of England, and have alone given it its characteristic colour. From various causes, the obligation of its formularies has lain lightly on the shoulders of many of its most loyal children. Its national character, which, if denied by the collector of contemporary statistics, no fair student of history will question, and the obvious compromise involved in the settlement of Elizabeth, have justified some thoughtful men in taking up a position intermediate between the extremes of Catholic and Protestant theory. They have looked upon the Prayer-book as a manual of devotion which they were bound to use, but upon which they might put their own meaning. They have regarded the Articles as Articles of peace, or as terms of comprehension, or as settlements of contemporary controversies, rather than as a Confession of Faith, every clause of which was separately and collectively binding upon the conscience of the signatory. With a large class of clergymen, the neglect of systematic theological study, till lately almost characteristic of their order, has tended in the same direction: they have lived and worked in their parishes, performing, as is the wont of the English parish priest, many secular and social duties with admirable efficiency, preaching ethical sermons, and not troubling themselves with schools of thought. The Arminian reaction against the severity of the Calvinistic scheme had a wide influence in England, though it came too late to leave its mark on any of the formularies of the Church: if on the one hand there have been many excellent clergymen who have never dreamed of realizing the sacerdotal powers bestowed upon them at their ordination, there have been as many who would be puzzled to reconcile their views of human nature and their theory of salvation with the seventeenth Article. Always there has been a distinct Latitudinarian party in the Church, though all Latitudinarianism has not arisen from the same source or manifested itself in the same way: men like Hales of Eton, or Whichcote and Smith of Cambridge, or the beloved disciple whose loss is yet fresh, Arthur Stanley, the natural bent of whose minds was towards a wide comprehension, and the reduction of the essentials of religion to the fewest, and the subordination of the dogmatic element in it to the ethical and the spiritual; or philosophizing theologians, like Cudworth and Henry More the Platonist, and, in a later time, Butler and Paley; or modern Broad-churchmen, who claim that the Articles interpose no obstacle in the way of the freest investigation of the character and claims of Scripture, and who seek a reconciliation between ancient faith and modern science. But when we turn from the masters of schools to their disciples, we find that there is an essential difference between schools within a church and sects without it. In the latter, diversities of faith always tend to become emphatic: their respective adherents stand to one another in an habitual attitude of opposition, and belief grows to be onesided in proportion as it is firmly held. But schools of thought are to some extent the arbitrary creation of the critic; they melt into one another by imperceptible gradations: there are men who without conscious inconsistency claim to belong to all schools, and men who do not think themselves unfaithful to truth in adhering to none. And the Church of England has always held, especially in the ranks of its laity, a large number of excellent Christians who have at once kept aloof from parties, and have exercised a moderating influence upon them. They have been content with a form of worship which came down to them from their forefathers, and with which their own religious affections were inextricably intertwined. They have as much liberty as they desire, and as much order as they need. They see that the system of the Church has grown up with the institutions of the country, and think it well fitted to satisfy the wants of the people. If we are at all able to speak of the Church of England as a whole, it is largely because of the existence in it of men like these.

The presence in the Church of England of a Catholic and a Protestant school, makes it difficult to define its position in regard to the authority of Scripture. If, on the one hand, there are theologians who adopt the dictum of Chillingworth, "The Bible, and the Bible only, the religion of Protestants," who, with the eighth Article, base the authority of the creeds on the fact that they may be proved by most certain warrants of Holy Scripture, and with the twentieth, subordinate the "authority" of the Church "in controversies of faith" to the final arbitrament of "God's word written"—there are certainly others who look upon the Bible as rather the witness and guarantee of the teaching of the Church than as the original source of doctrine, and lay a very real stress on the decisions of the first four Councils. There can be no doubt that the Church of England has always been eager, beyond other Protestant churches, in the study of Patristic theology. She has consulted the mind of antiquity. She has set Cyprian beside Augustine, and

Athanasius beside Jerome. The necessity of defending her episcopal constitution has sent her back to the ante-Nicene Fathers, and given her a personal interest in the problem of the Ignatian letters. In like manner, the scientific study and emendation of the New Testament text was early begun and has been zealously carried on in England. The first of the great MSS. of the New Testament to be carefully collated and printed were the Alexandrine (A), which in 1628 was sent to Charles I. by the Patriarch of Constantinople, Cyril Lucar; and that which Beza gave to the University of Cambridge (D). Bryan Walton's Polyglot, published in 1657, Mill's New Testament of 1707, the materials gathered by Bentley for his projected edition, lie at the basis of modern New Testament criticism, while Griesbach was enabled to accomplish his epoch-making work by pecuniary help from England. Of later labours in the same field, I will only say that the great edition of the New Testament which has lately been issued from Cambridge, shows that English scholarship need not fear even German rivalry in this most important branch of theological investigation. But the peculiarity of Anglican religion nowhere shows itself more characteristically than in its neglect of dogmatic theology. It has contributed almost nothing to the development of that Protestant scholasticism which was the subject of my last Lecture. When I have mentioned "Pearson on the Creed," I have said all. The very fact that the chief dogmatic book of the Church of England is based upon the Apostles' Creed, and not upon a series of *Loci Communes* capable of indefinite subdivision and multiplication, is full of meaning. For such "bodies of divinity" as our language possesses, we must go back to the days of triumphant Puritanism. The Church of England has abundantly defended her own theological position, has endeavoured to find a philosophical basis for religion, has contended more or less successfully with Deism, has produced many famous preachers and some few mystics; but she has nothing to set beside the mighty volumes of Gerhard or of Turretine. It is well for her that she has been content with the simplicity of her own formularies: had she made the deliberate attempt to enlarge and draw out the compromise of Elizabeth into a compact logical system, she would certainly have lost in comprehensiveness all that she might have gained in doctrinal coherence.

So founded and animated by such a spirit, the Church of England has always held, and still holds, a middle and a mediating place in Christendom. This is curiously illustrated by the character of a small class of men over whom she has exercised an attraction. I mention only in passing, Marc Antonio de Dominis, Archbishop of Spalato, for he was a man of doubtful character, who, after holding an English benefice, returned to the Church of Rome to die in her prisons. But there was Saravia, the friend and neighbour of Richard Hooker: there was Isaac Casaubon, who found that here he could reconcile with his sense of the abuses of the Papacy the reverence for antiquity natural to so great a scholar: there was Pierre Le Courayer, the friend of Atterbury, who, before he left France or the Catholic Church, wrote a defence of the validity of English orders: there was Grabe, the learned editor of the Septuagint, who quitted the Lutheran with the intention of joining the Roman Church, but finally found in England what he conceived to be the union of sound doctrine with apostolical order.[1] The list is perhaps not a long one, but the kind of name of which it is composed is significant. Nor has the idea of a re-union of Christendom, to be effected on the lines of her own constitution, ever been long absent from the mind of the English Church. Archbishop Wake, at the beginning of the last century, with this view actually opened communications—unhappily fruitless—both with the Gallican party of the French Church, and with leading Protestant theologians in Germany and Switzerland.[2] In our own time the Evangelical Alliance, the establishment of the Bishopric of Jerusalem in conjunction with Prussia, the Society for the Re-union of Christendom, the efforts at friendly intercourse with the Greek Church, the sympathy of churchmen of almost all parties with the old Catholics, are evidences of the same spirit. The difficulties in the way of any practical result are immense, probably insuperable; but the persistence of the desire is a strong testimony to the fact that the Church of England, taken as a whole, is both Protestant and Catholic—or neither.

I have regarded the English Reformation as having come to its close in the year 1662, when the Act of Uni-

---

[1] It is singular to note that of these Casaubon and Le Courayer are buried in Westminster Abbey, while Grabe has a monument there. We may add to the list given in the text the names of Gerhard Johann and Isaac Voss, father and son—two well-known and very learned theologians of the seventeenth century. The elder Voss (d. 1649) was recommended by Laud to Charles I., from whom he received a Canonry of Canterbury, with permission to reside abroad: the younger was during the latter part of his life Canon of Windsor, where he died in 1689.

[2] For some account of this movement and subsequent ones of the same kind, see Abbey and Overton, "The English Church in the Eighteenth Century," Vol. I. p. 352 et seq.

formity at once settled the Church of England on a basis which has not since been disturbed, and necessitated the separate existence of Dissent. To enter upon the subsequent history of the Dissenting churches would therefore both transcend the limits of my subject and introduce us to a fresh field of discussion, not only wide, but demanding very minute treatment. What can and must be said of Dissent in the general may be compressed into comparatively little space. The multiplication of sects is a phenomenon almost peculiar to English and American religion, and may, I think, be traced to the influence of free political institutions. Nations which have charge of their own business, and have conquered the right of unfettered discussion, cannot be compelled into a mechanical uniformity in religion. The same spirit which made the Lords and Commons of England pass the Act of Provisors under the Plantagenets, dictated the abandonment of their benefices by the Ejected Ministers of 1662, and has since kept in independent existence the numerous sects into which Nonconformity has developed. Some Dissenting churches represent a principle, theological, ecclesiastical, ritual; others are the result of attempts to feed a spiritually-neglected people; others again, it may be, little more than the children of dissatisfaction and revolt. I am not here to state, much less to estimate, the grounds on which each bases its Nonconformity: all I have to note is, how large a part of the nation's religious life flows in these channels. The pure mysticism of the early Friends, the steady devotion to liberty, civil and religious, of the English Presbyterians, the insistance upon personal piety of the Independents and the Baptists, the zeal for souls of every various sect of Methodist, the ethical view of religion so strongly urged by modern Unitarians, are all elements which have helped to give compass and richness to the religious life of England. Both the quality of piety has been enhanced and its quantity increased by the existence of Nonconformity. At the same time, it is the necessary tendency of a sect to exaggerate the importance of its own constituent principle and, to the neglect of others which may be of equal weight, to push it to an extreme; at once to over-value orthodoxy, and to give orthodoxy a narrow interpretation. And the reaction of Dissent upon the Church has been far from wholly favourable. The consciousness of rivalry has lessened its comprehensiveness and chilled its generosity. Churchmen have lavishly sent out beyond seas the sympathy which they have denied to fellow-christians at home. The fear of being thought to yield to Nonconformist pressure has stiffened the immobility of doctrine and practice natural to an ancient church. Had a policy of comprehension been frankly adopted in 1662, or when the opportunity came again in 1689, I am convinced that the tone of English theology to-day would have been far more accordant than it is with the best knowledge and the characteristic spirit of the age. *Sed Dis aliter visum:* and we can only look to the new Reformation to restore the unity which was shattered by the old.

LECTURE X.

THE GROWTH OF THE CRITICAL SPIRIT.

THE theology of the Reformation rests upon the assumption that the Bible is a whole, consistent in all its parts, dogmatically authoritative, and containing, either explicitly or implicitly, a minutely elaborate system of revealed truth. I have now to show the effect produced upon this assumption, and the doctrinal results which rest upon it, by the growth of the critical spirit in Europe during the last three hundred years. This effect is of two kinds. First, the Bible itself has been subjected to a process of literary and historical criticism which has made it henceforth impossible to use it as the Reformers did, and to draw from it the same kind of doctrinal inference. And next, the conjoint influence of philosophical speculation and the successful study of nature, has been to establish new canons of credibility and to undermine the authority of the record, even in cases where its witness cannot be disputed. The method, in one instance, is literary; in the other, philosophical: one puts the documents in a new light, the other criticises their contents. Possibly this division of the subject may be more logical than real; nor can I pretend that my treatment

will answer to it with minute accuracy. What we have
to deal with is the changed spirit of the age, which tries
truth by new tests, and finds incredible what men once
never thought of questioning. Secular movements of
the human mind are brought about only by many independent yet related forces subtly acting and interacting.

I shall speak to-day of the growth of literary and historical criticism in Europe, and of the change which it
has wrought in our conception of the Bible.

The Humanists and the Reformers soon began to part
company. For some students of classical antiquity, the
purely religious interests which prevailed at Wittenberg
had little attraction: other and graver scholars not only
had no sympathy with Luther's characteristic doctrine,
but thought the atmosphere of the elder church more
favourable to the intellectual freedom which was the
breath of their life. We have seen the choice which
Erasmus deliberately made. Reuchlin, who had given
Melancthon to Wittenberg, withdrew his friendship from
him when he saw his devotion to the cause of Reform.[1]
Mutianus Rufus became a more orthodox Catholic as
he grew older. Crotus Rubianus, the chief author, if
recent conjecture be correct, of the "Letters of the
Obscure Men," went back to Rome in his old age. When
Willibald Pirkheimer died, he was cordially at one with
neither communion. On the other hand, it was not

---

[1] Reuchlin, who was Melancthon's great uncle, revoked in his last
years the legacy of his very valuable library which he had intended
for him, and begged that he would write to him no more. That the
alienation was complete, we may infer from the fact that in the numerous letters which Melancthon wrote in 1522, he nowhere alludes to
Reuchlin's death. L. Geiger: Johann Reuchlin, p. 466.

unnatural that the men who, as they believed, had rediscovered the gospel and restored the Bible to the Church, should not rate very highly the study of the classics in and for themselves. To them, the cultivation of Greek and Latin letters had had its complete work in making possible a correct interpretation of Scripture. Luther, in rebelling against the schoolmen, had also rebelled against their great master, Aristotle: to him, the gospel was the one true philosophy, and all truth not contained in the Bible of only secondary importance. As years went on, he became more and more absorbed in theology: he even went so far as to say, that when once the Bible was in all men's hands, there would be an end of human writing of books: God's Word would be enough.[1]

Still, when Erasmus says more than once, with quite sufficient bitterness, that "wherever Lutheranism reigns, there good letters perish,"[2] it is to be noticed that he excepts Luther and Melancthon from the general censure. Luther was all his life a zealous promoter of education. He held that the establishment of schools was the duty of every city and village, and desired to divert in that direction part of the revenues of the Church. He was so far in advance of his age as to advocate the foundation of girls' schools. The whole of his active life was spent as a teacher in a university,

---

[1] Köstlin: M. Luther, I. 600.

[2] Ep. to Pirkheimer, 1528, Opp. III. 1139 B. Conf. Ep. to Reuchlin, 1520, III. 590 B. Epistola ad Fratres Germaniæ inferioris, X. 1598 A. Goethe seems to have been of the same opinion as Erasmus when he says:
    Franzthum drängt in diesen verworrenen Tagen, wie ehmals
      Lutherthum es gethan, ruhige Bildung zurück.
Vier Jahreszeiten, No. 63.

of which he was the animating and guiding spirit. At the same time, he looked upon classical learning as subordinate to theology, and as valuable only for theological purposes. When, in 1523, Eoban Hess writes to him expressing his fear "lest we Germans should become more barbarous than ever we were, by reason of the decline of letters brought about by our theology,"[1] his answer, though frankly admitting the necessity of literary culture, shows that he has always an outlook towards theological interests. A little later we find him eager to divert Melancthon from the teaching of Greek, which he contemptuously calls "a childish lecture," to the exposition of the Scriptures.[2] But I do not think it is possible to quote from his works or letters passages which tend to the serious disparagement of classical culture. And Melancthon was distinctly a humanist. He came to Wittenberg to teach Greek, and would willingly, but for the prevailing influence of Luther, have gone on teaching Greek all his life. By his persevering labour in annotating classics and compiling school books, he earned the title of *Præceptor Germaniæ*. His bosom friend and biographer, Joachim Camerarius, was the most conspicuous figure among the generation of German humanists who succeeded Erasmus. But even the influence of Melancthon could not prevent

---

[1] Briefe, ed. De Wette, II. 313, to Eoban Hess, March 29, 1523. "Cæterum timores isti vestri te nihil moveant, ubi timetis, fore, ut barbariores fiamus Germani, quam unquam fuerimus casu literarum per theologiam nostram. . . . . Ego persuasus sum, sine literarum peritia prorsus stare non posse sinceram theologiam, sicut hactenus ruentibus et jacentibus literis miserrime et cecidit et jacuit."

[2] Ibid. II. 491, to the Elector Frederick, March 23, 1524.

the new religious teaching from throwing the old learning into the shade. That it did so, we need not go to the complaints of the humanists themselves to prove: the evidence lies plentifully scattered through Melancthon's own letters. In 1522, he speaks of the signal folly of those "who at the present day think that piety consists only in the contempt of all good letters, of all ancient erudition."[1] He implores Spalatin to have an especial care of the literary studies of the University, complaining that the students are rather overwhelmed than instructed by the mass of theological lectures.[2] He bewails to Eoban Hess the decline of literature, adding, "Those, believe me, who profess their dislike of profane letters have no better opinion of theology, for this is only the excuse which they put forward for their laziness."[3] He writes to Baumgärtner, a senator of Nürnberg, that unless he and men like him defend and foster letters, a Scythian barbarism or something worse must settle upon Germany.[4] In face of this evidence and much more of the same kind, we can easily believe Erasmus when he says that it was easier to find professors than students to attend their lectures;[5] that

---

[1] Corp. Ref. I. 594. Ep. Eberhardo a Than, 1522. "Nam qui sacras literas sine aliarum artium atque literarum adminiculo tentant, nae illi sine pennis volaturi sibi videntur. Stultissime autem omnium sentiunt, qui hodie nihil esse pietatem, nisi contemptum omnium bonarum literarum omnis priscae eruditionis arbitrantur."

[2] Ibid. to Spalatin, July 1522, March 1523, I. 575, 604, 607.

[3] Ibid. I. 613, to Eoban Hess, April 1523. Conf. to Spalatin, Dec. 1524, I. 695: to Gottfried Hittorp, Feb. 1525, I. 726.

[4] Ibid. I. 1001, to Jerome Baumgärtner, Sept. 1528.

[5] Erasmi Ep. ad Fratres Germaniae inferioris, Opp. X. 1618 D, E. "Scripsi alicubi, ubicunque regnat Lutheranismus, ibi frigere litterarum

the booksellers declared that before Lutheranism came up they could sell three thousand volumes in less time than six hundred afterwards; that at Strasburg and elsewhere there were those who thought that the only thing a theologian needed to learn was Hebrew. No doubt the old humanist grew bitter in his last days, as he watched the triumphant progress of the movement from which he had deliberately turned aside. But it is plain that, in spite of Melancthon, there was a tendency to go back to the spirit of a time at which it was considered a perilous thing for a Christian to read heathen books.[1]

But the tide of reviving interest in classical culture, which had been slowly gathering strength for a century and a half, was far too mighty to be even temporarily arrested by any defection of the Reformers. While they

studium. Si hoc non erat verum, cur Lutherus tam sollicite coactus est homines ad litterarum amorem revocare? Cur idem coactus est facere Melancthon, qui non dissimulabat esse verum quod dico? Quam floreat Academia Wittenbergensis, nescio. Si quid est illic bonæ litteraturæ, Melancthoni debetur. Quid fiat in pagis, nescio. Certe nuper cœperunt aliquot civitates conducere Professores, sed opus erit ut et auditores conducantur. Tam ardet studiorum amor! Non excutio nunc, quo id consilio fiat. Conferat Academiam Wittenbergensem cum Lovaniensi aut Parisiensi, quanquam et hæ nonnihil detrimenti sentiunt ex Lutheranismo. Typographi narrant se ante hoc evangelium citius distrahere solitos tria voluminum millia, quam nunc distrahant sexcenta, vel hoc arguit quam floreant studia litterarum. Quid autem isti fere docent nisi linguas? Sed proferant nobis vel tres, qui in Lutheranismo feliciter in litteris progressi sunt." The letter from which the above extract is taken was published in August, 1530. It is one of the documents of a controversy in which Erasmus became involved with the Protestant divines of Strasburg. Conf. Letter to Melancthon, Dec. 1524, Opp. III. 832 D.

[1] I may refer here to a declamation written by Melancthon in 1557, in which he bewails in the strongest terms the decline of science and letters. Corp. Ref. XII. 240 et seq.

were occupied in internecine quarrels and the building up of rival systems of dogmatic theology, the work of recovering the mind of antiquity went steadily on. It was a longer and a more laborious task than from our present standpoint of culture we are easily able to conceive; and the men who accomplished it are not to be measured by the worth of their visible contributions to literature. When the convent libraries of east and west had been ransacked, and every fragment of ancient literature consigned to the safe keeping of the printing-press, the work was only begun. Texts had to be emended, grammars to be slowly compiled, the materials of dictionaries collected with almost infinite toil. The whole mass of learned tradition, on the basis of which a scholar now begins his work, had to be painfully brought together. When, by the labours of several generations, the philological part of the task was accomplished with tolerable completeness—when all educated men could read the classical authors in the original, and Greek and Latin were written by scholars with facility and even elegance —there remained the work of reproducing the life of the ancients; of understanding their law, their worship, their military systems, their amusements; of re-writing their history, and reducing their chronology to order. And this was a toil which lasted through the eighteenth century, if indeed it can be said to be even yet at an end. Italy soon gave up her place in the van of classical culture. Her scholarship became mere phrase-mongering and Ciceronianism. Not what a man had to say, but how he said it, was the all-important thing; while platitude was no offence at all, solecism was a mortal sin. I have already spoken of the lack of moral fibre in the

Italian scholars of the age of the despots: when Rome became serious under the influence of the Counter Reformation, humanists were warned off debateable ground, and bidden to employ their pens in her service, if at all.[1] The study of Greek fell into disfavour; and when Jesuit influence came to predominate in schools and colleges, those admirable educators had practical ends of their own, which they cared for more than the progress of philology. So the literary hegemony passed to France and to Holland. Budæus, Turnebus, Casaubon, Salmasius, are the glories of French scholarship. If the Scaligers boasted an Italian descent, the elder lived and wrote in France; the younger and greater, who was Huguenot to the heart, taught in Leiden. It would be difficult to enumerate the many profound scholars who toiled in the Universities of Holland to complete the long task the nature of which I have endeavoured to indicate. Their labours lie concealed in the grammars and dictionaries which to-day smooth the path of classical culture to our children; in the annotations which elucidate every difficult passage and explain every obscure allusion; in that knowledge of ancient life which is part of the intellectual air we breathe. The result was at

---

[1] For illustration of this statement, see the life of the great French scholar, M. A. Muret, by Charles De Job (Paris, 1881). Muret, or Muretus, as he is more commonly called, spent the last half of his life as Professor in the University of Rome, finally joining the Society of Jesus. He found it a hard service. On one occasion he was forbidden to make Plato the subject of his lectures; on another he was ordered to substitute Sallust's Conspiracy of Catiline for the Politics of Aristotle. At the same time, he did not hesitate, at the request of Gregory XIII., to celebrate, in the most flowing phrases of his Ciceronian Latinity, the massacre of St. Bartholomew.

once to restore that living connection with the mind of antiquity which Christian Europe deliberately abandoned in the sixth century, and to accumulate the materials upon which the higher and more constructive criticism of a later age has worked.

To narrate, even in the briefest summary, the history of that higher criticism, would be manifestly impossible in this place. But I may be allowed to say a word of each of three epoch-making books, which will sufficiently indicate the direction which the current of educated European thought was taking from the end of the seventeenth to the beginning of the nineteenth century. The first of these is Richard Bentley's immortal "Dissertation on the Epistles of Phalaris," which was published in 1699. Sir William Temple, ignorantly meddling in the foolish controversy as to the respective literary merits of ancients and moderns, had asserted that the Epistles of Phalaris, a Sicilian tyrant of the sixth century B.C., were not only the earliest in date, but the best ever written. An edition of the letters published upon this by the Hon. Charles Boyle, drew from Bentley, then young and comparatively unknown, a decisive opinion that they were a worthless forgery. All Christchurch, of which college Boyle was a member, rose in arms to defend him; and Bentley, in the opinion of contemporary critics, was completely crushed by the answer which, though published in Boyle's name, was really the production of a confederacy of scholars, of whom Atterbury was the chief. And it is to be noticed, as a gauge of the general state of learning in England, that even when Bentley in his "Dissertation" had overwhelmed his opponents in such a flood of impetuous learning as no other European scholar could have poured forth, public opinion was still on the side of Boyle. But the moral of the controversy—one that sank slowly but effectually into the minds of the learned—was, that the authorship of ancient books cannot be decided by the traditional titles which they bear, but must be determined, at least negatively, by a careful examination of their contents. The second book I have to mention is Friedrich August Wolf's "Prolegomena to Homer," published in 1795. In it was put forward the hypothesis that the Iliad and the Odyssey were not, as was supposed, the work of one supreme poet, but each a cycle of heroic ballads, handed down by oral tradition from an age when writing was not yet known, and reduced to external unity by an anonymous editor. Nothing could be more shocking to literary orthodoxy than this theory, yet it gradually made its way, and is now, in one form or other, generally adopted. Its result has been the acceptance, on wider than Homeric ground, of the principle, that an ancient book, which comes down to modern times as a whole under the name of a single author, may possibly be composed of many different documents of various age and origin, and that it is for criticism to decide, upon internal evidence, whether its unity is real or only apparent. The third book is Niebuhr's "History of Rome," the first volume of which was given to the world in 1811. Let the great critical historian speak in his own words. In the Preface to that memorable work, he says:[1]

"The history of Rome was treated, during the first two centuries after the revival of letters, with the same prostration of the

---

[1] Niebuhr: History of Rome, transl. Hare and Thirlwall, Preface, p. 1.

understanding and judgment to the written letter, and with the same fearfulness of going beyond it, which prevailed in all the other branches of knowledge. If any one had pretended to inquire into the credibility of the ancient writers and the value of their testimony, an outcry would have been raised against such atrocious presumption. The object aimed at was, in spite of everything like internal evidence, to combine what they related. At the utmost, one authority was made, in some one particular instance, to give way to another, and this was done as mildly as possible, and without leading to any further results."

But at the touch of the Ithuriel spear of Niebuhr's criticism, the basis of that stately edifice of Roman history which Livy had erected crumbled into dust, and Regal Rome, from being a tract of human story peopled by living men whose motives we could analyze and whose actions we could narrate, became a shadowy realm of legend, in which only the imagination of the historian could reconstruct the beginnings of law and order. Thenceforth, all primæval history was looked at with fresh eyes. Its only sure facts were discerned to be such as could be vouched for by the testimony of contemporaneous structures and surviving institutions. It was seen what large contributions had been made to its written record by national self-consciousness and family pride, expressing themselves in legend and poetry. The earliest historians of the beginnings of humanity were henceforth regarded as being, for all practical purposes, as distant from the events which they pretend to narrate as we ourselves are, and much less able to distinguish the false from the true.

From what I have already said, it will be plain that it is not possible in this connection to speak of literary and historical criticism as things apart. To determine the genuineness and trustworthiness of documents, is often to impugn or establish the credibility of the facts which they record. And literary and historical criticism blend into one when the task to be accomplished is the decipherment of inscriptions, and the pushing forward of knowledge into a region beyond the range of formal historical record. The first great step in this direction was made when, at the end of the last century, the discovery of the Rosetta stone gave Young and Champollion a clue to the mystery of Egyptian hieroglyphics. The result of their researches, followed up by long subsequent toil in the same field by other labourers, has been no less than the unveiling to modern eyes of a national life, stretching back to an antiquity which would once have been considered incredible, and yet known to us in its minutest details. The decipherment of the monuments has been followed by the reading of many papyri, wonderfully preserved in the dry air of Egypt; and if the result has been to show that Herodotus was more accurate and Manetho less boastful than was once believed, the history of the Nile valley has been enriched by many particulars unrecorded by either. In a word, Egypt is no longer the mere vague synonym for the mysterious and the profound, which it was not only in ancient but in mediæval times, the *terra incognita* where every wild theory could find an anchorage, but has taken its definite place in the history of civilization and the development of religious thought. A similar result has attended the decipherment of the cuneiform inscriptions, begun by Grotefend, and Burnouf, and Lassen, and continued by a host of successful followers. The primæval history of the great empires which pressed upon Palestine from the north and east, as did Egypt from the south-west, has been unrolled before our eyes. In turn, Assyria, Babylonia, Persia, have become known to us in the same way, and almost as minutely, as Egypt. Monument answers to monument; clay tablet to papyrus. But this second great triumph of decipherment added more unexpected elements to our knowledge of antiquity than the first. Behind the Assyrian, now known to be a Semite, stands the Accadian, a Turanian, who spoke an agglutinative language, but who had a distinctive civilization, and who handed down to the tribes which supplanted him arts and sciences which descend from a world as yet unknown. And it is one of the most startling as well as the most recent results of archæological and philological research, that, as the faded characters of a palimpsest re-appear under the cautious manipulation of the chemist, an empire which the world had all but forgotten has once more emerged into view. The Old Testament presents to us the Hittites as a Canaanitish people, often coupled with the Amorites, and maintaining an habitual attitude of hostility to Israel—but that is all. Now they are revealed as forming a powerful state, between the Euphrates and the Orontes, having their capital at Carchemish, and with a wide-spread influence in Asia Minor, which has left traces in the history of art and religious ideas. From the apologetic point of view these discoveries are important, as they tend to confirm or to correct the Biblical narrative. But to the philosophical historian they have a much higher value. They restore Israel to his true place and proportion in the ancient world. We see now, for the first time, the forces of civilization which were at work about the Hebrews while they were still a half-migratory tribe of Canaan, as well as the tremendous political pressure which in later years made the kingdom of David the sport of rival empires.

Contemporaneous with this gradual decipherment of ancient records, aiding and aided by it, has been the growth of the new science of comparative philology. It had its birth in the recognition of the true place of Sanskrit among the languages of the world. The existence of Sanskrit, which as the literary dialect of India can never be said to have been a dead language, had been long known to missionaries, and to some extent to philologists; but it was not till the last years of the eighteenth century that the labours of Sir William Jones and his colleagues of the Royal Asiatic Society began to display it in its true relations, nor till 1808 that Friedrich Schlegel, who possessed the vivid imagination which at certain turning-points of thought is the critic's best endowment, decisively pointed out its importance for the classification of language. I will not tell the familiar tale again, nor how the labours, first of Anquetil du Perron and then of Rask and Burnouf, restored the Zend to the catalogue of known tongues, and made Zerdusht once more a living prophet. But the result of thus establishing comparative philology on a basis the safety of which has been demonstrated by constantly fresh discovery, was, in virtue of the ethnological deductions surely drawn from it, first to extend our knowledge of primæval history far beyond the period of even the rudest monumental record, and next, to reduce to order a whole realm of facts which had hitherto received only conjectural interpretation. The separation of the Aryan peoples means also the segregation of the Semites, and the placing of Hebrew philology for the first time on a scientific foundation. I need hardly point out that in view of the sure outlook which we now have into that far distant past when the common ancestors of all Aryan peoples dwelt under the shadow of the Himalayas, already speaking a language which cannot be connected with any Semitic dialect—in face of the fact that a large part of the population of the world expresses its thought in agglutinative tongues, which almost seem to be framed upon a different theory of speech from our own—it is impossible any longer to dream dreams of Hebrew as the language of Paradise, and to trace back the disruption of human speech to the arrogance of the Tower of Babel. Indeed, it is much more than a question of invalidating the historical truth of this or that Old Testament story: we look back over an infinitely wider prospect, and the map of primæval humanity is other than it was. But the procedure of comparative philology has made another and perhaps a more important contribution to the higher criticism than is involved in anything I have yet said. One of its achievements has been to reveal the secret of the Greek mythology. These gods and heroes, these divine beings haunting the secret recesses of mountain and wood, these strange stories, so full of naive beauty, so empty of ethical meaning, about which the classical imagination disported itself, whose spell a seriously moral Christianity has often striven to shake off, are an open riddle now. Tracked to their source in Vedic religion, they stand confessed as nature myths, and their frank immorality is no more than the result of the expression of cosmic facts in terms of humanity. And it is thus to comparative philology that criticism owes the formation and clear definition of the idea of myth. Now at last the conception stands distinctly out by the side of that of legend, and can never again be confounded with it. No doubt, like all new intellectual instruments, the mythical theory has been too largely used, and has suffered from over-lavish application. But it answers to a real tendency of the human mind, especially in its earlier stages of development, and must henceforth take its place as a recognized factor of primæval history.

One general result of this long series of investigations has been the gradual growth of an art which, as distinguished from the mere formation and emendation of texts, has been called the higher criticism. It deals with the age and authorship of books: it decides whether a writing is an organic whole, or made up of fragments more or less cleverly combined: it attempts to go behind the letter, and to determine the writer's secret bent or conscious purpose. As applied to history, it sifts testimony before accepting it: it collects the witness of chance admissions, unconscious discrepancies: it questions rites, institutions, even language itself, in the hope of discovering the secrets which lie beneath the surface: it traces legend to its origin in long-descended custom or genealogical pride, and compels myth to yield up the thought which has bodied itself in story. When it inspects the history of religious thought, it judges in accordance with the principle of continuity: it distinguishes between an earlier and a later in the intellectual order: and it first accomplishes its purpose when it succeeds in tracing a sure line of development. Indeed, its method may almost be summed up in one word as the historical: it rejects all *à priori* views and reasonings: its endeavour is to take facts as they are, to understand their origin, and to trace their mutual relation and interdependence. I have called this higher criticism an art rather than a science, not only because its principles and rules do not readily lend themselves to precise statement, but because the success of its processes largely depends upon the skill and tact of the critic. Possibly its negative are more definite than its positive achievements. It is less difficult to say by whom an ancient book cannot have been written than to name its actual author. To prove that Paul is not the writer of the Epistle to the Hebrews is an easy thing; not so to decide between the conflicting claims of Apollos and Barnabas, and one knows not how many more. Criticism may pronounce a book to be made up of many fragments, of various date and origin, and yet fail to pick each separate stone out of the mosaic, and to say authoritatively where it came from. In the criticism of the Pentateuch, Elohist and Jehovist and Deuteronomist stand for facts, and not for fancies, though Ewald divide the text among them in one way, and Kuenen in another. It is the fashion in some quarters to deride the higher criticism as the mere product of individual caprice, to exaggerate the discrepancies of its results, and to imagine that they can be got rid of, like positive and negative quantities in an equation, by setting one against the other. But it is a mistake to suppose that this process, however far it may be carried, necessarily makes for the traditional view of things, which stands or falls by itself, and must meet its own difficulties. And criticism is making its sure way, from destruction to construction, from negative to positive results. Difficulties which the sharp sight of the eighteenth century detected, but which it could only solve by more or less ingenious guess-work, are rapidly receiving answers which, once fully understood, are felt to be final. Criticism now knows what legend is when it sees it. It can distinguish myth from either tradition or history. It can decide with adequate certainty delicate questions of authorship and genuineness and date. And the fresh triumphs which it is every day winning in the most obscure regions of primæval history make its claim to be heard on Biblical ground also, impossible to resist.

I have thus traced the growth of the critical spirit, in order that it may be quite clear that we are dealing with a general development of human thought, and not merely with a flux and reflux of the theological tide. There cannot well be a greater contrast than between the progress of truth within and beyond the reach of what are conceived to be religious interests. No sober scholar now questions the results of criticism as applied to Greek literature or Roman history; while, on the other hand, the battle still fiercely rages round positions which were held by the Reformers, yet which for a century past have been attacked by overwhelming and ever-accumulating forces. A finality is claimed for old views of the Bible, which in the case of any other literature would be laughed out of court; and the strangest devices, perpetually set up and perpetually abandoned, are used to blunt the edge of criticism and put the Scriptures in a place apart. And it is therefore expedient to show that these debates as to the literary constitution of the Bible do not belong to the class of theological logomachies which each generation is at liberty to renew with the old weapons and upon the old ground, but are an incident of the universal march of the human mind, which occupies new territory every day, and never abandons what it has once occupied. At first, and for some time, Biblical criticism was cultivated more by Catholic than by Protestant divines. It was the interest of the former to undermine the authority of Scripture for the benefit of the Church, while the latter were far too well satisfied with the foundation on which they built to pry too narrowly into its security. Besides, Protestants had other work to do. Their critical battle-field with Catholicism lay much more in the dark ages than in the first Christian centuries. The Centuriators of Magdeburg, Blondel, Scaliger, Daillé, convinced the world that the writings attributed to Dionysius the Areopagite were spurious, and exposed the forgery of the pseudo-Isidorian Decretals. In a work on "The Right Use of the Fathers," in which he was sarcastically said to have proved that they were of no use at all, Daillé again dealt a heavy blow at patristic theology. But in the mean time the beginnings of Biblical criticism, which, each in a different way, Luther and Carlstadt had made, were neglected. Within the orthodox churches of the Reform, Scripture was indeed studied, but only for dogmatic purposes.

The first impulse came from the outside, from Catholic divines, from Arminian heretics, from unbelieving philosophers. Hobbes[1] remarked that the name, "the Five Books of Moses," was no proof that Moses was their author, and went on to adduce some of the most obvious reasons why he could not have written a large part of

---

[1] Leviathan, III. c. xxxiii.

them. Spinoza interweaves with his *Tractatus Theologico-Politicus* a whole body of acute negative criticism, not only showing by internal evidence that Moses could not have written the Pentateuch in its present shape, but throughout the whole Bible detecting literary facts at variance with traditional statements of date and authorship. Richard Simon, a priest of the Oratory, in his "Critical History of the Old Testament," published in 1678, again gave reasons against the Mosaic authorship of the Pentateuch, a decision in which the Arminian Le Clerc, on some other grounds opposed to Simon, heartily concurred. But it was Astruc, a Catholic physician of Paris, who, in a work published in 1753, struck the key-note of subsequent debate. He believed that Moses wrote the Pentateuch, but he thought he could distinguish and disengage the materials that he had used. There was a document, he said, in which God was always called Elohim, another in which he was always called Jehovah, and these were manifestly by different authors. The theory, in the shape in which Astruc proprounded it, was crude, and so far untenable; but it was eagerly caught up and modified by Semler, Eichhorn, Michaelis, and by the beginning of the present century had become a commonplace of criticism. Meanwhile, the study of the New Testament had been running a parallel course. The literary problem presented by the likenesses and differences of the Synoptical Gospels was the first to attract attention. The great Arminian, Hugo Grotius, in his "Annotations on the New Testament," laid it down that Mark's Gospel was an abridgment of Matthew's, and that Luke had used the other two. Simon, whose labours were not confined to the Old Testament, came to the conclusion that the first Gospel, as we have it, could not be the original work of Matthew, and revived the recollection of the *Antilegomena* of the ancient Church —the Apocalypse, the letter to the Hebrews, some of the Catholic Epistles. Le Clerc thought that the Synoptists had all used the same documentary materials. Semler postponed the formation of the Canon to the end of the second century, and, in anticipation of the later Tübingen school, referred it to the influence of that Catholicism in which Jewish and Pauline Christianity found their reconciliation. But the very title of a treatise by Lessing, which was published in 1784, three years after his death, shows how far men had then wandered from the thought of the Reformation: "A New Hypothesis as to the Evangelists, considered as merely Human Writers of History." Nothing could more plainly indicate the breach made by literary criticism in the conception of the New Testament as an infallible record and authoritative compendium of doctrine.

I must pause here for a moment to notice a peculiar and very powerful influence exercised upon Biblical criticism by two great men whose active lives fall in the second half of the eighteenth century, Lessing and Herder. It would be easy to draw out points of contrast between them: in literary preference, Lessing belonged to the classical, Herder to the romantic school: the former would as little have written the "Spirit of Hebrew Poetry" as the latter the "Laokoon." Lessing exulted in the freedom of a man of letters, the fewness of whose wants left him at liberty to criticise all systems and to pay an undivided allegiance to truth: Herder fretted all his life long under the restraints of his clerical profession, and leaves behind him the vague impression of an unfinished life, and profound truths not rounded off into system. But both were humanists, in the widest sense of the word, before they were theologians. Lessing's characteristic idea is the divine education of the human race; Herder's greatest book, his "Contributions to a Philosophy of Human History." Both concurred in taking theology off the narrow Biblical ground to which the post-Reformation divines had confined it, and making it an affair of universal history and the natural capacities of man. What pregnancy was there in Lessing's conception of the Old Testament as the religious schoolbook adapted to the childhood of humanity! Nor, when he hinted that it was possible to regard the New Testament in a similar light, and darkly prophesied an eternal Gospel yet to be revealed, was he far from that thought of an universal faith which has been suggested to later times by comparative theology. He restored tradition to its true place in Christian history by the remark, that at the very time when primitive faith was brightest and purest, the New Testament did not yet exist: he threw down the wall which had hitherto separated the Jewish and Christian dispensation from the religious history of the world, by pointing out the root of all true religion in the heart of man. Perhaps Herder's characteristic efficacy of a similar kind lay in his intense appreciation of the human element in the Bible: not so much that he looked at it with an æsthetic eye, acknowledging its sublimity and praising its pathos, as that he heard in it the heart's cry of humanity towards God, and saw how it exhibited religion as closely interwoven with every other faculty and capacity of man. After these men had written, it was hard for Biblical criticism to go back to the dry dissection of texts, the discussion of merely literary controversies. Theology, without ceasing to be divine, had become fully human. The Bible is only one chapter, though the most important, in the religious history of the race. As much as God's speech to man, it is man's answer to God. If it breathes now the accent of Divine command, it thrills and trembles as often with the aspirations and despairs of humanity.

The inquiries and speculations indicated in what I have already said have been pursued with untiring energy during the eighty years of the present century. As critic has succeeded critic—as Kuenen has seemed to correct and supersede Ewald, and may probably be corrected and superseded in his turn—as the mythical theory of Strauss and the tendenz-theory of Baur have been proposed and rejected as the key which would unlock all mysteries—as no account of the mutual relations of the Synoptical Gospels can be said to be generally accepted—as the age and authorship of the Fourth are still matters of warm debate—it might appear at first sight as if nothing had been accomplished, and the sole result of criticism had been to throw our notions of the Bible into hopeless confusion. Even if it were so, its negative efficacy would be complete and undeniable. Where positive conclusions cannot be reached, it is better to rest in clear denials than in delusive affirmations. We are at all events nearer the truth when we look at the Pentateuch as made up of many fragments, put together we know not when or by whom, than when we confidently place it as the work of Moses at the beginning of Hebrew history. Which is the truer and therefore the more fruitful conception, the Book of Psalms as wholly or in large part the production of David, or as a collection of sacred lyrics, in which the whole spiritual life of Israel, in all his troubles and anguishes and varying moods of faith, is mirrored and expressed? So, in regard to the Gospels, even if we were unable to replace our negative by positive conclusions about them, we should still have got rid of the idea, so little accordant with fact, of the four independent witnesses, whose testimony it is necessary, in the interests of evangelical truth, to harmonize by every fair and unfair device of interpretation. The critics, whose principle it is to trace a line of continuity in human thought, to detect a natural line of development in human affairs, know very well that the traditional view of the Scriptures is precisely that which is most fruitful in difficulties. No new theory of Hebrew history can be so puzzling as that which places the Levitical legislation at the beginning of long ages, the records of which show almost no trace of its existence and observance. What can be more difficult to suppose than that the teaching of Christ waited for the interpretation that was to make it plain till Paul came—Paul, who had never known him in the flesh, and who carefully abstained from intercourse with those who had?

But nothing is less true than the allegation that no results have been attained which can justly be called positive. In the first place, the Biblical history has been brought into due relation with the general development of humanity. We are no longer invited to contemplate the beginnings of the race in the Garden of Eden six thousand years ago, or to connect the peopling of the globe with the dispersion of the family of Noah. Long before the date fixed by the old cosmogony for the creation of the world, we discern the existence of ancient empires, settled civilizations, substantial progress in the arts of life. We can trace the connection of the nomad tribe, which, though numerically so insignificant, was reserved for so great a destiny, with neighbours more powerful and more civilized than itself, who were also its kinsmen by blood. Its story is no longer the story of mankind: its cosmogony, however poetically sublime, is only one of many similar guesses into the origin of things: the myths and legends into which its history runs up, have their near analogues in those read off from Babylonian bricks. Its genealogies require to be translated into tribal history, and even so tell us no more than the vague traditions of national relationship preserved among a people whose outlook upon the world was narrow. There is a strange contrast, which every year's investigation makes stranger, between Israel's conception of his own material grandeur and his real place in the world: he thinks, in common with all ancient peoples, that he stands next to the beginning of things and can command its secret: he is in reality but an insignificant tribe, prisoned in a corner of Asia, pressed upon by tribes as insignificant as himself, once, and only once, emerging into a position of second-rate political importance, and counting for nothing in the shock of Mesopotamian and Egyptian empires. Yet in another way all this only brings into a more vivid light the grandeur of Israel's vocation, the strangeness of his fate. While ancient India, Assyria, Persia, Egypt, are almost forgotten, except by the scholars who painfully decipher the records of their life, Israel lives in human memory side by side with Greece and with Rome. He was powerless to resist the conquerors of the world; but he has avenged conquest by imposing upon them his religious ideas. He shares with Greece the distinction of being the teacher of mankind.

In like manner, criticism has re-read the Hebrew history, making the thread which binds it together not one of conscious prophecy looking forward to its fulfilment, but a natural intellectual and religious development, which in the far reach of its scope and the order of its sequence is divine without being miraculous. To attain this result, it was necessary to abandon all traditional accounts of the authorship of books, and to seek the secret in the unconscious revelations of the documents themselves. But in comparison with the historical inferences which this method yields, literary questions shrink into insignificance. That the Pentateuch is a composite book, which assumed its present shape when the independent political history of Israel was at an end—that the Book of Chronicles was written in the interest of the priestly caste—that the apparent unity of Isaiah's prophecy hides at least a dual authorship—that the books ascribed to Solomon are of different origin and much later date—that the prophecy of Daniel must be postponed to an era which is late enough to change prediction into history—are all important results of research in regard to which most competent critics agree. But the question of questions in the criticism of the Old Testament is this: Are we to place the Law at the beginning of national history, or at the end, when a restored but broken Israel begins a new life in a corner of the Persian empire? Was Israel sternly monotheistic from the day of his escape from Egypt, or did Jehovah slowly grow from a tribal God, worshipped under strange names and with half-idolatrous rites, into "the righteous Lord who loveth righteousness," before whom "all the Gods of the nations are idols"? Was prophecy a revolt against a priesthood already corrupt and a law fallen into disuse, or itself the first dawn of a pure faith and a noble religious life? Can we, except in fragments of legislation still preserved in the Pentateuch, trace the Law further back than its sudden production from the temple archives in the days of Josiah? And must we not descend to the time of Ezra for the epoch when, the voice of prophecy being silent, and almost its very remembrance faded out of the people's hearts, the legal conception of religion laid a stiffening grasp upon Israel which it never again relaxed? It is manifestly not for me to indicate, even in the briefest way, the evidence for this complete reversal of what once passed for Hebrew history; it is enough to say, that while every step in the reasoning can be sufficiently justified, the result of the whole is for the first time to present a reading of the record which conforms to a natural process of development. Now we see how Israel grew into what he was. We understand his perils, his temptations, his backslidings. He re-enters the field of ordinary history, and from a puppet of the Divine purposes becomes human once more.

Criticism has had a much less difficult, a much less destructive work to do on the New Testament; but the result has been the same—the conversion of a divine oracle into a human record. We do not now assume the New Testament as the beginning of the history of Christianity: we watch it gradually become what it is, in a

Church which was itself growing and gathering strength through a period of at least a century and a half. There is a time when only the Apocalypse and some Epistles of Paul's are in Christian hands: then come "Memoirs of the Apostles," which disengage themselves into separate Gospels, extant and lost: there is a fourth Gospel, which bears plain traces of a later date, and Hellenic, perhaps Alexandrian influence: the defining line of the Canon shifts, including and excluding doubtful books, until at last from the long and changeful process emerges the New Testament that we have, yet at a time when the Church is already far on her way towards recognition by the empire. When the literary history of the New Testament is thus set forth in all its details, when the different influences under which its separate books were written are drawn out, when it is plain that it was at one time possible that the Shepherd of Hermas might have found a place in the Canon and the Apocalypse have been shut out, how can it be any longer regarded as "one entire and perfect chrysolite" reflecting the unchangeable and infallible mind of God? We have to recognize the fundamental distinction between the words of Christ himself and the varying interpretation put upon them by apostles. We must separate the Palestinian tradition of his teaching preserved in the Synoptics from that which had passed through the strongly refracting medium of the powerful mind to which we owe the Fourth Gospel. We may learn from Strauss that the causes which produce myth and legend had not been wholly inoperative in shaping the evangelical history. We must set Paul and his gospel apart, as an efficient factor of the earliest Christianity. We must note the existence of other forms of apostolical interpretation of Christ, which were neither Paul's nor capable of reconciliation with his. We may see in the Apocalypse an outbreak of fiery Hebrew zeal, goaded to vision by the cruelties of Nero, and find in the Pastoral Epistles the traces of a Church slowly organizing itself years after Paul has vanished in the darkness. We may discern, if we will, with Baur, the conflict between Paul and the Twelve, between Judaism and Universalism, in the Apostolic Church, until at last both were reconciled in a Catholicism in the shadow of which the influence of the Apostle to the Gentiles paled, till it was revived by Augustine. But if all these things are so, what becomes of the one, minute, dogmatic faith which all the books of the New Testament are alleged to teach with accordant voice? Must we not substitute for this theory the conception of a Teacher, greater than any or all of his disciples, whose words have come down to us in records which rest upon a still earlier tradition, and whom apostles have interpreted, each as he could, each in accordance with the limitations of his own lesser soul? This New Testament, in which every word, no matter by whom written or when, is of equal inspiration and equal authority—still more, this New Testament of Luther's, in which Paul interprets Christ, and the true gospel is not the word of the Master but the comment of the servant—may be a literary miracle, but it is hardly the New Testament whose component parts we can distinguish, and whose history we can trace.

There are two elements of Hebrew history which have been relied upon to give it a quite peculiar character, as to each of which criticism has a word to say, miracle and prophecy. The first shows the special interposition of God in this particular line of human development; the second binds together all parts of the dispensation into an indissoluble whole. Of miracle, I shall have more to say in connection with another part of my subject: the lesson which criticism teaches in regard to it is, that the allegation of marvels is not confined to the Jewish history; that they form part of the furniture, so to speak, of all religion in a particular stage of development; that, given a certain habit of thought, a certain urgency of spiritual crisis, miracle is as sure to make its appearance as hysterical excitement to accompany emotional fanaticism, Cybelic or Bacchic, Catholic or Evangelical. It is much more a form of popular belief than of conscious imposture: it is the people's way of acknowledging the presence of God, as the devout man of science recognizes Him in inexorable law and unbroken order. So, again, the controversy as to prophecy has gradually changed its ground. It was once a question as to the fulfilment of prediction: the doubt now is, whether predictions were ever uttered. The prophet is no longer the mouthpiece of divine vaticination as to the future: when Israel, who, like every other ancient people, believed in prediction, burned to know the mind of the Lord or to compel the secret of what should be, it was not to the prophet that he turned, but to the diviners, to the priests, to Urim and Thummim, to the lot. The prophet is the teacher of spiritual religion, the servant of Jehovah, who calls back the people to their rightful allegiance, the rebuker of sin in high places and low. He is profoundly persuaded of the necessary connection of national prosperity with national righteousness, and he does not hesitate to promise good things to a people that serve the Lord. He is the preacher of the ideal; and the ideal lies always in the future. The darker, the more hopeless, is Israel's present fate, the clearer is the prophet's conviction that a deliverer must come, who, by lifting the people to a higher plane of faith and obedience, will end their misery too. Mingled with this, especially in the later Isaiah, is an ardent prevision of the part which Israel is destined to play in the religious education of the world. But all this is so far from answering to the ordinary idea of prediction, consciously uttered, accurately fulfilled, capable of being used as an evidence of Divine interposition, as to belong to quite another order of thought.

The re-reading of Hebrew history which the higher criticism thus compels, enormously increases the literary and human interest of the Bible. It is true that the mechanical ties and braces of type and antitype, prediction and fulfilment, covenant of law and covenant of grace, fall to pieces at its touch; but they are more than replaced by the living unity which it enables us to trace through every successive age of Biblical development. While the human element in Scripture and the history which it records is thus brought into more vivid relief, the divine remains, though possibly no longer clothed in the forms with which the uncritical mind of the Reformation was familiar. The more decisively Israel finds his place in ordinary history, the more singular that place is discerned to be. Whatever criticism may have to say as to the composition of the Gospels, it cannot touch the charm of the Christ, or weaken the force of his sweet reasonableness, or derogate from the victory of his faith. And it is only when the words and incidents of the Old Testament are released from the artificial necessity of proving this or answering to that—when, instead of being fitted into their places as parts of a theological system, they are allowed freedom of movement and the grace of self-manifestation—that we see the Hebrew literature as it is, and for the first time fully appreciate its marvellous religious depth and variety. These dim patriarchal times, whose story the piety of a later age tells with such an exquisite simplicity, so tender a grace: the first struggles of the people escaping from Egypt for a place in the world, and some fixed law, some stable order: the slow advance of Israel to the conception, not only of a single Ruler, but of a moral government of the world: the deep conviction of the prophets that the salvation of the nation lay in allegiance to a righteous God, and the persuasions, the complaints, the rebukes, the warnings, the encouragements, which they addressed to a people stiffnecked and only half convinced: the growth of the legal and sacerdotal conception of religion, which at last substituted the Rabbi for the Prophet, and enabled the Scribe and the Pharisee to sit in Moses' seat:—all prepare the way for the splendid outburst of the prophetic spirit which Israel was no longer able to comprehend, though it was welcomed by the world. But along the line of this development, once more discerned in its natural order, what free play of human emotion and passion, what interfusion of God's life with man's, what depth of reverent awe, what dizzy flights of aspiration, what stern faithfulness to duty, what restoring agonies of repentance! These things, disengaged now from the theological trammels which confined and disguised them, show themselves in their real force and beauty. This poor Semitic tribe, but one degree removed from the

Bedouin of the desert, no longer regarded as the mechanical mouthpiece of Omnipotence, is revealed in its native grandeur. We have religion, not now embodied in a dogmatic system, but interwoven with human life, unravelling its perplexities, inspiring its strength, sanctifying its sorrows,—at once the law of its development and the goal of its endeavour.

The theology of the Reformation begins and ends with the Bible. It disowns tradition, and accepts the testimony of the Fathers only in so far as it accords with its own interpretation of Scripture. But I have, finally, to point out to you that the New Testament, as included within the hard and fast line of the Canon, cannot be placed at the fountain-head of Christian development and treated as the sole source of sound doctrine. We have seen that it grew up side by side with the Church of at least the first century and a half. It is true that the same forces to some extent moulded both; but, on the one hand, many things conspire to prove that the New Testament contains, not a complete record of the influences which were at work, but only such a selection from them as the literary and religious sense of the third century judged worthy of preservation; while, on the other, nothing can be plainer than that the literary activity of Paul gave him a larger place in the Canon than in the contemporary Church. There was, first, a Church without a New Testament; next, a Church with a New Testament in process of compilation, and existing in different forms in different hands. What are we to say, then, of the relation to the New Testament of that Creed of Nicæa in which in the year 325 the Church for the first time formulated its faith? Can its doctrine be extracted from Scripture by fair process of literal interpretation? Can we say, as a matter of history, that Scripture was the sole source from which it was derived? Can its doctrine be shown to have been universally held throughout the second and third centuries, and to have been definitely drawn out in the fourth, only for the condemnation of Arian heresy? I may seem to be here treading upon delicate ground; but I should be untrue to myself and the theory which I am advocating, if I did not say that I regard it as a clear result of criticism that the history of Christian doctrine during the first ages is one of gradual development, affected by the impact of forces which were Greek as well as Jewish. I do not inquire whether that development involves an approach to or a retrogression from the truth: I only affirm that continuity is an active principle at all periods of the history of religious thought, and that it is contrary to the plainest evidence of fact to seek for finality even in the New Testament. There was more of Plato, more of Philo, in the Reformers' creed than they knew, though the germs which attained so luxuriant a growth in Patristic theology may have passed in the first instance through a New Testament medium. Human thought is but a single great sea, though with many sheltered bays and land-locked inlets: it rises and falls with a universal tide, and none of its waters can be completely or long severed from the rest.

Lecture XI.

THE DEVELOPMENT OF PHILOSOPHICAL METHOD AND SCIENTIFIC INVESTIGATION.

THROUGHOUT the last Lecture I confined myself strictly to the ground of Biblical criticism. I showed how a more accurate appreciation of the character of ancient literature, joined to a gradually accumulating knowledge of antiquity, compelled us to look at the books of the Bible in a fresh light; to re-read their testimony, and to substitute another principle of unity for that which had been supposed to bind them together. But although the first object of literary criticism, regarded as a method of investigating truth, is to ascertain the original form and true character of books, and to collect their direct or incidental testimony to facts, a second and more radical process of judgment is often involved in this; and even when the record is plainest and most authentic, it may be necessary, while still remaining on purely literary ground, to form an estimate of its credibility. Now, however, I have to speak of intellectual forces which have been at work since the Reformation, the characteristic of which is to approach the Bible and religion generally with à *priori* criteria of credibility, and to claim an absolute right of judging or moulding conceptions which are undoubtedly Biblical. The result of the higher criticism, as a whole, is to declare that the history, the structure, the religious constitution of the Bible, unfit it to stand in the relation to human faith in which the Reformers placed it. But the tendencies of thought which are now to occupy us take up an independent attitude of criticism to Biblical statements and ideas; and while they altogether reject some, demand that others shall be modified, as a condition of being recognized as certain constituents of knowledge. These may be classed under two heads, philosophical and scientific: the one being the result of modern ways of thinking, the other of a knowledge of nature which has become a permanent possession of the race. Here, again, I must call attention to the fact that these forces mutually act and re-act, and that the distinction between them cannot always be observed.

One important result of the Reformation was the dissolution of that union between philosophy and theology which had been effected by the Schoolmen. Up to the sixteenth century, there had been, with trifling exceptions—and those brand-marked as heretical—but one philosophy, as there was but one theology. I do not mean that the Schoolmen were speculatively agreed among themselves; that there were not Nominalists and Realists, Scotists and Thomists; but that opposition between philosophy and theology was a thing undreamed of. The Church might look upon one form of speculation as being more favourable to her claims than another, but all speculators declared themselves the supporters of orthodox doctrine and the Church's obedient servants. There were indeed subtle forms of philosophical as of theological heresy beneath the surface. Arabian thinkers, of whom Averrhoes may be taken as the representative, had drunk strange draughts at the same fountain-head of Greek thought as that at which the Schoolmen had quenched their thirst; but as a rule philosophy was orthodox, and orthodoxy willing to be thrown into philosophical form. But the great re-awakening of European thought, of which the Reformation was one result, completely changed all this. Luther's rebellion was almost as much against the Schoolmen and Aristotle as against the Pope; and although his followers, as I have tried to show, fell easily under the yoke of a scholasticism which was identical in spirit, though not in form, with the old, the impulse given to independent speculation was strong and lasting. From that time to this, theology and philosophy have pursued each its own way: rival powers, often conscious of secret hostility, often seeking reconciliation, but always, from the very fact of the separation, engaged in reciprocal criticism. Philosophy, laying claim to universal intellectual jurisdiction, has sometimes been willing to allow religion, upon certain fixed conditions, a subordinate and limited place: religion has anxiously gone about to find for herself a sure philosophical basis: while, again, each has flouted the other, each has claimed an undivided supremacy. The time of complete and permanent reconciliation may come yet; but there are few signs of its approach, and the joint history of philosophy and theology during the last three centuries is one of independent life and often sundered interests.

When we try to get behind these general statements, we are met by the difficulty that modern European philosophy can show no development in the direction of fixed and widely-accepted results of speculation. The continuity of thought is indeed not difficult to be traced: Descartes, Spinoza, Leibnitz, Kant, Fichte, Schelling, Hegel—between any one of these great thinkers and the next in succession, the critic may discern not merely the logical but often the actual link. Can we say as much, now that a considerable part of educated Germany has made the transition to Schopenhauer and to Hartmann? So in our own country we can establish a line of succession from Locke to Hume, from Hume to Spencer, with many deviations of more or less importance, by the road but who can say in what direction the development tends, or to what obvious goal it makes its way? Much more it seems to an outside critic that the motion of philosophy is rather in an orbit round a centre than in a direct line towards a mark: old problems continually recur: not even the solutions of them are always new: the pendulum swings between opposite poles of thought: a sensational philosophy now obtains, and now an intuitional: a nation is idealist in one generation and sceptical in the next. But whether there be any advance on the part of philosophy towards absolute truth, or in what direction that advance is being made, are not questions which we have to answer now. What we are concerned with is the relation of philosophy to theology. And here I fail to trace such a parallel course between the philosophy and the Christianity of the post-Reformation centuries, as would indicate a progressive influence of one upon the other. Minds naturally inclined to religion have justified their adhesion to it on every kind of philosophical principle. And, on the other hand, men in whom the religious sense is only rudimentary, and who have rarely felt the touch of divine awe upon their souls, never find any difficulty in persuading themselves that true philosophy leaves no place for faith.

If this were all, it would seem unnecessary to pursue this part of the subject farther. But that it is not so, will appear from the consideration that philosophy is not only an attempt to comprehend all knowledge in an intellectual unity, throughout which the same laws are valid and every subordinate part falls into its proper place, but also a method, an organon, which prescribes modes of investigation and declares laws of thought. And the work of philosophy, regarded in the latter light, has made a sensible approach to completion, which is recognized by all thoughtful men. Europe, since the time when Descartes first applied himself to the solution of the philosophical problem, has made enormous progress in the art of thinking. Nor do I now chiefly allude to the publication of certain great books on method, or the investigations which have been made into the principles of logic: here, as elsewhere, practice has to a large extent preceded theory. The problem of walking has been solved by walking, not by anatomical and mechanical disquisition; and when the historian of human thought is disposed to put Bacon at the head of the development of modern science, he should remember that, of the men who have actually made the discoveries and thought out the laws, not one in a hundred has ever read a line of his works. Philosophy and science, working now separately, now together, have painfully beaten out a method for themselves, which success has confirmed, which failure has helped to correct; and the result is, the formation of habits of thought, the laying down of canons of investigation, which are, if I may so speak, in the intellectual air, which are the common inheritance of inquirers, to which it is no signal merit to conform, but which it is absurd and disgraceful to neglect. To place a general reliance on the faculties of the human mind, to suffer, if possible, no unverified assumptions, to bring the most ancient and most widely accepted principles to the test of facts, to lay a broad basis of observation for every induction, to test what seems to be fresh truth by crucial experiment, to expect uniformity in the action of natural forces, are all rules which cannot now be formulated without a sound of commonplace. But those who are best able to contrast the working of the modern with that of the mediæval mind, will also know best how large a part of the fresh ground which humanity has won for itself since the Reformation, is covered by these homely maxims of common sense.

Philosophy has thus succeeded in bringing about, to a large extent, a unification of method in the pursuit of truth. Is theological truth to be considered as a thing *sui generis*, and to be distinguished from every other kind of intellectual possession which the mind conceives itself entitled to call its own? Must it be regarded as given, not attained, and, when given, to be received without question and held exempt from criticism? Possibly the answer to these questions is, as I have already indicated, more properly to be sought on the ground of fact than of theory. Can any revelation be produced which does not require for its acceptance the active exercise of human faculties, and in its structure imperatively invite criticism? Still, as these matters have been persistently argued in a purely *à priori* fashion, two things may be noticed: first, that the highest claims of divine authority have been made and defended by an appeal to that very reason which it is their object to put out of court; and next, that the numerous attempts to frame systems of religious evidence are really a settlement of the matter in dispute in favour of philosophy. When Lardner compiles proofs of the credibility of the gospel history, when Samuel Clarke constructs *à priori* demonstrations of the Christian verities, when Butler attempts to show that the course and constitution of nature present difficulties of the same kind as the scheme of revelation, when Paley infers the existence of God from the marks of design in creation, when Theodore Parker hears the voice of God in the conscience and sees the Divine lineaments mirrored in the soul—they are all, consciously or unconsciously, testifying to their belief that religious, must be sought by the same methods and tried by the same tests as other truth. The case of religious truth may indeed have elements peculiar to itself, as mathematics and morals, belonging to different departments of human thought, have each their own criteria, which differ in kind while they agree in principle. But no truth can be quite passively received. Even faith requires an antecedent mental process by which it feels itself justified.

Undoubtedly, therefore, the influence of philosophy has been steadily exerted in the direction of rationalism. I use this much decried word, in what is at once its etymological and its best sense, as meaning the application to religious data of such criteria as human faculties supply. There is indeed another and a bastard rationalism which has greatly prevailed, though not often in very close connection with earnest philosophical thinking; which, taking as its test common sense, or the ordinary course of things, or the light of nature, has rejected as unworthy of belief all religious phenomena which seemed to cut athwart or to transcend them. It is unfortunately not possible to change an established nomenclature; else, it seems to me, we should gain in clearness of perception by calling this particular manifestation by the name of naturalism. We might then be able to bring together in one category, as allied facts, the criticism of the English Deists, the crude and uncompromising disbelief of Voltaire and the Encyclopædists, and the attempt of Paulus to explain away the supernatural element in the Gospels. But philosophical rationalism, as I understand it, is a nobler and a wider principle than any of these. It admits whatever is involved in the pre-eminence of the infinite Object of religious thought over the finite powers by which it is sought to be apprehended, and expects an element of mystery, a region of inconceivableness. On the other hand, it does not limit the cognitive powers of man to the reason, either logical or practical, or to any faculty which deals only with ideas that can be clearly apprehended and facts that can be wholly grasped; but allows a real value to the straining of the imaginative intellect after the Infinite and the Absolute; the aspiration of the soul towards the eternal, the indwelling, the all-energizing Life; the revelation in the conscience of an ideal holiness. In other words, against the overwhelming mass of Divine

Being it sets the totality of human nature, and expects that, if there be a God, He is one who will approach man on every side and touch him at every point. This rationalism, therefore, is so far from being antithetical to revelation, as positively to look for it; in the sense, that is, not of a theological system reduced to form and order, and enshrined in a book subject to time and chance, but of a constant intercourse between God and the soul; gleams of insight, quickenings of conscience, inner tides of inspiration, all sweetening and strengthening graces, which interfuse the human with the Divine, and are in themselves the one sufficient proof of God. But at the same time it keeps the citadel of human individuality. A man can believe only that which has approved itself to him by some inward process, the efficacy of which he recognizes. Before he can even surrender his reason to authority, there must be some antecedent examination of its claims. And, on the other hand, to be thrilled by a sudden sense of the charm of Christ, and so to offer him the heart's allegiance, is as truly a rational process as to read every word of Paley's Evidences, and to surrender belief to the cogency of the reasoning.

There is one form in which the rational criterion is applied which deserves special mention. Men still dispute about the origin of moral ideas and analyze the secret of obligation, but they do not differ as to the ideas themselves. It is indeed a characteristic of the peculiar scepticism of the day, that almost in proportion as it loses hold of religious convictions, it clings to the supreme obligation of the moral law; while not only is there a general agreement as to the contents of morality, but such change as takes place in this respect is in the direction of admitted progress. As the race rises, so does its conception of duty; and with its conception of duty, its thought of God. Man cannot permanently worship that which is lower than his highest, inferior to his best. The character of the Deity reflects the moral status of the worshipper: cruel men believe in cruel divinities: to the licentious, not even the courts of heaven are pure. And therefore when, as constantly happens, old forms of belief survive into a better time and claim the authority of prescription, their accordance with the highest morality becomes a test which not only may, but must, be applied to them. No evidence of authority can stand for a moment against an awakened conscience. What a man once clearly sees to be cruel, or revengeful, or unjust, he cannot ascribe to God. There are, I know, innumerable moral and intellectual subtleties in which he may take refuge, in the hope of avoiding the antithesis which will show itself only in one light. But this force of doctrinal decay is always at work, and its efficacy is in proportion to the clearness of men's moral perceptions, and the degree in which they disengage themselves as an absolute law. It produces theories of atonement which avoid the naked substitution of the innocent for the guilty. It draws pictures of future retribution in which the omnipotent love of God is not baffled by the impenitent misery of an eternal hell.

I have spoken of one kind of bastard rationalism; there is another. Whatever theologians, even of the extreme Catholic type, may say, the application of reason to religion lies in the nature of things: the only question is as to the method and the degree. The vast folios of the Fathers, the elaborate disquisitions of the Schoolmen, the massive and minute systems of the Protestant dogmatists, are all essentially rationalistic. There is no mystery which they do not attempt to analyze, no religious fact too obscure to be made the subject of an inference, no divine reality too sublime to be woven into a system. If we may judge from the immemorial practice of Christendom, rationalism is the appropriate method of building up vast and complicated edifices of belief: it is out of place only when applied to the digging of foundations. Employ reason as much as you will in drawing inferences and establishing conclusions, but for the sake of all that is holy never use it to examine an assumption or to test a premiss! And it is curious and instructive to note how some of the last deliverances of philosophy tend to the acknowledgment of mystery in religion, and discourage the application of human faculties to matters that are essentially above them, and limit the province of formal logic to ideas that can be wholly grasped, and bid men speak of divine realities "with bated breath and whispered humbleness." In a sense that is only too true, philosophy declares God to be the Unknown and the Unknowable. We cannot shut up the Divine Infinitude in a syllogism. When we make God's attributes a link in a chain of reasoning, our argument runs up into contradictions. All we can do is to catch a glimpse of His Being and Perfectness, now on this side, now on that; and our attempts to combine them into a whole end in a dazzling confusion, like that which strikes us when we look at the sun, an excess of light that is almost darkness. It matters little whether reason be critical or only expository: there are some things which are too great for it, and confound it.

I turn now to the second half of my subject. The re-awakening of Europe in the fifteenth and sixteenth centuries was, as I have already stated, general: it left no department of intellectual activity untouched: literature, religion, philosophy, natural science, each in succession felt its influence. But it followed from the fact that the so-called ages of faith had passed in one long sleep of indifference to the exact study of nature, that science woke to life only when men had for some time been busy in the regions of literary culture and philosophical speculation. The Moors of Spain had, strange to say, proved themselves the heirs of Hellenic science: astronomy and geometry, favourite studies of the Greeks, they had pursued further than their masters: they had invented the numerals which make arithmetic easy: they had laid the foundations of algebra, and made discoveries which are still recorded in the nomenclature of chemistry. But I cannot see that this manifestation of intellect holds any natural place in the history of European development: it was Eastern in its origin, its triumphs were recorded in the obscurity of an Eastern tongue; and although we cannot altogether refuse it an influence upon Christian thought, its chief interest is perhaps that which belongs to a brilliant blossoming which has borne but little fruit. These Moors did good work for science, but it has had to be almost all done again: the martial and bigoted Christianity which subdued them was too ignorant to appropriate the results of their labours.[1] And Luther

---

[1] Conf. Whewell: History of the Inductive Sciences, I. 259. "At any rate, when these sciences (Mechanics, Hydrostatics, &c.) again became progressive, Europe had to start where Europe had stopped. There is no Arabian name which any one has thought of interposing

belonged to a generation which lived but in the first grey dawn of modern science. The world had just been widened by the three great voyages: Columbus had discovered America (1492), Vasco de Gama had doubled the Cape (1498), Magellan had united their discoveries into one by circumnavigating the earth (1522). Mark these dates: the Confession of Augsburg belongs to 1530: theology was already putting on the form of finality when natural science was but feeling, with the almost aimless fingers of an infant, after the truth. I gravely doubt whether Luther at all realized the meaning of what was going on around him: I look upon him as too much absorbed in the changeful fortunes of the Reform, and in his own personal struggles and temptations, to note the attempts that were being made to read the universe with a scientific eye.[1] But it is a characteristic fact that Melancthon was a firm believer in astrology, a

---

between Archimedes the ancient and Stevinus and Galileo the moderns."

[1] Luther seems to have stood absolutely outside the conception of natural law. In three sermons on Angels which are to be found in his Works, ed. Walch, X. 1233 et seq., he represents man as the object of a perpetual contention between good and bad angels, to whose differing disposition and opposed efforts are to be ascribed all the circumstances of his fate. "Wenn er (der Teufel) nun die Seele also gefasset hat, so greifet er nach dem Leibe auch: da schickt er Pestilenz, Hunger, Kummer, Krieg, Mord, &c. Den Jammer richtet der Teufel alle an. Dass nun einer ein Bein bricht, der andere ersäuft, der dritte einen Mord thut: wer richtet solches alles an? Niemand denn der Teufel." X. 1236. And again: "Also, sind die guten Engel stets um und bey uns, dass sie uns helfen, dass wir bey der Wahrheit bleiben, unser Leib und Leben, Weib, Kind, und was wir haben, vor dem Teufel behalten mögen. Dass nun die ganze Welt nicht lichterlohe brennet, dass nicht alle Städte und Flecken auf einem Haufen liegen, ist alles der lieben Engel Werk und Thun." X. 1241.

caster of horoscopes, a watcher of starry omens, and that both he and Luther put faith in strange monsters and portentous appearances, quaintly interpreting them of the fate of Popes and Monarchs.[1] Still there is one epoch-making discovery in science which belongs to the age of the Reformation. In 1543, three years, that is, before Luther's death, Copernicus published his work, *De Revolutionibus Orbium Cœlestium.* Astronomy, the oldest of the natural sciences, thus, though in an imperfect way, put on the form which it has ever since retained. But many years were still to elapse, and many bitter battles

---

[1] In 1523, Luther and Melancthon jointly published a pamphlet (Walch, XIX. 2403), illustrated with strange pictures, in exposition of a multiform monster called the "Papstesel," which it was asserted had been found dead in the Tiber in 1496, and of a monstrous calf, the "Mönchkalb," which had been born near Freiburg in Meissen. They seem to have given unsuspecting credence to these stories, and to have expounded the alleged physical peculiarities of these monsters as indications of the will of God in regard to the Papacy. It is worth while to note that these and similar follies of superstition were not approved by all their contemporaries. George Wizel, who went back from Lutheranism to the Church, though always striving to maintain a mediating position, says, in a passage quoted by Döllinger, Reformation, I. 118 : "Dass es in Schlesien stark blitzt, ist denn dass ein Mirakel ? Der Nordwind trägt Dächer ab, eilt denn desswegen der Herr von Himmel herab zum Gerichte ? Man hat feurige Kohlen gesehen, die Erde hat gebebt, der Donner gekracht, die Blitze geleuchtet, eine sehr dichte Wolke hat eine Stadt überschattet, aber geschieht denn das selten in der Welt? .... Oh ihr köstlichen Ausleger !" Nicholas Ellenbog, a Benedictine monk, wrote a "Vituli monachilis Lutheri confutatio pro monasticæ vitæ defensione," in which he makes the very sensible remark : "Monstra, Naturfehler, Geschöpfe, die gegen den gewöhnlichen Lauf des Lebens mit etwas Naturwidrigem behaftet erzeugt worden, seien überhaupt nicht im Stande für die Zukunft etwas vorherzusagen." Quoted by Janssen, "Geschichte des Deutschen Volkes seit dem Ausgang des Mittelalters," II. 283.

to be fought, before it could compel a general assent to its conclusions.

We live in so full a sunlight of natural knowledge, as often, I think, to fail to realize how modern a thing it is, and how completely the whole framework of our dogmatic theology was built up before natural science was born. Let me lay before you a few dates, which, if they do not too much try your patience, will coalesce into the proof of a very striking fact. It was in 1609 that Galileo invented the telescope, which he used in the following year for the discovery of Jupiter's moons: in 1616 that he was condemned by the Inquisition for asserting the motion of the earth. Kepler's three laws were published by him, the first two in 1609, the third in 1617: in 1686, Newton laid his *Principia* before the Royal Society. Since that turning-point in the history of men's knowledge of the universe, enormous progress has been made: mechanics, optics, mathematics, have put new and continually more powerful instruments into the hands of the astronomer, who now includes in the scope of his science ages so long as to defy the imagination to realize them, spaces so vast as to be described only by elaborate devices of calculation. As astronomy obtained its priority over other sciences from its connection with the primitive art of navigation, so anatomy took precedence from the necessities of medicine. Vesalius, the plates of whose book, *De Humani Corporis fabricâ*, are still among the most beautiful of their kind, was Charles V.'s physician. He was on the right track, for he dissected the human body and reported only what he saw: but it was not till 1628 that Harvey publicly announced his capital discovery of the circulation of the blood. Men, however, had long worked at both these sciences, beating out their great principles in a way which the brilliant performance of our own days tempts us to think clumsy and slow, before some of those branches of knowledge which now attract the largest attention had been cultivated at all. It was in the latter half of the eighteenth century that modern chemistry took its origin in the researches of Cavendish, Priestley and Lavoisier into the composition of air and water; but the Atomic theory, on which all its calculations are made, was the work of a philosopher whose reverend old age I well remember; while its last achievement, the Spectrum Analysis, which defines the physical constitution of sun and stars, is a triumph of yesterday. Again, a little more than a hundred years ago, geology, destined to succeed to astronomy as the science hated by theologians, was slowly struggling to the birth, though the principle of uniformity which now dominates it was formulated by Sir Charles Lyell only a few years ago, while the demonstration of the antiquity of man upon the earth is of later date still. The first great name in systematic botany is that of Linnæus, whose works appeared between 1731 and 1753, while the introduction of a natural classification is due to the elder and younger Jussieu, who belong to the latter half of the same century. Electricity and magnetism, sciences which at the present moment promise everything to their successful cultivators, may be traced back to the beginning of the eighteenth century; but the great names and great discoveries which illustrate them are all recent. And it is characteristic of the latest scientific activity, that sciences seem more and more to run into one another and coalesce; that one law is seen to prevail through many regions of thought; that forces are discerned to be interchangeable and guessed to be ultimately identical. The theory that heat is only a mode of motion has been proved by the actual determination of its mechanical equivalent: mechanical force is every day converted into electricity, and electricity into light, or mechanical force again. So in regard to the sciences of life, extending on one side into the secret processes which physiology aims to track, on the other to what were once conceived as the merely formal classifications of natural history—all are now combined into a majestic unity by the theory of evolution. But Cuvier's is almost the first great name in the annals of comparative anatomy; and the "Origin of Species," the *Principia* of our age, was not published till 1859.

During the whole of this period, a change, at first slow but afterwards rapid, has been taking place in men's conceptions of the universe. For the most part it has matured itself in entire independence of theological ideas. It is true that at some points of the frontier between religion and science skirmishes have been continually going on: first astronomy, then geology, bore the brunt of theological opposition: a post of honour which, until theologians saw, or thought they saw, that they could turn it to their own purposes, has last of all been occupied by the theory of evolution. But this guerilla warfare has attracted more attention than it deserved. The main forces on either side have not been engaged, nor has it been waged about the key of the position. Men of science have calmly pursued the path of investigation, leaving religion to accommodate itself as it best could to the results of their search: divines, in the most remarkable way, have repeated the old formulas, enforcing the ancient view of the universe and God's relation to it, as if science did not exist. The controversy as to whether it was possible to reconcile the first chapter of Genesis with the facts of geology, no one has greatly cared about; one explanation of the discrepancy has succeeded another; but the religious people were not in their hearts convinced that the facts of geology were facts, while the scientific people were too certain of them to care to look at the matter in another light. The real difficulty is, that the scenery in the midst of which the drama of religion is played—if I may use such a metaphor—has been wholly changed. We live in a widened world. The horizons of time and space are indefinitely enlarged. Throughout the whole of the universe, which thus opens upon us in inconceivable vastness and complexity, obtain one law, one order. When we take the Bible, the religious ideas of the Jews, the Pauline exposition of the Gospel, the millennial expectations of the early Church, out of the narrow and half-known world of Augustine or of Luther, and transport them into this fresh universe, will they fill the same place, can we look upon them in the same light? Will the systems of doctrine which have been elaborated from these materials tally any longer with the world of ascertained fact? And if these questions be answered, as they must be, in the negative, we are next compelled to ask, Can we reconcile old faith with new fact by dropping certain constituents of it, as merely local and temporary? Or is it unhappily necessary to recommence the labour of faith, and to demand from history, from philosophy, from nature, the religion which we can no longer inherit from simpler and less self-conscious ages?

In thus endeavouring to define the situation, I am conscious of having transcended the proper limits of my subject. I have not to say yea or nay to this crucial question, but only to point out, with such clearness and completeness as I can, the extent of the divergence between the doctrine of the Reformation and the science of to-day. And, first, let me indicate how much of a theological kind is involved in the change from the geocentric to the heliocentric system, and the remarkable developments which have since taken place in stellar astronomy. I will not trouble you with the repetition of quite familiar facts: the difficulty is not to apprehend them with the mind, but to give life and meaning to them by the imagination. They all tend one way: to enlarge the universe and to lessen man. This earth, from being the centre of created things, with its sun to rule by day, its moon and stars to rule by night, has dwindled to the tiniest atom of star-dust, a mere luminous point in a milky-way of worlds. We find ourselves, even within the limits of our own narrow system, in presence of secular changes which look forward and back over almost inconceivable areas of time. From day to day we watch, with such precision as an existence which is by comparison but momentary permits, a universe in perpetual process of development and decay: nebulæ slowly coalescing into suns, suns slowly "paling their ineffectual fires." But the whole scale is so vast as to convict all cosmogonies of childish presumption, and to take from us any clear conception of end or beginning. It seems to me that the attempt to conceive God becomes more trying to the imagination in proportion as the universe widens, than which He is wider, as the grandeur grows, than which He must be grander. We are, comparatively speaking, almost on a level with the tribal Jehovah who brought the Hebrews out of Egypt: we are still not hopelessly below the God who hung with shining lamps the solid firmament that stretches above the earth: but how shall we rise to the thought of Him who is the Lord of innumerable worlds, the Ruler of the boundless spaces, the Master of the eternal years? I may be told here that moral and material greatness are incommensurable quantities; that the moral law affected Kant with as much wonder and admiration as the starry order; and that the possession of a spiritual nature, however insignificant his physical frame, makes man free of the spiritual universe. True; but is this pin-point of earth the only spot of the universe upon which reasonable life exists, on which it is possible to praise and to pray, to sin and to aspire? From the very nature of the case, this question can never receive categorical reply; but I confess that it seems to me a quite inconceivable thing, upon any hypothesis, theistic or atheistic, that only a millionth part of the universe should be instinct with the fire of reason, and all the rest mere cold, dead matter. Did, then, God, and such a God as the all of things proves He must be, die for us? I say it with the deepest respect for the religious feelings of others, but I cannot but think that the whole system of atonement of which Anselm is the author, shrivels into inanity amid the light, the space, the silence of the stellar worlds.

To call in our speculation to narrower limits, I have already remarked that the various attempts to reconcile the cosmogony of the first chapters of Genesis with the ascertained facts of geology are of no real interest. They vary from year to year, and are satisfactory to few but their own inventors. On the one hand, the geologist observes that his own science affords the standard in conformity with which the Biblical narrative is sought to be interpreted; on the other, the literary critic claims the controversy as his own, and traces up the legend to a Chaldean or Accadian antiquity with which Moses had indisputably nothing to do. But the date at which man appeared upon the earth is a matter for purely scientific determination, and it can be fixed, at all events negatively, in a way for which the poor six thousand years of Biblical chronology altogether fail to provide. We are carried, as I have already shown, far back into a civilized antiquity by the newly-deciphered records of Egypt and Babylonia. The certain inferences which may be drawn from the history and structure of language reveal to us a period beyond written record, at which the ancestors of almost all the peoples of modern Europe lived in Northern India, already in possession of the arts of settled life. At this point geology takes up the story, introducing us to the tribes who lived in Irish crannoges, who built the Swiss lake dwellings, the refuse of whose food is heaped up in the kitchenmiddens of the Baltic—until we make our slow way backward to the men who chipped the flint instruments of the valleys of the Somme and the Ouse, at a time when England was not yet an island, and the rhinoceros and the elephant roamed over her plains and left their bones in her caves. And though now in a world strangely different in outward aspect from that in which we live, we are still on distinctly human ground.

Man, in full possession of his characteristic faculties, is fighting the battle of his race against nature. It is in virtue of brains that he is surviving. He uses tools, he builds, he cultivates. And if the pathetic record of the burial cave of Aurignac[1] may be trusted, he has already some dim outlook towards a life to come.

There is, however, one scientific principle of the greatest importance which underlies and justifies the projection of the reason and imagination over vast areas of space and time. It is trust in the uniformity and universality of law. A law of nature once established, we assume, until cause be shown to the contrary, that it is valid in the most distant star as on the earth's surface, a million years ago as now. And this is not so much an abstract principle as a practical confidence, slowly built up out of long experience of investigation. We can go back to a time when even among inquirers into nature a certain expectation of miracle prevailed, such as now exists in full force among the pilgrims to Lourdes or La Salette. But little by little, as more rigorous methods of research were adopted and accumulating scientific experience became more accurate, this expectation faded, and a quite contrary one took its place. Whatever record there might be of miracle in past times or in other circumstances, the investigator encountered none under his own scalpel or in the field of his own microscope, until at last it grew to be a silent assumption, underlying his whole method, that none would be encountered. It would be difficult to say into what force of universal cogency this has developed under the stimulus of the scientific activity of

---

[1] Lyell: Antiquity of Man, p. 193.

the last century. The invariability of law is the very atmosphere which the investigator breathes. He places a daily reliance upon it, and is not disappointed. It is the tacit condition on which he makes all his predictions, and for whatever other reason they fail, it is never for this. Philosophically speaking, believers in God cannot prove the impossibility of miracle: He can always, by an arbitrary exercise of will, interfere with the operation of His own laws. But every day adds to the already overwhelming accumulation of evidence that He never does. The controversy may still be conducted on *à priori* ground, so far as it is conducted at all, but a body of habitual opinion is being formed which takes no heed of it. The God of a scientific world must be conceived of as one who is absolutely faithful to His own methods, and who permits those methods to be scrutinized by men.

A new element has been introduced into the controversy between old modes of belief and new scientific ideas by the doctrine of evolution, which, first formulated in Darwin's "Origin of Species" twenty-four years ago, has so rapidly gained acceptance. The whole cycle of ideas put forward in that celebrated book were presented at first as one of those hypotheses in which the scientific imagination seeks to anticipate the results of minute inquiry, and which investigation may either confirm or modify or reject. But with quite unexampled rapidity the idea of evolution has established itself, not only in biology, but in almost every other department of human thought. What was a few years ago a daring supposition in one branch of investigation, has risen to the dignity of a general method: it is a doctrine of slow and minute changes, each brought about by natural forces, each surviving and perpetuating itself in proportion as it is adapted to the environment of the organism in which it takes place. In biology, we call it the struggle for existence and the survival of the fittest: in geology, it reveals itself as the theory which abolishes cataclysms in favour of the constant operation of ordinary forces through long periods of time: in history, it seeks to explain change and growth, by tracing each successive state to its origin in that which preceded it: in morals, it educes the conscience of a civilized age from the gregarious instincts of savage men, or the apes from which they grew. Whether, itself developed into a world philosophy, the theory of evolution will account for everything, as its devotees claim for it, may be gravely doubted: to trace man back from the ape to the ascidian, from the ascidian to I know not what more primitive germ—to discern the potentiality of all this various world in the original fire-cloud—is still much more a brilliant escapade of the imagination than a sober feat of reason. The geologist, the biologist, the physicist, cannot yet agree upon the number of millions of years required for such an evolutionary process; nor are the philosophical difficulties in the way by any means wholly overcome. But the fact remains, that if evolution will not account for everything, it indisputably explains much; that it can never again be left out of their reckoning, not only by biologists, but by historians, by moralists, by theologians; and that at almost every point it has opened up new questions as to God's relation to the world, and man's place in it, which imperatively ask reply.

For if the idea of evolution is to be accepted, we have

done with that of special creation. No doubt the former is much more conceivable than the latter, and therefore fits more easily into a scientific statement: while, again, it is obvious that what is really involved is not the abolition of Divine action upon matter, but a change in the method of its operation. No form in which the doctrine of evolution can be put dispenses with a *primum mobile:* there must be some force at work to produce the infinitesimal variations on which so much depends, and some general law by which the conjoint survival of the fittest tends in a given direction. Why but for this should ape rise out of ascidian, and man out of ape, the living all of things, lifting itself, as it were, to a higher level, tending to some unseen goal? But the conception of Divine action reconcilable with this process must be one of two: either God is the great Mechanician who, having started the complex contrivance, leaves it to work out its end according to pre-arranged and unchangeable law, or He is the Immanent Life, the All-energizing Force, sustaining, vivifying, developing all things in accordance with the necessities of His own nature. Each of these suppositions will serve to reconcile evolution with theism, though neither, I fear, will fit in with ordinary notions of providence and piety. And it is curious to note how in connection with the new doctrine have come up again the old difficulties as to the origin of evil and the prevalence of pain in the world. This struggle for existence, in which life and the possibilities of life are so prodigally wasted: this charnel-house of nature, in which the various tribes of animate things, preying on one another, slay and are slain continually: this upward progress, the wheels of whose car of Juggernauth pass over the bodies of countless innocent victims—have taken possession of the imaginations of men, and questions long silent are again asked as to their reconcilability with the omnipotence and perfect goodness of God. It is not for me now to indicate even in the briefest way a possible line of answer. I have only to note the existence of currents of thought against which accepted theological ideas will have to defend themselves or to suffer modification.

Closely connected with the idea of evolution is the doctrine of heredity. Every generation is implicitly contained in all those which have preceded it. Did we know *them* accurately, we might predict *it*. Our descent and our environment—of these two factors we are composed, and they account for all that is in us. This is an extreme statement of the case, and one which I am myself by no means disposed to adopt; but it represents a tone of thought which is rapidly gathering strength and receiving wider application. On the ground of observed fact, not on that of metaphysical reasoning, it is becoming harder to find a place for free-will in the constitution of man; while, even if its existence be still contended for, the area of its action must be indefinitely lessened. And so the doctrine of evolution involves a kind of natural Augustinianism. What the old divines called predestination, re-appears as a net of natural necessities, closing round the will on every side and preventing its free action. Our fate has been largely settled for us, if not in the eternal counsels before time was, yet by the generations which have gone before, and the circumstances in which we find ourselves. We thought that we were men wielding the divine prerogative of will;

but on this theory we are only physical phenomena, as calculable as any other; the subject of statistics, the material of averages. The problem of humanity is only a little more complicated and difficult than that of meteorology: patience, accumulated observation, a fresh calculus, will yet solve both.

In one particular, the theory of evolution lays hold of certain undisputed facts of human character which are the natural basis of theological doctrine, and gives them a quite new interpretation. Whence this strange intermingling of evil with good in man? Whence these brutal passions, this selfish indifference to suffering, this cool malignity of purpose, which are the dark threads of the chequered web of life? Whence this evil that we would not, rising up within us to overcome the good that we would? Christian theology has accounted for these things on the theory of a fall from a primæval state of innocence, the result of which has been the transmission of a vitiated nature from the first father to all his children. The historical foundation of this doctrine has been destroyed by the recognition of the mythical character of the narrative in Genesis; but certain facts still remain—the existence of the passions and tendencies, and their hereditary transmission in accumulating or diminishing strength—which every theory of human nature must take into account. What if for a fall, evolution substitutes a rise of man? What if the evil which is in us, and sometimes masters us, be the brute which is slowly dying out of our nature? These are secular changes, always gradual in their operation, accelerated now, and now retarded by various causes, within and outside of us. But it would at once fall in with the general scope of evolution, and answer to facts which neither religion nor philosophy can affect to ignore, to suppose that some survival of the fittest was taking place upon moral ground also; that the passions natural to a powerful animal were giving place to the affections, and passing under the control characteristic of civilized man; that we were losing the scars, outgrowing the mutilations, which we received in the long, hard struggle with nature; that new capacities were coming into play, a larger aim opening out before us; and that the traces we yet retain of that lower companionship out of which we have emerged, are themselves the guarantee of the upper air and the ampler life which remain for us in the future.

But a question of questions, which will have to be answered if religion is to come to terms with the idea of evolution, is as to the area to which that idea and others cognate with it legitimately apply. The theory has had its origin in the study of physical nature: it is the contribution which the scientific research of our day, gathering up its light into one focus, makes to general philosophy. On the one side, the tendency of thought fostered by Paley and the Bridgewater Treatises has been to expect nature to reveal the secret of God; on the other, the men of natural science, flushed with the delight of this brilliant generalization, have demanded that it shall be rigorously applied in every department of human thought. Everywhere, they say, we are in the grip of law: there is nothing in our life which is not accounted for by our inheritance and our environment: if God exists, He neither can nor will break in sunder the bonds of fate which tie us down: we cannot feel the touch of His hand upon our personal life, and the best that is left to us is the faith that somehow and in a general way, in which we too shall have our share, "good will be the final goal of ill." And the only escape from this spiritual imprisonment lies in keeping open a region of free and intimate intercourse between God and the human soul. There is the less difficulty in this, as the existence of such a region, the reality of such an intercourse, are precisely the message which religious men in all ages bring, out of the depths of their own experience, to those who have less insight than themselves. This they announce as "the fountain-light of all their day, the master-light of all their seeing," and not their light only, but their strength and their consolation. And as this experience involves a series of facts as real and as little to be pushed aside as the embryonic changes and the aborted organs which are rightly regarded as so full of meaning, Religion yet retains the right of reserving to herself a space in which spirit may meet with spirit, on the one side in impulse and support, on the other in aspiration and self-surrender. Perhaps we have been too hasty in expecting to see the character of a perfect God reflected in the mirror of a material world. We ought to have recollected that only soul answers to soul.

But I should commit a grave error if I left upon your minds the impression that the result of modern scientific inquiry was only to put new difficulties in the way of religion. I do not know that many of the ideas of which I have spoken are harder to deal with religiously than others whose place they are taking: all that my argument is designed to show is, that they cannot be dealt with in precisely the same way, and therefore necessitate some modification of theological conceptions. On the other hand, there are results of research which seem to me to assist a religious conception of the universe. From one point of view, the general effect of the newest science may be described as simplification. Chemistry reads us a list of some sixty-six primitive substances out of which everything is built up, and may yet, as new instruments for compelling the secrets of nature are devised, add to the number. At the same time, she is also beginning to guess, with that instinctive apprehension of the truth which often precedes discovery, that all these may be but one and the same primitive stuff variously compounded, and that when we have said matter we have said all. So, in like manner, one of the chief triumphs of the newest time is the convertibility of force; and it is a permissible speculation, to which many facts point, that one force, in different forms, moves and sustains the universe. But what is matter? This dull, dead stuff of the world, which makes its impression upon every sense, which was once taken as the quite comprehensible antithesis of incomprehensible spirit, turns out to be the most fathomless of mysteries, the abyss which transcendental physicists explore, finding always a deeper depth below. Idealists argue, with a plausibility not easy to refute, that it does not exist at all: materialists refine its coarser characteristics away, till it exhibits itself as one phase of a reality which on the other side is known as spirit. But can the distinction between force and matter be kept up, or must not even this simple duality be resolved into a unity which is simpler still? We may say, with Boscovich, that what we call atoms are only centres at which forces manifest themselves; and the more we think out the conception into its details, the more will it appear that the hypothesis of matter is superfluous, and its existence difficult to prove. But if, thus resolving our knowledge into its simplest elements, we find ourselves surrounded by an impenetrable mystery, and in presence of a single all-energizing force, what shall prevent us from uttering the name of God, the Incomprehensible, the One? The transition from force to person, from law to will, is one for which, I know only too well, science builds no bridge; but the wings of Faith are not yet clipped, and she flies lightly over the abyss.

Lecture XII.

CONCLUSION.

My task is now drawing to a close: all that I have yet to do is to re-state the general drift of my argument, and to give it what application I can to existing facts. My thesis is briefly this. The Reformation was the manifestation upon religious ground of that great re-awakening of intellectual life in Europe which in its first phase we call the Revival of Letters. In Italy, where that re-awakening began, it confined itself almost exclusively to literature and to art: it was in France, in England, in Switzerland, and especially in Germany, that it touched and transformed religion. There were reasons enough for this. One result of the services which Christianity had rendered to civilization, when the fabric of the Roman empire broke up under the incursions of the barbarians, was, that life throughout the middle ages was organized upon an ecclesiastical model; that literature, art, philosophy, education, were all in the hands and bound to the service of the Church. But, in addition to this, the practical abuses of the Papal system were many and confessed. The most shameful license was a matter of every-day occurrence among the clergy.

Popes competed with secular potentates in unscrupulous worldliness, and surpassed them in infamy. The maladministration of the sacramental system had sapped the foundations of public and private morality. The exactions of the Italian hierarchy at once drained the Northern nations dry, and undermined their allegiance to Rome. The cry for reform was universal: it had been demanded by churchmen, urged on by princes, made the theme of bitter satire and biting pasquinade, attempted by general councils, temporarily effected by monastic orders. But the wound, however staunched in part and for a time, always broke out afresh, and at the beginning of the sixteenth century was a running sore which threatened the entire corruption of the Church. What Luther, Zwingli, Calvin did, we know: I have pointed out the peculiar efficacy of the means they used to break up the mediæval system, and have described that which they established in its place. Indirectly, the separation from the Latin Church of the communions which they founded led to the amendment of its worst practical abuses: with Paul IV. began a new line of Popes, austere, devout, zealous, almost fanatic; and the Council of Trent marks the first stage of the Counter Reformation.

But Luther had been a monk, and was always a theologian; while the Revival of Letters was essentially an upheaval of the lay mind. I have insisted upon the distinction between the Italian and the German humanists: the one, throwing themselves with frank sympathy into the naturalness of classical life and thought; the other, never shaking off the moral restraints of religion, and anxious to bind the new learning to the service of Christianity. But when the Italian revival had spent itself in the production of scholars, who could express the emptiest platitudes in the most Ciceronian Latinity, the movement of thought, of which it was the fountain-head, took a new direction and spread itself out over a wider field. Men of a profound and laborious erudition completed the task of reconquering the mind of antiquity. The scientific study of nature, and the speculations of a philosophy which was careless of ecclesiastical restraint, divided between them the keenest intellects of Europe. The result is, that in every department of knowledge signal victories have been won. Philosophy, whatever the paucity of its positive results, has improved and developed the art of thinking. We look out upon a widened universe with more accurate eyes. Our knowledge of antiquity has been indefinitely increased. An art of criticism has grown up which enables us to use with confidence the materials bequeathed to us by primitive tradition and ancient learning. Nor does this triumphant progress of science as yet show any signs of arrest or retardation. The last three hundred years are distinguished from all that went before, in the fact that the increase of knowledge which they have brought with them is such as is not subject to reversal. Except in the sense in which complete is opposed to partial truth, there is no fear lest the twentieth century should contradict the nineteenth. It is impossible to conceive of our present achievements being neglected and forgotten, as Greek literature and science were neglected and forgotten in the middle ages. Our children will not have to go back and try for a fresh method, as Descartes and Spinoza had to break with the philosophical traditions of the Schoolmen.

But, in the mean time, what has been the history of

theology? While scholarship was still tentative, when the beginnings of natural science were hardly made, before philosophy had taken its first fresh flight, when antiquity was yet wholly misunderstood, the belief of the Reformation was crystallized into creeds which are still held to be binding on the great Protestant Churches. Nor was this all: in Germany, in Switzerland, in Holland, these creeds themselves became the nucleus of vast and elaborate systems of theology, which in spirit, in method, in all but name, were a revived scholasticism. But since then, how much has happened! The science of Biblical criticism has been born, and has grown to a vigorous maturity; a correct text of the New Testament has been formed; a more accurate philology has put us into fresh relations to the original languages of Scripture ; the Biblical history has been re-read. The general results of research have pressed upon theology with modifying effect; the history of man upon earth can no longer be compressed within the limits of scriptural chronology; Israel's place in the world is not what he was himself wont to think it; the patriarchal stories fall into the general category of primæval history, and undergo the same dissolvent analysis. The miracles which are so closely interwoven with the sacred story, look strange and out of place in a world where law is universal and invariable. The conception of nature, which is the inspiration o recent research, and seems to hold all the promise of the future, demands, if it is to be brought into conformity with religion, some modification of the traditional conception of nature's God. In brief, we are now called upon to make the ancient affirmations of the Churches, in an age when the evidence on which they were based has either changed or must be estimated by other canons of judgment. We cannot read the Bible, or interpret history, or look out upon nature, as the Reformers did. If we are to accept their creeds at all, it must be either by boldly putting our own meaning upon their phrases, or by resolutely shutting our eyes to the best knowledge of our time.

There is a sense in which the issue between progress and stagnation in theology may be said to be decided by the Reformation itself. For it was a revolt against finality, and it would be strange if finality were to be its result. If, as I have tried to prove, it was the first effect of the intellectual movement which is still in full operation, why should it withdraw itself from its influence in its latest and most important stage? I cannot help thinking that Luther, could he live now, would breathe the common air of the intellectual world, and answer to its inspiration as he did to that of his own time. About the greatest minds there is an ever fresh receptiveness: they stand close to the sources of truth, and desire no better than to drink and be satisfied: it is a second and weaker generation, accustomed *jurare in verba magistri*, who subject facts to creeds, and will not permit even God to contradict His own servants. I know of course how this argument is sought to be evaded: the Reformation, it may be said, though in appearance a forward, was really a backward step: it was a recurrence, past an intercalated period of corruption, to primitive purity of belief and a standard which is independent of intellectual progress. But this, after all, only begs the question. If it was admissible for Luther to examine the interpretation put by the Catholic Church upon the Bible and

Christian antiquity, it is equally admissible for us to examine Luther's. We are but following his example in testing religious ideas by the surest knowledge of our own day. What if it turns out that his work was only half done, and could be no more than half done with the materials at his command? What if the Bible shows by its history and structure that it is unfit to occupy that seat of authority from which, in its favour, he displaced the Church? The truth is, that one Reformation always carries in it the seed of another. There are two elements in religion, the permanent and the transient, the divine and the human—a duality which rests upon the fact that what is given by God can only be partially apprehended by man. And it is necessary, in order that the permanent should shine out in its pure and simple splendour, that the transient should gradually drop away.

These facts and arguments, I submit, establish the necessity of a new Reformation of religion. In what way are they met by those who deny that necessity? Without some attempted reply to this question, my exposition would be incomplete.

The Roman Catholic Church goes behind the Reformation, which she regards as a futile and criminal rebellion against her authority. She claims to be the sole depositary of religious truth, which she has not only received from the past at the hands of a practically infallible tradition, but which she has the power and the right to develope into fresh complexity and symmetry. At first sight, then, it would seem that her system is not touched by the intellectual forces which corrode the theology of the Reformation. And yet, if the Bible is to be carried on the shoulders of the Church, instead of standing on its own feet, the Church must be held responsible for the use which is made of it and the inferences which are drawn from it. To a certain extent, however, the literary difficulties involved in the structure of the Bible are thus evaded, and the Catholic replies to the assertion that the Scriptures are not fitted to be a dogmatic authority, that he does not want them to be, but looks for the exercise of that function to the Church. But even so, the antagonism between the ancient and the modern spirit not only remains, but is made more bitter. It is not now a religious system born at the re-awakening of the human mind which is opposed to historical criticism, to new speculation, to modern science, but one which was the product of the middle ages, and bears upon it the stamp of their childish ignorance, their gross superstition. It is true that in some respects Rome has modified her attitude of iron rigidity towards new knowledge. She has found out that the heliocentric theory of our system is consistent with orthodox belief. Father Sacchi and his Roman observatory are a curious comment upon Galileo's dealings with the Inquisition. There are other natural sciences which may be pursued, at least in their lower branches, without injury to the faith; while as to history, Rome is always skilful in narrating and interpreting it in her own way. But whatever real or apparent concessions the principle of ecclesiastical authority may make, it remains fundamentally at war with science. Here too is a claim to absolute and final authority which is daily establishing itself in men's minds, and which once recognized can never be abandoned. From a proved fact, from an established law, there is no appeal. Against them can be pleaded no force of tradition, no claim of authority. For a time the gravity of the issue may be conceded or evaded, but it must come out clear at last. The infallible Church on one side, the forces of science and reason on the other—these are in the last resort irreconcilable. If I may adapt to a new use the imagery of the Apocalypse, there must be at last an intellectual battle of Armageddon, in which either the Church or science will win a decisive victory.

I have been accustomed to think that the Roman Catholic Church is the only communion familiarly known to us which puts the principle of authority into a logical shape. It excludes as far as possible the opposing principle of reason, it openly bases the authority of the Bible on its own, it declares that it possesses a living power of determining dogma, and has not scrupled to exercise it. With the position of the Church of England, which, if we are to accept the joint witness of its Articles and its actual historical development, seeks to blend into one the authority of the Church and the authority of Scripture, I am not directly concerned. So far as the faith of that Church rests upon ecclesiastical authority, it can make no concessions to science, and must ultimately come into conflict with it; so far as it rests upon Scripture, it is open to the difficulties which are suggested by the literary structure of the Bible. I venture to think that there are only three intelligible—and those not equally intelligible—positions which it is possible to take up in regard to the reception of religious truth. We may accept it at the hands of a Church of whose infallible authority we have previously convinced ourselves. We may deduce it from Scripture by a process of interpretation which we believe to be divinely ordained to lead devoutly inquiring minds into the truth. We may apply the faculties of the mind and conscience to all sources of information—scripture, history, nature, our own constitution—examining, sifting, comparing, in obedience to the canons of scientific search. I believe that the third method is implicitly contained in the other two, and that we are therefore logically brought back to it as alone conclusive. But whether this is so or not, the seat of authority is not double but single. It must reside either in the Church, or in the Bible, or in Reason. You cannot plead the first two of these conjointly against the third.

In any case, however, the position of the Church of England must be that of ancient faith against new thought. It recites in its services the three Creeds. Its Liturgy draws a large part of its inspiration from mediæval forms of devotion. The Articles are founded upon the Confession of Augsburg. Nothing in its formularies, except a prayer published now and then for a special occasion, is more modern than the Caroline settlement. Something has been dropped from the Prayer-book since 1662, but nothing added to it. And it is not too much to say, that however clergy and laity have been affected by modern science and speculation, the set of opinion in the Church is strongly against any change in the formularies. There is, I believe, a Society for the Revision of the Prayer-book, but it conciliates little support and makes no progress. The outcry a few years ago against the use of the Athanasian Creed appeared to be both loud and deep, but the agitation for its disuse bore little fruit. Not only is the Prayer-book firmly rooted in the affections of churchmen—so firmly rooted as not merely to have become the indispensable expression of their religious emotions, but to have been almost identified with those emotions themselves—but the men who would reform it fear the beginnings of change, lest it should take a direction the very opposite to their wishes. Am I speaking too strongly, when I say that churchmen would almost as soon consent to a project for revising the Bible as the Prayer-book? Both, it may be said, are facts of religious and literary history which have come down to us from an antiquity nearer or more remote; and what we have to do, if we find them out of accord with present conviction, is not to change but to interpret them. But the pressure is not the same in the two cases. Few men are called upon to frame a theory which will unite the whole of the Bible into accord with itself and their own personal convictions, while, on the other hand, the hunger of the soul is always able to choose from its varied pastures abundant and fitting food. But the Prayer-book prescribes the form of daily worship, and any serious and devout spirit must come to some kind of intellectual reconciliation with its thoughts and phrases. And I suppose that this is what many laymen and some clergymen, who are touched by the spirit of the newer time, habitually do. They pour the new wine into the old bottles, without waiting or greatly caring for any specific result. They have many ways of satisfying themselves—ways which I shall not pause to criticise—that whatever evils may attend this course, do not outweigh its benefits. I do not imagine that if they had the opportunity of compiling the Prayer-book or enacting the Articles over again, they would make them what they are; and if so, I am justified in inferring that they look forward to a time at which the forms of belief and worship will receive some accommodation to the necessities of modern knowledge. But they take no steps towards that end, and in the mean time they put a meaning upon the formularies satisfactory to themselves, considering that they have done all that is necessary if in public and private explanation they make their position clear to others.

I am here much more to state facts than to argue about policies; and I forbear to criticise the Broad-church theory. Nor do I at all question the intellectual integrity of those who thus take up a position in which I could not myself stand, and with which I only imperfectly sympathize. While, on the one hand, it is a maxim of ecclesiastical law that *lex orandi est lex credendi*, and that a man must be held bound by the doctrinal implications of the prayers which he uses, I am ready to admit, on the other, that a fixed form of prayer must always be more or less in the nature of a compromise; that the congregation has its rights as well as the officiating minister; and still more, that in dealing with religion, and especially with an historical religion, perfect scientific accuracy of phrase is practically impossible. Even when the process of change in religious conviction is most rapidly and surely going on, it is fatal to emotion to break with the past too abruptly, too completely. Religion belongs to the conservative side of our nature; we pray best in familiar words; we are moved by old associations; the feeling of community counts for much: no generous or tender soul could renounce without a pang the fellowship of a great Church in full activity of beneficence, much less sever itself from the petitions and aspirations which were once upon the lips of the Church that is at rest. Then, there is the feeling that

God is only another name for the Ineffable and the Incomprehensible; that all our words to Him and about Him do but painfully and clumsily hover around the truth without ever settling upon it; and that there must be a certain poetic warmth and width of phrase in regard to realities which transcend all scientific apprehension. But while we give these considerations all the weight that belongs to them, they surely, in face of the facts on which I rely, form an argument for gradual and cautious change, rather than for no change at all. If it be not possible for religion to march side by side with science with equal step, accepting every sure addition to knowledge as soon as it is made, and at once translating it into the language of faith and aspiration, it is no reason why she should lag three centuries behind her comrade, and utterly refuse to try to lessen the interval. And even were the policy of simple interpretation defensible on other grounds, the experience of the last quarter of a century, it seems to me, practically condemns it. Eloquent expositions of freedom and progress come and go, but the formularies remain. In every cathedral and church throughout the land they are repeated from day to day, enforcing their authority more firmly on men's minds, exercising their ancient and various charm, gathering round themselves fresh associations to blend with the old, identifying themselves more and more with the emotions and affections which they express. These ingenious explanations, which aim to show that in some mysterious way the authors of the Creeds, the framers of the Articles, the writers of the Prayers, anticipated the difficulties and wants of centuries as remote as ours, are but as the waves which now quietly lap, now angrily beat against the steadfast crag, with no other result than that of proving its magnificent immovability. We have had a school of liberal theology in the Church of England more than once, and notably in our own times. With what result? Many noble books have been written: many devoted and successful labourers have toiled in her vineyard: she has been kept faithful in her allegiance to the sanctities of daily life. But it is also true that the breach between the clergy and the most actively intelligent of the laity has grown wider, that many sweet and strong souls have declined or abandoned her service, and that her formularies remain in all essential points what the Reformers made them.

But outside as well as within the Church of England there is a great body of Evangelical opinion which is wont to regard itself as in an especial way affiliated upon the theology of the Reformation. It is all directly or indirectly of Genevese origin, being either a Calvinism with its sharp edges rubbed off, or that milder form of faith which Arminius developed in the school of Beza. The Evangelicism of Dissent also has its written standards, though not such as are used in worship: the creeds, like an abridged Westminster Confession, which form the doctrinal clauses of Independent and Baptist trust-deeds, and, in one well-known case, the Sermons published by John Wesley. But it is curious for the student of dogmatic theology to note how far short these statements of doctrine fall of the amplitude, the minuteness, the precision of the old confessions; how distinctions which once divided the Protestant world into hostile camps are now passed over as unessential; how the word Evangelical is made to cover more than one church and theories of

Christianity which were once thought radically divergent. As you may suppose, I am far from lamenting this change: not only is it well that kindly sympathy and sincere co-operation among Christians should be independent of minute agreement, but theology, in my view, becomes saner in proportion as it recognizes the fact that its outlines cannot always be sharp, nor its distinctions precisely stated. But it is just the Evangelical faith which has shown itself least receptive of the influence of the newer time. It is true to the spirit of the Reformation in this, that it relies upon the letter of Scripture, interpreting what it thinks to be the gospel after the manner of Paul, and compelling all other Biblical voices into harmony with that. So, not unnaturally, it will not listen to the re-reading of the Old and New Testament which the higher criticism asks for. To tell the whole plain truth, it is not greatly in sympathy with learning, or science, or speculation of any kind: to all of them it opposes the simple gospel: it glories in the antithesis between faith that is spiritual and knowledge that is carnal. It is not indeed altogether uninfluenced by the spirit of the age, though it withdraws itself from it as much as it can, reading its own literature, absorbed in its own labours, content with its own life; but it yields nothing to new knowledge that it can by any artifice withhold, and when forced to give ground, gives it only slowly and grudgingly. It denies the validity of discoveries till long after all the rest of the world has been convinced; it exaggerates the differences of scientific men, making them an excuse for being altogether deaf to the voice of science; it reads history after a fashion of its own, and Scripture as if criticism did not exist. I do not know what comfort men of this school can have in the future; for they must see that they are driven back more and more upon the allegiance of the less educated part of society, and that forces are quickly gathering strength which must at last carry their fortress by storm. Perhaps they think, as Luther did, that theirs are the last days, and that the world's victorious unbelief will prove the prevailing invitation to the irresistible self-manifestation of the Lord, and the final triumph in which they will have their part.

One important question as to these various manifestations of religious belief, touches the conception of Christianity which underlies them. In contradistinction to the Catholic idea of a development of doctrine, conducted and watched over by a Church divinely guided, the Protestant theory is, that Christianity is purest at its source, and that that source is the New Testament. Few Protestants, however, are bold enough to follow this notion to its legitimate issue; to acknowledge that in the New Testament itself the process of interpreting Christ has already begun; and to set apart, as of superior authority, the words of the Master himself, in their pregnant and piercing simplicity, from the philosophical speculations of one apostle and the sacrificial theories of another. But, granting for the moment that it is possible to speak of primitive Christianity as of a defined body of doctrine, whether directly derivable from Scripture or gradually reduced to form and proportion by the Church, in what relation are we to conceive it to stand to the advancing knowledge, the accumulating experience, the ripening speculation of man? Is theology to grow with his growth, and to strengthen with his strength? Is it to advance step by step with the other sciences, acting upon them and receiving their modifying impact, or does it remain the one changeless thing in a world of intellectual change? Or, to put it in another way, is it a voice from heaven, which once heard is obligatory for ever, above doubt, subject to no question, or is it the cry of man to the Eternal, with which the answer of God is subtly mingled? There can be no doubt as to the reply which we shall give to these questions, when once we have taken the Hebrew history out of the category of the miraculous, and learned to interpret the Bible as we would any other book. So far as the Scripture record goes, it is a story of religious progress, chequered indeed and interrupted, but always steadily tending towards its goal. The Jehovah whom the tribes ruled by the Judges worshipped with half-pagan rites, was on a lower level than the God and Father of Jesus Christ. The morality of the Gospel is an unspeakable advance upon the retaliatory jurisprudence of Leviticus. There is a wide interval between the sensuous splendour of the Temple ceremonies and the worship of a Spirit "in spirit and in truth." Why should we suppose that the great designs of God for the religious education of the world came abruptly to a conclusion with the close of the New Testament canon? I do not know that any long roll of years can add spiritual depth to such a word as "the pure in heart shall see God," or give a more compelling obligation to the Golden Rule; but as the moral experience of mankind grows larger, and new experiments are tried in personal and social duty, these universal principles receive fresh and unexpected application, which surely find their way, if I may so speak, into man's thought of God.

I have tried in a former Lecture to show how science has widened the world, and so has given breadth and depth and many-sidedness to our conception of its Divine Ruler. And if, as I must needs believe on penalty of losing all hold on religion, an assured fact, in whatever department of knowledge, is a word of God not less authoritative than that which was placed of old on the lips of prophet or apostle, it might be permitted to a Newton, as he tracks the law which bids the apple fall from the tree and sustains the planet in its course—to a Darwin, as he reveals the hidden tie which binds all animate things together and almost makes them a single organism—to announce his discovery with the ancient "Thus saith the Lord." We are accustomed—though not, I think, in our worthiest moments—to lament that miracle is dead, that prophecy is silent: let us rather rejoice that we too live in an age of revelation, when in the sublimest majesty of self-manifestation God is laying bare His ways to the reverent scrutiny of man.

In all that I have said hitherto, I have taken for granted that the facts of religion are facts, and may be recognized as such by human faculties. It is true that I think that theology has been far too minute and precise; that it has attempted to define and distinguish when the only word upon its lips should have been an *O Altitudo;* that it has placed mysteries whose abyss no logic can sound, details of faith which no research can verify, on the same footing as the great truths, the cardinal principles, which alone feed the religious life. But I mean by religious facts something external to human emotions and aspirations; that which is indeed their object, and without which they could not long sustain themselves in life. Yet there are thinkers, whether few or many I hardly know, who, setting a real value on religion as the supreme agent in the softening, the sweetening, the elevating of human life, imagine that it can permanently exist without theology, and that so long as the characteristically religious emotions and affections are felt, it does not matter whether they have any intellectual basis or no. Ideals, they think, are just as good for all practical purposes as facts; the abstract conception of a perfect Being as operative as the conviction of a living God; and the charm of the Christ what it is, were the Gospels no more than the most consummate of religious fictions. And so no dogmas are worth anything; for the simplest statement of theological principle is tainted by the same presumption and unreality as the minutest definition of the *communicatio idiomatum*. I need not say how this theory of religion is fatal to the very idea of theology. It not only degrades it from the rank of a science, but takes it out of the category of things that may be known. Its history becomes a mere record of human folly and presumption, of wasted toil, foolish strivings, baffled aspirations. And if its past be thus melancholy, it can look forward to no future. It is not so much that its subject-matter is unsearchable, as that it has none. Human nature will continue to strain towards its ideal, learning gradually, we must suppose, to rely on other helps, to lean on other supports, than those which are afforded by a belief in divine realities; and in the mean time, as all dogmas are equally worthless, a wise man will accommodate himself to the prejudices of his age, and worship as his neighbours worship.

That, under such circumstances, men should worship at

all, is perhaps sufficient testimony to the reality of that religious emotion which seeks to justify itself so strangely. And I am disposed to explain this state of mind by the fact that it is a survival of religion after the death of theology. Men, whom an imperious intellectual necessity drives from outpost after outpost of faith, may yet be unwilling to lose their hold of affections which they know to be elevating, of associations which touch the secretest fibre of their hearts, of aspirations which they need as a counterbalance to the coarseness and commonness of the world. But I am bound to believe—else were my long labour wholly vain—that they are fundamentally in error, and that they mistake the impulse of old forces, which once moved them too powerfully to be ever wholly extinct, for a living manifestation of energy, which they can transmit to their children, and which will stir generations to come. I am far from depreciating the efficacy of some of those moral ideals, which are not religious either in their origin or their sanction, and which, under present circumstances of belief, may be expected to move and mould men more powerfully than ever before. But I do not think that their method of operation is the same as that of the religious ideals which most of us believe to be realized in fact, and it can serve no good purpose to confound them. I do not understand how men continue to pray, unless they are convinced that there is a listening ear. It seems to me that there is all the difference in the world between a Christ who actually walked the earth in the consummate beauty of holiness, and one who owes the strength and symmetry of his character to vivid ethical imagination and subtle literary skill. The last may still charm and raise and refine those who study him; but the first makes mankind richer, opens out new possibilities to human nature, effectually calls upon all who love him to come up into the mount of God. So, too, the mathematician may "scorn delights and live laborious days" for his science, which may screen him from all grosser temptations, and teach him the method of an innocent life: the unbelieving philanthropist, consumed by the enthusiasm of humanity, may wholly give his life to others, and in so doing learn the secret of self-forgetfulness. But even this, though a fine, is not the same thing as to feel the awful touch of God upon the soul; to obey a holier will, to lean upon a steadier strength than our own; to bind ourselves to the service of a living righteousness; and to find in trust of a personal lovingkindness the inspiration of courage and patience. The strain towards an unrealized ideal still allows man to think himself the highest and best thing that he knows: obedience to the Living God subdues him into humility and chastens him to self-distrust.

With those who affirm that religion is an emotion of the childhood of humanity which its maturer years have outgrown, I do not feel myself in this place called upon to argue. They are, in this country at least, very few in number, and not accustomed to maintain their position with a very rigid consistency. By an extension of the meaning of the word religion, which at this moment I neither approve nor blame, but which makes it include all the ideal and unselfish elements of life, it is not difficult to show that they are all religious in their own way and in conformity with their own convictions. But there is the less need thus to play with words which have an old and well-defined meaning, that I imagine I see a distinct and wide-spread desire on the part of philosophical and scientific thinkers, who have decisively broken with old forms of faith, to work their way back again to some standpoint of practical religion. It may not be to Christianity, as that word is commonly understood: even its simplest and least dogmatic forms may seem to them to state more of divine realities than can be fully proved: but it is to religion that their return is being made, to the recognition of something that is supersensual and divine, to the acknowledgment of a righteous order in the world, and the dependence of human nature for its best impulses upon an Infinite Holiness. And it is not only in the interests of these men, but in those of religion itself, that I plead for a bolder policy on the part of the churches, and ask for a revision of formularies, a relaxation of bonds. Scientific men have been educated, by the whole method and experience of their lives, into careful observation and accurate statement of facts. They want proof for all that they are to believe: they are accustomed to distinguish between hypothesis and reasonable certainty. They do not understand the principle of accommodation, of taking words in non-natural senses, of looking to the historical derivation of formularies rather than to their plain meaning. It is not their practice to make solemn and precise statements of belief, and then to explain them away. Possibly they are too exacting in their demands upon theology and theologians: they forget that the same methods of discovering and testing truth are not applicable in all departments of human thought: they do not sufficiently take into account the necessarily infinite character of religious realities, or recognize the fact that when logic has done all it can, there are yet place and work for faith and aspiration. But when all needful allowances have been made on either side, much remains to be done in assimilating the methods and results of theology with those of other sciences, if the men of whom I have spoken are to be reconciled with religion. Can theology, then, afford to be at variance with the keenest wits, the most judicial intellects of the day? Or is it of any use to bid them, in the old imperious fashion, submit their reason to the divine authority alleged to be embodied in Church or Bible? In that intellectual activity which is their very life, they live by reason, and must stand or fall by it.

And it must be recollected that scientific culture is rapidly extending. The number of educated men, whose chief intellectual training and interest lie in the study of natural science, increases every day. Such men, having little to do with literature except as a mental recreation, are apt to exhibit at once the strength and the weakness of the scientific intellect: its love of accuracy, its demand for strict reasoning, its passion for definite results, and at the same time its disbelief in other methods of ascertaining truth than those which it has itself found effectual. But whether this state of things be favourable to religion or not, it is a fact and must be reckoned with. On the other hand, it is no longer possible for theology to shut itself up in the cell of its own peculiar erudition, and to claim implicit credence for whatever oracles it chooses to utter. It finds its assumptions rudely questioned, its authorities carefully sifted. A dogmatic utterance of Augustine's, a rhetorical phrase of Jerome's, no longer weighs heavily on the mind of Christendom. Even were such a thing possible as a consensus of the Fathers upon any particular point of doctrine, criticism would at once reply by an investigation into the grounds of patristic authority. Ecclesiastical history, as now written, is inexorable in pointing out the mistakes of Reformers, the assumptions of Schoolmen, the inconsistencies of Fathers, the contradictions of Councils, the unfounded pretensions of Churches. Criticism asks of creeds, by whom they were enacted; of dogmatic systems, upon what foundation they repose; of the authority of Scripture, by what arguments it can be justified; and does not always receive an answer which it is willing to accept. Theology, in a word, has had to come down from the calm and lofty eminence of the temple, where she was wont to receive the unquestioning homage of her votaries, to mingle with men in their common haunts and daily avocations, to defend her own claims, and to rely for reverence on her intrinsic worth. That she can victoriously stand this test, I thoroughly believe: but it must be on condition that she frankly submits to it; that she is ready to abandon all untenable assumptions; that she throws off every needless dogmatic burthen; that she is simply faithful to the truths of which she is profoundly convinced. But the test is, year by year, being applied on a wider scale and with added stringency, and it is useless to try to evade it by retiring to the solitary heights of authority.

I must honestly confess that I see no evidence that Christ ever intended to teach any dogmatic system of theology at all. Separating, as I must do, between his own words and the interpretations put upon them by Apostle and Evangelist, I find in the Synoptical Gospels the earliest and most trustworthy tradition of his teaching. And, if this is so, it must be admitted that these documents—on other grounds the most valuable literary possession of the human race—are singularly ill-fitted for dogmatic purposes. They are a very incomplete record of what the Master actually said. Brief as they are, that incompleteness is increased by many repetitions. We cannot say that they submit theology or even religion to any systematic treatment. They are full of deep spiritual sayings, pregnant ethical precepts; but even these do not stand in logical connection, and are not rounded off into a whole. The only impression of Christ's method which we can derive from them is, that he intentionally adapted his instructions to the individual, almost to the occasional necessities of those who heard them, sowing his truth broadcast, and leaving the harvest to the good husbandry of God. It may have been otherwise: he may have formed a school and elaborated a system; but, if he did, the record fails to tell the tale, and we must look for his secret, not in the open page of the Gospels, but in the esoteric tradition of the Church. It is only when we consider the interpretations put upon Christ by lower and lesser minds than his, that we come upon the first traces of a system. That profound and penetrating religious genius to whom we owe the Fourth Gospel, wove Christianity into the web of a world philosophy, and strove to reconcile the simplicity of Hebrew monotheism with the breadth of Hellenic speculation. Paul, whose keen perception had grasped the fact, which was hidden from some at least of the Twelve, that the Gospel was not to add a new distinction to Judaism, but to become the religious life of humanity, found himself under the necessity of at once offering it to the Gentile and vindicating it to the Jew, and so tried to think out for himself an intelligible and a logical position. I need not say that, even while I place these two great men on a lower level of spiritual insight than their Master—and they would have been the last to claim for themselves that position of equality with him to which the doctrine of the infallible inspiration of the New Testament has practically elevated them—I acknowledge most fully the unspeakable obligation under which the Church of all ages lies to them. But not even in their writings will you find any system of religious thought which can compare in complexity and symmetry with those to which the Reformation gave birth, or such as are now considered to be the indispensable basis of church fellowship. In the Fourth Gospel are the germs of that doctrine of the Deity of Christ which the first three centuries developed into the statements of the Nicene, three centuries more into those of the Athanasian Creed. In the Pauline letters is the outline of that doctrine of Atonement which the early Church passed by almost in silence, but which, revived by Augustine, by Anselm, by Luther, has since, in one form or other, met with almost universal acceptance. These developments may have been in the mind of Christ and lie implicitly in his words. But I confess I can see no proof of it; and when I look at what alone we can suppose to have been the method of his intellectual training, and the attitude in which he consistently stood to Hebrew religious life, I must think it improbable as well as unproved.

I do not of course mean to assert that because the teaching of Christ, as we have it in its earliest records, embraces no dogmatic system, it is on that account not full of great and fruitful theological truths. Such a truth, the most fundamental, perhaps the most original of all, is the Fatherhood of God, and the relations of trust, love, obedience, awe, in which His human children stand to Him. A correlative truth is the Brotherhood of Man, a fraternity which transcends all differences of country, colour, speech. A third is the Kingdom of God,—the perfect society in which the new life poured into the individual heart was meant to issue. A fourth is the Future State, connected with this by the bond of those ethical principles which must be conceived of as tying all human life together. But it is remarkable how Christ is content with the simplest statement of these truths. He does not seek to develope them into what metaphysical theologians would now declare to be their necessary consequences; he does not attempt to bring them into logical co-ordination. In regard to the nature of God, he seems to me to stand on the plain ground of his ancestral monotheism. In regard to God's lovingkindness, equity, forbearance, forgiveness, omniscience, he is emphatic in statement, vivid in illustration; but of a philosophical doctrine of Divine attributes there is no trace. So, too, he is content to leave the future life under the veil of parable: he gives no encouragement to the theological scene-painters, who daub with their rude and staring colours the solemn chambers of human destiny. And it is even more to be noticed that he seems to consider these few and simple truths sufficient, not only for the instruction, but for the purification, the elevation, the impulse of human life. It is from them that his appeals derive all their winning charm; his warnings, all their awful significance. They are the food of his own religious life, and he considers them adequate to feed the religious life of others. It is not that, like a consummate artist, he is able in the strength and versatility of genius to produce the greatest effects with the simplest means, but that in the region of practical religion the simplest means are alone necessary and alone efficacious. There are no more solemn and moving truths than those of which I have spoken. When others of a more derivative and complex kind seem to sway the hearts of men, it is only in the hidden energy of these.

It will at once be objected that there is very little in what I have said to differentiate Christianity from other religions, and that, if it is to have a characteristic quality of its own, it must be described in terms less vague. But I, for one, consider it no discredit to Christianity that, thus reduced to its simplest elements, it comes very near to what some have called Absolute Religion; the quintessence, that is, of all that the wisest minds have thought, all that the tenderest hearts have felt, all that the keenest consciences have recognized as binding. Nor am I concerned to discuss the originality of Christ or the novelty of Christianity: the more these are magnified, the harder is it to find a place in the providential order for Hebrew faith and Hellenic wisdom. But, indeed, what Christ brought into the world was not so much new truth as fresh life—not so much ethical principles and precepts unknown before, as an enlarged capacity of moral obedience and growth. To discuss the secret of this spiritual life would lead me too far into thorny theological by-paths: I am content to rest in the fact. It is this which raises Christ above the level of the teacher, and gives him his claim to be called, however you may define the word, the Saviour of the world. It is this which justifies the contention of Evangelical divines of every school, that we go to him not to learn the outlines of a system, moral or theological, but to be inspired, moved, changed, saved. One of those deep sayings which seem to me to show that the author of the Fourth Gospel had access to a genuine fund of Christian tradition, which but for him would have perished, is, "I am come that they may have life, and may have it abundantly." And this I accept as an authoritative description of Christ's mission. But if it is so accepted, I must go on to point out that the possession of life must be taken as the proof of contact and communion with Christ; that the qualifications for standing in the line of Christian affiliation are not intellectual, but moral and spiritual; and that it ought to be impossible to deny the name of Christian to any who acknowledge Christ as their Master, and can show any genuine likeness to him. This test might unchurch some loudly professing believers; it would admit many heretics to the fold; but it would at last gather in from diverse communions the pure, the self-forgetting and the brave, and would make Christianity as wide a thing as Christendom.

I know that in thus pleading for the simplification of doctrine, for the enlargement of terms of communion, for the reconciliation of theology with new knowledge, I have never left the critical ground. We have looked at religion from the outside as a datum of history, a subject of speculation—a thing which it lies with ourselves to accept or reject according as it satisfies the tests by which our intellectual nature compels us to try it. And from one point of view it is and must be this. With the best will in the world, we cannot believe what is intrinsically incredible to us. Some *tour de force* of logic is necessary before we can abandon ourselves to the authority of a church, however complete may be our submission afterwards. But there is another attitude to religious truth which is not the critical, though we may call in the critical judgment to justify it when the first storm of enthusiasm which compelled us to assume it has spent its force. Sometimes, under happy stress of circumstance, we do not choose a religion, but religion chooses us. In this higher order of things, Christ's was the natural procedure: his apostles did not, after long hesitation and much questioning, attach themselves to him; but he chose them, he called them, he took possession of them, and they obeyed. They were carried away by a force generated beyond the bounds of their own nature; their enthusiasm was the motion of a God within. Changes of theological opinion are, I know, produced by intellectual causes and run an intellectual course; but when no religious impulses intervene, they are rarer than is commonly supposed, and all spiritual upliftings and transformations conform to the law of which I have spoken. And so I venture to think that to restore Christianity to the place which it has lost and is more and more losing in the hearts of thoughtful and educated men, still more to give back to it its old victorious energy in dealing with the sinful and the wretched, what is chiefly needed is a prophet of this latter day who, in the keenness and directness of his religious insight, will speak at once a piercing and a reconciling word. Such an one will be deeply penetrated with the scientific spirit, rejoicing in the interpretation of nature as an unveiling of God, and desiring only the plain truth of history that he may trace in it the working of the Divine Hand. But he will be too full of the awe of direct vision to lose himself in the arid wastes of criticism, or to be led astray by the pedantries of scientific investigation. I dare venture to predict that, like every other true prophet, the future will fill his eye and heart too completely to suffer him to be a bond-slave of the past: present revelations always overbear old theologies, and no living church ever supplies the model of the New Jerusalem. I have no fear lest he should fall out of the ranks of Christ's soldiers; for I do not believe that religion has anything to offer to man that the Gospel does not hold, and I notice that what is strong and inspiring in newer systems is Christian in essence, if not always in name. I know that when he speaks men will crowd to hear him, and lay their hearts and lives in his hands; for the religious instincts of humanity are ineradicable, and even if they sometimes sleep, wake always to life and energy again. And though his clear and penetrating accents may not fall upon our living ears, and we can do nothing to direct the operation of the Spirit of God, which, like the wind, "bloweth where it listeth," yet it belongs to us of this generation to make straight the way of his coming, by living and working in the light of our best knowledge and most intimate convictions. Intellectual difficulties we can to some extent reconcile: hindrances to church fellowship we can remove: we can go back to the simplicity of primitive piety: we can acknowledge the oneness of the religious life. So, as age follows age, and each pours fresh wealth into the treasury of human knowledge—as men accumulate a riper experience, solving ever more perfectly the problems of life and entering upon wider possibilities—Christianity too will receive a fuller development, and mankind, with the acknowledgment of mystery and the cry of imperfection always upon its lips, will penetrate more and more deeply into the glory and the wonder of God.

INDEX.

Abbot, Archbishop, 321, 322.
Adrian VI., 93, 97, 106.
Æneas Sylvius Piccolomini, vid. Pius II.
Agricola, Johann, 287.
Agricola, Rudolf, 31, 46, 47, 141.
Albigenses, the, 8.
Albrecht, Duke of Austria, 48.
Albrecht of Brandenburg, Elector Archbishop of Mainz, 48, 68, 69 n.
Aleander, 79.
Alexander III., 25, 308.
Alexander IV., 17 n.
Alexander V., 9.
Alexander VI., 32, 141.
Althammer, 215.
Altorf, Socinianism at, 274 n.
Alva, 96, 100, 110, 243, 261.
Amaury de Bène, 26 n.
Amsdorf, 288.
Andrewes, Bishop, 321, 325.
Anquetil du Perron, 349.
Anne of Bohemia, 28.
Anselm, 277, 307.
Apology of Confession of Augsburg, 283, 289, 290.
Aquinas, Thomas, 8.
Archimedes, 382 n.
Argyropulos, 53.
Ariosto, 43.

Arminius, 297, 413.
Articles, the Forty-two, 315, 316 n.
Articles, the Nine (of Lambeth), 320, 327.
Articles, the Six, 244, 304, 309, 315.
Articles, the Ten, 309.
Articles, the Thirteen, 315.
Articles, the Thirty-nine, 244, 300, 315, 316, 316 n., 318, 324, 325, 327, 328.
Astruc, 355.
Atterbury, Bishop, 332, 344.
Augsburg, Confession of, 122, 122 n., 267, 282, 289, 290, 310, 315, 316, 325, 327, 382, 409.
Augsburg, Diet of, 74, 87, 89, 104, 108.
Averrhoes, 372.

Bacon, 374.
Bainham, 306.
Barnes, 306.
Basel, Council of, 13, 43.
Basel, University of, 48.
Baumgärtner, 340.
Baur, F. C., 358, 364.
Bebel, 49.
Becket, Archbishop, 307, 308, 311.
Beghards, 20, 21.
Beguines, 20, 21.

Behem, Hans, 29 n.
Belgic Confession, 301.
Bembo, Cardinal, 41 n.
Benedict, St., 7.
Benedict XIII., 9.
Benedictines, 7.
Bentley, Richard, 331, 344.
Bernard, St., 7.
Bessarion, Cardinal, 31.
Beza, 251, 297, 331, 413.
Biandrata, 269, 275 n.
Bilney, 306.
Blasphemy, 173, 178.
Blondel, 354.
Boccaccio, 5, 39, 43.
Bohemian Reformation, 28.
Boiardo, 43.
Boleyn, Ann, 303, 317.
Bonaventura, 8.
Bora, Catharine von, 85, 142.
Boscovich, 399.
Bourbon, Constable of, 107.
Boyle, Hon. C., 344.
Brandt, Sebastian, 49.
Brenz, 138 n., 167, 174, 316.
Brethren of the Free Spirit, 19, 26 n.
Brethren of the Common Life, 21, 46.
Bucer, 101, 139, 176, 283, 310, 313 n., 314.
Budæus, 343.
Bugenhagen, 93, 166.
Bullinger, 242, 271.
Burnouf, 347, 349.
Busche, H. v. d., 51.
Butler, Bishop, 329, 376.

Cajetan, Cardinal, 83.
Calixt, George, 291.
Calov, Abr., 291, 292.
Calvin, on the authority of Scripture, 122. On the interpretation of Scripture, 125. Sacramental theory, 139. Calvin and Servetus, 180. A generation younger than Zwingli and Luther, 227. Relation to Zwingli and his theology, 228. Belongs to a later stage of the Reformation than Luther and Zwingli, 242. Director of the French Reformation, 244. Adviser of Edward VI., 244. Geneva a fortress of the Reform, 245. His prevailing influence there, 246. His theory of the Church, 246. Ecclesiastical discipline, 248. As set up in Geneva, 249. Its effects, 251. Calvin's theory of persecution, 253. Gruet, 253. Servetus, 254. Calvin's letter to the Protector Somerset, 254. Differences between Calvinistic and Lutheran theology, 255. Its leading idea the absolute supremacy of God, 256. Its relation to morals, 257. Theory of Scripture, 258. Calvin a more consistent scripturalist than Luther, 258. Calvinism the last word of orthodox Protestantism, 260. Rejects symbolism, 260. On the side of popular politics, 261. Calvin's "Institution," 293. Editions, 293. Contents, 294. Character, 295.
Calvin, other references, 37, 264, 269, 271, 278, 299, 305, 310, 326, 327, 402.
Camerarius, Joach., 93, 339.
Campanus, 125, 173.
Capito, 195, 206.
Capnio, vid. Reuchlin.
Carlstadt, 71 n., 84, 137, 141, 165, 169, 186, 190, 192, 198, 354.
Casaubon, Isaac, 332, 333 n., 343.

Cavendish, 385.
Caxton, William, 28.
Celtes, Conrad, 45 n., 49, 51.
Champollion, 347.
Charles I., 331, 333 n.
Charles IV. of Bohemia, 28.
Charles V., allegorical play at Augsburg, 74. His descent, 93. Elected Emperor, 93. His territories, 93. His scheme of universal dominion, 95. A Fleming, 96. His character, 96. His ministers, 96. Did not understand Luther, 97. No sympathy with Protestantism, 97. The centre of his policy Burgundian, 98. Dynastic selfishness, 98. Intended to put down Protestantism, 99. His interview with the Protestant Princes before the Diet at Augsburg, 104. Reasons why he did not crush Protestantism at once, 108. Battle of Mühlberg, 109. The Interim, 109. Charles' flight before Maurice, 110. Treaty of Passau, 110. Charles' retirement at Juste, 95, 111.
Charles V., other references, 243, 384.
Charles VII. of France, 14.
Charles the Bold, 94, 232.
Chaucer, 5.
Chieregati, 79.
Chigi, Agost., 106 n.
Chillingworth, 275.
"Christian Man, the Institution of a," 309.
"Christian Man, the Doctrine and Erudition of a," 309.
Clarke, S., 376.
Clement VII., 32, 85, 93, 107.
Cobham, Lord, 28.

Cochlæus, 287.
Colet, Dean, 225, 302.
Cologne, University of, 44, 44 n.
Colonna, Cardinal, vid. Martin V.
Columbus, 382.
Communicatio idiomatum, 256, 284, 285, 296.
CONCLUSION, 401. Recapitulation of the argument, 401. The revival of letters a movement of the lay mind, 402. Progress of philosophy and science, 403. Concurrent history of theology, 404. Reformation itself decides between progress and stagnation in theology, 405. Attitude of the Catholic Church, 406. Of the Church of England, 408. Its aversion to change, 409. A liturgy always a compromise, 411. The power of the formularies, 412. The practical issue of the Broad Church, 413. The Evangelical school, 413. Is Christianity susceptible of change and growth? 415. The revelation of science, 417. Can religious ideals replace religious facts? 418. A return of scientific thinkers towards religion, 421. Theology universally criticised, 422. Christ did not intend to teach any dogmatic system, 423. Systems of later origin, 424. The great truths of Christianity, 426. Christ brought fresh life into the world, 427. New conditions of church communion, 428. The prophet of the latter day, 429.
Confessio Tetrapolitana, 175, 282.
Constantine, Donation of, 4.
Constanz, Council of, 1, 10, 13, 43.

Copernicus, 383.
Corpora doctrinæ, 289, 290.
Corvinus, Matthias, 94 n.
Cossa, Balthazar, vid. John XXIII.
Courayer, P. le, 332, 333 n.
Cowper, William, 257.
Cranmer, Archbishop, 182, 244, 305, 306, 310, 311, 312, 313, 313 n., 315, 324.
Crell, 274.
CRITICAL SPIRIT, THE GROWTH OF THE, 336. Its double effect, 336. Humanists and Reformers part company, 337. Luther's view, 338. Melancthon's, 339. Erasmus's, 340. Revived interest in classical culture, 341. The task of the humanists, 342. Latter stage of the Italian revival, 342. Leadership passes to France and Holland, 343. Three epoch-making books, 344. Bentley's Phalaris, 344. Wolf's Prolegomena to Homer, 345. Niebuhr's Rome, 345. New view of primæval history, 346. Decipherment of Egyptian hieroglyphics, 347. Of the cuneiform inscriptions, 347. Re-discovery of the Hittite empire, 348. New science of comparative philology, 349. Its ethnological application, 350. Secret of the Greek mythology revealed, 350. The higher criticism, 351. Its negative more remarkable than its positive achievements, 352. A general development of human thought, 353. Biblical criticism at first more cultivated by Catholic than Protestant divines, 354. Hobbes, 354. Spinoza, 355. Simon, Le Clerc, Astruc, 355. Grotius on the Synoptical Gospels, 355. Lessing and Herder, 356. Clear negative conclusions of criticism, 358. Connection of Biblical with general history, 359. Contrast between Israel's conception of himself and his real position, 360. Hebrew history re-read, 361. Criticism applied to the New Testament, 362. Its results upon the Reformation theory, 364. Miracle in Hebrew history, 364. Prophecy, 365. Literary and human interest of the Bible increased, 366. Development of Christian doctrine in the three first centuries, 368.

Cromwell, Oliver, 257, 261.
Crotus Rubianus, 63, 63 n., 337.
Cruciger, Caspar, 195, 313 n.
Cudworth, 329.
Cunningham, Dr., 297.
Cuvier, 386.
Cyril Lucar, 331.

Daillé, 354.
Dalberg, Joh. v., 46.
Dante, 39, 43.
Darwin, 392.
Davalos, 96.
David, Franz, 275 n.
Denck, Joh., 125, 173, 204 et seq., 268.
Descartes, 373, 374, 403.
DEVELOPMENT OF PHILOSOPHICAL METHOD AND SCIENTIFIC INVESTIGATION, 370. Union of philosophy and theology effected by the Schoolmen now dissolved, 371. Their independent course since the Reformation, 372. No philosophical development in the direction of fixed results, 373.

Improvement of the art of thinking, 374. Is theological truth different from all other? 375. Philosophical treatment of religion, 376. Influence of philosophy in the direction of rationalism, 376. A bastard rationalism, 377. What philosophical rationalism is, 377. The rational criterion in an ethical form, 378. Orthodox and systematizing rationalism, 379. Re-awakening of science, 381. The Moors of Spain, 381. Three great voyages, 382. Melancthon's astrology, 382. His and Luther's belief in portents, 383. Copernicus, 383. Newness of modern science, 384. Astronomy, 384. Anatomy, 384. Chemistry, 385. Geology, botany, electricity and magnetism, 385. Theory of evolution, 386. Change in man's way of looking at the universe, 386. From geocentric to heliocentric system, 388. Its results, 388. Antiquity of man, 390. Uniformity of law, 391. Miracle, 391. The "Origin of Species," 392. Evolution a general scientific method, 393. Evolution and theism, 394. Origin of evil and prevalence of pain, 394. Doctrine of heredity, 395. A fall or a rise of man? 396. Is evolution of universal application? 397. Assistance given to religion by new scientific thought, 398. Mystery of matter, 399. Unification of force, 399. Leads to the conception of the one God, 400.
Diether, Elector Archbishop of Mainz, 48.

Dietrich, Veit, 87.
Dionysius the Areopagite, 354.
Dolcino, Fra, 18.
Dominicans, the, 8.
Dominis, M. A. de, 332.
Dordt, Synod of, 228, 297, 321.
Dringenberg, L., 46, 47, 48.
Dryander, 310.
Duns Scotus, 8, 9.
Dürer, A., 49, 215.

Eberbach, G., vid. Petrejus.
Eberhard, Duke of Würtemberg, 48, 54.
Eck, Joh., 29, 50, 51, 287.
Eckhart, 19, 21.
Edward VI., 226, 244, 304, 310, 312, 314, 314 n, 315, 319.
Eichhorn, 355.
Eitelwolf vom Stein, 48.
Elizabeth, Queen, 244, 304, 315, 317, 318, 319, 320, 323, 325, 326.
Ellenbog, N., 383 n.
Emser, 119.
ENGLAND, THE REFORMATION IN, 300. Its peculiarity, 300. Due to the same causes as German and Swiss Reformations, 301. Wiclif, 301. Erasmus and the new learning, 302. English Reform as much political as religious, 303. Depends largely upon character of Princes, 304. Produces no great heroes of faith, 305. W. Tyndale, 305. Cranmer, 305. Recantations, 306. Spoliation of the monasteries, 306. Royal supremacy, 307. Its assertion the last stage of a long process, 308. Wolsey and disciplinary reform, 309. Henry VIII.'s Catholic position, 309. Alliance with German

Protestantism impossible, 310. Protestantism of Edward VI., 310. Continuity of the Anglican Church, 311. Mediæval origin of the Prayer-book, 312. Quignon's Breviary, 312. Hermann von Wied's Consultation, 313. Revisions of the Prayer-book, 314. Elizabeth's Prayer-book, 314 n. The Thirty-nine Articles, 315. Changes from the forty-two Articles, 316. Reaction under Mary, 316. Elizabeth's forced Protestantism, 317. Armada, 318. Settlement under Elizabeth, 318. Discontent of the Marian exiles, 319. Growth of Puritanism, 320. Hampton Court Conference, 321. Reaction under Laud and Andrewes, 321. Struggle with Puritanism and final victory of the Church, 322. Alleged pettiness of Puritanism, 323. Church of England both Protestant and Catholic, 324. The Prayer-book a link with the mediæval Church, 326. The Articles Augustinian, if not Calvinist, 327. A middle party in the Church, 328. Latitudinarians, 329. Position of the Church towards Scripture, 330. Its love of Patristic theology, 330. Attention to criticism of the New Testament, 331. Neglect of dogmatic theology, 331. Holds a middle place in Christendom, 332. Attempts at re-union of Christendom, 333. Characteristics of English Dissent, 333.

"Epistolæ Clarorum Virorum," 59, 59 n.

"Epistolæ Illustrium Virorum," 59 n.

"Epistolæ Obscurorum Virorum," 60 et seq.

Erasmus republishes Valla's notes on the New Testament, 39, 66. Date of his birth, 43. Taught by A. Hegius, 47. Attitude to Church corruptions, 51. An eye of Germany, 53. On the Epp. Obsc. Vir., 61. The literary chief of Europe, 64. Circulation of his works, 64. Colloquies condemned, 64 n. His services to scientific theology, 65. Editions of the New Testament, 65. Paraphrases, 66. Ordered to be set up in every English parish church, 66. Editions of the Fathers, 66. Not wholly in accord with the Reuchlinists, 67. Tries to prevent Froben from printing Luther's works, 68. "Apotheosis of Reuchlin," 68. His answer to the Elector Frederick, 69. His timidity, 70. His belief in culture, 70. His theological opinions not Lutheran, 71. The "Encheiridion," 71. Luther's criticisms on him, 71 n., 72 n., 149. "De Libero Arbitrio," 72. "De amabili Ecclesiæ Concordia," 72 n. Estimate of his place in the Reformation, 72. On the literal interpretation of Scripture, 119, 120. Annotations on the New Testament, 150. His doctrinal hardihood, 151. His rationalism, 152. Erasmus in England, 302. His opinion on the damage done to literary culture by the Reformation, 337, 338, 340.

Erasmus, other references, 5, 67, 74, 91.
Erfurt, University of, 44, 44 n., 46, 58, 63 n.
Eugenius IV., 13.
Evangelical revival, the, 325.
"Everlasting Gospel," the, 17.
Ewald, 352, 358.

Fagius, 310.
Falck, Jac., 180.
Falkland, Lord, 275, 322.
Ferdinand of Austria, 95, 96, 98, 104, 213.
Ferrara, Council of, 13.
Fichte, 373.
Ficino, 38.
Filelfo, 38, 142.
Fisher, Bishop, 306.
Flacius Illyricus, 288.
Florence, Council of, 13.
Formula of Concord, 285.
Francis I., 73 n., 89, 95, 107, 108, 294.
Franciscans, 8, 9.
Franciscans, Spiritual, 9.
Franck, Seb., 204, 206, 215 et seq., 268, 280.
Frankenhausen, Battle of, 199.
Frankfurt-on-the-Oder, University of, 48.
Fratres Poloni, 274, 281.
Fratricelli, the, 17.
Frecht, M., 216.
Frederick the Wise, Elector of Saxony, 48, 69, 83, 91, 100, 101 et seq.
Frederick III., Emperor, 14, 44, 45.
Freiburg, University of, 48.
Friends of God, 19.
Froben, 66, 68, 83.

Galileo, 382 n., 384, 407.
Garrett, 306.

Gattinara, 96.
Gentile, 269.
George, Duke of Saxony, 79, 176, 303.
George, Margrave of Brandenburg, 104.
Gerard Sagarelli, 18.
Gerhard (Franciscan), 18 n.
Gerhard, Joh., 290, 299, 332.
Gerson, 10, 11, 12, 13.
Goch, John of, 30, 31.
Goethe, 65, 338 n.
Grabe, 332, 333 n.
Granvella, 96.
Gregory XII., 9.
Gregory XIII., 343 n.
Greifswalde, University of, 48.
Griesbach, 331.
Grindal, Archbishop, 320.
Grocyn, 302.
Groot, Gerhard, 21.
Grotefend, 347.
Grotius, 355.
Gruet, 253.
Guises, the, 243.
Gutenberg, 43.

Hales of Eton, 275, 329.
Hallam, Bishop, 11, 12.
Hampton Court Conference, 321, 323.
Hartmann, 373.
Harvey, 384.
Hausmann, Nicholas, 167.
Hegel, 373.
Hegius, Alex., 46, 47, 60.
Heidegger, 297.
Heidelberg, University of, 44, 44 n., 46, 48.
Helvetic Confession, 301.
Hemerken, Thomas (vid. Thomas à Kempis), 22 n.
Henry I., 307.

Henry II., 307, 308.
Henry VI., 14.
Henry VII., 302.
Henry VIII., 89, 244, 304, 306, 307, 308, 309, 310, 312, 317, 324.
Herbert, George, 322.
Herder, 356, 357.
Hermann, Elector of Cologne, 109, 313, 313 n.
Hermolaus Barbarus, 53.
Hess, Eoban, 50, 63 n., 339, 340.
Hetzer, L., 125, 206, 209 n., 210 n., 268.
Hobbes, 354.
"Homines intelligentiæ," 19 n.
Hoogstraten, Jac., 57, 58 n., 60, 62 n.
Hooker, Richard, 248, 332.
Hooper, Bishop, 306.
Hubmaier, Balthasar, 193, 195.
Hume, David, 373.
Huss, John, 10, 28, 29, 29 n., 30, 133, 270.
Hutchinson, Col., 322.
Hutten, Ulrich v.; republishes Valla on the Donation of Constantine, 39 n. Knight errant of the Revival, 51. Induces Sickingen to take Reuchlin's part, 58. His character, 62. How far the author of the Epp. Obsc. Vir., 62, 63, 63 n. Other references, 81, 199.

"Imitation of Christ," 16, 22.
Ingolstadt, University of, 48.
Innocent III., 4, 7, 308.
Innocent IV., 17 n.
Innocent VIII., 32.
Interim, the, 109, 243, 310.
Isidore, decretals of, 4, 354.
Italian religion, 41.

Jäger, Johann, vid. Crotus Rubianus.
James I., 261, 320, 321, 323.
Jerome of Prague, 11.
Joachim, Abbot, 18, 28.
Joachim of Brandenburg, 153.
Joanna of Spain, 94.
John Frederick, Elector of Saxony, 101, 102, 109.
John, King of England, 308.
John of Leiden, 193.
John of Parma, 18 n.
John the Steadfast, Elector of Saxony, 89, 101, 176, 177.
John XXII., 19.
John XXIII., 5, 10, 11.
Jones, Sir W., 349.
Julius II., 32, 36, 93, 106.
Jussieu, 385.
Justus, Jonas, 166.

Kant, 373, 389.
Kempis, Thomas à, 21, 22, 22 n., 46, 47.
Kepler, 292, 384.
Kessler, Johann, 206.
Knox, John, 86, 243, 244, 257, 305.
Krauth, Heintz, 196, 197.
Kuenen, 352, 358.

Lanfranc, 311.
Lange, Johann, 73 n.
Lange, Rudolf, 46, 47.
Lardner, 376.
La Rochelle, Confession of, 228, 296.
Lasco, John a, 182, 310.
Lassen, 347.
Latimer, Bishop, 306.
Laud, Archbishop, 321, 322, 325, 333 n.
Lavoisier, 385.

Le Clerc, 298, 355, 356.
Lefevre d'Etaples, 225.
Leibnitz, 373.
Leipzig, University of, 44.
Leo Jud., 242.
Leo X., 32, 36, 55, 58 n., 65 n., 68, 74, 93, 106.
Lessing, 356, 357.
Liber, Antonius, 46, 47.
Linacre, 302.
Linnæus, 385.
Locke, 373.
Louis XI. of France, 14, 94.
Louvain, University of, 58.
Lucius III., 25.
Luther, strong speech on Papal abuses, 5. Opinion of *Theologia Germanica*, 23. A Hussite without knowing it, 30. Independence of his German precursors, 32. Opinion of the Epp. Obsc. Vir., 61. Criticisms of Erasmus, 71 n., 72 n. Appeals to a Council, 78. His character, 80. A popular leader, 80. The grounds of his popularity, 81. Activity not political, 81. Eagerness of his nature, 82. Early and great popularity, 83. The centre figure of the Reformation, 84. Self-confidence, 84. Roughness of speech, 85. His domestic character, 85. His courage, 86. His prayerfulness, 86. His dark hours, 88. Position in the University of Wittenberg, 91. Makes no impression upon Charles V. at Worms, 97. Continues to believe in the Emperor, 97. Devotion to his Princes, 101. Substitutes authority of the Bible for that of the Church, 116. Discovers a Latin Bible at Erfurt, 117, conf. 117 n. Finds that *pænitentia* is not penance, but repentance, 118. His method of Biblical interpretation, 118. Scripture to be interpreted literally, 118. Strong assertion of the authority of Scripture, 121. Does not attempt to prove it, 121. Scripture easy to be interpreted, 124. Yet the results of interpretation very different, 125. Conception of the Bible as an organic whole, 126. Scripture to be interpreted by the gospel, not gospel by the Scriptures, 127. Doctrine of justification by faith alone, 128. False accusation of Antinomianism against Luther, 130. Justification involves complete change of character, 131. Double meaning of *glaube*, 131. Luther's idea of justification becomes more purely intellectual, 132. Efficacy of this doctrine as against the Catholic system, 132. Doctrine of the priesthood of the believer, 133. This the centre-point of the opposition to Catholicism, 134. Luther's sacramental theory, 135. Baptism 137. The Eucharist, 137. Insists upon taking the words of institution literally, 138, 139 n. Eucharistic doctrine the rock on which the Reformation was wrecked, 139. His revolt against ethical theories of the Middle Ages, 142. His marriage, 142. Its moral consequences, 144. Puts reason beside Scripture, 153. After abandonment of that position,

153. Reasons for reaction, 154. Opinions on reason, 154. Virulent abuse of reason, 156. Rationalistic opinions on matters Biblical, 157. On prophecy and miracles, 159. Discrepancies in Scripture, 160. Opposition between reason and faith, 161. Incredibility of orthodox doctrine, 162. The constant struggle in his mind, 163. Safety only in clinging to Scripture, 164. Diabolic visitations, 165. "Anfechtungen," 166. Luther's own account of them, 167. Their explanation, 168. Luther on Christian liberty, 170. On temporal authority and the obedience due to it, 171. Practical unfaithfulness to these principles, 172. Distinction set up between heresy and blasphemy, 173. Between the temporal and the spiritual half of life, 173. Luther at the Marburg Conference, 174. Political action of the Reformers limited by dogmatic agreement, 175. Luther and the Princes, 176. On religious liberty, 178. Against capital punishment of heretics, 179. Conduct to the Zwickau prophets, 191. On the steadfastness of the Anabaptists, 195. Tempted to make the Reformation political, 199. Relation to the Peasants' War, 200. Change which comes over him, 200. Relation to Schwenkfeld, 213. The centre-point of European Reform, 225. Rebellion against scholasticism, 264. Luther's dislike of the word Trinity, 267.
His relation to classical culture, 337, 338, 339. To scientific knowledge, 381, 382, 382 n., 383, 383 n.
Luther, other references, 37, 74, 225, 227, 228, 229, 230, 231, 232, 235, 236, 239, 240, 241, 242, 243, 245, 248, 258, 259, 260, 273, 278, 280, 282, 283, 284, 286, 288, 295, 299, 301, 303, 304, 305, 326, 327, 354, 364, 372, 387, 402, 405, 406, 415.
Lupfen, Count von, 201.
Lyell, Sir C., 385.
Lyra, Nicholas de, 55, 55 n.

Magdeburg Centuriators, 354.
Magellan, 382.
Mainz, University of, 48, 58.
Mantz, Felix, 179.
Marburg, Articles of, 282.
Marburg, Conference of, 84, 103, 138, 174.
Marburg, University of, 93.
Margaret, Duchess, 243.
Marozia, 32.
Martin V., 13.
Marvel, A., 275.
Mary of Burgundy, 94.
Mary, Queen of Scots, 243, 318.
Mary Tudor, 304, 308, 316, 317, 319.
Maurice of Saxony, 109, 110.
Maximilian, Emperor, 32, 56, 94, 101.
Medici, Catharine de, 107, 243.
Medici, Cosmo de, 272.
Medici, Lorenzo de, 38, 41.
Melancthon on Reuchlin's Hebrew learning, 53, 55. Holds Luther's pen, 84. Distress at Weimar, 86, 87. His character, 88. His in-

INDEX. 443

tellectual yieldingness, 89. Want of authority, 89. Really a humanist, 90. His misery in later life, 91. Faith in Charles V., 97. Obedient to princes, 101. On the authority of Scripture, 121. Idea of a consensus of theological opinion, 125. What he thought of Erasmus, 149, 152. At the Conference of Marburg, 174. On religious liberty, 177. On capital punishment of heretics, 180. Letter to Calvin on Servetus, 181. Opinions on the subject, 181 n. Conduct of the Zwickau prophets, 190. The Anabaptists of Jena, 195 et seq. Relation to Schwenkfeld, 213. To Franck, 213, 217. Change of position as to the Trinity, 268. Author of the Confession of Augsburg, 282. Of the Apology, 283. Of "Loci Communes," 286. Luther's praise of the "Loci Communes," 286. Editions, 287. Controversies after Luther's death, 288. "Corpus Doctrinæ Philippicum," 289. His share in Hermann's Consultation, 313 n., 314. His relation to classical culture, 337, 338, 339, 340, 341, 341 n. To scientific knowledge, 382, 383 n.
Melancthon, other references, 245, 248, 254, 264, 271, 273, 284, 290, 295, 296, 298, 304.
Meyer, Gerald, 236.
Michael Angelo, 116 n.
Michaelis, 355.
Mill, editor of New Testament, 331.
Milton, 261.
Mirandola, Pico della, 55.

Mochau, Anna, 142.
Mohr, Hans, 178.
Moller, Jobst, 196, 197, 198.
Moral effects of the Reformation, 145 n.
More, Henry, 329.
More, Sir Thomas, 61, 302, 306.
Morton, the Regent, 86.
Mühlberg, Battle of, 109, 243, 310.
Münster, Anabaptist kingdom of, 203.
Münzer, Th., 85, 186, 189, 190, 198, 199.
Muretus, 343.
Musa, Antonius, 195.
Mutianus Rufus, 50, 51, 53, 63 n., 145 n., 337.
Myconius, F., 92.
Myconius, Os., 242.

Newman, J. H., 324, 327.
Newton, Sir I., 292, 384.
Nicholas of Basel, 20.
Nicholas V., 14, 38, 39 n.
Niebuhr, 345, 346.
"Noble Lesson," the, 24.
Non-jurors, the, 325.
Nürnberg, Diet of, 79.
Nürnberg Gymnasium, 93.

Ochino, 269.
Ockham, William of, 8.
Œcolampadius, 143, 204, 205, 207, 227, 242.
"Ortlieber," the, 26 n.
Ortuinus Gratius, 60.
Osiander, 205, 288, 313 n.
Osmund, Bishop, 312.
Ostorodt, 274.
Oxford movement, the, 325.

Paley, 329, 376, 378, 397.
Pandulf, 308.

Paris, University of, 58.
Parker, Archbishop, 311, 312, 318, 320, 321, 324.
Parker, Theodore, 376.
Passau, Convention of, 110, 243.
Paul III., 93, 107, 244.
Paul IV., 244, 309, 402.
Paulus, 377.
Pearson, Bishop, 331.
Peasants' War, 199.
Peissker, Hans, 196.
Pellicanus, Conrad, 53 n.
Pescara, 96.
Peter Martyr, 310, 314.
Peto, William, 309.
Petrarch, 5, 37, 39, 43.
Petrejus, 63 n.
Peutinger, C., 49.
Peutingeriana, Tabula, 49 n.
Pfefferkorn, 54 n., 56, 57, 61.
Pflug, Julius, 72 n.
Philip II., 98, 243, 296, 318.
Philip of Hesse, 84, 93, 103, 104, 109, 138, 174.
Philip, son of Emperor Maximilian, 94.
Pirkheimer, W., 49, 145 n., 205, 215, 337.
Pisa, Council of, 9.
Pius II., 13, 44, 45.
Pius IV., 244.
Poggio Bracciolini, 38, 43.
Poland, religion in, 270.
Pole, Cardinal, 309, 311.
Politian, 38, 49.
Pontano, 38.
Poor Men of Lyons, 24, 141.
Prague, University of, 44, 44 n.
Priestley, 273, 385.
PRINCIPLES, THE, OF THE REFORMATION, 112. Catholicism objective, Protestantism subjective, 112. Two great Churches described, 113. The method of the Catholic Church, 114. Luther's attack upon it, 116. Substitutes authority of the Bible for that of the Church, 116. His method of literal interpretation, 118. The four senses of Scripture, 119. Erasmus on allegorical interpretation, 120. Reformers do not think of proving the authority of Scripture, 121. Calvin's theory, 122. Every believer to interpret Scripture for himself, 124. Yet how were differences to be reconciled? 125. The Bible an organic whole, 126. The Gospel in the Old Testament, 127. Presence of the Gospel a test of the value of Scripture books, 127. Justification by faith alone, 128. The belief and practice to which it was opposed, 129. Luther's ethical preaching, 130. Intellectual and moral meanings of the word faith, 131. *Glaube*, 131. Luther's conception of faith becomes intellectual, 132. The priesthood of the Christian believer, 133. This the centre-point of opposition to the Catholic system, 135. Sacraments, 135. Illogicalness of Luther's theory, 137. His insistance on the Real Presence, 138. His obstinacy at Marburg, 138. The Reformation a reaction against mediæval ethics, 140. Marriage of priests, 142. Luther's marriage and domestic character, 143.
Procopius, 29.

Protest of 1529, 102.
Pulci, 43.
Puritans, vid. Reformation in England.

Quignon, Cardinal, 312.

Racovian Catechism, 281 n.
Racow, Academy of, 273.
Rask, 349.
REFORM BEFORE THE REFORMATION, 1. Statement of objects of the course, 1. Oneness of the Mediæval Church, 3. Dissatisfaction with its practical working, 4. Efforts of the Church to reform itself, 6. The Catholic efforts, 6. Monastic orders, 6, 7. Outbreak of anti-sacerdotalism, 7. Mendicant orders, 8. The Spiritual Franciscans, 9. Council of Pisa, 9. Of Constanz, 10. Gerson's treatise on reform, 11. Council of Basel, 13. Of Ferrara and Florence, 13. Failure of this method of reform, 14. The Mystic efforts, 14. Characteristics of Mysticism, 14. Mystics in all churches, 16. Different developments of Mysticism, 17. The Fratricelli, 17. Brethren of the Free Spirit, 19. Eckhart, 19. "Homines intelligentiæ," 19 n. Nicholas of Basel, Tauler, *Theologia Germanica*, 20. Beghards and Beguines, 20. Ruysbroeck, 21. Brethren of the Common Life, 21. à Kempis and the "Imitation of Christ," 22. Luther on the *Theologia Germanica*, 23. Biblical efforts, 23. Waldenses, 24. Double origin, 24. Their principles, 24. Wide diffusion, 25. Born out of due season, 26. Wiclif, 26. A Biblical and anti-sacerdotal reformer, 27. Why his movement failed, 27. His influence revived in Bohemia, 28. John Huss, 28. Luther at the Leipzig disputation with Eck, 29. A Hussite without knowing it, 30. The German Reformers before the Reformation, 30. John of Goch, 30. John Wessel, 31. John of Wesel, 31. Luther's independence of them, 32. The evils of the Church still grew, 32. Moral infamy of the Popes, 32. Scholastic theology, 33. The intellectual revival of Europe the cause of Luther's success, 34.

REFORMATION IN ITS EXTERNAL ASPECTS, THE, 76. Large part of Germany in the hands of the Church, 76. Demand for a German Council, 77. Catholic demand for reform, 78. Council of Trent, 79. Luther a popular leader, 80. The reasons of his influence, 81. His activity purely religious, 81. His intense nature, 82. Strong personal influence and quick fame, 83. His self-confidence, 84. His violence of speech, 85. His home at Wittenberg, 85. His religious insight, 86. His prayerfulness, 86. His trials and temptations, 88. Melancthon, 88. His character, 89. A humanist, 90. The University of Wittenberg, 91. Luther's and Melancthon's influence on it, 92. The centre of German Protestantism, 93. Charles V.,

93. His birth and inheritance, 94. His policy, 95. His character, 96. No sympathy with Protestantism, 97. Charles' policy Burgundian, 98. Influence of the constitution of the empire on the fortunes of the Reformation, 99. The three Saxon Electors, 101. Philip of Hesse, 103. The Popes of the Reformation, 104. Belonged to the same class as the Italian despots, 105. Julius II., 106. Leo X., 106. Adrian VI., 106. Clement VII., 107. Paul III., 107. The progress of events, 108. The war breaks out, 109. Battle of Mühlberg, 109. Maurice changes sides again, 110. Convention of Passau, 110. Abdication of Charles V., 111.

REFORMATION, THE, IN RELATION TO REASON AND LIBERTY, 146. Reformation a triumph of the scientific spirit and an assertion of human liberty, 148. Theological rationalism of Erasmus, 149. Luther at Worms relies upon Scripture and reason, 153. Reaction under the influence of Anabaptism, 154. Passages in praise of reason, 154. In disparagement, 156. His rationalizing view of Scripture, 157. Criticism of its matter as well as of its form, 159. Scriptural truth opposed to reason, 161. Reason to be strangled, 163. Luther's *Anfechtungen*, 165. His belief in the devil, 165. His troubles of mind, 167. Arise out of his inner struggle between faith and reason, 168. The Reformation asserts the rights of conscience, 170. Luther on liberty of conscience, 171. Imperfect application of these principles, 172. Conference of Marburg, 174. Differences at the Diet of Augsburg and afterwards, 175. Intolerance involved in the practical transition from a Catholic to a Protestant Church, 176. The Saxon Visitation, 177. Blasphemy, 178. Luther's behaviour to heretics, 178. Zwingli's, 179. Melancthon's, 180. Calvin's, 180. Things are worse in the next generation, 181. Persecution of a Lasco and his fugitives from England, 182.

Reformed churches, vid. Reformation in Switzerland.

Reinecke Fuchs, 49.

Réné, Duchess of Ferrara, 259.

REVIVAL, THE, OF LETTERS IN ITALY AND GERMANY, 35. The age of the Renaissance, 35. The method of the revival, 36. Its inspiration classical, 38. Style all-important among the humanists, 39. Valla, 40. Prevalent immorality, 40. Classical travesty of Christian names and facts, 40. Peculiarity of Italian religion, 41. Italy too familiar with religion as it existed, 42. And gains by it, 42. Humanists of the first generation only learning the lessons of antiquity, 42. Second age of the revival creative, 43. Invention of printing, 43. Germany behind Italy in classical culture, 43. Poggio, 43. Æneas Sylvius, 43. The older Universities of Germany, 44. Poverty of instruction given in them, 44. à Kempis and his pupils, 46. Agricola, 46. Dringenberg, 46. Hegius, 46. New universities in the fifteenth century, 48. Distribution of culture all over Germany, 48, 49, 50. Knights errant of the revival, 51. Humanists did not agree in theological opinion, 51. Opposition between humanists and poets, 52. Reuchlin and the theologians of Cologne, 52. Reuchlin's birth and education, 53. A lawyer and a statesman, 54. His devotion to Hebrew studies, 55. Pfefferkorn and his errand, 56. Reuchlin's answer, 56. Controversy with the Dominicans of Cologne, 57. Case heard at Mainz, 57. Appeal to Rome, 57. Continued controversy, 58. The Reuchlinists, 59. "Clarorum Virorum Epistolæ," 59. "Epistolæ Obscurorum Virorum," 60. Prodigious effect, 61. Erasmus' opinion, 61. Luther's, 61. Who was their author? 62. Ulrich v. Hutten, 62. Crotus Rubianus, 63. Erasmus the greatest name of the German revival, 63. His enormous reputation, 64. Deserts in respect of scientific theology, 65. His Greek New Testament, 65. His Paraphrases, 66. Editions of the Fathers, 66. One of the religious humanists, 67. Yet does not act with the Reuchlinists, 67. Disavows Reuchlin in his letters, 68. "Apotheosis of Reuchlin," 68, 68 n. Interview with Frederick the Wise, 69. His theory of a Reformation produced by culture, 70. Dislike of Luther's theology, 71. The Jerome of the Reformation, 71. Is involved in controversy with Luther, 72. His merits and defects, 72, 73. Play in dumb show performed before Charles V., 73.

Reuchlin, 31, 43, 52, 62 n., 74, 90, 141, 337, 337 n.
Reyman, H., 180.
Richard II., 28.
Robert of Citeaux, 7.
Rostock, University of, 44.
Rovere, Franc. della, vid. Sixtus IV.
Ruarus, 274.
Ruysbroeck, 21.

Sacchi, 407.
Sachs, Hans, 215.
Salmasius, 343.
Sancta Clara, 324.
San Marco, Ant. di, 106.
Sannazaro, 38.
Saravia, 332.
Sarzana, Thomas of, vid. Nicholas V.
Sattler, M., 195.
Savonarola, 41.
Savoy Conference, 322.
Scaligers, the, 343, 354.
Schelling, 373.
Schism, Papal, 9.
Schlegel, F., 349.
Schmalkalden, Assembly of, 175, 213.
Schmalkalden, Articles of, 283.
SCHOLASTICISM, PROTESTANT, 262. Catholic scholasticism, 262. Luther's rebellion against it, 264. Formation of a Protestant coun-

terpart, 264. Assumptions contained in Protestant use of the Bible, 265. Three Protestant systems of theology, 266. Limits of Protestant dogmatic divergence from Rome, 267. Reformers on the Trinity, 267. Melancthon's Loci, 268. Southern rationalists, 269. Find refuge in Poland, 270. Socinian church there established, 270. Lælius Socinus, 271. Faustus Socinus, 272. His character, 273. The Polish Unitarian church, 273. Unitarians expelled from Poland, 274. Socinianism at Altorf, 274 n. Unitarians in Transylvania, 275. Reproach of Socinianism, 275. Its intellectual hardihood, 276. Its theological system, 277. Accepts the authority of Scripture, 278. At the opposite pole of thought from mysticism, 280. The Unitarian name, 281 n. Dogmatic development of Lutheranism, 282. Articles of Marburg, 282. Of Schwabach, 282. Confession of Augsburg, 282. Confessio Tetrapolitana, 282. Articles of Schmalkalden, 283. Concord of Wittenberg, 283. The *communicatio idiomatum*, 284. Its development, 285. The Formula of Concord, 285. Melancthon's Loci, 286. Periods of its development, 287. Lutheran controversies, 288. Polemical rage, 288. *Corpora doctrinæ*, 289. *Formula Concordiæ*, 290. Gerhard's Loci Theologici, 290. Calov's Systema, 291. Results of the dogmatic passion, 292. Calvin's "Institution," 293. Its contents, 294. Its character, 295. Supralapsarian controversy, 296. The Calvinistic systematizers of the seventeenth century, 297. Conclusion, 298.

Schopenhauer, 373.
Schwabach, Articles of, 282.
Schwabach, Assembly of, 175.
Schwenkfeld, Casp., 204, 212.
Schwenkfeldian church, 212 n.
SECTS, THE, OF THE REFORMATION, 184. The Biblically orthodox phase of the movement that which prevails, 184. Other phases, 185. The sects of the Reformation usually thought to be its reproach, 186. Influence of German mysticism on Luther, 187. The mysticism of the Reformation assumes the Anabaptist form, 189. Anabaptist principle of the continuity of Revelation, 189. The prophets of Zwickau, 190. Anabaptist views of Scripture, 191. Their literal interpretation of it, 192. Spread of Anabaptism, 193. Its individual character, 193. Persecution and steadfastness, 194. Melancthon's *Narratio de Anabaptistis*, 195. Connection of Anabaptism with revolutionary politics, 198. The Peasants' War, 199. Luther's changing attitude to it, 200. Religious colour of the Peasants' demands, 201. Anabaptist kingdom of Münster, 203. Antinomianism, 203. Three representative men, 204. Joh. Denck, 204. His life, 205. Character, 206. Cha-

INDEX. 449

racteristic opinions, 207. Caspar Schwenkfeld, 212. His life, 213. Peculiarity of his mysticism, 214. Seb. Franck, 215. His literary activity, 216. Character as an historian, 217. His theological opinions, 218. His conception of nature, 220. No Anabaptist, 221. Was he a Pantheist? 223. Relation of these men to future thought, 223.
Selnecker, 287 n.
Semler, 355, 356.
Servetus, 125, 180, 253, 254, 268, 269, 276.
"Ship of Fools," the, 49.
Sickingen, F. v., 58 n., 81, 199.
Sidney, Sir Philip, 318.
Sigismund, Emperor, 10, 11, 13.
Simon, R., 355.
Sixtus IV., 31, 32.
Smith, of Cambridge, 329.
Socini, the, 125, 269, 271, 271 n.
Socinus, Faustus, 265, 271, 272, 273, 276, 277, 278, 279.
Socinus, Lælius, 271.
Somerset, the Protector, 244, 254, 310.
Soner, E., 274 n.
Spalatin, G., 30, 69, 101, 286, 340.
Speier, Diet of, 102.
Spencer, H., 373.
Spener, 292.
Spiegelberg, M. v., 46.
Spinoza, 298, 355, 373, 403.
Stanley, Dean, 329.
Staupitz, Joh., 30, 83, 91.
Stephen Harding, 7.
Stevinus, 382 n.
Storch, Nich., 190, 192.
Strauss, D. F., 52, 358, 363.
Supralapsarian controversy, 296.

SWITZERLAND, THE REFORMATION IN, 225. Lutheran and Reformed churches, 225. Luther at first the chief figure of the Reformation, 225. Calvinism the missionary Protestantism, 226. Zwingli and Calvin, 227. Zwingli's doctrine Lutheranism with a difference, 229. Independent of Luther, 229. No mysticism in him, 230. Zwingli a humanist, 231. His sphere less Switzerland than the Rhineland, 232. Influence on him of Republican institutions, 232. His political purposes, 234. Similar influence of politics on ecclesiastical institutions, 235. Ethical character of Zwinglian religion, 236. Theory of Church and State, 237. Authority of Scripture, 239. Zwingli more Biblical than Pauline, 240. Does Zwingli rationalize? 241. His character and disposition, 242. Calvin belongs to a later stage of the Reform, 243. The only great Reformer who is international, 244. Geneva, 245. His theory of church authority, 246. Church discipline, 248. Relation of Church and State in Geneva in this respect, 249. Geneva under Calvin, 250. Did his rule succeed or fail? 251. Calvin's defence of persecution, 253. Case of Gruet, 253. Of Servetus, 254. Calvin's letter to the Protector Somerset, 254. Differences between Calvinistic and Lutheran type of theology, 255. Idea of supremacy of God runs through it, 256. Moral

2 G

effects of this kind of religion, 257. Calvin more completely Biblical than Luther, 258. Calvinism the last word of the orthodox Protestant Reformation, 258.

Tauler, Joh. 19, 21, 280.
Temple, Sir W., 344.
Tertiaries, Franciscan, 20.
Tetzel, 5.
Thamer, Theobald, 220 n.
Theodora, 32.
"Theologia Germanica," 16, 23, 280.
Thurius, Paulus, 293 n.
Titian, 96.
Tremellio, 310.
Trent, Council of, 79, 97, 109, 111, 402.
Trier, University of, 48.
Trithemius, 49, 51.
Tübingen, University of, 48.
Turlupins, 20 n.
Turretine, 297, 299, 332.
Tyler, Wat, 27.
Tyndale, W., 261, 305.

Unitarian church of Poland, 270. Of Transylvania, 274, 275.

Valla, Lorenzo, 39, 39 n., 40.
Van Mastricht, 297.
Vasco de Gama, 382.
Vaudois, the, 24.
Vesalius, 384.
Vida, 41 n.
Vienna, University of, 44, 44 n.
Visitation of the Saxon churches, 177.
Voltaire, 65, 377.
Voss, G. J., 333 n.
Voss, Is., 333 n.

Wake, Archbishop, 333.
Waldenses, the, 7, 24, 25, 25 n., 133.
Waldo, Peter, 24.
Walter de Mapes, 25 n.
Walton, Bryan, 331.
Warham, Archbishop, 302, 309, 311.
Weller, Hier., 168 n.
Wesel, John of, 30, 31.
Wesley, John, 24, 257, 413.
Wessel, John, 5, 31, 32, 55.
Westminster Confession, 228, 322, 413.
Whichcote, 329.
Whitgift, Archbishop, 320, 327.
Wiclif, John, 26, 27, 133, 141, 301, 303.
William, Duke of Bavaria, 194.
William of Nassau, 257, 296.
William Rufus, 307.
Wimpheling, Jacob, 48, 51.
"Winkeler," the, 25 n.
Witsius, 297.
Wittenberg, Concord of, 283.
Wittenberg, University of, 48, 91, 92, 93, 225, 337.
Wizel, G., 145 n., 383 n.
Woidowski, 274 n.
Wolf, F. A., 345.
Wollzogen, 274.
Wolsey, Cardinal, 68, 308, 309.
Worms, Diet of, 79, 96.
Worms, Edict of, 79, 80, 108.
Würtemberg, Confession of, 316.
Wyttenbach, Th., 231.

Ximenes, Cardinal, 97.

Young, Dr., 347.

Zasius, U., 49.
Ziska, 29.

Zwickau prophets, 169, 186, 189, 190, 191, 198.
Zwingli on indulgences, 5. Theory of sacraments, 136. At the Conference of Marburg, 174. On capital punishment of heretics, 179, 194. Early preaching at Einsiedeln, 225. His birth, 227. Scene of his activity German, 227, 232. Death at Cappel, 227. Calvin's relation to him, 228. Independence of Luther, 229. No mystic, 230. A humanist, 231. Classical studies, 231. Philosophical studies, 232. Political aims, 232. Social ideal of religion, 234. Connection of Swiss Republicanism with Presbyterianism, 235. Ethical spirit of Zwinglian religion, 236. Theory of Church and State, 237. Connection of this theory with persecution, 238. With church discipline, 238. Beginnings of Genevan discipline in Zürich, 239. Zwingli acknowledges authority of Scripture, 239. Distinction between his position and Luther's, 239. His scheme of Scripture instruction, 240. Common sense in Zwinglianism, 241. Personal character of Zwingli, 242.
Zwingli, other references, 23, 305, 402.

www.ingramcontent.com/pod-product-compliance
Lightning Source LLC
Chambersburg PA
CBHW032002300426
44117CB00008B/874